Microsoft®
Manual of Style,
Fourth Edition

Microsoft Corporation

PUBLISHED BY
Microsoft Press
A Division of Microsoft Corporation
One Microsoft Way
Redmond, Washington 98052-6399

Library of Congress Control Number: 2011942371
ISBN: 978-0-7356-4871-5

Microsoft Press books are available through booksellers and distributors worldwide. If you need support related to this book, email Microsoft Press Book Support at mspinput@microsoft.com. Please tell us what you think of this book at http://www.microsoft.com/learning/booksurvey.

Microsoft and the trademarks listed at http://www.microsoft.com/about/legal/en/us/IntellectualProperty /Trademarks/EN-US.aspx are trademarks of the Microsoft group of companies. All other marks are property of their respective owners.

The example companies, organizations, products, domain names, email addresses, logos, people, places, and events depicted herein are fictitious. No association with any real company, organization, product, domain name, email address, logo, person, place, or event is intended or should be inferred.

This book expresses the author's views and opinions. The information contained in this book is provided without any express, statutory, or implied warranties. Neither the authors, Microsoft Corporation, nor its resellers, or distributors will be held liable for any damages caused or alleged to be caused either directly or indirectly by this book.

Acquisitions Editor: Kim Spilker
Developmental Editor: Valerie Woolley
Project Editor: Valerie Woolley
Copy Editor: Roger LeBlanc
Indexer: Christina Yeager
Editorial Production: Waypoint Press
Cover: Ivan Silantyev

Contents

PART 1. GENERAL TOPICS

Chapter 1: Microsoft style and voice   3

Chapter 2: Content for the web   19

Chapter 3: Content for a worldwide audience   33

What do you think of this book? We want to hear from you!

Microsoft is interested in hearing your feedback so we can continually improve our books and learning resources for you. To participate in a brief online survey, please visit:

microsoft.com/learning/booksurvey

Chapter 8: Grammar — 177

Chapter 9: Punctuation — 189

Chapter 10: Indexes and keywords — 203

Chapter 11: Acronyms and other abbreviations — 215

PART 2. USAGE DICTIONARY

What do you think of this book? We want to hear from you!

Microsoft is interested in hearing your feedback so we can continually improve our books and learning resources for you. To participate in a brief online survey, please visit:

microsoft.com/learning/booksurvey

Foreword

Innovations in technology require great minds. Yet how many of those innovations would be lost on those they were created for without the dedication of writers and editors who are committed to ensuring their success? At Microsoft we are privileged to work every day with brilliant engineers who build amazing products for our customers. We are equally privileged to work with teams of creative writers and editors who, as the shepherds of language and quality, build the important bridges between the promise of technology and the ability to understand its use.

If you've spent any time at all as a writer or editor at Microsoft you've most likely had the experience of attending a session in one of our usability labs watching customers attempting to use early prototypes of a product. It's often with mixed emotions that we watch customers who are unable, or only partially able, to use a new feature simply because the words on the user interface aren't easy to follow or descriptive enough. We know the words in these early prototypes were probably created hastily by an overworked engineer using nerdy language that was not intended for primetime. We experience the frustration of both the engineer and the customer. And we know that, through language, we can make the customer experience much better.

The *Microsoft Manual of Style* is the reference tool that all teams at Microsoft use to help ensure language quality. This guide lays the foundation for the language in our products and services, which, at the time of this publication, reach more than 1.7 billion people worldwide in more than 100 languages. As the sponsor of this publication I am honored to have had the experience of working with Elizabeth Whitmire during the last year as she readied this reference for public use. Elizabeth, along with Microsoft Press, other members of my team and the talented team of editors who are members of the Microsoft Editorial Board, have worked diligently to create this reference. We hope that you will find the *Microsoft Manual of Style* useful, that it will save you a lot of time, and that your own endeavors with language quality and editorial excellence are innovative and fruitful!

Suzanne Sowinska
Director of Language Services
Microsoft Corporation
2011

Introduction to the Fourth Edition

At Microsoft, the guiding principles for how we communicate the ideas and concepts behind our technologies, software, hardware, and services have remained the same over the years: consistency, clarity, and accuracy, and our desire to inspire as well as inform. However, change occurs rapidly in the world of technology, and so do the ways we talk about technology. Even expert editors need a set of vetted guidelines that keep them up to date and protect them from making the same decisions repeatedly or in isolation. This edition of the *Microsoft Manual of Style* is about standardizing, clarifying, and simplifying the creation of content by providing the latest usage guidelines that apply across the genres of technical communication—1,000 decisions you don't have to make again.

A style guide is by nature a work in progress. Despite the evolutionary nature of a reference project like this, the time is right to make this version of the *Microsoft Manual of Style* available outside Microsoft. This edition includes guidelines for the wired and global audience, cloud computing, publication on devices, social media, search engine optimization (SEO), and the natural user interface (NUI). It also provides guidance for the many ways Microsoft writers and editors communicate about technology today, including web content, blogging, video, and more.

Gesture guidelines for the natural user interface (NUI) introduce what have been non-technical words such as *flick, pinch,* and *tap* into the realm of technical documentation. Terms from gaming, such as *achievement* and *badge,* make their way into the general vocabulary of technical communicators who are exploring social and interactive media. Other changes directly reflect shifts in the technology we write about. For example, the first version of the manual included abbreviation guidelines for *kilobyte* (abbreviated simply as K) and for *megabyte,* but not for *gigabyte.* In the world of cloud computing, we now include *terabyte* (TB), *petabyte* (PB), and on up to *yottabyte* (YB), or 10^{24}. Other entries reflect the way that rapid technological change has affected our everyday language. While the Third edition maintained the hyphen in *e-mail* and the status of *Web* as a proper noun in *Web site,* the ubiquity of these terms in our daily lives has accelerated the adoption of the more streamlined *email* and *website.* And of course many new terms and concepts have emerged since 2004, such as *app, cloud,* and *sync,* and many popular new acronyms too, such as *IM, PC, NUI,* and *SEO.*

Although this Fourth edition aims to include as many relevant neologisms as possible and to represent the most current thinking of senior editors at Microsoft about their usage, a printed manual is, by necessity, a snapshot. As always, style is a matter of convention and consensus; the guidance offered here does not describe the only correct way to write. Discerned through research and ongoing conversation within our company, these guidelines reflect the current state of our discussions about these concepts and terms.

You may notice that examples are labeled as "Microsoft style" and "Not Microsoft style" rather than as "Correct" and "Incorrect." We don't presume to say that the Microsoft way is the only correct way. It's simply the guidance that we follow in our workplace. In sharing it with others, we hope that the decisions we have made for our content professionals will help you in your own efforts to promote consistency, clarity, and accuracy.

What's inside

- **Microsoft style and voice**   This chapter highlights the shift toward a lighter, friendlier tone in Microsoft content, with succinct guidelines for writing in the Microsoft voice.

- **Content for the web**   This chapter can help you decide which type of web content best suits your intended audience. It offers guidance for the creation of effective text, video, and audio for the web and includes information about optimizing your content—including blogs and wikis—for readability, search engines, and social media.

- **Content for a worldwide audience**   This chapter reflects the pervasive internationalization of information in the software industry. The *Microsoft Manual of Style* now includes substantial information about writing for a global audience. "International considerations" sections throughout the manual call attention to issues of localization, global English, and machine translation.

- **Accessible content**   This chapter includes the latest guidance on accessibility for content, and how to describe accessibility features in software and hardware products and services. "Accessibility considerations" sections throughout the manual call attention to these concerns.

- **The user interface (UI)**   This chapter includes content for the NUI and Windows Phone UI, and features illustrations of touch and gesture guidelines. To help you write about the user interface in new ways, there are guidelines for writing content for multiple platforms and a checklist for creating UI text, and more.

- **Procedures and technical content** This chapter includes topics on document conventions, cloud computing style, and other general technical issues. It also includes new guidance about reference documentation and code examples for software developers, making the manual a more relevant resource for all content that is created for this audience—from websites, to Help, to software development kits (SDKs).

- **Practical issues of style** This chapter provides page layout guidelines and guidance for common style problems such as how to format titles and headings, lists, and numbers.

- **Acronyms and abbreviations** This list contains acronyms and abbreviations that are commonly used in the software industry and a table of abbreviations of measurements.

- **Grammar, Punctuation, Indexes and keywords** These chapters cover grammar and punctuation guidelines relevant to Microsoft style and provide resources for indexing content.

- **Usage Dictionary** This section includes individual guidance for more than 1,000 technical terms.

How to use this manual

The first part of the manual includes general topics that are organized by subject. The alphabetical usage dictionary follows with guidance about usage and spelling of general and computer-related terms. Topics provide information ranging from a simple note on the correct spelling of a term to a thorough review of what to do, why to do it, what to avoid, and what to do instead, with frequent examples.

Italic is used to call attention to words or phrases used as words rather than as a functional part of a sentence. For example: It is all right to use *sync* as an abbreviation for the verb *synchronize*. Examples of usage appear in quotation marks.

The *Microsoft Manual of Style* does not cover all terms or content issues that are specific to various Microsoft products and services. In addition, because legal guidelines change quickly and cannot be applied internationally, the *Microsoft Manual of Style* does not include content about legal issues. Information about Microsoft trademarking, including the trademark list, guidelines for usage, and licensing on a per-language basis can be found at *http://www.microsoft.com/about /legal/en/us/IntellectualProperty/Default.aspx*.

Other references

The following reference materials provide guidance for issues that are not included in the *Microsoft Manual of Style*:

American Heritage Dictionary of the English Language, 4th ed. Boston: Houghton Mifflin Company, 2000.

Chicago Manual of Style, 16th ed. Chicago: The University of Chicago Press, 2010.

Microsoft International Style Guides (http://www.microsoft.com/Language /en-US/StyleGuides.aspx), Microsoft Corp.

Windows User Experience Interaction Guidelines (http://msdn.microsoft.com/en-us /library/windows/desktop/aa511258.aspx), Microsoft Corp.

Associated Press Stylebook and Briefing on Media Law, 2010 ed. Associated Press, 2010.

Glenn, Cheryl and Gray, Loretta. *Hodges Harbrace Handbook*, 16th ed. Heinle Cengage Learning, 2007.

Acknowledgments

Throughout this project, I have relied heavily on the expertise, assistance, and support of my colleagues at Microsoft. My greatest thanks belong to the Microsoft Editorial Board. This edition would not have been possible without the substantial contributions, thoughtful research, careful review, and always lively discussions of this group of exceptional and generous editors: Handan Selamoglu, Dee Teodoro, Dana Fos, Thomas Olsen, Catherine Minden, Barb Roll, Elizabeth Reese, Karen Scipi, Robin Lombard, Elaine Morrison, Gail Erickson, and Elise Morrison. Working with the Editorial Style Board has been the most rewarding aspect of this project.

Other colleagues from across Microsoft provided subject matter expertise on important topics or helped prepare this edition for print. I would particularly like to thank Lisa Andrews, Deanna Armstrong, Alex Blanton, Linda Caputo, Monica Catunda, Cheryl Channing, Carl Diltz, James Dunn, Rob Haverty, Kay Hofmeester, Rio Jansen, Erik Jensen, Steve Kaczmarek, Alma Kharrat, Kristi Lee, Jennifer Linn, Michael Mikesell, Becky Montgomery, Cathy Moya, Jyotsna Natarajan, Colin O'Neill, John Osborne, Ken Pacquer, Palle Peterson, Mike Pope, Kim Spilker, Chris Wendt, Adam Wilson, Valerie Woolley, Michael Zuberbier, and especially Kathy Phillips, for her expert advice and legal review of the Fourth edition, and Katherine Robichaux and Suzanne Sowinska for sponsoring this project.

I owe a tremendous debt to the previous lead editors of this manual, who guided the content from an internal style sheet to an industry resource: Amanda Clark, Barb Roll, and especially Jim Purcell, who restructured the content to include conceptual chapters in the Third edition, and who carried the torch for Microsoft style for many years before my arrival.

And a special thank you goes out to the Microsoft editorial community—too many folks to name individually—who have enriched this resource with their comments, suggestions, and critiques. The engagement of this community in upholding and scrutinizing stylistic standards keeps the *Microsoft Manual of Style* relevant and accurate. I'd also like to thank the technical editors outside Microsoft who generously provided feedback about their experiences with previous editions and offered suggestions for making this content more useful to technical communicators across the industry. Thank you all for making this a better book!

Elizabeth Whitmire
Lead Editor, *Microsoft Manual of Style*
Microsoft Corporation
2011

Contact the Microsoft Editorial Board

The Microsoft Editorial Board welcomes your content suggestions and feedback about the Microsoft Manual of Style at *mmstyle@microsoft.com*. We read all feedback, but we cannot guarantee a personal response or that all suggestions will be addressed. Your contact information will be used solely to respond to any questions you may have and will not be retained. It will not be shared with any third party, and it will not be associated with other information you may have previously shared with Microsoft.

Microsoft respects your privacy. To learn more, please read our privacy statement at *http://go.microsoft.com/fwlink/?LinkId=81184*.

Errata & book support

We've made every effort to ensure the accuracy of this book and its companion content. Any errors that have been reported since this book was published are listed on our Microsoft Press site at oreilly.com:

http://go.microsoft.com/FWLink/?Linkid=237674

If you find an error that is not already listed, you can report it to us through the same page.

If you need additional support, email Microsoft Press Book Support at *mspinput@microsoft.com.*

Please note that product support for Microsoft software is not offered through the addresses above.

We want to hear from you

At Microsoft Press, your satisfaction is our top priority, and your feedback our most valuable asset. Please tell us what you think of this book at:

http://www.microsoft.com/learning/booksurvey

The survey is short, and we read every one of your comments and ideas. Thanks in advance for your input!

Stay in touch

Let's keep the conversation going! We're on Twitter: *http://twitter.com/MicrosoftPress*

PART 1

General Topics

CHAPTER 1

Microsoft style and voice

S tyle guidelines help make Microsoft products and services easier to understand and inspiring to use by establishing a consistent voice. In addition to providing technically accurate information, we want to convey our trustworthiness, responsibility, empathy, and passion. Style is not just *what* we say to our users, it's *how* we say it.

An essential aspect of style is establishing a consistent and friendly voice. Our voice represents the way Microsoft products, services, tools, and content speak to our users. Even though the content we produce varies widely depending on audience, subject matter, and intent, it's important that it share a consistent, recognizable voice. Whether we are writing an SDK, producing a video for a consumer audience, or crafting a Twitter post, a unified voice is critical for creating a relationship of trust and engagement with our users.

All the content we create should convey the same values regardless of the writer, subject, or medium. Using consistent rhetorical approaches can help establish and unify our voice. This chapter offers style guidelines that you can use to make our messages more effective.

Principles of Microsoft style

The following sections highlight some of the principles of Microsoft style that help us achieve a consistent voice in our content.

Consistency

Consistent terminology promotes learning technical concepts and a better understanding of them.	Inconsistency in terminology forces users and translators to figure out whether different words and actions mean the same thing, which leads to confusion. Using consistent terminology can also decrease translation and localization costs. Examples of inconsistent terminology include the following: ■ switch, toggle ■ start, launch, boot ■ burn, copy
Consistent syntax helps set users' expectations.	When users see the same type of information consistently expressed in the same syntactic structure, they know what to expect, and this makes content easier for them to understand. Use the same syntactic structures for things like introducing and writing procedures, guiding the user through the user interface, and for cross-referencing.

Consistent formatting reduces ambiguity.	Consistent formatting reduces ambiguity and increases a user's ability to scan our content quickly and with confidence. Our users shouldn't have to wonder what italic or bold formatting indicates in any given document.

Attitude

Be inspirational.	Emphasize what users can accomplish, rather than what they can't. Inspiring users is an important part of helping them realize their potential. We must help our users solve their problems, but we can also help them create opportunities by using our products and services in ways that they hadn't thought of before. *Microsoft style* You can add a personal touch to your computer by changing the computer's theme, color, sounds, desktop background, screen saver, font size, and user account picture.
Be responsible.	We have responsibilities beyond being a producer of great software. We think about how our comments will be perceived. We shouldn't dictate. *Microsoft style* Free technical support is available when you register with Microsoft. *Not Microsoft style* You must register with Microsoft to receive free technical support.
Be empathetic.	We understand the needs of our users, and we see meeting their needs as being in both our interests. We're more focused on helping users perform tasks and solving problems than on describing product or service features. Our content should strive to answer the questions "How do I do X?" and "What do I need to know before I do X?" rather than communicating "Let me tell you all about this product." *Microsoft style* To add messaging capabilities to your client application, you can use the Simple MAPI functions. The topics in this section cover the things that a Simple MAPI client needs to implement, such as the following: - Initializing your client - Creating messages - Managing attachments *Not Microsoft style* This overview describes Simple MAPI functionality. It lists the areas necessary to add messaging capabilities to the client application.
Be polite, supportive, and encouraging.	The user should never feel condescended to, blamed, or intimidated. *Microsoft style* This file is protected and can't be deleted without specific permission. *Not Microsoft style* Can't delete New Text Document: Access is denied.

Don't minimize complexity.	Avoid overusing subjective terms such as easy, fast, fun, and so on. If we say something is easy and the user finds it hard, we've risked alienating them. Being told over and over how easy and fun something is can lead to distrust. Instead, demonstrate that something is easy or fun.
	Microsoft style
	Plug in your device to launch the wizard, and then follow the steps.
	Not Microsoft style
	Nothing could be faster or easier. Just plug in your device.
Don't imply omniscience.	Don't assume that you know how someone is feeling. If there's a potential concern, you can anticipate and address it.
	Microsoft style
	Your files are automatically backed up before installation.
	Not Microsoft style
	Don't worry about losing data. It's backed up beforehand.
Use please and thank you judiciously.	Avoid please except in situations where the user is asked to do something inconvenient or the software is to blame for the situation. Use thank you when users have provided information that's difficult or inconvenient to collect
	Microsoft style
	Click Next. You were disconnected from the network. Please re-enter your password.
	Thank you for submitting a request. Please allow two days to process your request.
	Not Microsoft style
	Please click Next to continue.
	Please select an option.
	Please wait...
Use sorry only in error messages that result in serious problems for the user.	Serious problems include situations when data loss occurs, when the user can't continue to use the computer, when the user must get help from a technical representative, or when a product or service fails. Don't use sorry if the problem occurred during the normal functioning of the program, such as when the user needs to wait for a network connection to be found.
	Microsoft style
	We're sorry, but we detected a problem and your PC was shut down to protect your files and other data.
	Sorry, the service isn't available right now.
	Sorry, the Publishing Wizard couldn't start. Please try again later.
Don't try to be funny.	Jokes, slang, and sarcasm are context-specific and hard to translate and localize. What's funny to you might offend or alienate some portion of your audience, so it's best to avoid these rhetorical approaches.

Language

Use everyday words when you can, and avoid formal language that you wouldn't use when speaking to someone in person.	This guideline is especially important if you're explaining a complex technical concept or action. Imagine looking over the user's shoulder and explaining how to accomplish the task. *Microsoft style* Follow these steps to change your password. *Not Microsoft style* Use this procedure to change your password.
Use short, plain words as much as possible.	Shorter words are more conversational, save space on screen, and are easier to scan. Plain words are often easier for non-native English speakers and can reduce translation and localization costs. *Microsoft style* This section also shows you... Digital cameras use tiny microchips... *Not Microsoft style* In addition, this section shows you... Digital cameras utilize tiny microchips...
Don't invent words or apply new meanings to standard words.	Assume that users are more familiar with a word's established meaning than with a special meaning given to it by the technology industry. When an industry term is required, provide an in-context definition. Avoid jargon, but remember that some expressions specific to computer use, such as hacker, are already part of everyday speech. *Microsoft style* Use a real verb like categorize or group. *Not Microsoft style* Don't create a fake verb like bucketize from the noun bucket.
Don't make generalizations about people, countries, regions, and cultures, especially if the generalizations could be considered derogatory, and avoid culturally sensitive terms.	Military terms and analogies, some sports terms, as well as terms that reflect a U.S. world view, can offend worldwide users. *Microsoft style* ■ master/subordinate ■ coworker, colleague ■ perimeter network ■ stop responding *Not Microsoft style* ■ master/slave ■ collaborator ■ demilitarized zone (DMZ) ■ hang

Precision

Omit needless words.	Don't use two or three words when one will do.
	Microsoft style Follow these steps to change your password.
	Not Microsoft style Follow these steps in order to change your password.
Omit unnecessary adverbs.	*Microsoft style* It isn't difficult to change your password.
	Not Microsoft style It isn't terribly difficult to change your password.
Choose words with a clear meaning.	*Microsoft style* Because you created the table, you can make changes to it. Keep your firewall turned on, because turning it off could create a security risk.
	Not Microsoft style Since you created the table, you can make changes to it. Keep your firewall turned on, as turning it off could create a security risk.
Use context to reduce ambiguity.	Some words can be read as both verbs and nouns, such as file, post, input, screen, record, report, and map. When using these terms, ensure that the context and sentence structure reduce ambiguity.
Use words accurately and consistently.	Use words as they're defined in the dictionary or in your project style sheet. Use one term to represent one concept, and use terms consistently. This guideline is particularly important for technical terms, but it also applies to other words. Although the use of synonyms may be more interesting to read, users may assume that your choice of a different word indicates a subtle distinction.
	Microsoft style Set up operating units. A significant number of people access the website monthly.
	Not Microsoft style Setup operating units. A significant amount of people access the website monthly.
Choose single-word verbs over multiple-word verbs.	*Microsoft style* When you lock your computer...
	Not Microsoft style When you lock down your computer...

| Don't convert verbs to nouns and nouns to verbs. | *Microsoft style*
To protect your computer with a password...
To connect...
Open the invitation.

Not Microsoft style
To password-protect your computer...
To establish connectivity...
Open the invite. |

Sentence structure and grammatical choices

Because users scan text, make every word count.	Concise, simple sentences and paragraphs save space and can be the most effective means of conveying important ideas and actions. But you have to use your best judgment—make sentences tight, but not so tight that the tone seems abrupt and unfriendly. For more information about structuring content, see *Content for the web*.
Use parallelism.	Using parallel structures makes content easier to read and more predictable. For more information, see *Parallelism*.
Use present tense.	In technical writing, present tense is easier to read than past or future tense. Simple verbs are easier to read and understand than complex verbs, such as verbs in the progressive or perfect tense. *Microsoft style* Although the system is reliable, you should save important messages. The next section describes how to write an object-oriented program. *Not Microsoft style* Although the system has proven to be reliable, you should save important messages. The next section will describe how to write an object-oriented program. For more information, see *Verbs and verb forms* (Chapter 8).
In general, use active voice.	Active voice emphasizes the person or thing preforming the action. It's more direct than passive voice, which can be confusing or sound formal. *Microsoft style* You can arrange icons in alphabetical order. When you plug in any laptop... *Not Microsoft style* Icons can be arranged by name in alphabetical order. When a laptop is plugged in... For more information, see *Voice* (Chapter 8).

Use passive voice sparingly.	It is all right to use passive voice in the following situations: - To avoid a wordy or awkward construction. - When the action, not the doer, is the focus of the sentence. - When the subject is unknown. - In error messages, to avoid giving the impression that the user is to blame. *Microsoft style* The new icon is displayed in the upper-left corner. An error occurred while the update was being downloaded. For more information, see *Voice* (Chapter 8).
Use indicative mood to convey information.	Indicative mood expresses information such as facts, questions, assertions, or explanations. *Microsoft style* Style sheets are powerful tools for formatting complex documents. For more information, see *Mood* (Chapter 8).
Use imperative mood in procedures.	The imperative mood—a command or request—is direct and saves space, so it's appropriate for instructional text. *Microsoft style* Select the settings that you want, and then click Save changes. Insert the disc in the drive. For more information, see *Mood (Chapter 8), Procedures*.
Use questions sparingly.	While questions may support a friendlier tone, overuse of questions doesn't support a trustworthy voice. In general, users want us to give them answers, not to ask them questions. Questions can work well when users actually do have them, not when we invent them on their behalf. *Microsoft style* If you forgot your password, provide your secret answer. More nature themes are available online. Do you want to continue? *Not Microsoft style* Forgot your password? Provide your secret answer. Like what you see? Get more nature themes online.
In general, use second person.	Second person, also known as direct address, uses the personal pronoun you. Second person supports a friendly tone because it connects you with the user. It also helps avoid passive voice because it focuses the discussion on the user. *Microsoft style* You can always access these advanced settings later, if you need them. To apply these settings, click Next.

Use first person sparingly.	First person is appropriate when writing from the point of view of the user.
	Microsoft style
	Alert me when a new Bluetooth device wants to connect to my computer. (check box text)
	Use we judiciously. The first-person plural can suggest a daunting corporate presence. However, it can be preferable to using the name of the program. Use we recommend rather than it's recommended, and make sure you explain the reason for the recommendation.
	Microsoft style
	Choose the people you want to give permission to. We'll verify their identities before opening the document.
	Windows automatically downloads and installs security updates every day. You can change this, but we strongly recommend that you use the scheduled default setting because it's the easiest way to help ensure that your computer stays up to date.

Punctuation

Punctuation supports stylistic principles, but it isn't a substitute for good word choice. If you find yourself relying on punctuation marks to impart meaning, consider rewriting.

Use exclamation points sparingly.	The overuse of exclamation points can make content seem effusive or ingratiating. Save exclamation points for when they count.
	Microsoft style
	Warning! Resetting your phone will erase all your personal content. Do you want to continue?
Use semicolons sparingly.	Semicolons are associated with a more formal, academic writing style. When possible, create two sentences or a list instead of using semicolons.
	Microsoft style
	Antivirus software helps stop unwanted programs from accessing your computer. Make sure your antivirus software is up to date.
	Not Microsoft style
	Antivirus software helps stop unwanted programs from accessing your computer; ensure that your antivirus software is up to date.
	For more information, see *Semicolons* (Chapter 9).

Contractions

Use contractions to create a friendly, conversational tone.	The use of contractions supports a friendly, conversational style and tone, but it might not be appropriate in formal contexts or in certain technical content.
	If you do use contractions, follow these guidelines:
	■ Don't mix contractions and their spelled out words in user interface text such as a dialog box, wizard page, or error message.
	■ Never use a contraction with *Microsoft* or with a product or service name, as in "Microsoft's one of the fastest-growing companies in the computer industry" or "Microsoft Excel's the best-selling spreadsheet program."
	■ Never form a contraction from a noun and a verb. That is, never use a construction such as "Microsoft'll release a new version soon" or "the company's developing a lot of new products and services."
	■ Use common contractions, such as it's, you're, and don't, but avoid more ambiguous ones such as there'd, it'll, and they'll.

Colloquialisms and idioms

Be mindful of globalization and cultural considerations before you use colloquialisms or idioms.	Keep the diversity of your worldwide audience in mind.
	If your content might be used by non-native English speakers— either in English or in translation—it's best to avoid colloquialisms and idioms. Users might be confused or frustrated if they can't understand the language or need to look it up in a dictionary.
	Colloquialisms and idioms may be appropriate for some types of content for specific audiences. Consult your product style sheet, and make decisions based on your audience.
	For more information, see *Chapter 3, "Content for a worldwide audience."*

Bias-free communication

Microsoft supports, by policy and practice, the elimination of bias in both written and visual communication. Documentation and art should depict diverse individuals from all walks of life participating fully in various activities. Specifically, do not use terms that may show bias with regard to gender, race, culture, ability, age, sexual orientation, or socioeconomic class.

Use the following sections to evaluate your work and eliminate bias and stereotypes from it.

Do not use racial, cultural, sexual, and other stereotypes

Use gender-neutral or all-inclusive terms to refer to human beings, instead of terms using *man* and similar masculine terms.

Use these terms	Instead of
Chair, moderator	Chairman
Humanity, people, humankind	Man, mankind
Operates, staffs	Mans
Sales representative	Salesman
Synthetic, manufactured	Man-made
Workforce, staff, personnel	Manpower

- Do not use the generic masculine pronoun (he, his, him, himself) unless you have no other choice. Use the instead of his, or rewrite material in the second person (you) or in the plural. If necessary, use a plural pronoun such as they or their with an indefinite singular antecedent, such as everyone, or with multiple antecedents of different or unknown genders, such as Pat and Chris. Use his or her for the singular, possessive case if you can do so infrequently and only if nothing else works.

Microsoft style

A user can change the default settings.

You can change the default settings.

Someone may have the file checked out on his or her computer.

Pat and Chris each have their own profile.

The message remains there until your friend logs on to the Internet and retrieves his or her messages.

Not Microsoft style

A user can change his default settings.

Each employee can arrive when he wishes.

Each employee can arrive when s/he wishes.

- Do not use slang that may be considered profane or derogatory, such as *pimp* or *bitch*.

- Use a variety of first names, both male and female, that reflect different cultural backgrounds.

- In art, show men and women of all ages, members of all ethnic groups, and people with disabilities in a wide variety of professions, educational settings, locales, and economic settings.

- Do not use stereotypes relating to family structure, leisure activities, and purchasing power. If you show various family groupings, consider showing nontraditional and extended families.

- Ensure that examples represent diverse perspectives and circumstances. Avoid using examples that reflect primarily a Western, affluent lifestyle. For more information see *Chapter 3, "Content for a worldwide audience."*

Do not use stereotypes of people with disabilities

Not only should Microsoft products and documentation be accessible to all, regardless of disabilities, but documentation should positively portray people with disabilities.

Use these terms	Instead of
Blind, has low vision, visually impaired (this term encompasses people with blindness, low vision, or color anomalies)	Sight-impaired, vision-impaired, seeing-impaired
People who are deaf or hard of hearing	Hearing-impaired
Has limited dexterity, has motion disabilities, is physically disabled, uses a wheelchair	Crippled, lame, wheelchair-bound, confined to a wheelchair, restricted to a wheelchair
People with disabilities	The disabled, disabled people, people with handicaps, the handicapped
People without disabilities	Able-bodied, normal, regular, healthy
Cognitive disabilities, developmental disabilities	Slow learner, retarded, mentally handicapped
Has multiple sclerosis	Is affected by MS
Has cerebral palsy	CP victim
Has epilepsy or a seizure disorder	Is an epileptic
Has muscular dystrophy	Stricken by MD
Is unable to speak, or uses synthetic speech	Dumb, mute
Has mental retardation	Retarded, mentally defective

- Do not equate people with their disabilities. In general, focus on the person, not the disability. Whenever possible, use terms that refer to physical differences as nouns rather than adjectives. For example, use wording such as "customers who are blind or have low vision" and "users with limited dexterity."

> **Note** The phrases "she is blind" and "he is deaf" are all right to use.

- Do not use terms that depersonalize and group people as if they were identical, such as "the blind" and "the deaf."

Microsoft style

Customers who are blind can use these features.

Play-goers who are deaf or hard-of-hearing can attend signed performances.

Not Microsoft style

The blind can use these features.

Theaters now offer signed performances for the deaf.

- Do not use terms that engender discomfort, pity, or guilt, such as *suffers from, stricken with*, or *afflicted by*.

- Do not mention a disability unless it is pertinent.

- Include people with disabilities in art and illustrations, showing them integrated in an unremarkable way with other members of society. In drawings of buildings and blueprints, show ramps for wheelchair accessibility.

For more information, see *Chapter 4, "Accessible Content"*.

For background reading and in-depth information, see the following sources:

Dumond, Val. *The Elements of Nonsexist Usage: A Guide to Inclusive Spoken and Written English*. New York: Prentice Hall Press, 1990.

Guidelines for Bias-Free Publishing. New York: McGraw-Hill, n.d.

Maggio, Rosalie. *The Bias-Free Word Finder: A Dictionary of Nondiscriminatory Language*. Boston: Beacon Press, 1991.

Schwartz, Marilyn. *Guidelines for Bias-Free Writing*. Bloomington, Indiana: University Press, 1995.

Anthropomorphism

Anthropomorphism is attributing human characteristics or behavior to things that are not human. In technical writing there is an understandable temptation to anthropomorphize in order to make difficult material easier for the reader to relate to. Do not succumb to this temptation.

Because anthropomorphism is a form of metaphor, it can cause the same readability problems as other forms of metaphor. Not all readers will grasp the limits of the metaphor. Further, anthropomorphic metaphors may be interpreted differently by people from different cultures.

Anthropomorphism in technical writing is often the result of an imprecise or incomplete understanding of the topic at hand. While anthropomorphism may help you work toward a clearer understanding, your own content should reflect the result, not the process, of your learning.

Microsoft style

If you receive a confirmation message, the engine will store your data in the specified format.

Not Microsoft style

If you receive a confirmation message, the engine will behave as you requested.

Sometimes terminology forces anthropomorphism upon us. For example, in a hierarchical relationship, a *child* object is said to *inherit* attributes from its *parent* or *ancestors*. If, as in this case, the anthropomorphic metaphor is well established and limited and its limitations are clear, it is all right to use it, but take care to explain what some readers may not understand about the metaphor. Straining to avoid such usage would introduce more confusion than the metaphor itself, especially among initiated readers.

Be skeptical of established usage, though. If an anthropomorphism is not the predominant way a concept is expressed in edited publications or on websites, find another way to express the concept.

Sometimes the user interface or application programming interface of a feature is anthropomorphic. In dealing with wizards, assistants, guides, and other characters built into a program, you must let your professional judgment guide you in deciding how much the documentation should reinforce the anthropomorphism of the feature. But do not use words or phrases that convey intention or desire (such as *refuses* or *wants* or *is interested in*), intellect (*thinks*, *knows*, *realizes*), or emotion (*likes*).

Microsoft style

The speech recognition engine accepts only the following words.

Documents manage data; views display the data and accept operations on it.

You do not have to use the **sizeof** operator to find the size of a Date object, because the **new** operator encapsulates this behavior.

Not Microsoft style

The speech recognition engine is interested only in the following words.

Documents know how to manage data; views know how to display the data and accept operations on it.

You do not have to use the **sizeof** operator to find the size of a Date object, because the **new** operator can tell what size the object is.

Words to watch out for

The following words may be all right to use in the right context, but they often signal inappropriate anthropomorphism. Some are appropriate only for programmers or information technology professionals. This list is not exhaustive. When in doubt, check your project style sheet.

allow	interested in	recognize
answer	know	refuse
assume	let	remember
aware	like	see
behave	own	think
decide	permit	understand
demand	realize	want

Parallelism

Parallelism is ensuring that elements of sentences that are similar in purpose are also similar in structure. Parallel structures emphasize the similarities of the parallel elements, and they enhance readability by making the content more predictable.

Parallelism in lists

Items in a list should be parallel. For example, if the first item in a list begins with an imperative verb, all the items in the list should begin with an imperative verb.

Microsoft style

There are several ways to open documents in Windows:

Open your document from within the program that you used to create it.

Use the **Search** command on the **Start** menu to locate the document, and then open it.

Double-click the document icon to open a document.

Not Microsoft style

There are several ways to open documents in Windows:

You can open your document from within the program that you used to create it.

The **Search** command on the **Start** menu locates the document, and you can then open it.

Double-clicking a document icon opens a document.

Parallelism in procedures

In procedures, steps should be written in parallel style, typically sentences with imperative verbs.

Microsoft style

To share your printer

1. Click **Start**, point to **Settings**, and then click **Printers**.

2. In the Printers window, click the printer that you want to share.

3. On the **File** menu, click **Sharing**.

Not Microsoft style

To share your printer

1. Clicking **Start**, you point to **Settings**, and then click **Printers**.

2. In the Printers window, the printer that you want to share should be selected.

3. On the **File** menu, click **Sharing**.

Parallelism in sentences

For parallel structure, balance parts of a sentence with their correlating parts (nouns with nouns, prepositional phrases with prepositional phrases, and so on). Sometimes, to make the parallelism clear, you may need to repeat a preposition, an article *(a, an, the)*, the *to* in an infinitive, or the introductory word in a clause or phrase.

Microsoft style

The *User's Guide* contains common tasks, visual overviews, a catalog of features, and an illustrated glossary of terms. (Parallel objects, with the articles added.)

With this feature you can choose which components to install and which ones to file away for later use. (Parallel clauses.)

Other indicators can appear on the taskbar, such as a printer representing your print job or a battery representing power on your portable computer. (Parallel phrases.)

Not Microsoft style

The *User's Guide* contains common tasks, visual overviews, a catalog of features, and illustrated glossary of terms.

With this feature you can choose which components to install and the ones you will file away for later use.

Other indicators can appear on the taskbar, such as a printer to represent your print job or a battery representing power on your portable computer.

CHAPTER 2

Content for the web

The web provides us with new ways to think about connecting with users and creating content for them. We have greater flexibility in how and what types of information we deliver to users than we did when print was the dominant medium.

Content types now include text, images, audio, video, and interactive presentations. Publishing feels instantaneous compared to print. And the web has become the foremost—and sometimes only—method for communicating with users. As a result, having a web content strategy is critical to content teams. The topics in this chapter provide high-level guidance for creating content for the web.

Make the right content choices

To make the right content choices, first ask these high-level questions:

- Who is the intended audience?

- What is the user's goal? What is the user trying to accomplish?

- What is your goal for providing the content?

- What type of content will best meet the user's needs and your objectives?

- Will a user access the content from a desktop, phone or other mobile device, a console—or all of these?

- Will the content be translated or localized? For more information, see *Chapter 3, "Content for a worldwide audience"*.

- How will the user find the content?

- How will success be measured?

- What are the budget and schedule constraints?

Your answers to these questions will help narrow your options so that you can focus on the best approaches for your user. For example, you might decide that either text or video would be appropriate for your user, but you know that your content will be localized into at least five languages, and you have a small initial budget for the project. Creating and localizing high-quality video is expensive, so you might choose text as the best choice to begin with and then, as you measure the text's success, you might be able to justify the larger investment in localized video.

Use the following table to help choose the type of web content to create:

If your user needs	Consider this type of content	Examples
To learn about a simple task or feature in an application	Procedural text with screen shots Short screen-capture video, with or without audio	Procedure with screen shots: *Remove a page break* Screen-capture video with audio: *Search or move around in a document using the navigation pane*
To learn about a complex task or feature in an we	Screen-capture video, with or without audio Procedural text with screen shots Procedural text with embedded screen-capture video End-to-end scenario descriptions or conceptual topics Technical papers	Video with audio: *Protecting a Word document with AD RMS* Procedure with screen shots: *Add or remove text effects* Procedure with screen-capture video: *Create a theme* End-to-end scenarios: *DirectAccess Test Lab for Windows Server 2008 R2* *Network connection problems in Windows*
Ongoing, regular communications from you	Blog Microblog (such as Twitter) Newsletter	*OneNote, The Microsoft Office Blog; http://blogs.office.com/b/microsoft-onenote/* *Virtual PC Guy's blog* *TechNet Flash Newsletter*
Ongoing engagement and participation with a like-minded community	Wiki Forum	*TechNet wiki* *Exchange Server Forum* *Microsoft Answers; http://answers.microsoft.com/en-us*
To learn something complex that takes time and practice	Online training Technical white papers	*Windows Phone 7 Training Course* *Windows PowerShell Survival Guide*
To learn high-level concepts about technology subjects	Concept papers eBooks	*An Enterprise Approach to Gov 2.0. Microsoft download center:* *http://www.microsoft.com/download/en/default.aspx* *Cloud Basics: Security in the Cloud. Microsoft download center:* *http://www.microsoft.com/download/en/default.aspx*
Detailed information about a product or technology on an ongoing basis	Podcasts Technical white papers Technical blogs	*The Crabby Office Lady Podcasts* Microsoft SQL Azure Team Blog: *http://blogs.msdn.com/b/sqlazure/*
To learn tips and tricks	eBooks Microblogs (such as Twitter)	eBook: Windows 7 Tips and Tricks: *http://www.microsoft.com/download/en/default.aspx* Microblog: FedDidUKnow: You can easily turn your #Access database #applications into #SharePoint 2010 applications. *http://bit.ly/3UaScH #gov #governance*
To understand a complex or integrated feature or scenario	Interactive posters	*Windows Server 2008 R2 Hyper-V Component Architecture (with Service Pack 1)*

If your user needs	Consider this type of content	Examples
To learn complex trouble-shooting or decision making processes	Interactive flowcharts	*Software Update Deployment Superflow*

Text for the web

Users are more likely to scan online text than read it. They decide very quickly if content is relevant to them, and searching is their most common behavior. With a glance, users should be able to have a rough idea of what your content is about, so this means that every word counts: users scan titles, headings, and paragraphs to see if they want to continue reading. You need to adapt your writing style to the web to show users that your content is valuable.

Make text scannable

Because users scan web content, if they find something that they like (gleaned from just a few words), they'll continue reading.

Here are some general guidelines.

- **Headings**   Make headings and subheadings short and make every word count by using keywords. For details about keywords, see *Help customers find your content*.

- **TOCs**   For long webpages or large content sets, use Tables of Contents (TOCs) with links to every subheading. For long pages, include "back to top" links within your content. In general, it's best to use shorter pages when you can.

- **Lists**   When appropriate, use bulleted lists, which are easy to scan and more likely to be read than paragraphs of text.

Microsoft style

Use linked files when these criteria are met:

You will use the same computer to create and display your presentation.

Your files are larger than 100 KB.

You plan to make changes to the source files.

Not Microsoft style

Use a linked file if you are going to use the same computer to display your presentation as the one you created it on. If your files are large, making them linked files is better. Also, you can change things in the source file later and have the changes show up in both the source and destination file.

- **Content chunks**   Write your content in short, digestible paragraphs.

- **White space**   White space can help users scan the page and more easily identify what they need. Ensure that you include enough white space between the content "chunks" on your page.

- **Text placement**   Content that is on the first screen ("above the fold") is more likely to be read—users are unlikely to scroll down to find more information. This means that you need to reduce word count (preferred) or increase the total number of pages (by dividing a page into shorter, separate topics). Remember that where "the fold" is depends on factors that you might not control, such as the device used to view your content and the screen resolution.

  Eye chart, heat map, and usability studies have shown that most users look at specific areas on a page first, so put your most important information there. Generally, in left-to-right languages, the area in the upper-left quadrant of a page is where users look first. For example, if the most important text on your page is a button that says "Buy" or "Download," put the button where users look first (not below the fold, on the far right, or near the bottom). Ensure that the text on the right side of the main body text can't easily be mistaken for an advertisement.

Organize your text

A clear, well-reasoned approach to content organization can help your users locate the information that is important to them. Here are some general guidelines.

- **Use a hierarchical content structure**   Put the most important content first, in the content's title, headings, subheadings, and the first sentence of each paragraph.

- **Give the conclusion first**   This is called "inverted pyramid" style—you write the key points first by using keywords, so that users will see them and know whether they want to read on.

- **See Also**   For more information about keywords, see *Search Engine Optimization (SEO)* later in this chapter.

- **Use short, focused paragraphs**   State your point in the first sentence of each paragraph and stick with one idea per each short paragraph.

- **Use notes and tips**   Break these out of the main paragraph, which should focus on your key point.

- **Use plain language**   Use simple sentences and short words. Use keywords that users use and can relate to. For example, they want to "download," not to "experience the latest innovations." Also avoid technical terms and jargon that users may not understand and wouldn't search for.

Use links—lots of them

Using links to related information can help keep your content concise and scannable. The goal of a link is to help users find the information that they want, so descriptive link titles are critical.

Here are some general guidelines.

- Use the title or a description of the destination page as the link text. Don't use "click here" or "more info" or a long URL.

- Limit link text to four keywords or fewer, if possible. Short links are easier to scan.

- Link to background and related information rather than summarizing.

- If you're creating a large set of content, improve the ease of navigation by including many cross-references.

- For more information about links, see *Search Engine Optimization (SEO)*.

Video content for the web

Done well, video does a better job of showing many users what a product or service is and does and how to use it than explanatory text and still images can. For example, a screen-capture video for a program shows users exactly what to click and when to click it.

But video may not meet your accessibility goals, may require more bandwidth to view than simple text and low resolution pictures, may be expensive to produce and localize, and may not be the best medium if you're trying to teach users a long, complicated process.

Here are some general guidelines:

- Video titles should clearly indicate the content of the video.

- Keep videos short. Shorter than two minutes is a good target. For a more complex subject that requires a longer time to cover, consider creating several short segments or chapters that can be combined in a playlist. This gives the customer an opportunity to watch the segments over time or select only the ones in which they are most interested.

- Make your key points clear and memorable and foreground them the way you would written content. (See *Organize your text*.) Don't say or show more than the audience can easily take in.

- Videos should tell a story with a beginning, middle, and end. Simple narratives are best. A plot keeps viewers interested and attentive and wanting to see what happens next. For example, a good beginning to a video that teaches a task includes a brief statement of what the viewer should expect to learn by watching the video. A good ending leaves viewers wanting to try the new task or feature. A video about learning to use the mouse could conclude with, "Remember: point and click. That's all you need to master the mouse. Give it a try."

- Use the same voice that you use in your other content. The tone will likely be less formal and more conversational, but that will depend on the message that you're delivering.

  For more information, see *Chapter 1, "Microsoft style and voice"*.

- The pace of the audio and video should be consistent, as should the ratio of audio to video. Don't read too fast or too slowly. Practice reading at a clear pace and enunciating all the words. At first, it might feel odd to speak that way, but it will help viewers who are watching your video for the first time (think especially of viewers who have trouble hearing or who are non-native English speakers). Rushing through seemingly simple procedures can frustrate viewers. So, too, can long, audio-only preambles to any video action. Practice timing the actions with your words.

- Timing is difficult, but can make a big difference in the quality of the videos. A pause in the audio while actions are happening on screen is better than reading ahead of the action. The audio doesn't need to explain every action that appears on screen. For example, let the visual images communicate common actions, such as clicking **OK**.

- Avoid references to earlier parts of the video, unless references are essential. Viewers should be following along, not trying to remember what they saw or heard before. They can always replay the video. If you must refer to earlier parts of the video, do so generally. For example, "Earlier, you saw how to add X to Z. Here's something else you can do with X...."

- To improve accessibility, include captions. If possible, break closed captions into one-sentence chunks so that they're easier to read.

- Because creating and localizing video can be expensive and time-consuming, try to take an "evergreen" approach to the content. If you can, avoid mentioning specific dates and product version names or showing images that will quickly date your content.

- Consider a branding element to open and close your videos, and a URL where the user can get more information at the end. These elements give your video credibility by clearly identifying the source of the content.

For more information go to Jakob Neilsen's Talking-Head Video is Boring Online at *http://www.useit.com/alertbox/video.html*.

Blogs

Blogs are a good way to provide customers with ongoing, regular communications from subject matter experts, but only if you can commit resources to keeping the blog updated and fresh. Often, bloggers start out with good intentions, but fail to keep up the pace, and their blog languishes. A stale blog creates customer dissatisfaction and can impact your credibility. An active, credible blog invites customer comments and community promotion. Blog posts can contain text, photos, videos, and screen shots.

Here are some general guidelines:

- Blog frequently and on a regular schedule, if possible. Post as frequently as necessary to tell your story effectively, but don't distract your customers with meaningless posts. A good rule of thumb is at least one blog post a week—consider a team blog so you can share the workload.

- Identify subject areas to blog about in advance and develop a schedule. This is especially important for a team blog. This will help you establish a blogging routine and provide more structure for you and your readers. For example, you might want to introduce a subject in an initial post and advance the subject further in subsequent posts. By planning this in advance, you can quickly prepare for each post. It also lets you inform your readers in advance that the post is one in a series.

- Tone should be friendly and informal—be yourself! Apply the same common sense and guidelines to blogging that you would to any interaction or communications with customers, partners, and the press. That is, always bear in mind that what you write or say reflects you and the company. For more information, see *Chapter 1, "Microsoft style and voice"*.

- Respond promptly to customer comments. Comments and your responses can be as important as the blog post itself because it fosters an image of transparency and responsiveness, it can create meaningful dialog with important customers, and it can drive feedback to your product team.

- If you plan to archive your blog posts, you might consider adding a disclaimer to old content along these lines: "To the best of my [our] knowledge, the information in this blog post was accurate at the time of publication, but it might not be accurate now. If you're reading something here that was published a while ago, I [we] recommend that you search the web for a more recent source."

- If possible, tag each blog entry with keywords to help your readers find related entries or entries on topics of interest to them.

- Support your blog by using other social media tools, such as Twitter and Facebook, to raise awareness about it. For more information, see *Social Media Optimization (SMO)*, later in this chapter.

Community-provided content

Customers expect to interact with content. People still use the web as a source for receiving information, obviously, but it's now also a place to share their information and expertise and to learn from other people like them.

If appropriate, consider offering your customers a way to provide content for your site. There are different models for this, from "anybody can contribute" to "we've selected a few people to provide content." Anytime you have a community-contribution content model, you must consider how you will manage the content for appropriateness, accuracy, and adherence to standards.

Wikis

Wikis are a great example of a community creating content—anyone can view wiki content and, generally, anyone can contribute or edit wiki content. In theory, the community of wiki users manages the content. In practice, most wikis also have assigned editors, content managers, or councils to ensure that the wiki content is appropriate, to encourage use of the wiki, and to arbitrate disagreements.

If you have an enthusiastic community, such as a highly engaged technical community with lots of expertise to share, consider developing a wiki. And remember, the community doesn't mean just customers outside your organization—it can include internal employees such as customer support services developers, testers, marketers, salespeople, or anyone else who has a vested interest in your wiki.

Many types of content are appropriate for a wiki, but they depend on your audience. Types of content and coverage areas that work well on wikis include the following:

- Troubleshooting and workarounds
- Tips and tricks
- Best practices
- Interoperability information
- Scenario or solution-based content
- Product evaluations
- Beta content
- White papers
- Community or wiki lists
- Learning roadmaps

A wiki might not be the best method for communicating the following:

- Information that needs to be localized

- Release notes or other information that's essential to defining how the product works (because a wiki can be modified)

Consider using a private wiki that is limited to a designated group of internal or external users for content that cannot currently be released.

With wikis, as with all web content, you need to think about the best ways to organize your content and make it discoverable. Most wikis don't have a standard TOC structure. You can, however, create your own navigation articles that act as a TOC and provide links to your articles. Consider creating multiple TOC articles that are specific to your users. For example, you might want to have a TOC article that is oriented toward a specific type of customer, such as a software developer or an accountant, and another TOC article that links to topics specific to a solution or scenario and isn't role-specific.

Consider using social media both to promote your wiki content and to encourage community contribution to your articles.

For more information, see *Social Media Optimization (SMO)***,** and for more information about making wiki content discoverable, see *Search Engine Optimization (SEO)*.

There are a number of strategies you can use to encourage contribution. Use "stub topics" that are partially filled in to encourage community additions and enhancements. Start with content that encourages contribution, such as troubleshooting, or tips and tricks. Be willing to experiment with content types (with the understanding and support of your product, legal, and localization teams), and be open to changing your approach to wiki content and community contributions based on the feedback you receive from the community. For more information, see *Getting Over the Barriers to Wiki Adoption (Alan Porter, 2010); http://arstechnica.com/business/news/2010/02/getting-over-the-barriers-to-wiki-adoption.ars*.

Evaluate your content

By publishing content on the web, you can get immediate feedback in a variety of ways from your customers. Using customer feedback, you can change or update your content to better meet your customers' needs—and you can get this improved content to your customer much more quickly.

Some websites have built-in feedback mechanisms so that customers can rate and comment on content. For example, some content includes a feedback survey at the bottom of each page.

If your content has many customers, you might want to use tools to help with data mining and analysis of customer feedback.

A/B testing

If you can't support sophisticated customer feedback tools and analysis, you might try the A/B content testing method, which is done through controlled online experiments. In A/B testing, customers are exposed to (A) control content and (B) treated content. Comparing the two by using the metrics that make sense for your site (number of downloads, sales, page views, and so on), you can make gradual and systematic improvements to your site.

Task analysis

Task analysis—understanding what your customers need to do and how they're using your content to do it—is another way of evaluating your content. In general, the task analysis process is as follows:

- Identify the top tasks that customers need to complete by using your content.

- Have participants use your content to do the tasks.

- Use metrics to measure their success rates.

Some metrics include the following:

- Task completion rate

- Disaster rate (percentage of failed attempts)

- Time it takes to complete the task

After you have identified areas of weakness in your content based on task analysis, you can make changes and remeasure as necessary to achieve an optimal success rate. For more information, see *Customer Carewords: Top Task Management for Websites*, *http://www.customercarewords.com/task-performance-indicator.html*.

Help users find your content

How can you help ensure that your customers will find your great content? First, it's critical that your content is optimized for search. Because algorithms and keyword usage can change rapidly, it's important to understand the latest research in these areas so that you use the right approach to optimize your content for search.

Second, take advantage of the community to promote your content by using *Social Media Optimization (SMO)* and *Tags*.

Search Engine Optimization (SEO)

SEO is the work that you do to improve the visibility of a website or a webpage in unpaid, algorithmic search engine results. Because most customers click one of the first few search results, it's important to do all that you can to ensure that your content is returned at the top of a search engine result page.

The four main areas to focus on for SEO are keywords, links, titles, and descriptions.

Keywords

Know the words and terms that customers use (not the words and terms that you use) to search for your information, and use these words as early and as often as possible in the following places in your content:

- Titles
- Headings and subheadings
- Summaries
- Overviews
- Introductions
- Page descriptions
- Paragraph text
- Link text
- Image and table alt text

There are specific tools that you can use to learn what search terms customers use—just search for "SEO."

Note Video and audio files are non-textual content, so search engines can't find them on their own. Add a text description near the asset, and add an alternative text description, if possible.

Links

In addition to including keywords in link text, you should link liberally to other content. If you have many incoming and outgoing links that use your keywords, you'll help improve your position in search results. The highest value is given to incoming links that match your keywords and which are from pages that also use your keywords.

Each page on your site should include some type of "share this" feature so that readers can easily link to your content from their content. This will take advantage of social media technologies and help increase the number of well-formed inbound links to your content. For more information, see *Social Media Optimization (SMO)*.

Ensure that your links are not circular (that is, don't link back to the same content), because search engines discount these links (and it can be a lousy experience for your customers).

Fix any broken links that occur in your content—if a search engine can't search your content because of a broken link, your ranking will be lower.

Titles

Titles are used by search engines to determine ranking and are then used as the page's heading (anchor text) in the search engine's results page. Use the following guidelines for titles:

- Use no more than 10 to 12 words, or about 65 characters.

- Use the most important keywords early in the title.

- Unless brand names must appear first in the title or unless the page is mostly about the brand, important keywords should precede brand names.

- The title should be specific and include what is unique about the content.

Descriptions

The page description appears in search results as a short paragraph between the title and the body of your content. It's important that you provide this text because if you don't, the search engine will decide what text to present. Use the following guidelines for descriptions:

- Include keywords in the description and put them as close as possible to the beginning of the description.

- A description should be no more than 160 to 170 characters.

- Write from specific to general.

- Use active words that clearly state what the page is about and that compel customers to access your content (without sounding like a sales pitch).

- Descriptions should be grammatically correct complete sentences.

- Avoid superfluous words. Don't begin with stock phrases, such as "This article discusses" or "In this technical article, we will …."

- For white papers and other long articles, indicate the length of the document.

Tags

"Tags" are keywords and terms chosen by the content's creator or by other users of the item (depending on the system) to classify the content. Tags are a kind of metadata that helps customers find the content by browsing or searching. Tags are often specific to the systems in which the content is published. That is, tags are useful within a specific wiki, but do not necessarily increase discoverability from external search engines.

As with keywords, use tags that customers would use, not just the tags that you would use.

Many blogging and wiki systems allow authors to add free-form tags to a post, placing the post into categories. For example, a post might display that it has been tagged with "Windows" and "operating system." Each of these tags is usually a link leading to an index page that lists all of the posts associated with that tag. The blog or wiki might have a sidebar listing all the tags in use, with each tag leading to an index page. In many systems, the font size of the tag title will be bigger or smaller, depending on the popularity (measured by customer use) of the tag. This gives customers a visual indicator of what content on the blog or wiki is most popular.

Social Media Optimization (SMO)

You can use social media like Twitter, Facebook, forums, newsgroups, and YouTube to promote your content and identify content needs. It's another strategy—complementary to *Search Engine Optimization (SEO)*—for making people aware of your content and increasing the amount of traffic to your site.

Social media evolves rapidly, so the approaches that you take to optimize your content today might need to be different six months from now. Because of this rapidly changing environment, the following information is limited to high-level approaches; there are resources available online for detailed information.

There are four main ways to approach SMO:

- Understand the social media "community of influencers" that might have developed in your area of expertise. Engage with them to promote your content, and use social media tools yourself.

- Collaborate with a partner team, such as your organization's marketing team, to promote your content.

- Monitor social media sites for common customer problems and use this data to identify gaps in your content. For example, in addition to responding to a forum or newsgroup post, you might need to add or correct content in your portfolio.

- Use social media technologies, such as bookmarking, blogging, RSS feeds, and other sharing technologies, to improve SEO by increasing the number of well-formed inbound links to your content.

To understand your community of influencers, you can use various listening and monitoring tools, known as "listening platforms." Listening platforms not only monitor and track what is being said about you, they also offer insight to help shape your strategy, giving you knowledge about sentiment, influence analysis, community, and engagement.

With social media, as with blogging, you need to have the resources to post and monitor frequently (once a week is a reasonable target) and respond to customer feedback promptly (a 24-hour to 48-hour response time is a good goal).

International considerations for web content

As with printed content, it's important to partner early with your localization team to share content plans and to understand the implications of your web-content strategy.

Certain types of web content, including video, are expensive to localize and this may affect your content choices. For more information about creating content for a global audience, see *Chapter 3, "Content for a worldwide audience"*.

Accessibility considerations for web content

There are certain accessibility standards that you must follow when you create content for the web. As you develop your web content strategy, partner early with your accessibility contact to share content plans, to understand accessibility implications, and to ensure that you understand the accessibility standards that you need to follow. For more information, see *Chapter 4, "Accessible content"*.

Legal considerations for web content

Any content created for the web—including blogs, wikis, Facebook and Twitter posts, and videos— must follow your corporate legal guidelines.

CHAPTER 3

Content for a worldwide audience

Because Microsoft sells its products and services worldwide, content from Microsoft must be suitable for a worldwide audience. Microsoft makes content usable worldwide in these ways:

- By globalizing content

- By localizing content

- By machine translation of content

- Through content curation and support of community-based contributions

Writers and editors globalize content by creating content that is easy to read and translate. Content is localized by translating the content into other languages and ensuring that any country or region specific information in the content is made appropriate for the target audience. Machine translation is used for content that is not translated by localizers in order to make as much content as possible available to worldwide users in their native languages.

Making content usable worldwide begins with globalization. The topics in this section show you how to globalize your content.

Global English syntax

For the most part, syntax that is good for a worldwide audience is also good for native English speakers. The following guidelines are helpful to all users of technical content, but they are especially helpful to non-native English speakers.

Note If you know beforehand that machine translation will be used to translate your content, also use *Machine translation syntax*. Doing so will significantly improve the quality of machine-translated content.

Guideline	More information
Avoid long, convoluted sentences.	Even if they are well written, they are hard for non-native English speakers to understand. Long sentences may also cause difficulty for localizers.
Use lists and tables instead of complicated sentence and paragraph structures.	Lists and tables can often simplify syntax and aid scanning.
Limit your use of sentence fragments.	Sentence fragments are often ambiguous and may cause difficulty for localizers.
Use language that is likely to be understood by English speakers worldwide.	Avoid idioms, regionalisms, colloquial expressions, and other culture-specific references. Although these forms add color and interest to writing for some users, they are almost always confusing for non-native English speakers, and they can be difficult or impossible to translate.
Use optional pronouns such as that and who.	Optional words often eliminate ambiguity by clarifying sentence structure. *Microsoft style* Inspect the database to ensure that all tables, data, and relationships were correctly migrated. This tool simplifies the tasks that you have to perform. *Not Microsoft style* Inspect the database to ensure all tables, data, and relationships were correctly migrated. This tool simplifies the tasks you have to perform.
Use optional articles such as the.	Articles help mark nouns in a sentence so that they cannot be confused for other parts of speech.
Include optional punctuation.	Optional punctuation, such as a comma after an introductory phrase and after the last item in a series, makes sentence structure explicit.
Avoid modifier stacks.	Long chains of modifying words, whether they are nouns or adjectives, increase the risk of ambiguity and are confusing even to native English speakers.
Let active voice and indicative mood predominate. Use imperative mood in procedures.	Use passive voice only in the following situations: ■ To avoid a wordy or awkward construction. ■ When the subject is unknown or the emphasis is on the receiver of the action. ■ If casting the user as the subject might sound blaming or condescending, especially in error messages and troubleshooting content.
Keep adjectives and adverbs close to the words they modify, and do not place them too close to other words that they might modify instead.	Pay particular attention to the placement of only.

For more information, see *Machine translation syntax, Words ending in -ing*

Machine translation syntax

Machine translation (MT) is a method for translating text automatically from one language to another. Machine translation is used to speed up the process of delivering products, services, and content to non-English speaking markets, and to increase the number of languages in which products, services, and content are available.

Machine translation takes sentences in a source language as input, and produces a translation of the source sentences in a specified target language. The output of machine translation is sometimes post-edited by human translators, and sometimes published without a review by a human.

The style of the source language has significant impact on the quality if the translation and how well the translated content can be understood.

If machine translation will be used to translate your content, use the following guidelines in addition to the global English syntax guidelines.

Guideline	More information
Write in Standard English.	Machine translation (MT) software is programmed to recognize the rules of Standard English grammar and punctuation. Therefore, content that follows these rules has the best chance of being translated correctly. *Good for MT* If you do not want to add tags to every picture, you can add tags to a batch of pictures. *Not good for MT* If adding tags to every picture sounds time-consuming, don't worry—you can add tags to a whole batch of pictures at once.
Ensure that your content is free of grammar, punctuation, and spelling errors.	Unlike human readers, MT cannot compensate for most errors in grammar, punctuation, and spelling. For example, if "window" is misspelled as "widow," MT will translate "widow" as "a person whose spouse has died," which will look very strange in the machine-translated content.
Avoid writing sentences of more than 25 words, but do include determiners such as a, the, your, or this to avoid ambiguity.	The longer a sentence is, the more decisions the MT software has to make about how the clauses and phrases are related. The fewer the number of subjects, verbs, and phrases in a sentence, the better the chance that the sentence will be translated accurately. *Good for MT* When you publish your webpage to a website or post it to a server, be sure to publish the subfolder also. The subfolder contains all the supporting files that are necessary to properly display your drawing. *Not good for MT* When you publish your webpage to a website or post it to a server, be sure to publish the subfolder as well, because it contains all the supporting files necessary to properly display your drawing.

Guideline	More information
Avoid writing very short sentences and headings.	With very short sentences and headings, MT may not have enough information to figure out the syntax of the text. Ensure that a short sentence or heading has the syntactical information that MT needs to translate the text correctly. *Good for MT* Empty the container. The empty container Access is denied. *Not good for MT* Empty container Access denied.
Do not use sentence fragments.	Because sentence fragments are, by definition, fragments of language instead of complete expression, they often lead to poor machine translations.
Reduce the ambiguity of verb-like words that end in "-ing."	A verb-like word that ends in "-ing" can be highly ambiguous because it can function as an adjective, noun, or gerund. Whenever it isn't clear from the syntax what the function of such a word is, disambiguate it. Note that the following sentence is ambiguous: ■ This is blocking code. ■ You can remove the ambiguity by rewriting this sentence as follows: ■ This is blocking the code. ■ This is the blocking code. For more information, see *Words Ending in -ing*

Reduce the ambiguity of verb-like words that end in "-ed."	A verb-like word that ends in "-ed" can be highly ambiguous. Whenever it isn't clear from the syntax what the function of such a word is, disambiguate it. You can do so in three ways, depending on the context:
	
	Add a determiner (a, an, the, this) either before or after the "-ed" form.
	
	Good for MT
	They have an added functionality.
	
	Not good for MT
	They have added functionality.
	
	    Turn the "-ed" phrase into a clause that uses a form of the verb be.
	
	Good for MT
	You should also configure limits for the backup size that are based on the amount of disk space available.
	
	Not good for MT
	You should also configure limits for the backup size based on the amount of disk space available.
	
	Note If a modifier such as "based on" can modify more than one noun, MT will join it to the closest noun. In this example, note that the *based on* can modify either *limits* or *size*. Because *size* is the closest noun, that's the one that the MT system will join it to. But note that this is not correct. *Based on* modifies *limits*. The example under "Good for MT" makes this clear by adding "that are" (a plural verb that can only modify the plural noun "limits"). You can also disambiguate the sentence in this example by writing it as two sentences, as is done in the next example.
	
	    Write the idea as two sentences.
	
	Good for MT
	You can also configure limits for the backup size. These limits should be based on the amount of disk space available.

Guideline	More information
Avoid linking more than three phrases or clauses by using coordinate conjunctions such as and, or, or but.	For every and, or, and but in a sentence, MT has to determine which sentence elements are being coordinated, and that becomes more difficult as the number of these coordinate conjunctions increase in a sentence. Therefore, try to keep them to a minimum.
	Good for MT
	Other computers may be able to acquire usage rights and play the songs if they have a connection to the Internet. However, devices such as portable CD players and car stereos will not be able to acquire those rights. Therefore, they will not be able to play protected content.
	Not good for MT
	Other computers may be able to acquire usage rights and play the songs if they have a connection to the Internet, but devices such as portable CD players and car stereos will not be able to acquire those rights, and will not be able to play protected content.
Do not use abbreviations unless they are standard abbreviations, such as CD for compact disc.	If you use an abbreviation that is not in the MT dictionaries, the abbreviation will not be translated. For example, if you decide to abbreviate "not permitted" in a table as "NP" after first mention, "not permitted" will be translated, but NP will not be translated. It will remain NP in the target language, and may be confusing or unintelligible to the reader.
	Good for MT
	To open SQL Server Configuration Manager on the target computer, double-click the file.
	Not good for MT
	To open SQL Server CM on the target computer, double-click the file.
Use correct capitalization.	Correct capitalization helps improves MT because capitalization clearly marks beginnings of sentences and identifies proper nouns. Note that the sentences in the following examples may not be translated the same way because "Start" is not capitalized in the "Not good for MT" example.
	Good for MT
	Learn how to use the Windows Start menu to open programs and folders.
	Not good for MT
	Learn how to use the Windows start menu to open programs and folders.
	Note Because MT can use capitalization to disambiguate words, sentence-style capitalization is better for headings than title capitalization.

Terminology and word choice

Precision and accuracy in terminology and word choices help with comprehension make the translation and localization processes easier. For more information about using terminology consistently, see *Chapter 1, "Microsoft style and voice"*.

Technical terms

If you are writing for a general audience, consider your use of technical terms. People who do not think of themselves as computer professionals often consider technical terms to be a major stumbling block to understanding. Whenever possible, you should get your point across by using common English words. It is all right to use technical terms when they are necessary for precise communication, even with a general audience, but do not write as if everybody understands these terms or will immediately grasp their meaning. Define terms in the text as you introduce them. Provide a glossary with your content, and provide links from the main text to the glossary if you are writing for online Help or for the web.

If you are writing for a technical audience, use domain-specific terminology only when the terminology is necessary to make your content precise and accurate. Be sure to use technical terms as they are defined at Microsoft and industry wide. To verify the industry-wide meaning, use authoritative resources, not unedited websites. For example, you can use domain books and dictionaries such as the *American Heritage Dictionary*. You can use authoritative terminology websites such as Webopedia.com, BusinessDictionary.com, and Whatis.com, and industry standard sites such as the W3C site. For recent usage citations of words that may be too new for dictionaries, you can refer to websites such as those for trade and consumer magazines. If you are writing about terminology for another product or service, you can check that group's project style sheet. Even for a technical audience, define terms in the text as you introduce them. Provide a glossary with your content, and provide links from the main text to the glossary if you are writing for online Help or for the web.

Use the same terms in marketing materials as those that are used in the product, service, tool, or website. Do not create a new term if a term describing a concept already exists. If you must create a new term, verify that the term that you select is not already in use to mean something else. Regardless of audience, avoid giving specific technical meaning to common English words. Even if new terms are well grounded in the everyday definition of a word, those reading your content may not be attuned to the subtleties of meaning that underlie such terms, and they may try to make sense of the material by using the common definition. For more information, see *Jargon*.

Jargon

Jargon, as a general reference to the technical language that is used by some particular profession or other group, is a neutral concept. In the right context, for a particular audience, jargon can serve as verbal shorthand for well-understood concepts. For example, technical terms are usually all right to use in content for a technical audience that expects a higher level of technical rigor.

However, in the wrong context, jargon is little more than technical slang that makes technology more difficult for many users. Many acronyms and abbreviations fall into this category. This category of jargon affects nearly all uninitiated users at least some of the time, especially worldwide users. In many cases, jargon is difficult to translate and can cause geopolitical or cultural misunderstandings.

Do not use jargon if any of the following is true:

- You could easily use a more familiar term.

- The term obscures rather than clarifies meaning. Be particularly wary of terms that are familiar to only a small segment of your customers, such as the term *glyph* to mean *symbol*.

- The term is not specific to computer software, networks, operating systems, and the like. That is, avoid marketing and journalistic jargon. For example, don't use *leverage the new technology* to mean "to take advantage of the new technology."

Testing for jargon

If you are familiar with a term, how can you tell whether it is jargon that you should avoid? If the term is not listed either in MSTP or your project style sheet, consider the following:

- If you are not sure, consider it jargon.

- If an editor or reviewer questions the use of a term, it may be jargon.

- If the term is used in newspapers, such as *The Wall Street Journal* or *The New York Times*, or in general interest magazines, such as *Time* or *Newsweek*, it is may be all right to use for some audiences.

- If the term is used in technical periodicals such as CNET (http://www.cnet.com), it is probably all right to use for a technical audience. However, be aware that technical magazines often adopt a more idiomatic style than is appropriate for a worldwide audience, and that magazine style can include usages that would be considered slang.

Latin and other non-English words

Do not use non-English words or phrases, such as *de facto* or *ad hoc*, in English content, even if you think these terms are generally known and understood. They may not be, or the language may not be understood by a translator or by the machine translation process. Find a straightforward substitute in English instead.

In general, do not use Latin abbreviations for common English phrases.

Use these terms	Instead of these abbreviations
for example	e.g.
that is	i.e.
namely	viz.
therefore	ergo

It is all right to use *etc.* (meaning "and the rest"), but only in situations where space is too limited for an alternative, such as on a button label. Otherwise, see *and so on* for alternatives.

Global art

Art presents many globalization issues. Colors and images that are unexceptionable in one place may be offensive somewhere else. Art that relies on metaphor may not be understood everywhere. In some cases, art can even raise legal problems. To globalize your art, use the guidelines in the following table.

Guideline	More information
Choose colors carefully.	Many colors have religious or political significance, such as those that are found on flags or used for country or region–specific holidays. Neutral colors are usually all right.
Choose simple or generic images that are appropriate worldwide.	Soccer players and equipment, generic landscapes, pens and pencils, international highway signs, and historic artifacts such as the Egyptian pyramids are examples of worldwide images.
	Be especially careful to avoid images that are offensive in some cultures, such as holiday images and situations, whether work or social, involving men and women. Do not use hand signs: nearly every hand sign is offensive somewhere.
	Do not use art based on English idioms, such as using a line of cars and a jam jar to indicate a traffic jam.
	Limit graphics and animations on the web. In some countries or regions, users pay for telephone calls by the minute, and long page loading times can be expensive.
For localized content, do not use text in graphics unless you have no other choice.	Some worldwide users use automatic translation software to read English content. This software does not translate text in graphics. In addition, it is expensive to localize graphics, and graphics can present accessibility issues. Use captions instead, or provide an explanation in the main text.
	Create descriptive alt text for each image, especially for button images. Users who do not understand the image can rely on alt text for an explanation. If you use art to label buttons, include text that describes the function of the button.
	Whenever possible, store art in a separate file and link to it from within a document. Subsidiaries or localizers can modify linked art. If a static copy of the art is embedded in the document, localizers might need to re-create the art, which is expensive.
Ensure that you are legally permitted to distribute the art worldwide.	Check whether worldwide distribution affects royalties. Check expiration dates on art licensing and ensure that you can remove the art before the license expires. Verify that copyright statements will protect the art anywhere it may be seen.
	Check for restrictions on imported content in countries or regions where your product, service, or website is likely to be used. For example, maps are often subject to government review before they can be imported. If you include maps in your content, be careful about treatment of disputed territories. Improper treatment of a disputed area might be illegal as well as offensive.

Examples and scenarios

Fictitious examples that include names of people, places, or organizations are always potentially sensitive, both legally and from a worldwide perspective. Use-case scenarios, which are detailed descriptions of specific user interactions with a product, service, or technology, present similar problems. To globalize examples and use-case scenarios, use the guidelines in the following table.

Guideline	More information
Vary examples in content.	From example to example, vary the national identity of business and personal names, addresses, telephone numbers, email addresses, currency, and URLs. You might need to include a disclaimer noting that any similarity to real people, places, or things is coincidental.
Be sensitive to how the cultural aspects of a use-case scenario will be interpreted by other cultures.	Social situations, politics, religion, events, holidays, sports, traditions, and legal and business practices vary worldwide. For example, greeting cards are uncommon in many parts of the world, and in some cultures men and women do not touch in public, even to shake hands.
Avoid mentioning real places altogether, or use the names of international cities that are easily recognized.	If you must mention real places, vary the locales that are represented from one example to the next. For example, you might mention Tokyo, Paris, and New York.
Do not discuss technologies and standards that are not used worldwide unless you have no other choice.	Standards for telephone, cellular phone, email, and wireless technologies, as well as electrical and video standards, vary worldwide.
Do not assume that United States standards are familiar to everyone.	Keyboard layouts, default paper and envelope sizes, common printers, monitor resolutions, character sets, text direction, and input methods vary worldwide.

International currency

The names of international currencies are always lowercase. Examples are the euro and the dollar. If a country or region name is used to specify the currency name, the country or region name is capitalized. Examples are the U.S dollar and the Hong Kong dollar. For official international currency names, see ISO 4217 currency and funds name and code elements.

Time and place

To globalize information for time and place, use the guidelines in the following table.

Guideline	More information
Use international time formats.	Do not use A.M. and P.M. notation unless you have no other choice. Use 24-hour time format.
If you give a time for an event, include the time zone and the corresponding GMT zone.	*Microsoft style* 13:00 Eastern Time (UTC5)
Begin calendars on Monday, not Sunday.	This is the custom in much of the world.

Guideline	More information
Spell out names of months.	Use the format month dd, yyyy. *Microsoft style* January 5, 2011 Do not use numbers to represent months. For example, do not use 6/12/2010. This example could be read in different parts of the world as June 12, 2011, or as December 6, 2011.
Do not refer to seasons unless you have no other choice.	Remember, summer in the northern hemisphere is winter in the southern hemisphere. Use months or calendar quarters instead. If you must mention a season in other than the most general way, establish which hemisphere you are referring to. *Microsoft style* The product is scheduled for release in July. The event takes place in northern summer. Flowers bloom in the spring. *Not Microsoft style* The product is scheduled for release in summer.
Include the country or region name in event locations.	None.
Do not name countries, regions, cities, or land features in disputed areas.	Errors in names of disputed territory can be highly offensive and even illegal in some countries.

For more information, see *A.M., P.M.; Dates; Time zones.*

Names and contact information

If you are creating a form that collects personal information, whether as a webpage or as a content example, globalize your form by using the guidelines in the following table.

Guideline	More information
Use first name or given name and surname in describing parts of a person's name.	Given name is preferable to first name. In many countries, the surname comes first.
Be aware that not all cultures use middle names.	It is all right to have a middle name field in a form, but do not make it required information.
Use title, not honorific, to describe words such as Mr. or Ms.	Not all cultures may have an equivalent to some titles that are common in the United States, such as Ms.
Provide text fields that take international addresses into account.	Make text fields large enough for the user to enter the entire address so that the user can include whatever information is appropriate for the locale. At a minimum, do not require the user to complete fields that do not apply everywhere, such as state.
Use postal code instead of ZIP Code.	Allow for at least ten characters for a postal code, and allow for a combination of letters and numbers.
Use state or province instead of state by itself.	Do not require an entry in this field.

Guideline	More information
Include a field for country/region instead of just country to accommodate disputed territories.	None.
If you need information for mailing between European countries or regions, include a field for the country/region code.	None.
Provide enough space for long international telephone numbers.	For details about formatting international telephone numbers, see *Phone numbers* (Chapter 7).

Be aware that many countries strictly control what personal information can be legally collected, stored, and shared.

If you are creating content that includes information about how to contact you, be aware that toll-free telephone numbers are not always available worldwide. Provide an alternate way for customers to contact you.

Try to avoid references to specific third-party companies or organizations in the United States, even very large ones. In particular, avoid referring users to United States resources. If you must provide a vendor, supplier, or retailer reference, state that it is a United States company or organization, and suggest where the user outside the United States might look for local resources.

Fonts

Use the following table as guidance for fonts.

Guideline	More information
Use fonts that are available in browsers and operating systems worldwide.	Among the common fonts are Times New Roman, Arial, Courier New, and Verdana. Alternatively, you can design your content so that fonts on the user's system will be substituted if the specified font is not available.
Avoid hand-drawn fonts or fonts that are hard-coded in text or code.	None.

Web, software, and HTML issues

Content that is published on the web attracts a worldwide audience. However, not all worldwide web users have the latest browsers. Broadband Internet access is not always available outside major cities, and Internet service providers do not always charge a flat monthly rate for access. To accommodate worldwide users, use the guidelines in the following table.

Guideline	More information
Use standard HTML tags.	Avoid proprietary tags. If you are developing HTML text with scripted code, globalize any text that is generated by the scripts, too.
Keep download issues in mind.	Charges for Internet service vary greatly depending on locale. Keep page size under 100 KB when possible, and consider including a text-only version of the page for larger content.
Design pages so that text loads first, followed by graphics.	This sequence ensures that the page is usable before it is fully loaded.
Keep in mind that some products and formats are not available worldwide.	Localized versions of new and updated products and formats may lag behind U.S. availability.
Provide support for browsers likely to be used by the worldwide audience.	If you are supporting earlier versions of browsers, you might need to do the following: ■ Provide a no-frames version. ■ Avoid certain elements in scripts. ■ Include some design information (such as background color) in the document files instead of the style sheet. ■ Avoid nested tables.
Use the simplest possible design techniques.	None.
Account for worldwide users who read from right to left or from top to bottom.	You may not be able to provide an ideal site for these users, but page design can help. For example, you might provide key information, such as home page links, at both the upper-right and upper-left sides of the page to increase your chances of reaching all users.
If your content will be localized or might be localized in the future, allow space for text expansion.	Some languages require many more words to express an idea that may be expressed compactly in English. Even if text will not be localized, be aware that many worldwide users translate English text by using an automated translation engine, such as Bing Translator. (*http://www.microsofttranslator.com/*)
Provide support for double-byte text entry in software.	None.
Follow laws for software restrictions.	If software contains code subject to export restrictions in the United States or legal requirements in other countries or regions, remove the code from versions that do not meet those requirements.
Exercise care when you provide software for download or on a multiproduct CD.	United States laws restrict the delivery of certain information and technologies internationally. Verify that the download complies with United States laws.
Be aware of the restrictions for downloads in a country or region.	Marketing statements, political statements, and names of people, places, and landmarks are restricted by law in some countries or regions. Restrict downloads that make reference to such information unless you are sure that the download is legal in the country or region.
If possible, link only to globalized sites and to publications that are available worldwide.	None.
If possible, link to a site where the user can specify the appropriate country or region.	None.
Identify links and cross-references that are not globally relevant.	If you must link to a site or refer to a publication that is not globalized, inform your users.
Monitor requests for email newsletters to determine user location.	Email notes that are sent to users outside the United States must be globalized, localized, or customized to meet local requirements.

Legal issues with worldwide content

Content is subject to the laws of the countries where it is distributed. The laws governing product documentation, advertising, sales promotion, and other kinds of content vary significantly from one country or region to the next. The information in this topic is not exhaustive, but it covers some important areas where U.S. and international law may affect what you write.

Guideline	More information
If you are writing about a discount or another special offer, be specific, and include any limitations on availability of the offer.	For each country or region where the offer is valid, give any price information in the currency unit for the country or region, and mention any taxes for the country or region that apply.
Specify the "where and when" of events, products, contests, and special offers.	■ Specify where events, products, contests, and special offers are available, and use *only* if necessary to exclude any place not specifically mentioned. State where items can be shipped, and note any additional charges, including international shipping, if appropriate. ■ State an expiration date, if there is one. If the offer is limited to available inventory, say so. ■ If release dates or events differ by country or region, provide a link to a list of release dates or give information that can be customized based on the user's location. ■ Include contact information for customers outside of the United States.
Use standard legal language.	Include legal statements that are required in countries or regions. A copyright or trade lawyer can help you determine what you must do to comply with Internet, copyright, privacy, and business laws in various countries and regions.
Be aware of privacy laws in other countries.	None
Use copyright and trademark information correctly.	In online content, you can include a link to copyright and legal information that can be updated for specific countries or regions.
Know the restrictions on product claims.	Marketing statements and political statements are restricted by law in some countries and regions. Do not compare one product with another product. Some countries and regions have strict requirements of documented proof for such comparisons. Others require the permission of the competitor. Still others restrict specific comparisons such as "more clip art than Brand X" (where Brand X is a named product). Do not use superlatives, such as, "The world's best word processor." It is all right to compare your product with earlier versions of the same product, such as, "Our fastest version yet." Third-party recommendations must be provided willingly. Paid endorsements are illegal in some countries and regions.
Include any media ratings required in the countries and regions where your product will be distributed.	For example, game software and hardware may require an epilepsy warning in some countries or regions.
Be aware of restrictions on using names of people, places, and landmarks.	The use of names of people, places, and landmarks is restricted by law in some countries and regions. Do not name countries or regions, cities, or land features in disputed areas, and avoid showing them on maps. Errors in names or boundaries of disputed territory can be highly offensive and even illegal in some countries or regions.

Guideline	More information
Ensure that you can legally use the third-party content that you want to use.	Ensure that you are legally permitted to distribute licensed third-party content worldwide, and check whether worldwide distribution affects royalties. Check expiration dates on third-party licensing, and ensure that you can remove the content before the license expires. Verify that copyright statements protect the content anywhere that it may be seen. Check for restrictions on imported content in countries or regions where your product or website is likely to be used. For example, maps are often subject to government review before they can be imported. And some of the free clip art that is available on Microsoft websites is provide by third-parties and may not be available for us to use freely in content.
Be aware of download requirements.	Exercise care when providing software for download or on a multi-product CD. United States laws restrict the delivery of certain information and technology internationally. Verify that providing the download will not break United States laws.

Additional globalization resources

To be more aware of issues of concern to the worldwide audience, become a consumer of worldwide information and media. Subscribe to email newsletters in the countries and regions where your audience lives. Do not assume that your customer knows anything about your country, region, or history. Examine the worldwide implications of anything that you say or do instinctively. To better understand strategies for worldwide content, visit these sites on the web:

- Microsoft International Style Guides, *http://www.microsoft.com/Language/en-US/StyleGuides.aspx*

- Plain Language Action Network (U.S.), *http://www.plainlanguage.gov/*

- World Time Zones, *http://www.worldtimeserver.com/*

- W3C Internationalization Activity, *http://www.w3.org/International/*

Print resources

Kohl, John R. *The Global English Style Guide: Writing Clear, Translatable Documentation for a Global Market*. Cary, NC: SAS Institute, Inc., 2008.

Weiss, Edmond H. *The Elements of International English Style: A Guide to Writing Correspondence, Reports, Technical Documents, and Internet Pages for a Global Audience*. M.E. Sharpe, 2005.

CHAPTER 4

Accessible content

Microsoft is committed to creating products, services, tools, and content that are easy for everyone to use. Content should be created in such a way as to maximize accessibility for people with disabilities and to support users of various input methods and devices, including mice, keyboards, touch screens, game controllers, gesture, and voice. This topic includes information about progress at Microsoft toward maximizing accessibility and guidelines about what everyone can do to assist in this effort.

Follow these guidelines for designing content to maximize accessibility for people with disabilities and to support users who use various input methods and devices:

- Conform to established accessibility guidelines and requirements.

- Follow standards for accessible webpages.

- Write clearly and concisely.

- Use graphics and design that enable comprehension.

- Use appropriate terminology.

Accessibility guidelines and requirements

It is Microsoft policy that all content be accessible. Compliance with the Microsoft Corporate Accessibility Policy is achieved by ensuring that content meets the necessary Microsoft Accessibility Standard (MAS) requirements. MAS contains a compilation of national and international standards and regulations that affect all components of software and hardware development, including web content and multimedia. It also includes information about implementing and testing each standard.

To learn about guidelines for making products, services, tools, and websites accessible, see the following resources:

- The Microsoft Accessibility website: *http://www.microsoft.com/enable/*

- Accessibility information for software developers on the Windows Accessibility website on MSDN: *http://msdn.microsoft.com/en-us/windows/bb735024.aspx*

- Section 508 of the Rehabilitation Act of 1998: *http://www.section508.gov/index.cfm*

- Trace Research and Development Center at the University of Wisconsin: *http://trace.wisc.edu/*

- W3C Web Content Accessibility Guidelines (WCAG): *http://www.w3.org/standards /techs/wcag#w3c_all*

Accessible webpages

Keep in mind that your website needs to be accessible not only to people with disabilities but also to people who use various kinds of browsers, who have graphics turned off, or who may be using older technology. The following guidelines are brief reminders. You can find more details about the rationale for these guidelines and some ways to accommodate them in the resources listed earlier in this topic.

To enhance the accessibility of webpages for people who use screen readers, follow these guidelines and the guidelines provided in the Web Content Accessibility Guidelines (WCAG) 2.0 (*http://www.w3.org/TR/WCAG20/*):

- Always provide *alternative text* for elements that are not text, including graphics, audio, and video. For simple elements, a brief but accurate description is enough. Use an asterisk (*) or the word *bullet* for bullets, not a description such as *little blue ball*. Do not include information about invisible placeholders. For more complex elements, provide a link to a separate page with more details. For further guidelines for HTML accessibility, see the Web Content Accessibility Guidelines (WCAG) 2.0.

- Provide text links in addition to image maps.

- Write link text that is meaningful but brief. Do not use phrases such as "click here." Use links that can stand alone in a list.

- Make link text distinct. Use redundant visual cues, such as both color and underline, so that color-blind users can identify link text.

- Plan links and image-map links so that navigation with the Tab key moves appropriately for bidirectional text.

- If you use frames, provide alternative pages without them.

- If you use tables, ensure that they are formatted according to production guidelines for your team and the Web Content Accessibility Guidelines (WCAG) 2.0.

- Provide closed captions, transcripts, or descriptions of audio and video content.

- Do not use scrolling marquees unless you have no other choice.

Accessible writing

Many of the following suggestions for maximizing accessibility also help make documentation clearer and more useful for everyone, and better for localization purposes:

- Provide clear, concise descriptions of the product and initial setup, including a section or card that gets the user up and running with the basic features.

- Put key information near the beginning of the content.

- Use a bulleted list or headings to emphasize important points.

- Keep paragraphs short or create small sections or text groupings.

- Minimize the number of steps in a procedure. Individuals who have cognitive impairments may have difficulty following procedures that have many steps. Keep the steps simple, and keep the user oriented.

- Keep sentence structure simple. Try to limit sentences to one clause. Individuals who have language difficulties, non-native English speakers, and some people who are deaf or hard of hearing may have difficulty understanding longer, complicated sentences.

- Provide descriptions that do not require pictures, or provide both pictures and written descriptions. Using only diagrams causes difficulty transcribing to other media. To test whether the writing is effective, try removing, one at a time, first the words and then the pictures. With only one method, can you still figure out what to do?

- Do not use directional terms (left, right, up, down) as the only clue to location. Individuals who have cognitive impairments may have difficulty interpreting them, as do users who rely on screen-reading software. A directional term is all right to use if another indication of location, such as *in the* **Save As** *dialog box, on the* **Standard** *toolbar*, or *in the title bar*, is also included. Directional terms are also all right to use when a sighted user with dyslexia can clearly see a change in the interface as the result of an action, such as a change in the right pane when an option in the left pane is clicked. However, directional terms can cause translation issues for bidirectional text.

- In product documentation, document all keyboard shortcuts. Describe all supported modes of interaction, such as mouse, keyboard, game controller, and gesture, with the user interface of your product. That way, users who have screen readers can hear the task before they hear the keyboard shortcut. Organize keyboard shortcuts in task groupings so that related shortcuts appear close together.

Accessible graphics and design

It is possible to work within the requirements of Microsoft standard design templates to make written content as visually accessible as possible. For example, use short paragraphs and break up long passages of text with subheadings.

Follow these guidelines for visually accessible documents:

- Do not use color coding alone. Use additional cues such as textual annotations or underlines. Alternatively, use patterns in addition to colors to indicate different types of information in charts and graphs.

- Do not use hard-coded colors. Hard-coded colors can become unreadable when using a high-contrast theme, as in a table, chart, or graph.

- Do not use hard-to-read color combinations, such as red and green or light green and white. People who have some types of color blindness may have difficulty seeing the differences between the colors.

- Do not use art that has screens or tints applied. Do not use text on a screened background, which is difficult to see and for a machine to scan. For the same reason, do not use shaded backgrounds and watermarks or other images behind text.

- Do not print text outside a rectangular grid. People who have low vision may have difficulty seeing text outside an established grid. Try to keep text in a uniform space for both visibility and ease of scanning.

Acceptable terminology

In general, refer to *a person who has a kind of disability*, not *a disabled person*.

If necessary, use the following terms to describe people with disabilities or the disabilities themselves.

Use these terms	Instead of
Blind, has low vision	Sight-impaired, vision impaired
Deaf or hard-of-hearing	Hearing-impaired
Has limited dexterity, has motion disabilities	Crippled, lame
Without disabilities	Normal, able-bodied, healthy
One-handed, people who type with one hand	Single-handed
People with disabilities	The disabled, disabled people, people with handicaps, the handicapped
Cognitive disabilities, developmental disabilities	Slow learner, retarded, mentally handicapped
TTY (to refer to the telecommunication device)	TT/TTD

CHAPTER 5

The user interface

I n the last decade, the types of electronic devices that a person can interact with have proliferated. In addition to computers, many people now have smartphones and game consoles, and they're interacting with them by using their voices, fingers, hands, and even their whole bodies.

The term used for these new types of interfaces is *natural user interface (NUI)*. The natural user interface is designed and programmed to enable a user to interact more naturally with a computer or program through gestures and speech instead of an input device such as a keyboard, mouse, or game controller. For example, a user can give a command or select an option by touching the screen with a finger or hand. With a device that has a camera or sensor, a user can perform a gesture with an arm, a foot, or even the entire body to interact with a character on the screen. With a device that has a microphone, a user can say a command, clap, or whistle to cause a program to react in a logical or expected manner. Additional interactions can include holding up something for the program to digitize and show on the screen, and then working with that item through an avatar. Programs can also read facial features to recognize a user, read lips, and even reply to a user's voice. Natural user interface technology can also enable a program to determine the location of a user and to react to that location.

As natural user interfaces develop, writing and editing content for the interface will undoubtedly generate the need for a new style and new terminology. This version of the *Microsoft Manual of Style* introduces the first wave of this new style and terminology with the intent to set some groundwork for future guidelines.

Windows user interface

The following illustrations show a Windows desktop, the desktop access points, an open window, a browser window, and a webpage, with the various elements that appear on them called out.

Elements that appear in more than one illustration are not necessarily called out on each illustration. For example, the scroll bar and the Close button appear in all windows, so they are only called out in the illustration of an open window.

For the names of dialog box elements, see *Dialog boxes*. For the names of items on a ribbon, menu, or toolbar, see those topics. For more information, also see *User interface formatting*, and the names of individual items.

Windows desktop

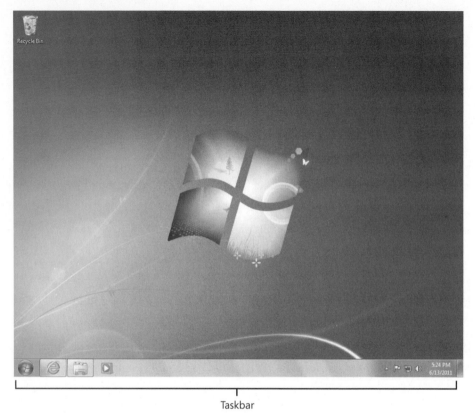

Taskbar

Desktop access points

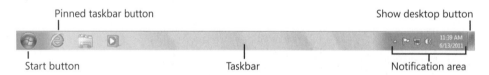

Pinned taskbar button

Show desktop button

Start button

Taskbar

Notification area

Open window

Menu bar   Address bar

Search box

Minimize Maximize Close
button   button   button

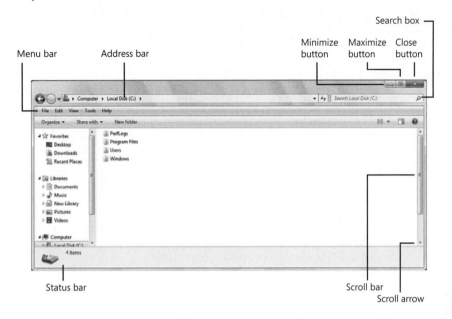

Status bar   Scroll bar

Scroll arrow

Browser

Favorites bar   Address bar

Home   Favorites Tools
button   button   button

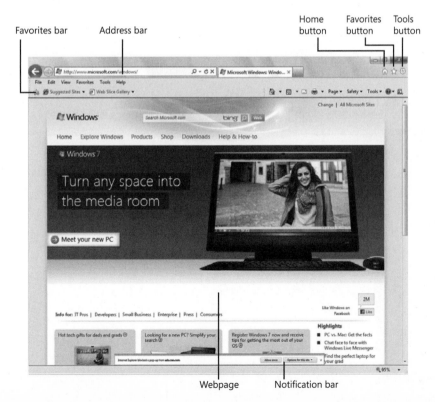

Webpage   Notification bar

Webpage

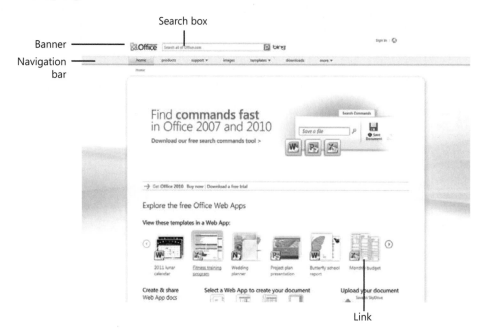

Banner

Navigation
bar

Search box

Link

Windows Phone user interface

The following illustrations show Windows Phone screens and the various elements that appear on them.

Start screen and Tiles

For a general audience, use **Start**, rather than *Start screen* or *Home screen* to describe this screen.

For a developer audience, if necessary, you can use *Start screen*.

Use *Tile* to refer to objects on **Start** that the user can move around, such as the Phone Tile and the Calendar Tile. Tiles are shortcuts to apps or other content. Always capitalize *Tile*.

Use *Live Tile* to refer to a Tile that updates automatically and shows content updates on **Start**.

In procedures, use the name of the Tile, such as **Messaging**, to refer to the Tile.

Refer to the arrow in a circle on the Windows Phone user interface generically as *the arrow*.

Microsoft style for Windows Phone

On **Start**, tap **Messaging**

You can pin Tiles to **Start**.

Other screen elements

Screen title

Pivot control

More icon

Icons

Application bar

In general, use the name of an icon and its image instead of the word *icon* in procedures.

Refer to the text at the top of a screen as the *screen title* or *application title*.

Don't use the terms *Pivot control* and *Application Bar* for a general audience. Both terms can be used in documentation for developers.

Microsoft style for Windows Phone

In Maps, tap **More** ▦, and then tap **Show traffic**.

Tap the check box next to each email that you want to delete, and then tap **Delete**.

The Pivot control provides a quick way to manage views of large sets of data within an application. (Developer audience)

The Application Bar is a set of one to four buttons that can be displayed along the bottom of the phone's screen. (Developer audience)

App list

The App list shows apps installed on Windows Phone. When referring to the App list, capitalize *App*. Do not use *Application list*.

Microsoft style for Windows Phone

On **Start**, flick left to the **App** list.

Hub

Don't refer to a *Hub* unless absolutely necessary. Instead, in procedures, use the name of the Hub, such as "In Marketplace..." or "In Pictures...," to refer to the front page of a Hub for a user action. If you do refer to a Hub, capitalize *Hub*.

Microsoft style for Windows Phone

In **Pictures**, find a picture, and tap to open it.

The Pictures Hub is where you go to see all the pictures on your phone and the latest pictures your friends have posted to Windows Live.

Menu

Use *menu* to refer to a context-specific menu that appears when the user taps the **More** icon.

Dialog box

Dialog box elements include text boxes, check boxes, and buttons.

Lock screen

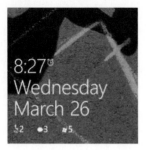

The lock screen appears when the phone is turned on. Refer to the lock screen by name or generically as *your phone's screen*.

Microsoft style for Windows Phone

To unlock your phone, turn it on, and then flick your finger upward on your phone's screen until you can see the keypad for entering your password.

If you haven't checked your phone for a while, you can get a lot of information from the lock screen, including how many new text messages, missed calls, emails, and voicemails you've received.

Keyboard

Refer to keyboard elements as *keys*. Examples are the *Enter key* and the *Shift key*.

Use *type* to refer to using alphanumeric keys; use *tap* to refer to functional keys.

Microsoft style for Windows Phone

Tap the message box, and then type your message.

Type your password, and then tap **Enter**.

User interface elements

User interface elements enable users to interact with programs, applications, and with pages and services on websites. These elements, which include controls and commands, can be presented to the user in various graphical forms, such as in ribbons, menus, toolbars, dialog boxes, property sheets, or web forms. Or they can be individual elements such as hyperlinks or download buttons on webpages.

User interface terminology

In content for software developers, buttons and other dialog box elements are called *controls*, especially in discussions about creating them. Do not use *control* in content for a general audience.

> **Note** In some hardware products, buttons, switches, and so on are called controls because they give the user control over various actions. For example, users use joystick controls to move around the screen in games. This usage is all right as long as the meaning is clear.

User interface syntax

The following terms are most commonly used to describe how users interact with controls and commands:

- *Click:* Use for commands, command buttons, option buttons, and options in a list, gallery, or palette.

- *Select* and *clear:* Use for check boxes.

- *Remove the checkmark:* Use for checked and unchecked commands.

- *Type or select:* Use to refer to an item (as in a combo box) that the user can either type or select in the accompanying text box. You can use *enter* instead if there is no possibility of confusion.

Except for the identifiers *box, list, check box*, and *tab*, the generic name of a control (*button, option*, and so on) should not follow the label of a control, especially within procedures.

Use bold formatting for dialog box titles, labels, and options. Do not use bold formatting for the title of a webpage. Instead, insert a hyperlink if appropriate or use regular type. For more information, see *dialog boxes*, *Document conventions* (Chapter 6), *Procedures* (Chapter 6), *User interface formatting*, *Windows user interface*.

The following example shows typical procedure wording for dialog box controls and webpage controls.

Microsoft style (for dialog boxes)

To view bookmarks

1. On the **Tools** menu, click **Options**, and then click the **View** tab.

2. Select the **Bookmarks** check box.

Microsoft style (for webpages)

To create a free website

1. Go to *http://officelive.com*.

2. On the Office Live Small Business sign-up page, click **Create a free website**. A sign-up page appears.

5 Ribbons, menus, and toolbars

Ribbons, menus, and toolbars are three methods that programs can use to show users what commands are available in those programs.

Ribbons

The ribbon is a rectangular area that fits across the top of an application window. It was introduced as a component of the Microsoft Office Fluent user interface in Office 2007.

The ribbon is composed of several tabs, each of which represents a subset of program functionality. The tabs contain related commands that are organized, grouped, and labeled.

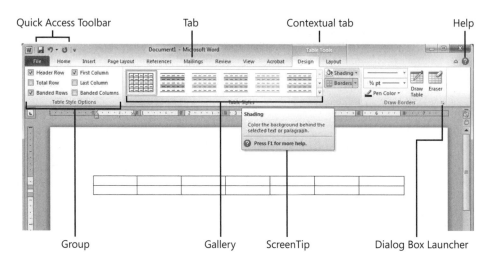

The ribbon has several elements. They are listed and described in the following table, using examples from Microsoft Word.

Element	Description
Tools	Context-sensitive tabs that appear on the ribbon under certain circumstances. For example, if you select an image in a document, the **Picture Tools** tab appears on the ribbon. If you select or are working in a table, the **Table Tools** tab appears on the ribbon. The tools tab disappears when the user clicks away from the selected item.
tab	A rectangular region on a ribbon that represents a subset of the program's functionality. In the following example, the **Home** tab is open.
group	A rectangular region on a tab that contains a set of related controls and commands. The following example shows the **Paragraph** group on the **Home** tab.
gallery	A rectangular window or menu that presents an array or grid of visual choices to a user. For example, when a user clicks an image in a document and then clicks the **Picture Tools** tab, the **Picture Styles** gallery becomes available.
mini toolbar	A set of controls that appears in context when an object is selected. A user can use these controls to perform actions upon the object. For example, when a user selects text, the formatting mini toolbar automatically appears above the text. As the mouse pointer moves closer to the mini toolbar, the toolbar becomes more visible. As the mouse pointer moves away from it, the toolbar fades away or disappears altogether.
ScreenTip	A ScreenTip is a small window that displays descriptive text when a mouse pointer rests on a command or control. A ScreenTip may include a link to a Help topic.
Quick Access Toolbar	A collection of icons, located on a program's title bar, that provides shortcuts to commonly used commands. Users can add icons to this toolbar or remove them.

5

Element	Description
Dialog Box Launcher	A specific icon that is used within a group to launch a related dialog box. It is located in the lower-right corner of a group.

Dialog Box Launcher

Element	Description
KeyTips	Small keyboard tips that indicate what key to press to access program functionality. The user must press the Alt key to see the KeyTips and then press the indicated number or letter to run the associated command. In the following example, pressing the number 1 saves a Word document.

Ribbon terminology

In Office 2007, *Ribbon* is capitalized. In Office 2010, *ribbon* is lowercase. Use *on* the ribbon, not *in* the ribbon.

Microsoft style

On the ribbon, click the appropriate tab or group to display the command that you want to add to the Quick Access Toolbar.

Not Microsoft style

Some tabs display in the ribbon only when they are relevant to the task at hand, such as when formatting a table or an image.

Do not use the possessive form of *ribbon*.

Microsoft style

One of the benefits of using the ribbon is its clear visual layout.

Not Microsoft style

One of the ribbon's benefits is its clear visual layout.

Spell out Quick Access Toolbar. Do not abbreviate it to QAT.

Microsoft style

You can add or remove commands from the Quick Access Toolbar.

Not Microsoft style

You can add or remove commands from the Quick Access Toolbar (QAT).

You can add or remove commands from the QAT.

To refer to tools, use the following format: Under **x** on the **y** tab, in the **z** group, click **zz**.

Microsoft style

Under **Table Tools**, on the **Layout** tab, in the **Data** group, click **Repeat Header Rows**.

Not Microsoft style

Click the **Layout** tab under **Table Tools**, and then in the **Data** group, click **Repeat Header Rows**.

To refer to the Dialog Box Launcher, use the following format: On the **x** tab, in the **y** group, click the **z** Dialog Box Launcher.

Microsoft style

On the **Home** tab, in the **Font** group, click the **Font** Dialog Box Launcher.

Not Microsoft style

Click the **Home** tab, and click the **Font** Dialog Box Launcher in the **Font** group.

On the **Home** tab, in the **Font** group, click the **Font** box down-arrow.

When writing procedures that involve the ribbon, use the following format:

- On the **x** tab, in the **y** group, click **z**.

- On the **x** tab, in the **y** group, click **z**, and then click **zz**.

Microsoft style

On the **Review** tab, in the **Comments** group, click **New Comment**.

On the **Home** tab, in the **Font** group, click the arrow next to the **Text Highlight Color** icon, and then click the color that you want.

Not Microsoft style

Click the **Review** tab, and then click **New Comment** in the **Comments** group.

On the **Review** tab, under **Comments**, click **New**.

Menus

A menu is a group of the main commands of a program arranged by category such as *File*, *Edit*, *Format*, *View*, and *Help*. Menus are usually displayed on a menu bar typically located near the top of a window.

Menus contain commands. Do not refer to a menu command as a *choice* or an *option*. Also do not refer to a menu command as a *menu item*, except in content for software developers about the user interface.

To describe user interaction with menus and menu commands, use *click*. Do not use *choose*, *select* or *pick*. If you must refer to the user action of opening a menu, use *click*. To open a submenu, the user *points to* a command on the main menu, which causes the submenu to open, and then *clicks* the appropriate command.

Microsoft style

On the **File** menu, click **Open**.

On the **View** menu, point to **Sort by**, and then click **Date**.

The following illustration shows elements of menus. In most content, you should not have to refer to user interface elements by their technical names. The usual practice, here as elsewhere in the user interface, is to refer to elements by their labels.

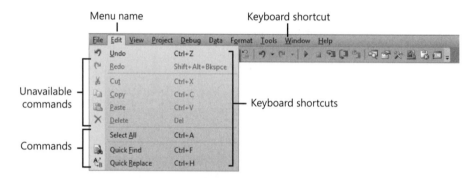

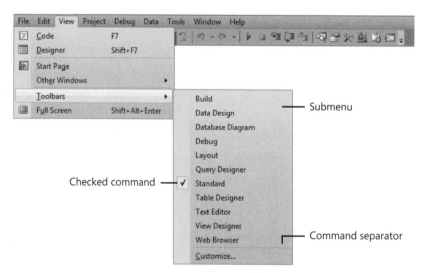

Menu terminology

When referring to a specific menu, use lowercase for the word *menu*, as in "the **Edit** menu."

In general, refer to unavailable commands and options as *unavailable*, not as *dimmed, disabled*, or *grayed* unless you are describing their appearance. In that case, use *dimmed*, but not *grayed* or *disabled*. In content for a technical audience, it is all right to refer to unavailable commands as *disabled*.

Microsoft style

There are several unavailable commands on the **Edit** menu.

If the **Paste** command is unavailable, first select the text that you want to paste, and then click **Cut** or **Copy**.

The **Paste** command appears dimmed because it is unavailable.

A disabled control is unavailable to the user. (In content for software developers.)

Not Microsoft style

There are several dimmed commands on the **Edit** menu.

If the **Paste** command is disabled, first select the text that you want to paste, and then choose **Cut** or **Copy**.

The **Paste** command appears grayed because it is unavailable.

In general, mention the name of the menu the first time that you refer to a particular command. However, if the location of the command is clear from the immediate context, you do not have to mention the menu name. An example is a topic about the **Edit** menu.

Microsoft style

If the **Paste** command on the **Edit** menu is unavailable, first select the text that you want to paste, and then click **Cut** or **Copy**. You now should be able to click **Paste** to insert the text in its new location.

Kinds of menus

In content for a general audience, do not qualify the term *menu* with the adjectives *cascading*, *drop-down, pull-down, pop-up, shortcut,* or *submenu* unless the way that the menu works needs to be emphasized as a feature of the product. *Shortcut menu* is all right to use, although in most cases, you can avoid it. Do not use any of these terms as verbs.

Microsoft style

Click the **File** menu.

When you click the right mouse button, a shortcut menu appears.

Not Microsoft style

Drop down the **File** menu.

When you click the right mouse button, a shortcut menu pops up.

In content for software developers about the user interface, you might need to detail specific kinds of menus.

Style of menu names and commands

Always surround menu names with the words *the* and *menu* both in text and in procedures.

Microsoft style

On the **File** menu, click **Open**.

Not Microsoft style

On **File**, click **Open**.

From **File**, click **Open**.

In procedures, do not surround command names with the words *the* and *command*. In text, you can use "the ... command" for clarity.

Microsoft style

On the **File** menu, click **Open**.

Not Microsoft style

On the **File** menu, click the **Open** command.

Do not use the possessive form of menu and command names.

Microsoft style

The **Open** command on the **File** menu opens the file.

Not Microsoft style

The **File** menu's **Open** command opens the file.

Follow the user interface for capitalization and use bold formatting both in text and procedures. Do not capitalize the identifier, such as *menu* or *command*.

Microsoft style

On the **Options** menu, click **Keep Help on Top**.

Not Microsoft style

On the **Options** menu, click **Keep Help On Top**.

Toolbars

A toolbar is a grouping of commands optimized for efficient access. Unlike a menu, which contains a comprehensive list of commands, a toolbar contains the most frequently used commands. Most toolbars are customizable, enabling users to add or remove toolbars, change their size and location, and even change their contents. Some toolbars are called *bars*. An example is the Command bar in Internet Explorer. Always follow the user interface.

Toolbars contain buttons. A toolbar button can have a submenu, which is indicated by an arrow next to it. A toolbar button with a submenu is called a *menu button* if the user can click either the button or the arrow to open the submenu, and it is called a *split button* if clicking the button carries out the command, but clicking the arrow opens the submenu. Do not refer to a toolbar button as a *choice* or an *option*. Also do not refer to a toolbar button as a toolbar *item* or a toolbar *control* except in content for software developers about the user interface.

To describe user interaction with toolbars and toolbar buttons, use *click* for toolbar buttons and submenu commands, and *click*, *type*, or *enter* for submenu commands that require users to provide information. Do not use *choose*, *select,* or *pick*.

Microsoft style

To read mail in Internet Explorer, click **Read mail** on the Command bar.

On the Command bar, click **Tools**, and then click **Internet options**.

The following illustrations show examples of toolbars. In most content, you should not have to refer to user interface elements by their technical names. The usual practice, here as elsewhere in the user interface, is to refer to elements by their labels.

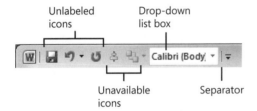

Toolbar Terminology

When referring to a specific toolbar, use lowercase for the word *toolbar*, unless the word *Toolbar* appears in uppercase in the user interface, as is the case with the Quick Access Toolbar in programs that use a ribbon, such as Word 2010. *Toolbar* is one word.

If there is only one toolbar, refer to it as the *toolbar*. If there are multiple toolbars, refer to them by name, followed by the word *toolbar*.

Refer to the main toolbar that is on by default and contains buttons for basic tasks, such as opening and printing a file, as the **Standard** *toolbar*, unless it is named in the user interface, as is the case with the Quick Access Toolbar.

Refer to named toolbar buttons by their user-interface names. Refer to unnamed toolbar buttons by their tooltip labels. Use the exact label text, including its capitalization, but do not include the shortcut key, the explanation, or the ellipsis for buttons that have them.

Refer to toolbar menu buttons and split buttons by their labels and the word *menu*. Use the exact label text, including its capitalization.

Microsoft style

On the Quick Access Toolbar, click **New.**

On the Quick Access Toolbar, click the arrow next to the **Font color** menu, and then click the color that you want.

On the Command bar, click **Feeds**.

On the Command bar, click the **Print** menu, and then click **Print Preview.**

Not Microsoft style

On the Quick Access Toolbar, click **New (Ctrl+N).**

On the Quick Access Toolbar, click the arrow next to **Font color**, and then click the color that you want.

On the Command bar, click the **No feeds detected on this page** button.

On the Command bar, click the **Print** menu, and then click **Print Preview....**

In general, refer to unavailable commands and options as *unavailable*, not as *dimmed, disabled,* or *grayed*, unless you are describing their appearance. In that case, use *dimmed*, but not *grayed* or *disabled*. In content for a technical audience, it is all right to refer to unavailable commands as *disabled*.

Microsoft style

There are several unavailable buttons on the Quick Access Toolbar.

When Word first opens, the **Can't Undo** and **Can't Repeat** buttons are dimmed because they are not available until there is something to undo or repeat.

In Microsoft Visual Basic .NET, the **Stop Debugging** button is disabled when a program is not in the process of being debugged. (In content for software developers.)

Not Microsoft style

There are several dimmed buttons on the Quick Access Toolbar.

When Word first opens, the **Can't Undo** and **Can't Repeat** buttons are disabled.

In Microsoft Visual Basic .NET, the **Stop Debugging** button is grayed when a program is not in the process of being debugged.

Kinds of toolbars

In content for a general audience, do not qualify the term *toolbar menu button* or *toolbar split button* with the adjective *cascading, drop-down, pull-down, pop-up,* or *submenu* unless the way that the menu works needs to be emphasized as a feature of the product. *Shortcut menu* is all right to use, although in most cases, you can avoid it. Do not use any of these terms as verbs.

Microsoft style

On the **Windows Help and Support** toolbar, click the **Options** menu.

On the **Options** menu, point to **Text Size**, and then click **Largest**.

Not Microsoft style

On the **Windows Help and Support** toolbar, open the **Options** pull-down menu.

On the **Options** menu, point to **Text Size**, and then click **Largest** on the submenu.

In content for software developers about the user interface, you might need to detail specific kinds of toolbars.

Style of toolbar names and buttons

In general, do not use the words *the* and *button* with toolbar buttons.

Microsoft style

To start a new document, click **New** on the Quick Access Toolbar.

Not Microsoft style

To start a new document, click the **New** button on the Quick Access Toolbar.

In general, do use *the* and *menu* with toolbar menu buttons and split buttons, but do not use the word *button*.

Microsoft style

To change Internet options, click the **Tools** menu on the Command bar, and then click **Internet Options**.

Not Microsoft style

To change Internet options, click **Tools** on the Command bar, and then click the **Internet Options** button.

To describe removing a check mark from a menu command, use click to remove the check mark. Do not use clear.

Microsoft style

To remove the **Desktop** toolbar from the taskbar, right-click the taskbar, and then click **Desktop** to remove the check mark.

Not Microsoft style

To remove the **Desktop** toolbar, right-click the taskbar, and then click **Desktop** to clear the check mark.

Do not use the possessive form of toolbars and toolbar buttons.

5

Microsoft style

To read mail, click **Read Mail** on the Command bar.

Not Microsoft style

You can read mail by clicking the Command bar's **Read Mail** button.

Follow the interface for capitalization and use bold formatting for toolbar names and buttons. Do not capitalize the identifier, such as toolbar or button.

Microsoft style

In Windows Help and Support, click **Help and Support home** on the toolbar.

Not Microsoft style

In Windows Help and Support, click the **Help And Support Home** button on the toolbar.

5 Webpage controls, dialog boxes, and property sheets

Here are some specifics on webpage controls, dialog boxes, and property sheets.

Webpage controls

Webpages contain such controls as hyperlinks, text boxes, and download buttons. A typical webpage with controls looks as follows.

Dialog boxes

Dialog boxes contain such controls as command buttons and list boxes through which users can carry out a particular command or task. For example, in the **Save As** dialog box, the user must indicate in which folder and under what name the document should be saved. A typical dialog box looks as follows.

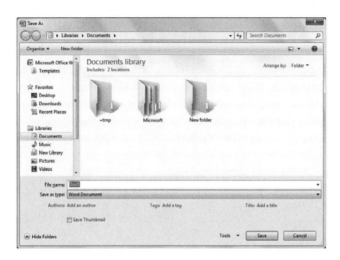

Property sheets

A *property sheet* is a dialog box that displays information about an object (the object's properties). For example, the **Internet Properties** property sheet shows information about Internet security settings. Property sheets contain such controls as check boxes and sliders. A typical property sheet looks as follows.

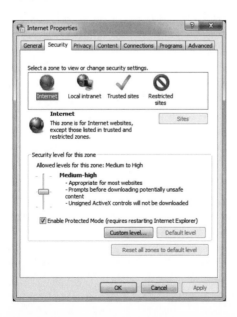

In general, avoid using *dialog box* or *property sheet* as a descriptor. If you cannot avoid a descriptor, use *dialog box* for both property sheets and dialog boxes unless your project style sheet provides different guidance. The distinction may be important for a technical audience, but do not distinguish in content for a general audience. For more information, also see *dialog boxes*, *Document conventions* (Chapter 6), *User interface text*.

Backstage view

Although the term *Backstage view* does not appear in the user interface, writers use it to refer to the page that a user sees upon clicking the **File** tab of any Microsoft Office 2010 program. The Backstage view, which is part of the Microsoft Office Fluent user interface, exposes information and metadata about the currently active document, lists recently opened documents and network places, and provides a variety of user options, such as opening, saving, printing, and versioning.

Note   The File tab replaces the Microsoft Office Button and the File menu that appeared in earlier versions of Office.

How to refer to Backstage view

Use the following guidelines to refer to Backstage view.

- On first mention, precede *Backstage + descriptor* with *Microsoft Office*, and use the appropriate trademark symbols for printed content. The descriptor that follows *Backstage* is usually *view*.

  Example: Microsoft® Office Backstage® view

- On subsequent mentions, you may omit *Microsoft Office* but you may not omit the descriptor. The only exception to this rule is if space is limited.

- Always capitalize *Backstage*.

- Always follow *Backstage* with a descriptor to explain what it is and what it works with. In most cases, the descriptor is the word *view*. Use *Backstage* only as an adjective; do not use *Backstage* as a noun, verb, or an adverb.

- In printed material, apply the trademark on first mention. Because it is trademarked, *Backstage* is not localized. However, the word *view* can be localized.

- It is acceptable, but not required, to precede *Backstage view* with the definite article *the*.

- In procedures, treat items in the Backstage view, such as tab names, headings, and button labels in accordance with the *Microsoft Manual of Style* guidelines.

- The items on the side of the Backstage view, such as Info, Recent, New, and Print, are called tabs.

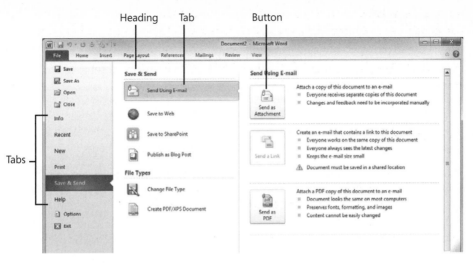

Heading   Tab   Button

Tabs

- Do not refer to the Backstage view as "the outspace."

- Do not refer to sections of the Backstage view as slabs, billboards, hero buttons, forms, panes, or windows except in content for software developers (if these terms appear in code samples or in content that documents these controls).

- Do not refer to the Backstage view as new.

- Do not apply a version number to the Backstage view.

Microsoft style

The Backstage view is where you manage your documents and related data about them.

Click the **File** tab. The Microsoft Office Backstage view appears.

After you create your document, go to the Backstage view to print it.

Not Microsoft style

After you create your document, go Backstage to print it.

The Office Backstage lets you inspect your document before you share it with others.

Clicking the **File** tab opens the Backstage.

The Office 2010 Backstage view lets you open previous versions of the active document.

Control Panel

With Control Panel, users can configure system-level features and perform related tasks. Examples of system-level feature configuration include hardware and software setup and configuration, security, system maintenance, and user account management.

The term *Control Panel* refers to the entire Windows Control Panel feature. Individual control panels are referred to as *control panel items*. A control panel item is considered *top-level* when it is directly accessible from the control panel home page or a category page.

The *control panel home page* is the main entry point for all control panel items. It lists the items by their category, along with the most common tasks. It is displayed when users click **Control Panel** on the **Start** menu.

A *control panel category page* lists the items within a single category, along with the most common tasks. It is displayed when users click a category name on the home page.

Control Panel contains icons that represent different control panel items. Do not use *applets*, *programs*, *tools*, or *control panels* to refer to either the icons or the items. Use bold formatting for the names of the icons and items.

If you must identify Control Panel by a category, use *the Control Panel application* in content for a technical audience, or *the Control Panel program* in content for a general audience. For a mixed audience, use *program*.

When documenting an alternate path to control panel items, use "To open <name of item>", and use bold formatting for the name of the item.

When referring to Control Panel itself, use regular type except when you are referring to the command on the **Start** menu. In that case, use bold formatting.

In documentation for a technical audience, refer to *control panel home page* and *control panel category page*, without capitalizing any of the words. A preceding definite article is optional.

When referring to a control panel item's hub page, use "main <control panel item name> page".

Do not use *the* when referring to Control Panel.

Microsoft style

In Control Panel, click **Network and Internet**, and then click **Internet Options**.

To open **Internet Options**, click **Start**, click **Control Panel**, and then click **Network and Internet**.

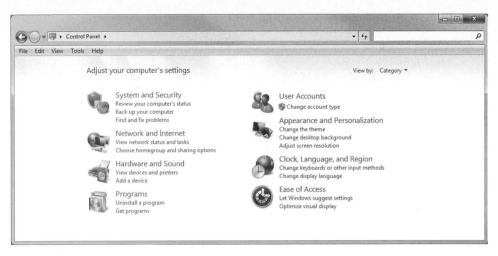

For more information about Control Panel, see the *Control Panels* section of the *Windows User Experience Interaction Guidelines* on MSDN.

Messages

When explaining a message, include the situation in which the message occurs, the message text, and what the user should do to continue. Do not use special formatting (such as monospace or bold) or title capitalization to set off messages from surrounding text unless specified in your product style guide. Instead, set the text off on a separate line or enclose it in quotation marks, as appropriate.

Programs use four types of messages:

- Errors
- Warnings
- Confirmations
- Notifications

Errors

An *error message* alerts a user about a problem that has already occurred. Error messages can be presented by using modal dialog boxes, in-place messages, notifications, or balloons.

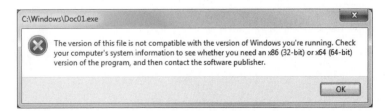

When referring to errors, follow these guidelines:

- In content for a general audience, refer to errors as *messages*, not *alerts, error messages, message boxes,* or *prompts.*

- For acceptable uses of alert, see *alert.*

- *Error message* is all right to use in content for a technical audience to describe messages that indicate an error condition. It is also all right if you must follow the user interface.

- Refer to errors by their main instruction. Use the exact text, including its capitalization. If the main instruction is long or detailed, summarize it.

Microsoft style

If you receive a "There is no CD disc in the drive" message, insert a new CD disc in the drive and try again.

If you receive Windows Update error 80072ee7 while checking for updates, you might need to change or remove static IP addresses for the Windows Update service.

International considerations

For machine-translated content, do not embed error message text that forms a completed sentence inside the sentence that makes a statement about the error message. Instead, structure the sentence so that the error message text is set off on a separate line or rewrite the sentence so that the error message text becomes a grammatical part of the sentence in which it is embedded.

For example, consider the following sentence:

> *If you receive a "There is no CD disc" in the drive message, insert a new CD disc in the drive and try again.*

To make this sentence better for machine translation, restructure this sentence as follows:

> *If you receive the following message, insert a new CD disc in the drive and try again: "There is no CD disc in the drive."*

> or

> *If you receive a message that states that there is no CD in the drive, insert a new CD disc in the drive and try again.*

Set error messages that are not completed sentences off on a separate line if you can. If you cannot, enclose the error-message text in quotation marks to mark the text as one unit.

For example, the following sentence may cause mistranslation:

> *If you receive Windows Update error 80072ee7 while checking for updates, you might need to change or remove static IP addresses for the Windows Update service.*

For better machine translation, restructure this sentence as follows:

If you receive the following Windows Update error while checking for updates, you might need to change or remove static IP addresses for the Windows Update service: 80072ee7

or

If you receive "Windows Update error 80072ee7" while checking for updates, you might need to change or remove static IP addresses for the Windows Update service.

Warnings

A *warning message* is a modal dialog box, in-place message, notification, or balloon that alerts the user of a condition that might cause a problem in the future.

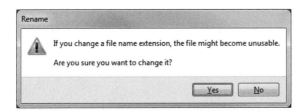

When referring to warnings, follow these guidelines:

- In content for a general audience, refer to warnings as *messages*, not *alerts*, *warning messages*, *message boxes*, or *prompts*.

- *Warning message* is all right to use in content for a technical audience to describe messages that indicate an error condition. It is also all right to use if you must follow the user interface. However, do not use *warning* without the word *message*.

- Refer to the warning message by its main instruction, which may be a question. Use the exact text, including its capitalization. If the text is long or detailed, summarize it.

Microsoft style

If you receive the "This file has been modified outside of the source editor. Do you want to reload it?" message, click Yes.

Confirmations

A *confirmation* is a modal dialog box that asks if the user wants to proceed with an action.

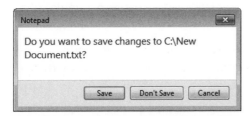

When referring to confirmations, follow these guidelines:

- Refer to confirmations as *messages*, not *alerts*, *warning messages*, *message boxes*, or *prompts*.

- Refer to the confirmation by its main instruction, which may be a question. Use the exact text, including its capitalization. If the text is long or detailed, summarize it.

Notifications

A *notification* informs a user of events that are unrelated to the current user activity, by briefly displaying a balloon from an icon in the notification area. The notification could result from a user action or significant system event, or could offer potentially useful information from Windows or an application.

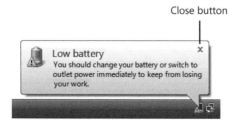

When referring to notifications, follow these guidelines:

- Refer to a notification as a *notification*, not as a *message*, a *balloon*, or an *alert*.

- Refer to a notification by its main instruction. Use the exact text, including its capitalization. If the main instruction is long or detailed, summarize it.

- Refer to the notification area as the *notification area*, not the *system tray*.

Microsoft style

The **Offline Files** icon in the notification area intermittently displays the "You are working offline. You are no longer connected to Server" notification.

For information about how to write messages, see the *Messages* section of the *Windows User Experience Interaction Guidelines* on MSDN.

Other user interface elements

In most content, especially for a general audience, do not differentiate between drop-down combo boxes, list boxes, and text boxes. Refer to such a control by its label, and use a descriptor only if necessary for clarity. If you must use a descriptor, use *list* or *box*. Do use the term *check box*, however.

The following table describes the various controls that can appear in dialog boxes and on webpages. Unless otherwise noted, avoid using the control name except in a discussion about designing a user interface. Use lowercase for the name of the control ("the **Spaces** check box"). In general, use sentence-style capitalization for the specific descriptor.

Control name	Definition	Usage	Example
Check box*	Square box that is selected or cleared to turn on or off an option. More than one check box can be selected.	Select the **Spaces** check box. Click to clear the **Bookmarks** check box. Under **Show**, select the **Draft font** check box. **Note** Always include *check box* with the label name.	
Combo box	Text box with a list box attached. The list is always visible. Because users can either type or select their choice, you can use *enter* to describe the action. Follow your project style sheet.	In the **Font** box, type or select the font you want to use. or In the **File Name** box, enter a file name.	
Command button	Rectangular button that initiates an action. A command button label ending with ellipses indicates that another dialog box will appear. More information is needed before the action can be completed.	Click **Options**.	
Command link	Command links enable users to make a choice among a set of mutually exclusive, related choices. Insert a hyperlink for the link text. If the user must click the link, refer to the text without using *link* or *hyperlink*. If the user must make a selection, refer to the links as *options*.	Click **Browse the Internet** now. or Click one of the following options:	
Drop-down arrow	Arrow associated with a drop-down combo or list box or some toolbar buttons, indicating a list the user can view by clicking the arrow.	Click the **Size** arrow to see more options.	

5

Control name	Definition	Usage	Example
Drop-down combo box	Closed version of a combo box with an arrow next to it. Clicking the arrow opens the list.	In the **Size** box, type or select a point size.	
Drop-down list box	Closed version of a list box with an arrow next to it. Clicking the arrow opens the list. Depending on the type of list, use either *list* or *box*, whichever is clearer.	In the **Item** list, click **Desktop**.	
Group box	Frame or box that encloses a set of related options. In some prograrms, a group box can be indicated by a single line that unifies the options below it. The group box is a visual device only. If necessary for clarity, you can use either *under* followed by the label or *in the <name of group> area.*	Click **Small Caps**. or Under **Effects**, click **SmallCaps**. or In the **Effects** area, click **Small Caps**.	
Label (do not use *caption*)	Text attached to any option, box, command, and so on. Refer to any option, box, and so on by its label.	In the **Font** list, click **Arial**.	Font:
Links	Links enable a user to go to another page, window, or Help topic; display a definition; initiate a command, or select an option. Insert a hyperlink for the link text, and then refer to the text without using the word *link* or *hyperlink*.	Click **Check for updates.**	

5

Control name	Definition	Usage	Example
List box	Any type of box containing a list of items the user can select. The user cannot type a selection in a list box.\n\nDepending on the type of list, use either *list* or *box*, whichever is clearer.	In the **Wallpaper** list, click the background wallpaper of your choice.	
List view	List views enable users to view and interact with a collection of data objects, using either single selection or multiple selection. Refer to a list view as a *list*.	In the **Picture library** list, click **Forest Flowers**.	
Option button (do not use *radio button* except in developer content.)	Round button used to select one of a group of mutually exclusive options.	Click **Portrait**.	
Progress bar	Progress bars enable users to follow the progress of a lengthy operation.	While the Memory Diagnostics Tool runs, you see a progress bar that indicates the status of the test.	
Progressive disclosure controls	Progressive disclosure controls enable users to show or hide additional information including data, options, or commands.\n\nRefer to individual controls by name. You can also use the name and a symbol in parentheses or an image.	To expand or collapse the folder, click the plus sign (+) or the minus sign (-) next to the folder name.\n\nor\n\nClick the chevron to expand your current network profile.	

Control name	Definition	Usage	Example
Slider* (also called *trackbar control* in some developer content)	Indicator on a gauge that displays and sets a value from a continuous range, such as speed, brightness, or volume.	Move the slider to the right to increase the volume.	
Spin box (do not use *spinner* or other labels)	Text box with up and down arrows that the user clicks to move through a set of fixed values. The user can also type a valid value in the box.	In the **Date** box, type or select the part of the date that you want to change.	
Tab* (also called *tabbed page* in technical documentation)	Labeled group of options used for many similar kinds of settings.	On the **Tools** menu, click **Options**, and then click the **View** tab. **Note** Always include *tab* with the label name.	
Text box	Rectangular box in which the user can type text. If the box already contains text, the user can select that default text or delete it and type new text.	In the **Size** box, select **10** or type a new font size. In the **Size** box, enter a font size. **Note** You can use *enter* if there is no chance of confusion.	
Title (do not use *caption*)	Title of the dialog box. It usually, but not always, matches the title of the command name. Refer to the dialog box by its title when necessary, especially if the user needs to go to a new tab.	In the **Options** dialog box, click the **View** tab.	
Unfold button	Command button with two "greater than" signs (>>) that enlarges a secondary window to reveal more options or information.	Click **Profiles** for more information.	

* *Check box, tab,* and *slider* are the only terms in this table that should typically be used in end-user documentation

For the names and functions of some other controls not included in this list, see the *Controls* section of the *Windows User Experience Interaction Guidelines* on MSDN.

Unnamed buttons

If you refer to an unnamed button that appears in the interface, use the name of the tooltip, and then insert a bitmap showing the button, if possible. For more information, see *dialog boxes*, *Document conventions* (Chapter 6), *User interface text***.**

Microsoft style

Click the **Minimize** button .

If you need help, click the Microsoft Word **Help** button .

If you cannot use inline graphics, use the name only.

Microsoft style

Click the **Minimize** button.

Modes of interaction

This section describes modes of interacting with the user interface.

Gesture

Use *gesture* to refer to a motion that the user can make to interact with hardware such as a touchpad, or a software program such as a game.

An *air gesture* can be a movement made by any part of a user's body to give an instruction to the program via a sensor or camera, or a pose that the user makes in front of a sensor or camera to which an avatar will react.

A *contact gesture* can be a motion made with a user's finger or hand directly on a screen or surface. If such a gesture is made above the screen or surface, it is an air gesture.

It is all right to use title capitalization for gesture names. Consult your project style sheet for the appropriate capitalization for your content. However, do not capitalize a gesture when it is used as a verb.

Microsoft style

The Help Me gesture displays the Help screen.

Draw a question mark to get help.

To speed through the intersection, perform the Boost gesture by quickly raising both arms above your head.

Now boost through the intersection.

Not Microsoft style

The help me gesture displays the Help screen.

Perform the boost gesture by quickly raising both arms above your head.

Now Boost through the intersection.

For more information about referring to gestures, see the following:

- drag
- flick
- hover over
- pan
- pinch
- pointer
- pointing device
- scroll
- stretch
- swipe
- tap
- turn
- vibration

Speech

Users of a natural user interface with speech recognition functionality can interact with a program by using voice commands. A voice command is a structured verbal input from the user that a program will respond to.

Enclose voice commands in quotation marks. Use punctuation at the end of the command or sentence that includes a command, but punctuation preceding or within the command is not necessary unless needed to avoid ambiguity. Always capitalize the first word in a voice command.

Microsoft style

To call Sean, say "Call Sean Bentley mobile."

"Find local pizza."

"Open Marketplace."

If you want your cub to roll on the ground, just say "Roll over."

Mouse terminology

This topic includes the following sections:

- How to refer to the mouse.

- How to refer to mouse pointers.

- Which verbs to use to refer to mouse actions.

- How to document mouse procedures.

How to refer to the mouse

If you need to refer to more than one mouse, use *mouse devices* if you can. Otherwise, use *mice*.

In general, use *mouse button* to indicate the left mouse button. Use *left mouse button* only to teach beginning skills or in a discussion of more than one mouse button when not referring to *the left mouse button* would create ambiguity.

Use *right mouse button*, not other terms such as *mouse button 2* or *secondary mouse button*. Regardless of accuracy, users understand this term and users who reprogram their buttons make the mental shift.

When more than one mouse button is used within a procedure, identify only the least commonly used button.

Microsoft style

With the right mouse button, double-click the icon.

Click the **Badges** tab, and then use the right mouse button to double-click the badge that you want to edit.

Use *wheel button* to refer to the third or middle button on the mouse. Users rotate the wheel itself, and they click the wheel button.

How to refer to mouse pointers

Refer to the mouse pointer as *the pointer*. Use *cursor* only in content for a technical audience.

For pointers that have activity indicators, use *busy pointer* for the pointer that consists of only an activity indicator and *working in background pointer* for the combination pointer and activity indicator.

It is best to use a graphic to describe the various ways the mouse pointer can appear on the screen. If that is not possible, use descriptive labels for mouse pointers. However, do not use a graphic or a descriptive label as a synonym for *pointer*.

Microsoft style

When the pointer becomes a ⬌, drag the pointer to move the split line.

When the pointer becomes a double-headed arrow, drag the pointer to move the split line.

Not Microsoft style

When the pointer becomes a double-headed arrow, drag the double-headed arrow to move the split line.

Which verbs to use to refer to mouse actions

In general, use *point to*, not *move the mouse pointer to*. Use the latter only in teaching beginning skills.

Microsoft style

Point to the window border.

> Use *click*, not *click on*.

Microsoft style

Using the mouse, click the **Minimize** button.

Click the image to select it.

> Use *click* with a file, command, or option name, as in "Click **OK**," but use *in* to refer to clicking in a general area within a window or dialog box.

Microsoft style

To see the **Control** menu, right-click anywhere in the window.

Click in the window to make it active.

Not Microsoft style

To see the **Control** menu, right-click the window.

Click the **Styles** box.

> Always hyphenate *double-click* and *right-click* as verbs.

Microsoft style

Double-click the **Word** icon.

Right-click to see the shortcut menu.

> Use *right-click* to mean click with the right mouse button.

Microsoft style

Right-click the selected text, and then click Copy.

- Use *press and hold the mouse button* only to teach beginning skills.

- Use *drag*, not *click and drag*. Use *press and drag* only to teach beginning skills. The *drag* action includes holding down a button while moving the mouse and then releasing the button.

- Use *drag*, not *drag-and-drop*, for the action of moving a document or folder. It is all right to use *drag-and-drop* as an adjective, as in "moving the folder is a drag-and-drop operation." It is also all right to use *drop* by itself if *drag* is not precise enough. For more information, see *drag, drag-and-drop*.

Microsoft style

Drag the folder to the desktop.

Drop your files here.

Use *rotate*, not *roll*, to refer to rotating the wheel button.

Microsoft style

Rotate the wheel button forward to scroll up in the document.

How to document mouse procedures

Be consistent in the way that you list mouse procedures. For example, always list the mouse method before listing the keyboard method if you document both.

Do not combine keyboard and mouse actions as if they were keyboard shortcuts.

Microsoft style

Hold down Shift while clicking the right mouse button.

Not Microsoft style

Shift+click the right mouse button.

Key names

In general, spell key names as they appear in the following list, whether the name appears in text or in a procedure. Capitalize as indicated.

> **Note** This list applies to Microsoft and PC-type keyboards unless otherwise noted. Differences with the Mac keyboard are noted.

Microsoft style

Alt

arrow keys (not *direction keys, directional keys,* or *movement keys*)

Backspace

Break

Caps Lock

Clear

Command (the Mac keyboard only. Use the bitmap to show this key whenever possible, because the key is not named on the keyboard.)

Control (the Mac keyboard only. Does not always map to the Ctrl key on the PC keyboard. Use correctly.)

Ctrl

Del (the Mac keyboard only. Use to refer to the forward delete key.)

Delete (Use to refer to the back delete key on the Mac keyboard.)

Down Arrow (Use the definite article *the* and *key* with the arrow keys except in key combinations or key sequences. Always spell out. Do not use graphical arrows.)

End

Enter (On the Mac, use only when functionality requires it.)

Esc (Always use Esc, not Escape, especially on the Mac.)

F1 - F12

Help (the Mac keyboard only. Always use "the HELP key" to avoid confusion with the **Help** button.)

Home

Insert

Left Arrow (Use the definite article *the* and *key* with the arrow keys except in key combinations or key sequences.)

Num Lock

Option (the Mac keyboard only)

Page Down

Page Up

Pause

Print Screen

Reset

Return (the Mac keyboard only)

Right Arrow (Use the definite article *the* and *key* with the arrow keys except in key combinations or key sequences.)

Scroll Lock

Select

Shift

Spacebar (Precede with the definite article *the* except in procedures, key combinations, or key sequences.)

Tab (Use the definite article *the* and *key* except in key combinations or key sequences.)

Up Arrow (Use the definite article *the* and *key* with the arrow keys except in key combinations or key sequences.)

Windows logo key

Spell key names that do not appear in this list as they appear on the keyboard. Use title capitalization.

When telling a user to press a letter key, capitalize the letter. When telling a user to type a letter key, use lowercase for the letter and use bold formatting, unless an uppercase letter is required.

Microsoft style

Press Y.

Type **y**.

> **Note** Format punctuation according to intended use. If the user must type the punctuation, use bold formatting. If not, use regular type.

On first mention, you can use the definite article *the* and *key* with the key name if necessary for clarity. For example, use "the F1 key." On subsequent mention, refer to the key only by its name. For example, use "press F1."

For the arrow keys and the Tab key, list only the key name in key combinations without the definite article *the* and *key*.

Microsoft style

To move the insertion point, use the Left Arrow key.

To extend the selection, press Shift+Arrow.

Special character names

Because special character names could be confused with an action (such as +) or be difficult to see, always spell out the following special character names: Plus Sign, Minus Sign, Hyphen, Period, and Comma.

Microsoft style

Shift+Plus Sign

Press Alt, Hyphen, C

Press Comma

Press Command+Period

Type an em dash

Press the Plus Sign (+)

Not Microsoft style

Shift+ +

Shift+ -

Press +.

It is all right to add the symbol in parentheses after the special character to avoid confusion, as in *Plus Sign (+)*. This is probably not necessary for commonly used symbols such as *Period (.)*.

Names of keyboard "quick access" keys

Terms in current or recent use are listed in the following table. See the specific topics for more details.

Keyboard "quick access" keys

Name	Alternative name	Definition	Audience
Accelerator key		Now obsolete in all uses.	Do not use.
Access key	Keyboard shortcut	Keyboard sequence corresponding to underlined letter on a menu name or command.	Use with a technical audience only. If a term is necessary in documentation for a general audience, use *keyboard shortcut*.
Application key		Key that opens a shortcut menu containing commands related to a selection in a program. Equivalent to right-clicking the selection.	All
Back key		Key that performs the same action as the Back button in a browser.	All
Forward key		Key that performs the same action as the Forward button in a browser.	All

Name	Alternative name	Definition	Audience
Hot key		Key that activates a TSR (memory-resident program).	Obsolete. Use *keyboard shortcut*.
Quick key			Do not use.
Shortcut key	Keyboard shortcut	Key that corresponds to a command name on a menu, such as Ctrl+Z.	Use with a technical audience only. If a term is necessary in documentation for a general audience, use *keyboard shortcut*.
Speed key			Do not use.
Start key		Key that opens the Windows Start menu.	All.

Keyboard shortcuts

In most situations, it should be sufficient to refer to a *key combination* or *key sequence* by the keys that make it up. To specify a key combination, use the plus sign between the keys to be pressed. To specify a key sequence, use commas and spaces to indicate the sequence in which the keys must be pressed.

Microsoft style

To undo the last action, press Ctrl+Z.

To open a file, press Alt, F, O.

To show a key combination that includes punctuation that requires use of the Shift key, such as the question mark, add Shift to the combination and give the name or symbol of the shifted key. Using the name of the unshifted key, such as 4 rather than $, could be confusing to users or even wrong. For example, the ? and / characters are not always shifted keys on every keyboard. However, do spell out the names of the plus and minus signs, hyphen, period, and comma.

Microsoft style

Ctrl+Shift+?

Ctrl+Shift+*

Ctrl+Shift+Comma

Not Microsoft style

Ctrl+Shift+/

Ctrl+?

Ctrl+Shift+8

Ctrl+*

If you must use a term to describe a keyboard shortcut, use *keyboard shortcut*. In content for software developers or in content that pertains to customizing the user interface, a more specific term such as *key combination* or *key sequence* may be needed.

Content for multiple platforms

With the proliferation in new technologies, writers and editors face new challenges in creating content that is appropriate for devices as diverse as computers, phones, TVs, and game consoles. When you create content that will be published on different devices, you must decide what terminology to use and how to write for screens of various sizes.

Before you start writing content or user interface text that will appear on different devices, consult with designers, developers, and localizers on your project to establish the guiding principles that will be used to govern the design, user flows, and user interface text. Ensure that everyone is working from the same frame of reference. Examples of guiding design principles include the following:

- There will be virtually no differences among the user interfaces of various devices.

- There will be some differences in the user interfaces to ensure that the user isn't confused about where to perform actions.

- There will be a number of differences in the user interface to accommodate the various devices.

After the design principles have been established, consider the following guidelines when writing the content:

- Be as specific as possible when referring to the device being used. For example, if you're talking about a phone, and only a phone, use *phone*. Don't use *device*, especially if you are writing content for a general audience.

- If your content refers to more than one device, such as a phone and a computer, *device* is most likely the appropriate term.

- Decide how you will document device-specific user interactions when the user interface or user action varies across devices. For example, you might use a table, as in the following example.

To spin 180 degrees

On this device	Do this
Xbox	Press **Y**.
PC	Click **Spin**.
Phone	Tap **Y**.

For more information about documenting alternative procedures, see *Chapter 6, "Procedures and technical content."*

User interface text

User interface (UI) text appears on UI surfaces such as dialog boxes, property sheets, buttons, and wizards. User interface text is as important to the overall design of a product or service as its functionality is. UI text is the most direct means that you have of communicating with your users. Therefore, your text must be clear and helpful. And although UI text must be short, it must still follow the same voice and tone guidelines as any other content. In addition, if your content will be localized, the text must allow for text expansion, which can be as high as 30 percent for some languages. That's the challenge that UI text poses—maintaining clarity and a consistent voice, while working within the unique constraints of the user interface.

This topic contains a brief list of guidelines and a checklist to help you develop great UI text. For more detailed information about writing UI text, see the extended discussion of UI text on the User Interface Text page of the *Windows User Experience Interaction Guidelines* on MSDN (*http://msdn.microsoft.com/en-us/library/aa511258.aspx*).

If you only do six things

1. Start writing UI text early, because UI text problems often reveal product or service design problems.

2. Think like a customer and ensure that you understand the entire workflow process:

   - How do customers get to this surface?

   - What is the essential information that they need to accomplish the task on this surface?

   - Where are they going from here?

3. Design your text for scanning. For more information, see the Layout page of the *Windows User Experience Interaction Guidelines* on MSDN.

4. Be concise, eliminate redundant text, and don't over-communicate. Too much text discourages reading.

5. Provide links to Help content for more detailed information only when necessary. Don't rely on Help to solve a design problem.

6. Use a consistent voice and consistent terminology across the product or service. For more information, see *Chapter 1, "Microsoft style and voice."*

High-level UI text checklist

- Is the text that describes the flow to and from the given UI surface logical? For more information, see the *Windows User Experience Interaction Guidelines* on MSDN.

- Is the point of the UI surface clear?

- Did you provide enough information for users to make a smart decision? Can they scan the text and still be successful?

- Did you use plain, straightforward words that your audience will understand?

- Did you use terms consistently? Is the voice consistent? For more information, see *Chapter 1, "Microsoft style and voice."*

- Could you use fewer words while still ensuring that the customer will succeed?

- Is the UI text easy to localize? Will the text still work with the visual design if the text were to be 30 percent longer after translation?

- Does the text inspire users' confidence that they can complete the task at hand?

User interface formatting

Consistent text formatting helps users locate and interpret information easily. Nowhere is this more important than in helping users navigate program user interfaces. For user interface elements, follow the capitalization and bold formatting guidelines in the following sections. For formatting conventions of elements that are not part of the user interface, see *Document conventions* (Chapter 6).

Capitalization

Use the following capitalization guidelines for user interface elements:

- For menu names, command names, command button names, dialog box titles, and tab names, follow the capitalization of the user interface. If the user interface is inconsistent, use title capitalization.

- For dialog box and page elements, follow the capitalization of the user interface. Current style calls for these items to use sentence-style capitalization. If the interface is inconsistent, use sentence-style capitalization.

- For functional elements that do not have a label in the user interface, such as toolbars (the **Standard** toolbar) and toolbar buttons (the **Insert Table** button), use title capitalization. However, do not capitalize the element type such as toolbar, button, menu, scroll bar, and icon.

- For labels in the interface that are all lowercase or all uppercase, title capitalization is recommended.

Always consult your project style sheet for terms that require specific capitalization or for terms that are traditionally all uppercase or all lowercase.

Bold formatting

In general, use bold formatting for user interface elements, both in procedures and in other text in instructional content. An exception is in content designed to generate interest, such as presales materials or overview content on the web, or if following this guidance would make content unreadable, it is all right not to use bold formatting for UI elements. When in doubt, consult your project style sheet.

Microsoft style

The Word 2010 ribbon has such tabs as the **Home** tab, the **Insert** tab, and the **Page Layout** tab.

On the **Home** tab, in the **Clipboard** group, click **Copy**.

Do not use bold formatting for feature names unless the user must click the feature name.

For more information, see *Controls*; *Document conventions* (Chapter 6); *Ribbons, menus, and toolbars*; *Procedures* (Chapter 6)

Microsoft style

When the Track Changes feature is turned on, you can view all changes that you make in a document.

On the **Review** tab, in the **Tracking** group, click **Track Changes**.

With Remote Desktop Connection, you can connect to your work computer from your home computer.

To open Remote Desktop Connection, click **Start**, point to **All Programs**, click **Accessories**, and then click **Remote Desktop Connection**.

Not Microsoft style

When the **Track Changes** feature is turned on, you can view all of the changes that you make in a document.

With **Remote Desktop Connection**, you can connect to your work computer from your home computer.

To open **Remote Desktop Connection**, click **Start**, point to **All Programs**, click **Accessories**, and then click **Remote Desktop Connection**.

Use the following bold formatting guidelines for user interface elements. For some elements, special capitalization guidance is also mentioned.

Element	Convention	Example
Button names	Bold.	On the **Standard** toolbar, click **Toolbox**. On the **Debug** toolbar, click **Immediate**.
Commands on menus, toolbars, and ribbons	Bold.	On the **View** menu, point to **Other Windows**, and then click **Solution Explorer**. On the **Outlining** toolbar, select the level that you want in the **Outline Level** box. On the **Review** tab, in the **Comments** group, click **New Comment**.
Dialog box options	Bold.	In the **Find and Replace** dialog box, type the text that you want Word to search for in the **Find what** box. Click the **More** button to display more options. If All is not selected in the **Search** box, click the arrow next to the **Search** box, and then click **All**. Click the **Replace** tab, and then type the text that you want Word to replace in the **Replace with** box. Click to select the **Match case** and **Find whole words only** check boxes.
Dialog box titles	Bold.	You can also set a document's password in the **Protect Document** dialog box. You can add text entries in the **AutoCorrect** dialog box.
File names (system-defined)	Bold in procedures if the user must click the file name or type the name as shown. Capitalization follows that of the user interface unless the name is all uppercase or all lowercase. If the name of the file is all uppercase or all lowercase, use title capitalization.	Double-click the **Scanpst.exe** file to open the Inbox Repair Tool. The SignedManagedObject.cer file The Iexplore.exe file (iexplore in UI) The Acwzmain.mdb file (ACWZMAIN.mdb in UI)
Folder and directory names (system defined)	Bold in procedures if the user must click the folder or directory name or type the name as shown. Capitalization follows that of the user interface unless the name is all uppercase or all lowercase. If the name of the folder or directory is all uppercase or all lowercase, use title capitalization, unless the folder or directory name is named in part or wholly after an acronym. Then, keep the acronym part of the name in uppercase letters.	Click the **Music** folder. The Microsoft shared folder (microsoft shared in UI) The Errorrep folder (ERRORREP in the UI) The PChealth folder (PCHEALTH in the UI) The OEM folder
Icon names	Usually bold. Treatment may vary, so always consult your project style sheet.	Drag the file to the **Recycle Bin**. In Control Panel, click **Add New Hardware**.
List names	Bold.	In the **Wallpaper** list, click…
Menu names	Bold.	**Debug** menu **Favorites** menu

Element	Convention	Example
Panes, named	Usually bold only when clicking a command. Treatment may vary, so always consult your project style sheet.	If you don't see the navigation pane on the left side of an open window, click **Organize**, point to **Layout**, and then click **Navigation pane** to display it. When the Navigation Pane is open, you can close it to increase your workspace.
Panes, unnamed or generic use	Sentence capitalization.	The navigation pane The annotation pane
Tab names	Bold.	Click the **View** tab.
Toolbar names	Usually bold. Treatment may vary, so always consult your project style sheet.	On the **Data Designer** toolbar, click **Relationship**. On the **Text To Speech** toolbar, click the command that you want to use.
Views, named	Bold only when clicking a command.	Switch to Design view by right-clicking the form, and then clicking **Design View**.
Views, unnamed	Sentence capitalization.	In outline view In chart view
Windows, named	Usually bold. Treatment may vary, so always consult your project style sheet.	Copy and paste the code from the **Immediate** window into the **Code** window. Double-click the table to open the **Database Properties** window.
Windows, unnamed	Sentence capitalization.	In the document window
Wizard names	Bold only if clicked.	On the **Create** tab, in the **Forms** group, click **More Forms**, and then click **Form Wizard**. The Form Wizard can create a variety of results depending on the options that you select
Wizard page names	Bold.	On the **Identify Fact and Dimension Tables** page, the fact and dimension tables identified by the wizard are displayed.

5

CHAPTER 6

Procedures and technical content

Consistent formatting of procedures and other technical content helps users find important information quickly and efficiently. The topics in this section show you how to create technical content with consistent formatting and layout.

Procedures

In technical writing, a procedure is a series of steps that a user takes to complete a specific task. Procedures are set off from the main text by their formatting. In product documentation, a procedure is usually a discrete topic. In other content, such as Knowledge Base articles and white papers, a procedure is usually only a part of the content.

If you document only one method for performing a procedure, document the preferred method, the method that best reflects the needs of the user. For example, the preferred method might be to use mouse actions, or it might be to use keyboard actions.

For information about documenting multiple or alternative input methods, see *Multiple input methods and branching within procedures* later in this topic.

How to format procedures

Although a procedure can be written in paragraph format, most procedures consist of sequential steps formatted as a numbered list. There are several ways to introduce a numbered list. For more information, see *Lists*.

Multiple-step procedures

For multiple-step procedures, follow these general guidelines:

- Set individual steps as separate, numbered entries. However, you can combine short steps if they occur in the same place, such as within one dialog box.

- Both of the following examples follow Microsoft style, although the first is more commonly used.

Microsoft style

1. On the **Tools** menu, click **Options**, and then click the **Edit** tab.

2. <Next step of the procedure.>

1. On the **Tools** menu, click **Options**.

2. Click the **Edit** tab.

- Use complete sentences.

- Use parallel structure.

- Capitalize the first word in each step.

- Use a period after each step. An exception is when you are instructing users to type input that does not include end punctuation. In this case, try to format the text so that the user input appears on a new line.

- Write procedures so that all the steps fit on one screen. For printed content, try to keep all steps in a procedure on one page or a left-right (verso-recto) page spread, and avoid continuing a procedure across a right-left (recto-verso) break.

- Do not bury procedural information in narrative text because the procedure will be difficult to find and follow.

Single-step procedures

Use a bullet to mark a single-step procedure. Never number a single-step procedure.

Microsoft style

To look at the PERT Chart

- On the **View** menu, click **PERT Chart**.

Not Microsoft style

To look at the PERT Chart

1. On the **View** menu, click **PERT Chart**.

How to write procedure steps

In general, tell the user where the action should take place before describing the action to take. This prevents users from doing the right thing in the wrong place. However, avoid overloading procedures with locators. Assume that the user is looking at the screen and is starting from the position where the procedure begins. For example, the following phrasing is typical: "On the **View** menu, click **Zoom**."

However, if there is a chance that the user might be confused about where the action should take place or if an introductory phrase is needed, use the following wording: "To magnify your document, click **View**, and then click **Zoom**," or "In Control Panel, double-click **Passwords**, and then click **Change Passwords**."

The following sections give brief guidelines about how to tell users to interact with folders and icons, commands, and dialog box options.

Folders and icons

Users *click* or *double-click* a folder or an icon to initiate an action such as starting a program or viewing a list of subfolders.

When you want the user to	Use this syntax
Switch to a program that is already running on the desktop	On the taskbar, click the **Microsoft Excel** button. Switch to Microsoft Excel.
Start a program	Click **Start**, and then point to **All Programs**. Point to **Microsoft Office**, and then click **Microsoft Word 2010**.
Select an icon before changing its properties, moving it, or taking some other action	Right-click **Microsoft PowerPoint 2010**, and then click **Properties**.
Start a Control Panel item	In Control Panel, double-click **Network and Internet**.
Choose any other icon, such as a folder icon or a drive icon	Double-click **Recycle Bin**.

Commands

When you want the user to	Use this syntax
Run a command on a menu	On the **Debug** menu, click **Start Debugging**.
Run a command, and then select an option in a dialog box	On the **Page Layout** tab, in the **Page Setup** group, click **Hyphenation**, and then click **Automatic**.
Click a button in a dialog box	Click **Apply**.
Run a command on a submenu	On the **Tools** menu, point to **Settings**, and then click **Reset**. Click **Start**, point to the arrow next to **Shut down**, and then click **Restart**.

> **Note** You do not have to end a procedure with "click **OK**" or "tap **OK**" unless there is some possibility of confusion.

Dialog box options

Use *click* for selecting dialog box options, tabs, and command buttons.

Tell users to *type* in text boxes or *enter* an element such as a file name that they can either type or select from a list. When you are referring generally to a feature, *turn off* and *turn on* are all right to use, but use *select* and *clear* to refer to check boxes that turn the feature on and off. You can say "click to select" if the action may not be obvious to the user.

The following table gives a few examples.

When you want the user to	Use this syntax
Select an option	In the **Print** dialog box, click **All**.
Open a tabbed section in a dialog box	In the **Options** dialog box, click **Text Editor Basic**, and then click **VB Specific**.
Insert text in a combo box	In the **File name** box, enter the name of the file.
Select multiple check boxes	In the **Options** dialog box, click **Text Editor Basic**, click **Editor**, and then select the **Word wrap** and **Line numbers** check boxes.
Select items in a group box	Under **Find options**, select the **Match case** and **Match whole word** check boxes.

Right angle brackets for menu items

Some products such as Windows Phone use a right angle bracket (>) to show users how to open a series of menus. Although this is not the method generally used in Microsoft content, it is all right to use for groups who have determined that this is the best way to communicate menu interactions for their platform or audience. If you use the bracket format, include a space before and after the bracket.

Microsoft style (for groups that use the bracket format)

To sort the email in a folder other than your Inbox, tap **Menu** > **Go To** > **Folders**, and then click the folder that you want to use.

In most content, continue to use the traditional method for telling users how to interact with menus. Consult your project style sheet to see whether it is all right to use the angle bracket format in your content.

Accessibility considerations

Using the angle bracket format may cause screen readers to skip over the brackets and read instructions such as **Menu** > **Go To** > **Folders** as "Menu Go To Folders," which may be confusing to the user.

Document conventions in procedures

Follow these standard document conventions in procedures:

- Follow interface capitalization. Capitalization of dialog box options varies. When in doubt, or if necessary for consistency, use sentence-capitalization style. Use bold formatting for labels to help the user parse the sentence correctly.

Microsoft style

Click Date and Time.

Select the Provide feedback with sound check box.

■ If a command name or dialog box option ends with a colon or ellipsis, do not include this punctuation.

Microsoft style

Click **Save As**.

Not Microsoft style

Click **Save As** ...

■ Do not use the descriptors *button* and *option button* unless the descriptor helps avoid confusing or awkward phrasing or is necessary to avoid confusion with another element.

■ Use bold formatting for user input and italic formatting for placeholders. User input can be on the same line as the procedural step, or it can be by itself on a new line. If the user input is on the same line, what the user types should be the last word or words of the step. If the user input is on a new line, what the user types should not be followed by end punctuation unless the user must type the end punctuation.

Microsoft style

In the **Date** box, type **April 1**.

In the **Date** box, type:

April 1

Type *password*.

■ Use a monospace font for program input and output text.

For more information, see *Document conventions*; *Ribbons, menus, and toolbars* (Chapter 5); and *User interface formatting* (Chapter 5)

Mouse procedures

When referring to mouse actions, use terms such as *click, double-click, double-clicking,* and *point to*. For more information, see *Mouse terminology* (Chapter 5).

Keyboard procedures

When referring to keyboard actions, use terms such as *press, use,* and *enter*. For more information about documenting key commands, see *Key names* (Chapter 5).

Pen-computing procedures

When referring to pen computing, use the words *tap* and *double-tap*.

Touch procedures

- When referring to hardware buttons and the keyboard, use *press*.

- When referring to buttons, icons, and other elements on the screen, use *tap* and *double-tap*.

- When referring to moving one or more fingers to scroll through items on the screen, use *flick*. Do not use *scroll*.

Sensor procedures

- When referring to buttons, icons, and other elements on the screen, use *hover over*.

- When referring to scrolling through items on the screen using a hand or arm, use *swipe*.

Joystick procedures

Assume that the mouse is the primary input device. Include joystick information in a table along with other alternative input devices.

Multiple input methods and branching within procedures

You can document multiple input methods for procedures in various ways, depending on content design, space restrictions, and other considerations. For example, you can do the following:

- List the steps in a table and provide a separate column for each input method.

  Microsoft style

  Choose colors to use on webpages

  To make webpages easier to see, you can change the text, background, link, and hover colors in Internet Explorer.

No.	Mouse actions	Keyboard actions
1	On the **Start** menu: ■ Click **Internet Explorer**.	Display the **Start** menu by pressing the Windows logo key ⊞. Select **Internet Explorer** by using the arrow keys, and then press Enter.
2	In Internet Explorer: **1.** Click the **Tools** menu. **2.** Click **Internet Options**.	In Internet Explorer: **1.** Select the **Tools** menu by pressing Alt+T. **2.** Select **Internet Options** by pressing O.

- Document the primary input method and provide the alternative instructions in parentheses or separate sentences after the main instructions.

Microsoft style

To pan, slide one finger in any direction (or drag the mouse pointer, or use the arrow keys).

To copy the selection, click **Copy** on the toolbar. You can also press Ctrl+C.

Not Microsoft style

To copy the selection, use the **Copy** button on the toolbar or Ctrl+C.

Consult your project style sheet for more specific guidelines about how to document and format multiple input methods.

If there are multiple ways to perform an entire procedure, and if you must describe each alternative, use a table to detail the alternatives, as in the following example. This approach helps the user know when to use which method.

Microsoft style

To	Do this
Save changes to the existing file and continue working	On the **File** menu, click **Save**.
Save changes to the existing file and exit the program	On the **File** menu, click **Exit**. If a dialog box asks whether you want to save changes, click **Yes**.

If one step has an alternative, that alternative should be a separate paragraph in the step. In a single-step procedure, an alternative can be separated by the word *or* to make it clearer to the user that an alternative is available.

Microsoft style

Press the key for the underlined letter in the menu name.

You can also use the Left Arrow key or the Right Arrow key to move to another menu.

To open a menu

Press Alt+*the key for the underlined letter in the menu name.*

or

Use the Left Arrow key or the Right Arrow key to move to another menu.

Not Microsoft style

Press Alt+*the key for the underlined letter in the menu name.* You can also use the Left Arrow key or the Right Arrow key to move to another menu.

Press the key for the underlined letter in the menu name; or,

Use the Left Arrow key or the Right Arrow key to move to another menu.

For several choices within one procedure step, use a bulleted list.

Microsoft style

1. Select the text that you want to move or copy.

2. Do one of the following:

    *   To move the selection, click **Cut** on the Quick Access Toolbar.

    *   To copy the selection, click **Copy** on the Quick Access Toolbar.

3. Right-click where you want to insert the text, and then click **Paste** on the Quick Access Toolbar.

Supplementary information and text within procedures

In general, users go to procedures for instruction, not for reference. Therefore, do not put supplementary information, such as special cases or behaviors that are not essential for completing the procedure, in the procedure itself. If supplementary information is necessary, put it in a single paragraph after the procedure. If absolutely necessary, put the supplementary information after the step that it explains, and indent it to align with the procedure text. If the supplementary information includes steps, make it a separate procedure and provide a cross-reference.

Avoid explicit descriptions of system responses. If necessary to orient the user, describe the system response in the step before the system response happens or in the step immediately following the system response.

Microsoft style

Click **Options**, and then select the **Reverse Print Order** check box.

1. To display more options, click **Options**.
2. Select the **Reverse Print Order** check box.

1. Click **Options**.
2. In the expanded list of options, select the **Reverse Print Order** check box.

Not Microsoft style

1. Click **Options**.

    The dialog box expands to display more options.

2. Select the **Reverse Print Order** check box.

6

Document conventions

Consistent text formatting helps users locate and interpret information easily. The following guidelines present some specific conventions for elements that are not part of the user interface. Use these document conventions both in procedures and in regular text. For the document conventions for user interface elements, see *User interface formatting* (Chapter5).

When capitalization style is to follow that of the user interface, consider making an exception for labels in the interface that are all lowercase or all uppercase: Title capitalization is recommended in these instances.

Some elements may not appear here. Consult your project style sheet.

Element	Convention	Example
Attributes	Bold. Capitalization varies.	**IfOutputPrecision**
Book titles	Title capitalization. Italic.	See *Visual Basic Custom Control Reference*.
Chapter titles	Usually title capitalization. Enclose in quotation marks.	See *Chapter 9, "Extending Forms."*
Classes (predefined)	Bold. Capitalization varies.	**ios** **filebuf** **BitArray**
Classes (user-defined)	Capitalization varies. See also *Code examples*	`BlueTimerControl`
Code samples, including keywords and variables within text and as separate paragraphs, and user-defined program elements within text	Monospace. See also *Code examples*	`#include <iostream.h>` `void main ()`
Command-line commands and options (switches)	All lowercase. Bold.	**copy** command **/a** option
Constants	Usually bold. Capitalization varies. Treatment of constants may vary, so always refer to your project style sheet.	**INT_MAX** **dbDenyWrite** **CS**
Control classes	All uppercase.	EDIT control class
Data formats	All uppercase.	CF_DIB
Data structures and their members (predefined)	Bold. Capitalization varies.	**BITMAP** **bmbits** **CREATESTRUCT** **hInstance**

6

Element	Convention	Example
Data types	Bold. Capitalization follows that of the application programming interface.	**DWORD** **float** **HANDLE**
Database names	Bold. Treatment of database names may vary, so always refer to your project style sheet.	**WingtipToys** database
Device names	All uppercase.	LPT1 COM1
Dialog box titles	Bold. Title capitalization.	**Protect Document** dialog box **Import/Export Setup** dialog box
Directives	Bold.	**#include** **#define**
Environment variables	All uppercase.	INCLUDE SESSION_SIGNON
Error message names	Sentence-style capitalization.	Access denied
Event names	Bold. Treatment of event names may vary, so always consult your project style sheet.	In the **OnClick** event procedure...
Fields (members of a class or structure)	Bold. Treatment may vary, so always consult your project style sheet.	**IfHeight** **biPlanes**
File extensions	All lowercase.	.mdb .doc
File names (user-defined examples)	Bold in procedures if the user must click or type the name as shown. Title capitalization. All right to use internal caps in file names for readability.	My Taxes for 2011 MyTaxesFor2011
Folder and directory names (user-defined examples)	Bold in procedures if the user is expected to click or type the name as shown. Title capitalization. All right to use internal caps in folder and directory names for readability.	Vacation and Sick Pay MyFiles\\Accounting\Payroll\VacPay
Functions (predefined)	Usually bold. Capitalization varies. Treatment may vary, so always consult your project style sheet.	**CompactDatabase** **CWnd::CreateEx** **FadePic**
Game titles	Title capitalization. Italic.	*Halo: Reach* *Kinect Adventures!*
Handles	All uppercase.	HWND
Key names, combinations, and sequences	Initial caps.	Ctrl, Tab Ctrl+Alt+Del Shift, F7 Alt, F, O Spacebar

Element	Convention	Example

Keywords (language and operating system)	Bold. Capitalization follows that of the application programming interface.	`main`
		`True`
		`AddNew`

Logical operators	All uppercase. Bold.	`AND` `XOR`
Macros	Usually all uppercase. Bold if predefined. May be monospace if user-defined. Treatment may vary, so always consult your project style sheet.	`LOWORD` MASKROP

Markup language elements (tags)	Bold. Case varies.	`<img>`
		`<input type=text>`
		`<message>`

Mathematical constants and variables	Italic.	$a2 + b2 = c2$
Members	Bold. Capitalization varies.	`ulNumCharsAllowed`
Methods	Bold. Capitalization varies.	`OpenForm` `GetPrevious`
New terms or emphasis	Italic on first mention, unless your project style sheet specifies otherwise. Italic. **Note** Italic type does not always show up well online. If necessary to accommodate low-resolution monitors, enclose new terms in quotation marks. Use italic formatting for emphasis sparingly.	Microsoft Exchange consists of both *server* and *client* components. You *must* close the window before you exit.
Operators	Bold.	`+, -` `sizeof`
Options (command-line)	Bold. Case exactly as it must be typed.	**copy** command **/a** option **/Aw**
Parameters	Italic. Capitalization varies.	*hdc* *grfFlag* *ClientBinding*
Placeholders (in syntax and in user input)	Italic.	/v: *version* Type *password*.
Programs, including utility and accessory programs	Usually title capitalization. Check the Microsoft trademark list for other styles of capitalization.	Microsoft Word Notepad Network Connections Nmake

6

Element	Convention	Example
Properties	Usually bold. Capitalization varies. Treatment may vary, so always consult your project style sheet.	**M_bClipped** **AbsolutePosition** **Message ID**
Registers	All uppercase.	DS
Registry settings	Subtrees (first-level items) are all uppercase. Separated by underscores. Usually bold. Registry keys (second-level items) follow the capitalization of the user interface. Registry subkeys (below the second level) follow the capitalization of the user interface. Treatment may vary, so always consult your project style sheet.	**HKEY_CLASSES_ROOT** **HKEY_LOCAL_MACHINE** **SOFTWARE** **ApplicationIdentifier** **Microsoft**
Song titles	All words capitalized (per industry standard).	You Are The Sunshine Of My Life Sittin' On The Dock Of The Bay
Statements	Bold. Case varies.	**IMPORTS** **LIBRARY**
Strings	Sentence-style capitalization. Enclosed in quotation marks.	"Now is the time"
Structures	Usually bold. Case varies.	**ACCESSTIMEOUT**
Switches	Usually lowercase. Bold.	**build: commands**
System commands	All uppercase.	SC_HOTLIST
URLs	All lowercase for fully specified URLs. If necessary, break long URLs before a forward slash. Do not hyphenate. See also *URLs, addresses* (Chapter 7)	http://www.microsoft.com/ seattle.sidewalk.com /music/ //www.microsoft.com/
User input	Usually lowercase, unless case sensitive. Bold or italic, depending on element. If the user input string contains placeholder text, use italic for that text.	Type **hello world** Type **-p** *password*
Utilities	Usually title capitalization.	Makefile RC Program
Values	All uppercase.	DIB_PAL_COLORS
Variables	Treatment may vary, so always consult your project style sheet.	bEmpty **m_nParams** file_name
XML schema elements	Bold. Case varies.	**ElementType** element **Xml:space** attribute

For more information, see *Capitalization* (Chapter 7); *Command syntax*; *File names and extensions*; *Fonts* (Chapter 3); *HTML tag, element, and attribute formatting*; *Key names* (Chapter 5); *Ribbons, Menus, and toolbars* (Chapter 5); *User interface formatting* (Chapter 5); *XML tag, element, and attribute formatting*.

Cloud computing style

Cloud computing is a type of computing in which groups of servers and scalable resources are used to provide a computing platform, individual applications, or both, over the Internet. As defined by the Word document, "The NIST Definition of Cloud Computing", found at the National Institute of Standards and Technology website (*http://csrc.nist.gov/*), cloud computing is "a model for enabling convenient, on-demand network access to a shared pool of configurable computing resources (for example, networks, servers, storage, applications, and services) that can be rapidly provisioned and released with minimal management effort or service provider interaction."

Two dimensions are used to classify the various deployment models for cloud computing:

- Where the service is running: on customer's premises or in a service provider's data center

- Level of access: shared or dedicated

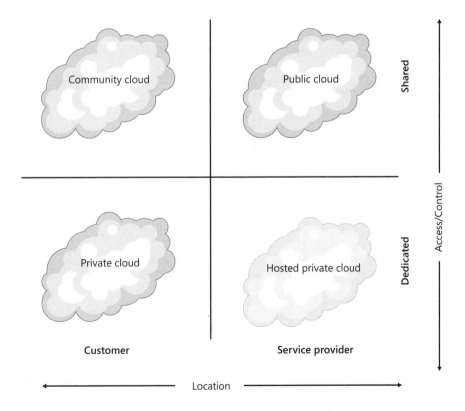

Cloud terminology

Cloud computing terminology is increasing and evolving. To present a cohesive, clear message to customers, it is important for groups across Microsoft to adopt consistent terminology and definitions. Use the following terms, and do not coin new terms unless you must introduce a new concept for which an established term doesn't already exist.

Cloud computing terminology is most likely to be used with a technical or business-decision-maker audience. However, consumers are increasingly being exposed to the subject of cloud computing, and therefore it is important to define terms and establish a clear context in content created for them.

Term	Definition	Usage note
cloud	A virtualized server environment that can host a web service or application for multiple tenants. For technical audiences, the term *cloud computing* typically refers to a specialized, virtual environment that houses applications, data, and/or computing resources in a single location and provides access to those resources over the Internet. For a general audience, *cloud computing* refers to applications and services that are accessed over the Internet, rather than to applications that are installed on a user's local computer.	The cloud is an emerging concept for many of our users, especially for the general audience and the worldwide audience. Define the term or give it context on first mention by using the definition that is appropriate for your audience. Use *cloud* as an adjective. *Cloud* may be used sparingly as a noun in content for a technical audience or in informal contexts. Do not use *cloud* interchangeably with *Internet* or *web*.
cloud platform	The cloud operating system that provides the computing, storage, hosting, and management services for hosting customer-developed applications and services.	Use only in content for a technical audience. In content for a general audience, it's probably not necessary to distinguish types of offerings, and referring to *cloud services* is preferred.
cloud service	A service, IT solution, or application that is delivered and consumed in real time over the Internet or an intranet ("the cloud"). Services range from email to entire IT platforms.	
community cloud	A cloud infrastructure that is shared by a group of organizations with shared goals or concerns, such as civil agencies. It can be managed by the group or by a third party, and it can be hosted on-premises or off-premises.	To keep the topic straightforward for customers, avoid using this term; most contexts can be described without introducing yet another term. Because the deployment models are not widely understood, when the term must be used, define it on first mention. See also *hybrid cloud*, *private cloud*, and *public cloud*.
elastic service capacity	The flexible allocation of computing resources over the Internet as demand changes.	Not *dynamic service capacity*. Define on first mention for audiences that may not be familiar with the concept.
hosted service	A service, IT solution, or application that is hosted by a service provider and made available to a customer over the Internet.	None
hosting provider	A third-party service provider that offers scalable infrastructure services to multiple customers.	May also use *cloud hosting provider* and *web hosting provider* if necessary to establish the context or distinguish cloud service providers from web hosts, such as Go Daddy. Do not use *hoster*.

Term	Definition	Usage note
hybrid cloud	A cloud infrastructure that uses a combination of public, community, and private clouds, with each discrete entity connected to enable data and application portability between them. A hybrid cloud addresses an organization's unique application and data storage needs and privacy concerns.	Use with a technical audience that is comfortable with cloud technology. For other users, it may be more useful to talk about a hybrid model. Because the deployment models are not widely understood, define on first mention. See also *community cloud*, *private cloud*, and *public cloud*.
infrastructure as a service (IaaS)	Flexible computing capacity, such as servers, storage, and networking, that is managed by a cloud services provider and made available to the customer over the Internet. In the infrastructure as a service (IaaS) model, hardware provisioning (such as for compute, storage, and networking) is controlled by the provider, but the customer maintains control of the operating system and applications.	All right to use *IaaS* after the full term has been spelled out on first mention. Do not capitalize as *IAAS*.
IT as a service (ITaaS)	IT as a service describes all three layers (IaaS, PaaS, SaaS) of IT services consumed by organizations and businesses. Examples of ITaaS services include hardware selection, configuration, and optimization, in addition to software configuration and patching.	Use only in content for a technical or business-decision-maker audience. In content for a general audience, refer to the specific type of service being provided (such as applying software updates) in a cloud computing model. All right to use *ITaaS* after the full term has been spelled out on first mention. Do not capitalize as *ITAAS*.
measured service	Service levels are contractually defined, and usage is metered—often per user or per hour. Customers pay only for what they use.	None
on-premises, off-premises	Terms used to distinguish local computing—in which computing resources are located within a customer's own facilities—from remote computing, in which computing resources are provided partially or totally through cloud computing.	Hyphenate in all positions. Note that *premises* is plural. Do not use *on-premise*, *off-premise*. Do not use *on-premises cloud* or *off-premises cloud*.
platform as a service (PaaS)	An operating environment that is made available to an organization over the Internet. Typically, a vendor manages the operating environment itself (which may include storage and servers), and the customer manages the end-user applications that are delivered in the operating environment. PaaS offerings provide a platform for the development, testing, deployment, and ongoing maintenance of applications without the cost of buying and maintaining the underlying infrastructure and operating environments.	All right to use *PaaS* after the full term has been spelled out on first mention. Do not capitalize as *PAAS*.
private cloud, hosted private cloud	A cloud infrastructure that is dedicated to an organization (not shared with other organizations). A private cloud can be managed by the organization or hosted by a third-party service provider, in which case it is referred to as a *hosted private cloud*. A private cloud can be located on-premises or off-premises.	Because the deployment models are not widely understood, define on first mention. See also *community cloud*, *hybrid cloud*, and *public cloud*.

6

Term	Definition	Usage note
public cloud	A cloud infrastructure typically owned and managed by an organization that provisions cloud services to the general public or a large group.	Because the deployment models are not widely understood, define on first mention. See also *community cloud*, *hybrid cloud*, and *private cloud*.
service-oriented architecture	A software architecture that uses policies, practices, and frameworks to enable application functionality to be provided and consumed as sets of services.	Note the hyphen. All right to use the acronym *SOA* after the full term has been spelled out on first mention.
software as a service (SaaS)	Software that is consumed over the Internet rather than installed on-premises. Typically, a vendor manages the cloud infrastructure, including hardware, storage, operating system, and applications.	All right to use *SaaS* after the full term has been spelled out on first mention. Do not capitalize as *SAAS*.
tenant	An organization that consumes cloud computing resources from a service provider but is ultimately responsible for the data stored in or transferred by the cloud resources. In a multitenant environment, the resources are shared by multiple organizations. In a single-tenant environment, the cloud resources are dedicated to a single tenant.	None

Reference documentation

Reference documentation provides comprehensive information about the programming elements that are associated with technologies such as ASP.NET or Windows Presentation Foundation, or programming languages such as C++, C#, or Visual Basic. Reference topics are typically used to document class libraries, object models, and programming language constructs.

Note Information such as configuration schemas, compiler options, and error messages might also be documented in reference topics, and will not necessarily follow the guidelines described in this section.

Standardization and consistency

Software developers consult reference documentation to look up specific programming elements, not to read about programming concepts or product features. Developers often compare programming elements to determine how they relate and to decide which one to use for a particular scenario.

Therefore, standardization and consistency are essential in helping users get the information they need as quickly as possible. If your reference topics use a standard topic design, predictable headings and structure, and consistent wording, users will know what to look for and where to find it on the page.

Reference topic titles

Generally, reference topics are titled by using the name of a programming element (such as Clear), followed by an element type (such as Class, Method, Property, or Event). If the name is shared by multiple elements, you can add a differentiator such as the parent element name or the product or technology name. The differentiators are especially important if your content coexists with other reference documentation in a large content repository such as the Microsoft Developer Network (MSDN) Library.

Microsoft style for reference topic titles

Clear Method

Device.Clear Method

Clear Method (Microsoft Ajax)

Not Microsoft style for reference topic titles

Clear

What to include in a reference topic

The following table lists the information that is typically provided in reference topics. Not all sections will appear in all topics. For example, the "Property value" or "Field value" section appears only in reference topics for properties. Sections will also vary, depending on the language, product, or technology being documented.

Section	Contains
Description	Typically, one or two sentences that describe the programming element. Whenever possible, explain what the element does or represents as concisely as possible without repeating the wording in the element name. For example, the description of a property named **Control.AllowDrop** might be "Gets or sets a value that indicates whether the control can accept data that the user drags onto it."
Declaration/Syntax	The code signature that defines the programming element. This section might also provide usage syntax. If you are documenting a technology that can be used with multiple programming languages, provide the syntax for each language.

Section	Contains

Parameters	If the programming element has parameters, a description of each parameter and its data type. If appropriate, indicate whether the parameter is required or optional, and whether it represents input or output. Descriptions should provide as much useful detail as possible instead of just repeating the words in the parameter name or repeating the data type.
	
	Microsoft style
	visible
	Type: System.Boolean
	true to specify that the box is rendered; **false** to specify that it is not rendered.
	input
	    Type: System.String
	    The text to convert.
	
	Not Microsoft style
	visible
	Type: System.Boolean
	A System.Boolean.
	input
	    Type: System.String
	    The input.

Return value	If the programming element returns a value, a description of that value and information about its data type. If the value is a Boolean that indicates the presence of a condition, describe the associated condition.
Property/Field value	A description of the value of a property or field. If the property or field has a default value, describe that as well. Include the data type of the property or field value if applicable.
Exceptions/Error codes	If the programming element can throw exceptions or raise errors when it is called, the list of those exceptions or errors, and descriptions of the conditions under which they occur.
Permissions	Security permissions that apply to the programming element, if required.
Remarks	Additional information about the programming element and important details that may not be obvious from its syntax, parameters, or return value. For example, the "Remarks" section might explain what the element does in more detail, compare it with similar elements, and identify any potential issues in its use.
Example	A code example that illustrates how to use the programming element. (For more information, see *Code examples*.)
Requirements	Language or platform requirements for using the programming element.
See also	References or links to topics or articles that provide more information about how to use the programming element, and references or links to related elements.

Some of this information, such as syntax, parameter names and types, and return values and types, can sometimes be generated directly from the source code of the technology that is being documented. Some organizations also export code comments from the source code and use that information to fill in sections, such as the programming element description, parameter descriptions, and remarks. If you decide to auto-generate your reference documentation from code comments, be sure to review the quality and appropriateness of the comments. Code developers might leave out details that seem obvious to them but that might not be obvious to users. In addition, developers use comments to provide implementation or internal details, to flag areas that might change, and to document aspects of the code for maintenance purposes. This information might be useful to other internal code developers, but it might not be suitable for user documentation.

For examples of technical reference topics, see the .NET Framework Class Library section (*http://msdn.microsoft.com/en-us/library/gg145045.aspx*) of the Microsoft Developer Network (MSDN) Library (*http://msdn.microsoft.com/library/*).

Code examples

Code examples illustrate how to use a programming element to implement specific functionality. They may include simple, one-line examples interspersed with text; short, self-contained examples that demonstrate specific points; and lengthy samples that illustrate multiple features, complex scenarios, or best practices.

Code examples are used by developers in all aspects of their work: during planning (to assess a technology through its API), when learning or exploring a language or technology, and when writing and debugging code. Developers often copy the examples that they find in the documentation to their own code, or adapt them to their own needs.

To create useful code examples, first identify the tasks and scenarios that are meaningful for your audience, and then create examples that illustrate those scenarios. Code examples that demonstrate product features are not useful unless they explicitly address the problems developers are trying to solve.

General guidelines

- Create concise examples that exemplify key development tasks. Start with simple examples and build up complexity after you cover common scenarios.

- If you can't provide examples for all programming elements, focus on frequently used elements and elements that may be difficult to understand or tricky to use.

- Don't create code examples that are too complex to scan or understand easily. Reserve complicated examples for tutorials and walkthroughs, where you can provide a step-by-step explanation of how the example works.

- Don't use code examples to illustrate points that are obvious or scenarios that are contrived.

- Add an introduction to describe the scenario that the code example illustrates and to explain anything that might not be clear from the code. List the requirements and dependencies for using or running the example.

- Design your code for reuse by making it easy for users to determine what to modify. Add comments to explain details, but don't over-comment. Don't state the obvious.

- Show expected output, either in a separate section after the code example or by using code comments within the code example.

- For code that creates UI, consider accessibility requirements. For example, include alternate text for images.

- Write secure code. For example, always validate user input, never hardcode passwords in code, and use code analysis tools to detect security issues.

- Show exception handling only when it is intrinsic to the example. Do not catch exceptions that are thrown when invalid arguments are passed to parameters.

- Always compile and test your code.

- If you're publishing your content on the web, provide an easy way for users to copy and run the code. If the code example demonstrates interactive and animated features, consider providing a way for the user to run the example directly from your content page.

- If you're publishing your content on the web, use the appropriate keywords, linking strategies, and other search engine optimization (SEO) techniques to improve the visibility and usability of the code example. For example, add links to relevant code example pages and content pages to improve SEO across your content.

For more information, see *Help customers find your content* (Chapter 2).

Code formatting and naming guidelines

- Use white space and indentation to improve the readability of your code. The Microsoft convention is to use four spaces per indent level for most programming languages, and two spaces per indent level for markup languages (HTML and XML).

- Use blank lines to separate individual tasks or components in the code.

- Avoid long lines of code; if possible, break these into multiple lines to improve readability.

- Use a monospace font for all code examples, whether they're embedded in text or displayed as separate paragraphs.

- If you omit part of the example for clarity or length considerations, insert a comment at the point of omission to explain what should be added to make the code compile, or use an ellipsis (in a comment) to indicate that code segments have been omitted. Identify code that users must edit or add before the code can be compiled. If your documentation will be localized, consider putting this information in the body of the topic as well.

- Observe the casing and coding conventions for the technology or language that you are documenting. For HTML, follow XHTML guidelines.

- Use fictitious people names, company names, email addresses, and URLs.

- Remember worldwide users. Do not use examples that include U.S.-centric data, such as zip codes or sports teams.

- Do not use sensitive geographic and cultural references.

- Do not use offensive language or slang. For example, do not use foo or bar or their derivatives when naming coding constructs.

- Use descriptive construct names. Do not use names that are too generic or that include the prefix My. For example, use the property name **MessageString** instead of **MyProperty** or **Data**.

Code commenting guidelines

- Use descriptive phrases that explain what the code does.

- Use the correct delimiter for the programming language that you are using. For example, use two forward slashes (//) followed by a space to denote a comment for C++, C#, and JScript code. Use an apostrophe (') followed by a space to denote a comment for Visual Basic code.

- Place each comment on its own line and before the code that it's describing. If you must use trailing comments (on the same line as the code), keep the comment short, especially if the comments will be localized.

- If your comment is lengthy, consider including that information within the body of the topic instead.

- For multiline comments, use the comment delimiter, such as two forward slashes (//), on each line. Do not use the /* ...*/ convention, which could cause problems when users copy and paste portions of the code into their own applications.

- Consider localization when you decide whether to include information in a comment or in the body of a topic. Comments are sometimes not localized because of cost considerations.

- Use complete sentences whenever possible, and observe standard rules of punctuation and grammar.

- Do not use first person. For example, do not say "Here we display a list of customers." Use present tense for comments that describe a code block, and use imperative mood to describe the action within that code block. Also use imperative mood to provide instructions for using the code example, as follows.

```
// Displays a list of customer information in the console. public void
PrintCustomers(List<Customer> customerList)
{
    // Display the name for each customer.
    foreach (var customer in customerList)
    {
        Console.WriteLine("Name: {0}, {1}",
            customer.LastName, customer.FirstName);
    }
}
// Insert code for get and set accessors.
```

- If you use comments to display the output of the code example, introduce the output with a comment such as "This code displays the following output." If the output varies, say "This code displays output similar to the following" instead.

Referring to code examples

Use *code example* to refer to source code that is included in content to illustrate a development task. Code examples are usually code fragments but may also include complete examples that users can copy to their computers, compile, and run. Introduce a code example with a complete sentence that ends with a period, not a colon.

Use *code sample* to refer to source code files that users can download to their computers and use in their development projects. For example, the *Samples Gallery* on MSDN provides code samples that users can download and use in Visual Studio.

Do not use *code snippet*.

Additional resources for writing code

- Cwalina, Krzysztof and Brad Abrams. *Framework Design Guidelines: Conventions, Idioms, and Patterns for Reusable .NET Libraries*. 2nd ed. Addison-Wesley, 2008.

- Howard, Michael and David LeBlanc. *Writing Secure Code*. 2nd ed. Redmond, WA: Microsoft Press, 2003.

- McConnell, Steve. *Code Complete*. 2nd ed. Redmond, WA: Microsoft Press, 2004.

- The Design guidelines for developing class libraries section of the MSDN Library describes the conventions and recommendations for developing .NET Framework classes and components.

- The Visual Studio languages section of the MSDN Library provides programming information about Visual Basic, C#, C++, JScript, and F#.

- The Program structure and code conventions (Visual Basic) section of the MSDN Library discusses program structure and code conventions in Visual Basic.

Security

Do not make statements that convey the impression or promise of absolute security, safety, or privacy. Instead, focus on technologies or features that help achieve security, safety, or privacy.

Be careful when you use the words *safe*, *private*, *secure*, *protect*, and their synonyms or derivatives. Use qualifiers such as *helps* and *can help* with these words.

Microsoft style

The default security settings in Windows Internet Explorer can help protect your computer from viruses.

Not Microsoft style

The default security settings in Windows Internet Explorer protect your computer from viruses.

For a full list of security-related terms and their definitions, see the Microsoft Malware Encyclopedia (*http://www.microsoft.com/security/portal/Threat/Encyclopedia/Glossary.aspx*). The *Microsoft Manual of Style* provides guidance for the following terms:

- antimalware
- antivirus
- antispyware
- bot
- deceptive software
- firewall
- hack, hacker
- malicious code
- malicious user
- malware, malicious software
- spyware
- trojan horse, trojan
- unwanted software
- vulnerability

Command syntax

Although computer users today use the user interface to do most of their work, there are still many tasks that require typing commands or running programs at a command prompt.

For elements that the user must type as they appear in the text, use bold. For elements that are placeholders representing information that the user must supply, use italic.

Note In text files where formatting is unavailable, substitute all uppercase for bold and all lowercase for italic.

The general form for presenting command syntax is as follows:

sample {**+r** | **r**} *arguments* [*options*]

where:

Element	Meaning
sample	Specifies the name of the command or utility.
{ }	Indicates a set of choices from which the user must choose one.
|	Separates two mutually exclusive choices in a syntax line. The user types one of these choices, not the symbol.
arguments	Specify a variable name or other information the user must provide, such as a path and file name.
...	Indicates that the user can type multiple arguments of the same type. The user types only the information, not the ellipsis (...).
[ ]	Indicates optional items. The user types only the information within the brackets, not the brackets themselves.

Microsoft style

chkdsk [*volume*:][*Path*] [*FileName*] [**/v**][**/r**][**/x**][**/i**][**/c**][**/l**:*size*]

doskey {**/reinstall** | **/listsize**=*size* | **/macros**:[{**all** | *exename*}] | **/history** | **/insert** | **/overstrike** | **/ exename**=*exename* | **/macrofile**=*FileName* | **macroname**=[*text*]}

For more information, see *Document conventions, Procedures*

File names and extensions

In content for Windows and the Mac, use title capitalization for file names, folders, and drive names. Use all lowercase for extensions.

Microsoft style

.htm file

C:\Taxes\April2010

My Tax File, 2010

It is all right to use internal capitalization for readability in concatenated file names if they cannot be confused with function names.

Microsoft style

MyTaxFile

Mytaxfile

Do not use the file name extension to identify the type of file under discussion unless you have no other choice. Use more descriptive language instead.

Microsoft style

A Microsoft Excel workbook contains one or more spreadsheets. Store the result as a text file.

Not Microsoft style

An .xlsx file contains one or more spreadsheets. Store the result as a .txt file.

If you must use the file name extension as a word, precede the extension with a period. If you must use an indefinite article (*a* or *an*), use the one that applies to the sound of the first letter of the extension, as though the period (or "dot") is not pronounced, as in "a .com file" and "an .exe file." In contexts that require title capitalization, capitalize as you would other common nouns.

Microsoft style

Initialization information is stored in an .ini file.

Save an .Rtf File as a .Doc File

Sometimes the file name extension corresponds to the abbreviation of the generic term for the file. For example, a .dll file contains a dynamic-link library (DLL). Do not confuse the abbreviation with the file name extension. For example, a .dll file (not a DLL file) contains a DLL.

When instructing users to type literal file names and paths, use lowercase for the file names and paths, and use bold formatting. Use italic formatting for placeholders.

Microsoft style

At the command prompt, type **c:\msmail\msmail.mmf** *password*

 Note Do not use *Foo, Fu, Foo.bar*, or a similar word as a placeholder for a file name. Use a substitute, such as *Sample File* or *MySample* instead.

For more information, see *Capitalization* (Chapter 7), *Document conventions*, *File names and extensions*

Version identifiers

Microsoft product and product component names can include version information by special identifier (Windows Vista), by year of release (Windows Server 2008), or by chronological version number (Windows 7).

When you list different versions of a product, list the most recent version first.

Microsoft style

Windows 7, Windows Vista, and Windows XP

Not Microsoft style

Windows XP, Windows Vista, and Windows 7

A complete product version number has three components:

- Major release identifier: **X**.x.x

- Minor release identifier: x.**X**.x

- Update identifier: x.x.**X**

Only the major and minor release identifiers are usually significant to the user. Update identifiers appear in the Help About information in products and in Knowledge Base articles and other content describing the update, but usually they do not appear elsewhere.

Microsoft style

Internet Explorer 4.0

Microsoft Exchange Server 4.0.829

Some products and product components may be identified by just their major release identifiers.

Microsoft style

Internet Explorer 8

Windows Media Player 9

In these cases, the version identifier by itself also encompasses minor releases of the same version. For example, Internet Explorer 5 identifies both the original release and minor releases such as Internet Explorer 5.1 and Internet Explorer 5.5. To identify only the original release of such a product, append *.0* as the minor release identifier.

Microsoft style

Internet Explorer 5   (Refers to major release and all minor releases of Internet Explorer 5.)

Internet Explorer 5.0   (Refers only to major release of Internet Explorer 5.)

Use *edition* to refer to the different Windows Vista and Windows 7 SKUs. For example, Windows 7 Home Basic is one edition, and Windows 7 Ultimate is another edition. Use *version* only to refer to different operating systems, such as Windows Vista and Windows 7.

General guidelines

Do not specify a particular version unless it is necessary for the context. For example, you may need to specify the version number when comparing current and previous versions of the same product or for reasons of clarity and technical accuracy. Do not include the update identifier of a product unless it is technically relevant.

If you must mention a version number, specify it on first mention in a topic or section. Thereafter, refer only to the product name without the version identifier. For products whose original release identifier includes *.0*, use *.x* (in italic type) to indicate all release numbers of a product.

Microsoft style

This topic applies to .NET Framework 3.*x*. (Indicates all releases of .NET Framework.)

You may use *earlier* if the statement is accurate for all preceding releases. For example, you can use "Windows 2000 or earlier" as long as the statement is accurate for all preceding releases, including Windows 1.0.

Do not use *later*.

Microsoft style

Windows XP with SP2, Windows XP with SP1, and Windows XP

Not Microsoft style

Windows XP and later

> Do not precede version numbers with the word version.

Microsoft style

If you are using Windows NT Server 4.0…

Not Microsoft style

If you are using Windows NT Server version 4.0…

> Do not refer to a product just by its release identifier.

Microsoft style

Windows 7, Windows Vista, and Windows XP

Not Microsoft style

Windows 7, Vista, and XP

> For more information, see also *earlier, later* in the Usage Dictionary.

Out-of-band release terminology

Use one of the following terms to refer to software that is released outside the regular product release cycle:

- To refer to bug fixes that are security-related: *security update*

- To refer to bug fixes that are not security-related: *update, critical update, definition update*

- To refer to cumulative sets of updates: *update rollup, hotfix, service pack*

- To refer to product functionality updates: *feature pack*

- To refer generically to out-of-band releases: *software update*

Do not use *bug fix, patch, software patch*, or *QFE* to describe an out-of-band release.

Protocols

A protocol is a standard for communication between computers. Most protocols are referred to by their abbreviations. For example, SMTP is an abbreviation for Simple Mail Transfer Protocol.

In URLs, the protocol used by the web server appears in lowercase before a colon. In text, protocol abbreviations typically appear in uppercase. Typical web protocols are HTTP, FTP, news, and so on.

Use title capitalization for the spelled-out form of protocol names (except in URLs) unless you know the name is handled differently. When in doubt, check the *Microsoft Manual of Style* index, or consult your project style sheet.

Microsoft style

http://www.microsoft.com

Internet Explorer supports Hypertext Transfer Protocol (HTTP).

XML tag, element, and attribute formatting

> **Note** These guidelines apply also to Extensible Hypertext Markup Language (XHTML), Extensible Stylesheet Language (XSL), Extensible Stylesheet Language for Transformations (XSLT), and XML Path Language (XPath).

Elements vs. tags

An element includes the tags, the attributes, and the content, if any. For example, consider the following:

```
<xsl:apply-templates
order-by="sort-criteria-list"
select=expression
mode=QName>
</xsl:apply-templates>
```

In this example, the <xsl:apply-templates> element consists of the start tag (<xsl:apply-templates>); the **order-by**, **select**, and **mode** attributes; and the end tag (</xsl:apply-templates>).

Note that XML can have empty tags, such as <doctitle/> or <elementName att1Name="att1Value" att2Name="att2Value"/>. Empty tags have no textual content, whether or not they have attributes.

Capitalization

XML is a case-sensitive language, so be sure to follow the capitalization of the code, unless otherwise noted. Many items are in lowercase, but not all. When in doubt, check with the author.

Element name formatting

Predefined XSL Transformation (XSLT) element names are always placed inside angle brackets. An example is the <xsl:attribute> element.

An element name can be presented in angle brackets if you are specifically referencing an example or code sample. An example is the <schema> element.

When you are working with document type definitions (DTDs) instead of schemas, you may notice that some primary element names appear in all uppercase letters. They should remain styled as such. An example is the DOCTYPE element.

When you are working with schemas instead of DTDs, used bold formatting for schema element names. An example is the **ElementType** element.

Use regular type for the name of any user-defined element. Examples are an author element and the bookstore element.

Attribute formatting

Capitalize attributes as they appear in the code and use bold formatting. Examples are the **xml:space** attribute and the **STYLE** attribute.

Tag and node formatting

In schemas, place tags and nodes inside angle brackets, as shown in the following example. Capitalization should match what the user must type.

the <first> and </last> tags of the <Schema> node

> **Note** In DTDs, some tags consist of all uppercase letters. An example is the DOCTYPE tag.

Other formatting

Use bold formatting for collections, data types, functions, interfaces, methods, objects, properties, and scopes. For more information, see *Document conventions; HTML tag, element, and attribute formatting*.

Use bold formatting for namespaces. An example is the **BookInfo** namespace.

Use italic formatting for parameters. An example is the *output-stylesheet* parameter.

HTML tag, element, and attribute formatting

Elements vs. tags

An element includes the tags, the attributes, and the content, if any. For example, consider the following:

<h1 align="center">This is a heading</h1>

In this example, the H1 element consists of the start tag (<h1>), including the **align** attribute, the **"center"** value of the **align** attribute, the content ("This is a heading"), and the end tag (</h1>).

Some elements, such as META and IMG (image), do not have start and end tags; they only have a single tag with attributes.

Formatting guidelines

- Use all uppercase for element names, and surround the element name with the definite article *the* and *element*. Examples are the H1 element and the FONT element.

- Use angle brackets and lowercase for tags. Examples are the <h1> tag and the <font> tag.

- Use bold formatting and lowercase for attributes and their values. An example is the **"center"** value of the **align** attribute.

Microsoft style

The FONT element includes start and end tags, attributes, and any content within the tags. The start <font> tag begins the FONT element, and the end </font> tag ends the FONT element. In the FONT element, you can use attributes such as **face**, **size**, and **color**.

> **Note** HTML is not case-sensitive.

For more information, see *Document conventions*; *XML tag, element, and attribute formatting*

Readme files and release notes

Readme files and release notes often contain similar types of information, and you can usually treat them in the same way. The main difference is that readme files provide late-breaking information about a newly released product and release notes provide information about test and beta releases.

Capitalize *Readme* when you refer to the specific file. Otherwise, you can use *readme file* or *readme*.

Microsoft style

For late-breaking information about the mission editor, look in the Readme file in the Editor folder of the game's root directory.

Look in the Readme file on Disk A for current information.

As far as practical, apply the same rules of style and usage to readme files that you would to all other documentation. Readme files should not contain jargon or overly technical language and they should otherwise conform to Microsoft style.

> **Note** Do not use trademark symbols or notes in readme files.

Readme files are usually HTML files, formatted with bold headings and other style conventions. Use the following guidelines for the front matter of your readme file to ensure that its information will be helpful to its intended reader:

- Title of the file left-aligned, with the date (month and year) left-aligned one line below. Standard Microsoft copyright notice, left-aligned under the title. Introductory paragraph explaining the purpose of the file. Contents listing all section headings.

- Standard Microsoft copyright notice, left-aligned under the title.

- Introductory paragraph explaining the purpose of the file.

- Contents listing all section headings.

In general, order the readme file with the most important information or information of the most general interest first. List errata and changes to the documentation last. Section numbers are optional.

6

CHAPTER 7

Practical issues of style

Unlike grammatical rules, the formatting of style elements such as dates, numbers, and measurements can be open to interpretation. As a result, users are faced with inconsistent styles that can lead to confusion and misunderstanding. By using a consistent style to present these elements, you can make your content more readable and easier to understand. This section discusses the most common style problems and provides you with guidelines to address them.

Capitalization

In general, follow the capitalization rules of Standard English. The following guidelines discuss the specific capitalization guidelines that are used in Microsoft content:

- Never use all uppercase for emphasis. Use sentence structure for emphasis instead. It's best to avoid formatting for emphasis, but if you must use formatting for emphasis, use italic formatting instead of all uppercase.

- Follow the capitalization guidelines or conventions for software or for a specific product or service as necessary, such as case-sensitive keywords or product or service names with internal capitalization.

- Do not capitalize the spelled-out form of an acronym unless the spelled-out form is a proper noun. When in doubt, see the *Acronyms and other abbreviations*, or consult your project style sheet.

- Do not use capitalization randomly. Use lowercase unless there is a specific reason for capitalizing.

After consulting your project style sheet and this manual, use the *American Heritage Dictionary* as the primary reference for proper capitalization of specific words and *The Chicago Manual of Style* for general guidelines.

Capitalization of feature names and technologies

As a general rule, be conservative in capitalizing the names of new features and technologies. To determine whether to capitalize a feature or technology name, follow these guidelines:

- Capitalize the name for legal reasons, such as efforts to establish a trademark or to respect a trademark registered by another company.

- Capitalize the name if it is capitalized in a marketing or branding campaign.

- Capitalize the name to distinguish a component or product, such as SQL Server, from a general technology with a similar name, such as an SQL database server.

- Capitalize industry-standard terms only if the rest of the industry does so. Search the *American Heritage Dictionary*, the Internet, and industry-specific dictionaries. Do not rely on unedited websites.

For new names and terms, work toward consistency in capitalization with other company products, services, documents, packaging, and marketing.

International considerations

Before you decide on the capitalization of a new name or term, consider how capitalizing will affect localization. If possible, check with a localization expert.

Capitalization of titles and headings

Over the years, design guidelines have become less formal, and many groups at Microsoft as well as at other companies are now using sentence-style capitalization for titles and headings. Sentence-style capitalization is also easier for the worldwide audience to read and for machine translation to translate. For these reasons, *Microsoft Manual of Style* recommends using sentence-style capitalization for titles and all headings, regardless of level.

Microsoft style

Copy music to a CD

Find a file

Not Microsoft style

Copy Music to a CD

Find a File

Title capitalization

If your content still uses title capitalization, the following guidelines answer questions about capitalization of various constructions and parts of speech.

- Capitalize all nouns, verbs (including *is* and other forms of *be*), adverbs (including *than* and *when*), adjectives (including *this* and *that*), and pronouns (including *its*).

- Capitalize the first and last words, regardless of their parts of speech ("The Text to Look For").

- Capitalize prepositions that are part of a verb phrase ("Backing Up Your Disk").

- Do not capitalize articles (*a, an, the*) unless the article is the first word in the title.

- Do not capitalize coordinate conjunctions (*and, but, for, nor, or, yet, so*) unless the conjunction is the first word in the title.

- Do not capitalize prepositions of four or fewer letters unless the preposition is the first or the last word in the title.

- Do not capitalize *to* in an infinitive phrase ("How to Format Your Hard Disk") unless the phrase is the first word in the title.

- Capitalize the second part of a hyphenated compound if it would be capitalized without the hyphen. Always capitalize the second part of a hyphenated compound if it is the last word of a heading or title.

  Microsoft style

  Installing Add-ins in Word

  Installing an Add-In

  Run-Time Error Codes

  Not Microsoft style

  Installing Add-Ins in Word

  Installing an Add-in

  Run-time Error Codes

- Capitalize user interface and application programming interface terms that you would not ordinarily capitalize unless they are case-sensitive ("The **fdisk** Command"). Follow the traditional capitalization of keywords and other special terms in programming languages ("The **printf** Function," "Using the EVEN and ALIGN Directives").

For more information, see *Lists, Tables*.

Capitalization and punctuation

Always use lowercase after a colon within a sentence, except when:

- A colon introduces a direct quotation.

- The first word after the colon is a proper noun.

For more information, see *Colons* (Chapter 9).

Do not capitalize the word following an em dash unless it is a proper noun, even if the text following the em dash is a complete sentence.

Always capitalize the first word of a new sentence. Rewrite sentences that start with a case-sensitive lowercase word.

Microsoft style

The **printf** function is the most frequently used C function.

The most frequently used C function is **printf**.

Not Microsoft style

printf is the most frequently used C function.

For information about capitalization of user interface elements, see *User interface formatting* (Chapter 5).

Titles and headings

Titles and headings of content should convey as much information as possible about the text that follows to help readers locate information quickly.

> **Note** Title and heading style varies among content teams. The guidelines in this topic are widely used and can make it easier to share files across teams. However, if your team follows a different practice, use your team's style consistently.

Title and heading style and conventions

- Use sentence-style capitalization for titles and for headings, regardless of level. For more information, see *Capitalization*.

- In general, use imperative constructions in conceptual or informational topics for both the title and the headings. Describe what the user wants to do in the user's language.

Microsoft style in titles and headings

Run programs and manage files

Find a file

Copy music to a CD

Not Microsoft style in titles and headings

To run programs and manage files

How to copy music to a CD

Microsoft style in procedure settings

To find a file

Not Microsoft style in procedure settings

Finding a file

Find a file

> **Note** There is considerable variation across content teams in the heading style for procedural topics. If the differences are generally based on valid assessments of user needs, there is nothing wrong with them. Some content teams provide only an infinitive heading and the procedure, reasoning that the work the user is doing at the time provides the necessary context. Other teams use "how to" in headings to avoid ambiguity for localization. Still other teams use the imperative form of the verb in topic headings. Consult your project style sheet, and whatever you do, use one form consistently.

- For material that does not describe a task, use a noun phrase, not a gerund phrase, a prepositional phrase, or a clause.

  Microsoft style

  Error messages and their meanings

  Visual Basic controls

  Accessory programs

  Not Microsoft style

  Understanding error messages and their meanings

  About Visual Basic controls

  Things that you can do with accessory programs

- Because users usually act on one thing at a time, headings should use singular nouns if possible. It is all right to use plural nouns when the plural is obviously more suitable.

  Microsoft style

  Format a disk

  Open a new document

  Manage folders

- Do not use ampersands (&) in headings unless you are specifically reflecting the user interface or the application programming interface.

- Use italic type if it would be required in body text. For example, use italic type for variable names. Follow the capitalization of any case-sensitive terms, even if the capitalization conflicts with the guidance for heading style.

  Microsoft style

  Dereference the *pszlUnknown* pointer

  Not Microsoft style

  Dereference the pszlUnknown pointer

  Dereference the PszlUnknown Pointer

7

- Use vs., not v. or versus, in headings.

  Microsoft style

  Daily backups vs. weekly backups

- In the first sentence following any heading, do not assume that the reader has read the heading.

  Microsoft style

  Find information in Help

  When you click **Help** on the menu bar, Help commands appear.

  Not Microsoft style

  Find information in Help

  This is easy to do from the menu bar.

- In printed content, avoid titles and headings of more than one line. If a title or heading must have two lines, try to make the first line longer than the second. For information about acceptable line breaks in headings, see *Line breaks*.

For additional considerations for titling webpages, see *Help users find your content* (Chapter 2).

Organizational guidelines

Headings help orient users and make content easier to scan. First-level headings usually apply to the most general material, and subsequent–level headings deal with more specific topics.

Follow these organizational guidelines:

- Ensure that all headings at the same level are grammatically parallel.

- Apply the rules for outlining when organizing headings. When dividing a section, try to make the material fall under at least two subheadings. It is all right to have only one subsection within a section, but only if other methods, such as restructuring the section, will not convey the meaning as well.

- In general, do not have two headings in a row without intervening text. However, avoid inserting "filler" text just to adhere to this rule. The intervening text should help the user decide whether what follows will be of interest. For example, a description of a user problem that the content will help solve can save the time of users who have a different problem. However, intervening text that seems perfunctory or lacking in content can indicate that restructuring is in order.

  Microsoft style

  System Requirements

  The following system requirements include software, hardware, network, and storage requirements for a quick migration scenario.

Software Requirements

Following are the software requirements for...

Not Microsoft style

System Requirements

Software Requirements

Following are the software requirements for...

For information about page breaks with headings, see *Page breaks*. For additional information, see *Capitalization, Help users find your content* (Chapter 2), *Line breaks, Lists, Tables*.

Microsoft in product and service names

On first mention, precede the name of a Microsoft product or service with *Microsoft*, except for references to the following products and services:

Windows Server 2008 R2

Windows Server 2008

Windows Server 2003

Windows 7

Windows Vista

Windows XP

Windows Internet Explorer

Windows Azure

SQL Azure

Xbox

On subsequent mention, you do not have to precede the product or service name with *Microsoft*, except for the following two names that must always be preceded with *Microsoft:*

Microsoft Dynamics

Microsoft Surface

When the first mention of a product or service occurs in a heading, a procedure, link text, a glossary definition, or art, do not precede the reference with *Microsoft*. Instead, precede the first mention that appears outside these elements with *Microsoft*.

On first mention of multiple versions of the same product or service in a sentence or multiple products or services under the same category title, such as the products in Microsoft Office, you must precede only the name of the first version or product or service with *Microsoft,* although it is all right to precede all of them with *Microsoft* if you think it is necessary.

Microsoft style on first mention

Microsoft Word 2010, PowerPoint 2010, and Excel 2010

Microsoft Word 2010, Microsoft PowerPoint 2010, and Microsoft Excel 2010

However, in a bulleted list, a column list, or a table that contains both first and subsequent mentions of multiple versions or multiple products or services under the same category title, follow the "on first mention" guideline for each product or service in the list.

Microsoft style on first mention in a list or table

- Microsoft Word 2010

- Microsoft PowerPoint 2010

- Microsoft Excel 2010

Not Microsoft style on first mention in a list or table

- Microsoft Word 2010

- PowerPoint 2010

- Excel 2010

Lists

Depending on the type of content that you are writing, you can choose among several types of lists: bulleted, numbered, unnumbered single-column, unnumbered multicolumn, or "term list." A list can incorporate a nested comment, an untitled table, or no more than one nested list.

A *table* is an arrangement of data with two or more columns in which the information in the first column in each row is related to the information in the other column or columns of the same row. A list of similar entries that is arranged in multiple columns is not a table but a multicolumn list. An example is a list of commands. A table usually has column headings and may have a title. For more information, see *Tables.*

How to punctuate lists

Introduce a list with a heading or with a sentence or fragment ending with a colon. Begin each entry in a bulleted or numbered list with a capital letter.

Make entries in a list parallel. End each entry with a period if all entries are complete sentences, if they are a mixture of fragments and complete sentences, or if they all complete the introductory sentence or fragment. An exception is when all entries are short phrases (three words or fewer) or single words. These entries do not need ending punctuation. If all entries are fragments that together with the introductory phrase do not form a complete sentence, do not end them with periods.

If you introduce a list with a fragment, do not treat the list and its introduction as one continuous sentence. That is, do not use semicolons or commas to end list items, and do not insert *and* before the last list element.

International considerations

If your content will be localized, be aware that the grammar and syntax of different languages can make it difficult to match the structure in English of an introductory fragment that is completed by each list element. Introductory fragments may also lead to mistranslation in content that is machine translated.

Microsoft style

> If you use printer fonts:
>
> - Choose a printer before creating a presentation.
>
> - Install all the fonts and printers that you will use by selecting them in the **Print Setup** dialog box.
>
> The database includes the following:
>
> - Reports
>
> - Forms
>
> - Tables
>
> - Modules

Not Microsoft style

> The database includes the following:
>
> - Reports,
>
> - Forms,
>
> - Tables, and
>
> - Modules.

Bulleted lists

Use a bulleted list for an unordered series of concepts, items, or options. Capitalize the first word of each bulleted entry.

Microsoft style

The database owner can:

- Create and delete a database.

- Add, delete, or modify a document.

- Add, delete, or modify any information in the database.

Numbered lists

Use a numbered list for procedures or other sequential lists. You can introduce a procedure in two ways:

- With a heading that uses an infinitive phrase.

- With a sentence in the imperative mood (including an infinitive phrase) or in the indicative mood.

If you introduce a procedure with a heading, do not use explanatory text after the heading. Also, do not use a colon after the heading.

Microsoft style (heading)

To log on to a database

1. On the **File** menu, click **Open Database**.

2. In **User Name**, type your name.

3. In **Password**, type your password, and then click **OK**.

Microsoft style (infinitive phrase)

To log on to a database, follow these steps:

1. On the **File** menu, click **Open Database**.

2. In **User Name**, type your name.

3. In **Password**, type your password, and then click OK.

Microsoft style (imperative mood)

Use the Pencil tool to draw thin, free-form lines or curves:

1. On the **Home** tab, in the **Tools** group, click the **Pencil** tool.

2. In the **Colors** group, click **Color 1**, click a color, and then drag the pointer in the picture to draw.

Microsoft style (indicative mood)

The basic steps for adding scrolling to your application are as follows:

1. Define a size for your documents.

2. Derive your view class from **CScrollView**.

3. Pass the documents' size to the **SetScrollSizes** method of **CScrollView** whenever the size changes.

4. Convert between logical coordinates and device coordinates if you are passing points between GDI and non-GDI functions.

Unnumbered single-column and multicolumn lists

An unnumbered list consists of one or more columns of list entries, all of which are very short, so no bullets or numbers are required to separate one entry from another. Use an unnumbered list to group similar items, such as a list of keywords. Use a single column for six or fewer items and balanced, multiple columns for seven or more items. In general, if columns are of different lengths, make the left column or columns longer. For example, if a two-column list contains nine one-line items, use five items in the left column and four in the right column. You do not have to capitalize entries. If the list is alphabetical, alphabetize down the columns, not across rows, if possible.

Because there are no page breaks in online content, long multicolumn lists can be difficult to read. In this case, you can alphabetize from left to right (for shorter lists) or sort in labeled alphabetical sections. Alphabetical sections make navigating in long lists of items, such as functions, easier.

International considerations

Alphabetical sort order often changes when a list is localized, so keep alphabetical lists as simple as possible so that localizers can easily change the alphabetical sort order if necessary.

Microsoft style for unnumbered single-column lists

addprocedure

checkpointrule

errorexitsum

nonclusteredtriggerover

Microsoft style for unnumbered multicolumn lists

Graphics Interchange Format (GIF)	Run-length encoded (RLE)
Joint Photographic Experts Group (JPEG)	Device-independent bitmap (DIB)
Macintosh PICT	Windows Enhanced Metafile (EMF)
Portable Network Graphics (PNG)	Windows Metafile (WMF)
Windows bitmap (BMP)	

Microsoft style for long unnumbered lists sorted in alphabetical sections

A-C

AbsCDbl

AscChoose

AtnChr, Chr$

AvgCIntCLng

CcurCodeDB

D-E

Date, Date$ErrError, Error$

DateAddErl

Environ, Environ$EOF

Term lists

Use term lists, also called term-def lists, for a series of terms, parameters, or similar items that are followed by a brief explanation or definition. You can use one of two formats for a term list:

- A term can be listed on its own line, usually in bold type, with the definition indented under it. In this format, the term may use additional character formatting if appropriate.

- A term can be listed in italic type, followed by a period, with the definition immediately following it on the same line.

Microsoft style

Computer name

The name by which the local area network identifies a server or workstation. Each computer name on the network must be unique.

Computer name. The name by which the local area network identifies a server or workstation. Each computer name on the network must be unique.

Not Microsoft style

Computer name   The name by which the local area network identifies a server or workstation. Each computer name on the network must be unique.

Computer name   The name by which the local area network identifies a server or workstation. Each computer name on the network must be unique.

For more information, see also *Parallelism* (Chapter 1).

Tables

A table is an arrangement of data with two or more rows and two or more columns. Typically, the information in the first column describes something whose attributes are shown in the other columns. A single row shows all the attributes for one item. The format of a table can vary, depending on the project style.

A list of similar entries that is arranged in multiple columns is not a table but a multicolumn list. An example is a list of commands. For details about lists, see *Lists*.

A table usually has column headings, and it can optionally have a title. Introduce a table with a sentence that ends with a period, not a fragment that ends with a colon. If a table is titled, an introductory sentence does not have to immediately precede the table. The title appears above the table.

Keep in mind these additional points:

- Table dimensions must be visible on a minimum screen resolution, typically 800 pixels by 600 pixels.

- Tables can be used to simulate frames. In this case, tables are better because older browsers cannot always process frames correctly.

Accessibility considerations

Screen readers for the blind can form table text into columns, ignoring the table column format. Providing summary information about the table can help. If possible, arrange the data in the table so that it makes sense when read in a linear fashion.

Capitalization and punctuation

Use sentence-style capitalization for the table title and for column headings.

> **Note** It is all right to use lowercase for the first word in column entries if capitalization might cause confusion. An example is a column of keywords that must be lowercase.

End each entry with a period if all entries are complete sentences or are a mixture of fragments and sentences. An exception is when all entries are short imperative sentences (only a few words). These entries do not need a period. If all entries are fragments, do not end them with periods.

Number tables in white papers or similar printable content if they are not adjacent to their text references or if a list of tables appears in the front matter. Do not number tables on webpages. If you decide to number tables, use numbers consistently throughout the document. The numbers include the chapter number and a sequential table number, such as Table 2.1, Table 2.2, and so on.

Microsoft style

TABLE 7.4 Formatting flags

Formatting flag	Action
\a	Anchors text for cross-references
\b, \B	Turns bold formatting on or off

Content

Follow these guidelines for organizing your table:

- Place information that identifies the contents of a row in the leftmost column of the table. For example, in a table that describes commands, put the command names in the left column. Place information about the item in the left column in the subsequent columns.

- Make entries in a table parallel. For example, in a description column, be consistent in beginning the entries with a verb or noun.

Microsoft style

Device name	Description
COM1	Serial port 1. This device is the first serial port in your computer.
CON	System console. This device consists of both the keyboard and the screen.
LPT1	Parallel port 1. This device represents a parallel port.

Command	Action
Bold	Turns bold formatting on or off
Italic	Turns italic formatting on or off

To move the insertion point	Press
To the first record	The Tab key
To a record that you specify	Enter

Not Microsoft style

To	Do This
Close a window	Click the **Close** button.
Size a window	Press Ctrl+F8

- Do not leave a column entry blank. That is, if the information doesn't apply, use *Not applicable* or *None*. Do not use em dashes

Microsoft style

Task	In Windows	On the Mac
Copy a picture	Not applicable	Command+Shift+T

Column headings

Make column headings as concise and as precise as possible, but include information that is common to all column entries in the heading, instead of repeating it in each entry. Do not use ellipses.

In tables that list procedures, use active voice in column headings, preferably in phrases that reduce repetition in the entries in the table.

International considerations

Some tables are organized so that the headings and table entries, when read from left to right, form a complete sentence. It is all right to structure a table this way if you have no other choice, but this will make the content more difficult to localize and may lead to mistranslation in machine-translated content. The grammar and syntax of different languages can make it difficult to match the English structure. For example, infinitives in many languages are only one word, so although all of the following examples are Microsoft style, the first example is preferable if the table will be localized or translated.

Microsoft style

Task	Action
To open a webpage	Type the address in the **Address** bar, and then press **Enter**.
To add a webpage to your favorites list	Click **Favorites**, and then click **Add to Favorites**.

To save a document	Do this
To a folder	Click **Save**.
With a new name	Click **Save As**.
To a network location	Connect to the server location and folder, and then click **Save**.

Not Microsoft style

To	Do this
Close a window	Click **Minimize**.
Size a window	Press Ctrl+F8.

Formatting

For some content teams, some table formatting may be done in design templates. The following guidelines suggest ways to make tables more readable.

- Try to limit tables with long entries to two or three columns. Four or more columns can be difficult to read unless they contain brief, numeric entries. The second column in the following example is approaching maximum readable length.

Addressing declared with Microsoft keywords

Keyword	Data	Code	Arithmetic
__near	Data resides in the default data segment; addresses are 16 bits.	Functions reside in the current code segment; addresses are 16 bits.	16 bits
__far	Data can be anywhere in memory, not necessarily in the default data segment; addresses are 32 bits.	Functions can be called from anywhere in memory; addresses are 32 bits.	16 bits
__huge	Data can be anywhere in memory, not necessarily in the default data segment. Individual data items (arrays) can exceed 64 KB in size; addresses are 32 bits.	Not applicable; code cannot be declared __huge.	32 bits (data only)

- Use rules between rows if the column information varies.

Footnotes

Put footnote explanations at the end of the table, not at the bottom of the page.

Your choice of footnote designator depends on the material in the table. For example, if the table contains statistical information, use a letter or symbol to designate a footnote. The order of preference for footnote symbols is numbers, letters, and symbols. For a list of symbols, see *The Chicago Manual of Style*. For more information, also see *Lists*.

Cross-references

Use cross-references to direct users to related information that might add to their understanding of a concept.

Try to write and edit so that you use cross-references only for information that is not essential to the task at hand. For example, users should not have to look up information to complete a procedure. If your content has too many cross-references, consider restructuring it.

Content for a technical audience can have more cross-references than content for a general audience.

Different teams have different requirements and methods for referring to other information. Always consult your project style sheet for how to use and format cross-references.

Do not provide cross-references to a product or service, its user interface, or its application programming interface. Refer only to content about the product or service.

Microsoft style

For information about available storage formats, see *Saving your document*.

Not Microsoft style

For information about available storage formats, see the **Save As** dialog box.

Unless you have no other choice, do not make cross-references to information that is not within your control, especially hyperlinks. Websites are always being modified and reorganized, and few things are as frustrating to the user as an invalid cross-reference.

Blind cross-references

Do not use blind cross-references. They provide no information about why you are using the cross-reference. The user should know whether it is worth interrupting the current topic for the cross-referenced information before following the cross-reference.

Microsoft style

For more information about modifying Visual Basic source code and installing Visual Basic forms, see Chapter 9, "Extending forms."

Not Microsoft style

See Chapter 9, "Extending forms."

It is all right to use blind cross-references in a "See also" or "Related links" type section or at the end of glossary entries.

Structure and style of cross-references

Information about why a cross-reference might be of interest should precede the cross-reference itself. That way, if the reason for following the cross-reference is not compelling, the user can move on quickly.

Microsoft style

For more information about modifying Visual Basic source code and installing Visual Basic forms, see Chapter 9, "Extending forms."

Not Microsoft style

See Chapter 9, "Extending forms," for more information about modifying Visual Basic source code and installing Visual Basic forms.

For cross-references that provide additional information, use "For more information *about*," not "For more information *on*." Many non-native English speakers have trouble with the latter phrase.

If the cross-referenced information provides an extended discussion of the current topic, the introduction to the cross-reference can be general.

Microsoft style

For details, see Chapter 9, "Extending forms."

For cross-references to books or manuals, provide both a chapter number and title. If the cross-reference is to information in the same chapter or short document (such as an article or white paper), provide a section title. In this case, explicitly note that the cross-reference is to the current chapter or document. Use *earlier* or *later*, not *above* or *below*.

If a cross-reference is to a section within a chapter or to a chapter in another publication, structure the cross-reference from the most specific to the most general reference, that is, section first, then chapter, then book title.

Microsoft style

For information about creating new pages, see "Working with page files" in Chapter 6, *Creating your pages*.

For information about arithmetic conversions, see "Usual arithmetic conversions" earlier in this white paper.

Not Microsoft style

For details, see "Extending forms."

For information about creating new pages, see Chapter 6, *Creating your pages*, under the topic "Working with page files."

For online cross-references that are formatted as hyperlinks, use descriptive text for the hyperlink; do not use an empty expression, such as "Click here." If the hyperlink comes at the end of a sentence, do not make the ending punctuation part of the hyperlink.

Microsoft style

For more information about modifying Visual Basic source code and installing Visual Basic forms, see Extending forms.

Not Microsoft style

For more information about modifying Visual Basic source code and installing Visual Basic forms, see Extending forms.

For more information about modifying Visual Basic source code and installing Visual Basic forms, click here.

Web-style hyperlinks, in which the reason for the cross-reference is implicit in the text, can be effective. Ensure, however, that the purpose of the link is clear.

Microsoft style

You can save your document in a variety of storage formats.

Format of cross-references

Format cross-references by using sentence-style capitalization, even if what you are referring to uses title capitalization.

Microsoft style

For more information about modifying Visual Basic source code and installing Visual Basic forms, see Extending forms.

Not Microsoft style

For more information about modifying Visual Basic source code and installing Visual Basic forms, see Extending Forms.

Accessibility considerations

Do not rely on color by itself to indicate hyperlink text. Color-blind users will not be able to see the links. Always provide a redundant visual cue, such as underlining.

Cross-references in "See also" sections

The style of providing "See also" sections can vary, depending on the needs of the audience and the type of content that you are writing. For example, a "See also" section in a programming reference is usually very basic, providing only blind cross-references to documentation for programming elements similar to the one under discussion. A "See also" section in a white paper, by contrast, might provide extensive information about each cross-referenced item.

Titles of "See also" sections can also vary. For example, such sections might be called "Related topics" or, for cross-references that are exclusively hyperlinks, "Related links." These sections can be formatted as pop-up windows, lists, or even marginal text. Because such variations are project-specific, consult your project style sheet, and be consistent in the way you format these sections.

Cross-references to art

Do not make cross-references to untitled or unnumbered art or tables unless the art or table immediately precedes or follows the reference.

Marginal cross-references

Cross-references that appear in the margin of a document can direct the user to additional help or ideas without interrupting the flow of the main text. These marginal cross-references can follow standard cross-reference style, using a complete sentence and ending with a period, or they can include a graphic (such as the **Help** button) with a heading and the cross-reference. Use a consistent format within your content.

Microsoft style

For more ideas, see
"Writing and correspondence"
in *Getting started*.

See *Getting started*

The following are some basic guidelines for marginal cross-references:

- Do not clutter a page with too many marginal cross-references; some teams limit notations to three per page.

- Try to limit marginal cross-references to about three or four lines. They expand when localized.

- Break lines so that they are about the same length.

- Follow the design for a specific project to determine whether to apply character formatting in marginal notations.

For more information, see *Art, captions and callouts; Marginal notes; Notes and tips; Tables*

Notes and tips

Notes call the user's attention to information of special importance or information that cannot otherwise be suitably presented in the main text. Notes include general notes, tips, important notes, and cautions. Use notes sparingly so that they remain effective in drawing the user's attention.

If your content is cluttered with notes, you probably need to reorganize the information. In general, try to use only one note in a Help topic. For example, if you must have two notes of the same type, such as a tip and a caution, combine them into one note with two paragraphs, or integrate one or both of the notes in the main text. Never include two or more paragraphs formatted as notes without intervening text. If you need to put two notes together, format them as an unordered list within the note heading.

You can include lists within notes.

The type of note (distinguished by the heading of the note or its bitmap) depends on the type of information given, the purpose of the information, and its relative urgency. The following sections explain the types of notes used in Microsoft content and their rank, from neutral to most critical.

Notes

A *note* with the heading "Note" indicates neutral or positive information that emphasizes or supplements important points of the main text. A note supplies information that may apply only in special cases. Examples are memory limitations, equipment configurations, or details that apply to specific versions of a program.

> **Note** If Windows prompts you for a network password at startup, your network is already set up, and you can skip this section.

Tips

A *tip* is a type of note that helps users apply the techniques and procedures described in the text to their specific needs. A tip suggests alternative methods that may not be obvious and helps users understand the benefits and capabilities of the product. A tip is not essential to the basic understanding of the text.

In Microsoft content, a tip icon signals a tip, with or without the heading "Tip." It is also all right to use the word "Tip" without an icon.

Microsoft style

  You can also use this procedure to copy a file and give it a new name or location.

Tip You can also use this procedure to copy a file and give it a new name or location.

Important notes

An *important note* provides information that is essential to the completion of a task. Users can disregard information in a note and still complete a task, but they should not disregard an important note.

Microsoft style

> **Important** You must be logged on as a member of the Administrators group to complete this procedure.

Cautions

A *caution* is a type of note that advises users that failure to take or avoid a specific action could result in loss of data. Also see *Messages*.

Microsoft style

> **Caution** To avoid damaging files, always shut down your computer before you turn it off.

For information about warnings and other UI notifications, see *Messages* (Chapter 5).

Numbers

The sections in this topic discuss when to use numerals and when to spell out numbers, how to treat fractions and ordinal numbers, when to use commas in numbers, and how to treat ranges of numbers.

Numerals vs. words

The use of numerals versus words is primarily a matter of convention. For consistency in Microsoft documentation, follow these conventions:

In body text, use numerals for 10 and greater. Spell out zero through nine if the number does not precede a unit of measure or is not used as input. For round numbers of 1 million or more, use a numeral plus the word, even if the numeral is less than 10.

Microsoft style

10 screen savers

3 centimeters

Type **5**, and then click **OK**.

1,000

five databases

zero probability

7 million

7,990,000

Not Microsoft style

2 disks

0 offset

eighteen books

twelve functions

1 thousand

7 million 990 thousand

Use numerals for all measurements, even if the number is less than 10. This is true whether the measurement is spelled out, abbreviated, or replaced by a symbol. Measurements include distance, temperature, volume, size, weight, points, picas, and so on, but generally not days, weeks, or other units of time. Bits and bytes are also considered units of measure.

Microsoft style

0 inches

3 feet, 5 inches

3.5-inch disk

0.75 gram

35mm camera

8 bits

1-byte error value

24 hours a day

seven days a week

two years

Not Microsoft Style

24/7

If it is necessary to save space in areas such as tables and the user interface, you can use all numerals, even for zero through nine.

Use numerals in dimensions. In most general text, spell out *by*, except for screen resolutions. For those, use the multiplication sign × (in HTML, ×).

Microsoft style

8.5-by-11-inch paper

640 × 480

Use numerals to indicate the time of day.

International considerations

To accommodate the worldwide audience, use the 24-hour time notation if you can. Use *00:00*, not *24:00*, to indicate midnight. If you must use *A.M.* and *P.M.*, use capital letters and periods. Using *12:00 A.M.* or *12:00 P.M.* to refer to noon or midnight is confusing. If you are consistently using 24-hour notation, *00:00* and *12:00* are unambiguous. In any case, just specifying *noon* or *midnight* is sufficient.

Microsoft style

The meeting is at noon.

The show begins at 19:00 Pacific Time (UTC-8).

The date changes at exactly midnight.

The meeting is at 12 P.M.

The show begins at seven o'clock in the evening Pacific Time (UTC-8).

The date changes at exactly at 12:00 A.M. .

To avoid confusion, always spell out the name of the month. The positions of the month and day are different in different countries. For example, 6/12/2000 can be interpreted as either June 12, 2000, or December 6, 2000.

Microsoft style

June 12, 2010

December 6, 2010

Not Microsoft style

6/12/10

12/6/09

Maintain consistency among categories of information; that is, if one number in a category requires a numeral, use numerals for all numbers in that category. When two numbers that refer to separate categories must appear together, spell out one of them.

Microsoft style

One booklet has 16 pages, one has 7 pages, and the third has only 5 pages.

ten 12-page booklets

Use numerals to indicate the coordinates of tables or worksheets and numbered sections of documents.

Microsoft style

row 3, column 4

Volume 2

Chapter 10

Part 5

step 1

Represent numbers taken from examples or the user interface exactly as they appear in the example or the user interface.

Use an en dash, not a hyphen, to form negative numbers: –79.

Do not start a sentence with a numeral unless you have no other choice. If necessary, add a modifier before a number. If starting a sentence with a number cannot be avoided, spell out the number.

Microsoft style

Lotus 1-2-3 presents options in the menu.

Microsoft Excel has 144 functions.

Eleven screen savers are included.

The value 7 represents the average.

Not Microsoft style

1-2-3 presents options in the menu.

144 functions are available in Microsoft Excel.

11 screen savers are included.

7 represents the average.

Hyphenate compound numbers when they are spelled out.

Microsoft style

Twenty-five fonts are included.

the forty-first user

Fractions as words and decimals

Express fractions in words or as decimals, whichever is most appropriate for the context. Do not express fractions with numerals separated by a slash mark except as noted later in this section.

Hyphenate spelled-out fractions used as adjectives or nouns. Connect the numerator and denominator with a hyphen unless either already contains a hyphen.

Microsoft style

one-third of the page

two-thirds completed

three sixty-fourths

In tables, align decimals on the decimal point.

Insert a zero before the decimal point for decimal fractions less than one. When representing user input, however, do not include a zero if it is unnecessary for the user to type one.

Microsoft style

0.5 inch

type **.5 inch**

When units of measure are not abbreviated, use the singular for quantities of one or less, except for zero, which takes the plural.

Microsoft style

0.5 inch

0 inches

5 inches

If an equation containing fractions occurs in text, you can use the Microsoft Word Equation Editor to format it. Or, to insert a simple fraction, use a slash mark (/) between the numerator and the denominator.

Microsoft style

1/2 + 1/2 = 1

Ordinal numbers

Ordinal numbers designate the place of an item in a sequence, such as *first*, *second*, and so on.

Cardinal numbers	Ordinal numbers
One, two	First, second
31, 32	Thirty-first, thirty-second
161	One hundred sixty-first

Spell out ordinal numbers in text, even when more than nine; that is, do not use 1st, 2nd, 12th, and so on.

Microsoft style

The line wraps at the eighty-first column.

Not Microsoft style

The line wraps at the 81st column.

Do not use ordinal numbers for dates.

Microsoft style

The meeting is scheduled for April 1.

Not Microsoft style

The meeting is scheduled for April 1st.

Do not add *ly*, as in *firstly* and *secondly*.

Commas in numbers

In general, use commas in numbers that have four or more digits, regardless of how the numbers appear in the interface. When designating years, however, use commas only when the number has five or more digits.

Do not use commas in page numbers, addresses, and decimal fractions.

Microsoft style

1,024 bytes

page 1091

1,093 pages

1.06377 units

2500 B.C.

10,000 B.C.

15601 Northeast 40th Street

Not Microsoft style

1024 bytes

page 1,091

1093 pages

1.063,77 units

2,500 B.C.

10000 B.C.

9,600 baud

15,601 Northeast 40th Street

Ranges of numbers

Use *from* and *through* to describe inclusive ranges of numbers most accurately, except in a range of pages, where an en dash is preferred. Where space is a problem, as in tables and online material, use an en dash to separate ranges of numbers. You can use hyphens to indicate page ranges in an index if you need to conserve space.

Do not use *from* before a range indicated by an en dash. Do not use *between* and *and* to describe an inclusive range of numbers because it can be ambiguous. For more information, also see *Dates*, *Dashes* (Chapter 9), *less vs. fewer vs. under* (Usage Dictionary), *Measurements and units of measure*, *more than vs. over* (Usage Dictionary)

Microsoft style

from 9 through 17

2008–2010

pages 112–120

Not Microsoft style

between 9 and 17

from 2008–2010

Dates

Use the following format to indicate a date: *month day, year,* as in July 31, 2010. Do not use *day month year* or an all-number method. Do not use ordinal numbers to indicate a date.

Microsoft style

February 23, 2011

June 11, 2007

Not Microsoft style

23 February 2011

6/10/11

11/6/07

April 21st

When a date appears in the middle of a sentence, set off the year with commas.

Microsoft style

The February 23, 2011, issue of the *New York Times* ....

Not Microsoft style

The February 23, 2011 issue of the *New York Times* ....

The February 23 2011 issue of the *New York Times* ....

To indicate a month and year only, do not use commas.

Microsoft style

The February 2011 issue of *MSDN Magazine* ....

Do not use abbreviations of months unless necessary to save space. If you must use abbreviations, use three-letter abbreviations: *Jan., Feb., Mar., Apr., May, Jun., Jul., Aug., Sep., Oct., Nov.,* and *Dec.*

Phone numbers

For U.S. telephone numbers, use parentheses to separate the area code from the seven-digit phone number, not a hyphen. In domestic telephone lists, do not precede the area code with 1 to indicate the long distance access code. Do add 1 in international lists to indicate the country code for the United States, as described later in this topic.

Microsoft style

(425) 555-0150

(317) 555-0123

Not Microsoft style

425-555-0150

1-317-555-0123

In North America, some 800 (toll-free) phone numbers are accessible to both U.S. and Canadian callers, and some serve only one country or the other. If a number serves only one country, indicate that the number or the service it provides is not available outside that country.

Microsoft style

(800) 000-0000 (Canada only)

International phone numbers

Precede local phone numbers with country and city codes if your content will be published in more than one country or if you list phone numbers from more than one country. City codes contain one, two, or three digits and are equivalent to U.S. area codes. Separate the country and city codes from the local phone numbers with parentheses, not hyphens or spaces. For local phone numbers, follow the convention of the country that users will call.

In the first example, 44 is the country code for the United Kingdom, 71 is the city code for London, and 0000 000 0000 is the local phone number. In the United Kingdom, the convention for displaying phone numbers is to insert spaces as shown in the first example of Microsoft style. The second example shows the convention for displaying local phone numbers in Japan.

Microsoft style

(44) (71) 0000 000 0000 (U.K.)

(81) (3) 0000-0000 (Japan)

Not Microsoft style

(44) (71) 0000-000-0000

44-71-0000-000-0000

81-3-0000-0000

In most U.S. cities, you can find a list of international country and major city codes in your local telephone directory.

Do not include the access code for international long distance in phone lists. Access codes vary from one country to the next and, within countries, they can vary from one phone service provider to the next. Do not put a plus sign (+) in front of a phone number to indicate the need for an access code.

Microsoft style

(81) (3) 000-000

(425) 555-0150 (when only domestic numbers are provided)

(1) (425) 555-0150 (when both domestic and international numbers are provided)

Not Microsoft style

+(81) (3) 000-000

011-81-3-000-000

(1) (425) 555-0150 (when only domestic numbers are provided)

Fictitious phone numbers

For fictitious phone numbers in North America, use the prefix 555 and a four-digit number between 0100 and 0199. For example, use 555-0187. These numbers are not assigned to any lines in regional area codes in North America. For fictitious phone numbers outside North America, determine the local phone system's policy regarding phone numbers reserved for examples or for use in works of fiction. If there is no such policy, get legal clearance before creating a fictitious phone number.

Time zones

The names of time zones should be treated as proper nouns. A time zone is a geographical area. Do not specify standard time and daylight time, which refer to clock settings within a time zone at specific times of the year, unless you are referring to an event, such as a webcast, where this information is important.

Microsoft style

Central Time

Eastern Time

Coordinated Universal Time

Pacific Time

Not Microsoft style

Central Daylight Time

eastern time

eastern standard time

Pacific time

It you are referring to a time zone as a geographical area, as opposed to indicating a time within that area, make explicit reference to the time zone as such.

Microsoft style

The event begins at 21:00 Eastern Time. Broadcast times may be different in the Pacific Time zone.

Do not use *Greenwich Mean Time* or *GMT* by itself unless you have no other choice. The current internationally accepted name for *Greenwich Mean Time* is *Coordinated Universal Time.* Because not everyone may be familiar with this name, it is all right on first mention to refer to *Coordinated Universal Time (Greenwich Mean Time).* If you must abbreviate Coordinated Universal Time, do not use *CUT.* By international agreement, the universal abbreviation is *UTC.* Do not refer to Coordinated Universal Time as *Universal Time Coordinate* or *Universal Time Coordinated.*

Do not abbreviate the names of time zones, such as *PT, ET,* and *UTC,* unless space is severely limited.

If you do not define a context, some time zone names can be ambiguous. For example, North America and Australia both have an Eastern Time zone. Unless you are creating a generic example where geographic location is not important, be sure to resolve such ambiguities. The simplest way to do so is to denote an offset from Coordinated Universal Time that uses standard (not daylight) time. In this case, it is all right to use the abbreviation UTC, as in the following examples:

- Eastern Time (UTC-5)

- Eastern Time (UTC+10)

Not all time zones have names. For time zones without names, refer to the offset from Coordinated Universal Time, as follows:

UTC+7

See also *A.M., P.M.*

Measurements and units of measure

Do not use measurements unnecessarily, especially in examples. When you do use measurements, follow these conventions:

- Use numerals for all measurements, even if the number is less than 10, whether the unit of measure is spelled out or abbreviated. For the purposes of this discussion, units of measure

7

include units of distance, temperature, volume, size, weight, points, and picas, but not units of time. Bits and bytes are also considered units of measure.

Microsoft style

5 inches

0.5 inch

8 bits

64 pixels wide

■ For two or more quantities, repeat the unit of measure.

Microsoft style

17-inch to 19-inch monitor

64 MB and 128 MB

Not Microsoft style

17- to 19-inch monitor

64 and 128 MB

■ Connect the number to the unit of measure with a hyphen only if you are using the measurement as an adjective.

Microsoft style

25-pixel square

14-inch monitor

8.5-by-11-inch paper

64 MB of memory

■ Use the multiplication sign (×), not *by*, to specify screen resolutions. In HTML, the multiplication sign is specified as &times or &#0215. Insert a space on each side of the multiplication sign. If possible, do not use a lowercase or uppercase *x* as a multiplication sign.

Microsoft style

1280 × 1024 monitor

See also *gigabyte, kilobyte, megabyte, terabyte* (Usage Dictionary).

Abbreviations of measurements

As a general rule, do not abbreviate units of measure except for kilobytes (KB), megabytes (MB), and gigabytes (GB), which can be abbreviated when used with numbers. If space is limited, as it might be in a table, use the abbreviations in the *Abbreviations of measurements* section of *Acronyms and other abbreviations* (Chapter 11).

URLs, addresses

A uniform (*not* universal) resource locator (URL) is an address, specified in a standard format, that locates a specific resource on the Internet or an intranet. In content for a general audience, use *address* rather than *URL*. In content for a technical audience, do not spell out *URL* on first mention.

The appropriate indefinite article for URL is *a*, not *an*.

A URL consists of an Internet protocol name; a domain name; and optionally other elements such as a port, directory, and file name. Use lowercase for each of these main elements, unless case is important.

In a typical URL, separate the protocol name (such as *http:*) from the rest of the destination with two slash marks, and separate the domain name and other main elements from each other with one slash mark, as in the following examples of URLs:

- *http://www.microsoft.com/security/articles/steps_default.asp*

- *http://www.microsoft.com/*

- *http://www.microsoft.com/business/*

When you specify a web address, it is not usually necessary to include *http://*. Most browsers today automatically add this information to the URL if a protocol name is not specified. If the protocol is something other than HTTP, such as File Transfer Protocol (FTP) or Gopher, you must specify the protocol with the URL. When the URL does not specify a file name, a final closing slash mark is optional.

7

Microsoft style

www.microsoft.com/business

www.microsoft.com/business/

ftp://www.example.com/downloads/myfile.txt

To refer to an entire website, as opposed to the home page of the site, it is all right to drop the *www.* at the beginning of the site address. If you do so, capitalize only the initial letter of the address, even if the name associated with the site is capitalized differently.

Microsoft style

The Gotdotnet.com website is the home of the GotDotNet user community.

If you include *www.* in the site address, with or without the protocol name, the entire address is in lowercase.

Microsoft style

Visit the GotDotNet website at *www.gotdotnet.com*.

Visit the GotDotNet website at *http://www.gotdotnet.com*.

In conceptual information, use *of* in discussions of the URL of a resource. Use the preposition *at* with the location of an address.

Microsoft style

For each webpage found, the search results include the URL of the page.

You can find information about Microsoft products and services at *www.microsoft.com*.

URLs often appear at the end of a sentence. If there is a possibility that your users will interpret the ending period as part of the URL, rewrite the sentence or set the URL off.

Microsoft style

Visit *www.microsoft.com* to find information about Microsoft products and services.

To find information about Microsoft, visit our website: www.microsoft.com

When indicating hyperlinks in webpages, use the title or a description of the new webpage as the link, rather than an empty phrase such as *click here*. The Alt text for graphical links should make clear that the graphic is a link.

Microsoft style

Visit the <u>Editorial Webpage</u> for up-to-date style information.

<Image> Alt text: Link to picture of a woman talking on a phone

Not Microsoft style

Click <u>here</u> for up-to-date style information.

<Image> Alt text: Picture

Although email and newsgroup addresses are structured differently from website addresses, they are also considered URLs. Format the entire address in lowercase, as in the following examples:

- microsoft.public.dotnet.framework

- news.announce.newusers

- someone@example.com

- mailto:someone@example.com

See also *Names and contact information* (*Chapter 3*), *link, HTTP* in the Usage Dictionary, *Protocols* (Chapter 6).

Names of special characters

Use the terms in the following table to describe the special characters shown.

Character	Name
´	acute accent (not *accent acute*)
&	ampersand
< >	angle brackets
’	apostrophe (publishing character)
'	apostrophe (user-typed text)
*	asterisk (not *star*)
@	at sign
\	backslash
{ }	braces (not *curly brackets*)
[ ]	brackets
^	caret, circumflex (not *accent circumflex*)
¢	cent sign
« »	chevrons, opening and closing. Microsoft term, seldom used, especially in documentation. Also referred to as *merge field characters* in Word.
©	copyright symbol
†	dagger
°	degree symbol
÷	division sign
$	dollar sign
[[ ]]	double brackets
…	ellipsis (s), ellipses (pl). Do not add space between ellipsis points.
—	em dash
–	en dash
=	equal sign (not *equals* sign)
€	euro symbol
!	exclamation point (not *exclamation mark* or *bang*)
`	grave accent (not *accent grave*)
>	greater than sign. If used in conjunction with the less than sign to enclose a character string such an HTML or XML tag, *right angle bracket* is all right.
≥	greater than or equal to sign
-	hyphen
"	inch mark

Character	Name
<	less than sign. If used in conjunction with the greater than sign to enclose a character string such an HTML or XML tag, *left angle bracket* is all right.
≤	less than or equal to sign
–	minus sign (use en dash)
×	multiplication sign (use * if necessary to match software)
≠	not equal to
#	number sign in most cases, but *pound key* when referring to the telephone
¶	paragraph mark
( )	parentheses (pl), opening or closing parenthesis (s)
%	percent
π	pi
|	pipe, vertical bar, or **OR** logical operator
+	plus sign
±	plus or minus sign
?	question mark
" "	quotation marks (not *quotes* or *quote marks*). *Curly quotation marks* is all right if necessary to distinguish from straight quotation marks.
" "	straight quotation marks (not *quotes* or *quote marks*)
' '	single curly quotation marks (not *quotes* or *quote marks*)
' '	single straight quotation marks (not *quotes* or *quote marks*)
®	registered trademark symbol
§	section
/	slash mark (not *virgule*)
~	tilde
™	trademark symbol
_	underscore

Art, captions, and callouts

Art can be effective in providing an example of the topic under discussion or in showing hierarchies or complex relationships that are difficult to explain in words. However, use art only if it is the best method for communicating a point.

Ensure that your art complements or supplements ideas that are also expressed in text. If you make your point only in art, blind and sight-impaired users will not get the information. Provide alt text that is brief but as descriptive as possible.

Do not rely on color alone to communicate the point of an illustration. Users who are color-blind will not see what you are highlighting.

Be aware of the impact of your art on the worldwide audience. Images that are perfectly innocuous for the U.S. audience may be deeply offensive elsewhere. Images and other elements of art, including color, can raise serious cultural or geopolitical issues. For details about creating art that is suitable for the worldwide audience, see *Global Art* (Chapter 3).

If your content is localized, do not include screen shots and illustrations that include text unless you have no other choice. Text in art is expensive to localize, and screen shots are unnecessary if the user has access to the user interface.

The appearance and placement of art are determined by the specific design guidelines for your content. Consult your designer or any available documentation of your document template for guidelines on the placement and appearance of art, captions, and callouts.

Cross-references to art

Unless you have no other choice, do not make cross-references to art unless the art immediately precedes or follows the reference within the Help topic or on the page.

Use *preceding* and *following* (or more specific references) when referring to art, not *above, below, earlier,* or *later.* End the introductory sentence with a period, not a colon.

Microsoft style

The following illustration shows file sharing with user-level access control.

Make cross-references to untitled or unnumbered art only if the relation of the art to the text is not immediately apparent or the content of the art furthers the explanation found in the text. In that case, a reference to the art can be helpful; however, the art should appear as close to the reference as possible so that you can refer to the art with a phrase such as *the following illustration*.

When to use captions and callouts

Not all art needs captions or callouts, even within the same document. Use editorial judgment or consult your project style sheet.

Always provide a brief description (see *alt text* in the Usage Dictionary) or a caption for a graphic on a webpage.

In printed content, information that appears in captions and callouts should also generally appear in text, unless there is no possibility of misreading or confusion and the art appears in the immediate textual context. However, online content and some printed documents require essential or procedural information to be placed solely in captions and callouts. This is acceptable but can affect accessibility.

Captions

You can use both title captions and descriptive captions within the same document. Use sentence-style capitalization for both kinds of captions.

Descriptive captions explain something about the art but do not necessarily point to or call out anything in particular about the art. Writers and editors determine how to write descriptive captions and when to use them. Use end punctuation only if the caption is a complete sentence or a mixture of fragments and sentences.

Title captions label a piece of art and should be concise. Do not use end punctuation. Some teams use numbered titles for art. In that case, the pieces are referred to as "figures," such as "Figure 7.1 Arcs."

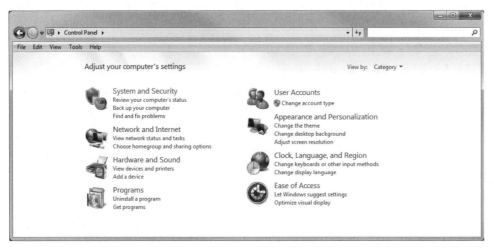

FIGURE 10.1 Windows 7 Control Panel

Callouts

A callout points to a specific item that the user should notice in an illustration. Observe the following rules when writing callouts:

- Capitalize each callout unless it begins with an ellipsis.

- End the callout with a period only if the callout is a complete sentence.

- Try not to mix fragments and complete sentences as callouts for the same piece of art. If you must mix them, use the end punctuation that is appropriate for each callout.

- For multiple-part callouts with ellipses, use lowercase for the first word in the second part of the callout. Leave one space between the ellipsis and the text that accompanies it, as shown in the example.

See also *Capitalization*; *Chapter 3, "Content for a worldwide audience"*; *Titles and headings*.

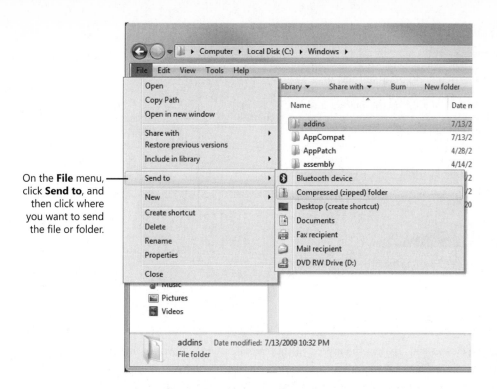

On the **File** menu, click **Send to**, and then click where you want to send the file or folder.

When you apply a design template ...

Title

- Lorem ipsum dolor sit amet, consectetur adipiscing elit. Aliquam sed urna at nisl vestibulum tincidunt sit amet quis ligula. Nullam blandit mattis manga a tempus. Proin egestas felis a ligula tempus vitae molestie massa tincidunt.
- Bullet 1
  - Bullet 2
    - Bullet 3
- Bullet 4
  - Bullet 5
    - Bullet 6

7

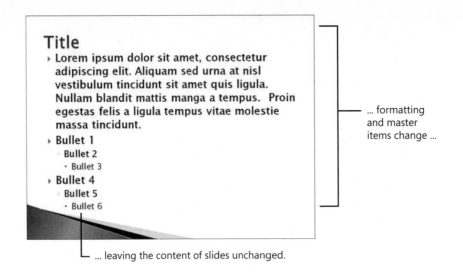

Title

▸ Lorem ipsum dolor sit amet, consectetur adipiscing elit. Aliquam sed urna at nisl vestibulum tincidunt sit amet quis ligula. Nullam blandit mattis manga a tempus. Proin egestas felis a ligula tempus vitae molestie massa tincidunt.
▸ Bullet 1
 ◦ Bullet 2
  • Bullet 3
▸ Bullet 4
 ◦ Bullet 5
  • Bullet 6

... formatting and master items change ...

... leaving the content of slides unchanged.

Bibliographies and citations

Scholarly works require documentation of source material in a bibliography. Other works also occasionally require that you cite source material or direct the user to a publication for further information. If you need to provide a bibliography or provide a formal citation, follow the examples listed here.

Citing books and printed articles

To cite books and printed articles, follow *The Chicago Manual of Style* "Documentation I" format. Exception: Follow the United States Postal Service abbreviations for states.

Bibliographies are usually formatted with a hanging indent. If a design template does not support hanging indents, separate each entry with a line of white space.

Only basic bibliographic entries are listed here. For more information, see "Bibliographies and reference lists" in *The Chicago Manual of Style*.

Books, general bibliographic style

The following paragraph lists the order and punctuation for each element in the citation of a book.

Author's name (surname first for the first author, given name first for additional authors). *Title: Subtitle*. Any additional information about the work, including editor's or translator's name and volume number. Edition number, if not the first. Place of publication: publisher, date.

Books, examples

Dupre, Lyn. *Bugs in Writing: A Guide to Debugging Your Prose*. Reading, MA: Addison-Wesley Publishing Co., 1995.

Li, Xia, and Nancy B. Crane. *Electronic Styles: A Handbook for Citing Electronic Information*. Rev. ed. Medford, NJ, Information Today, 1996.

Printed magazine and journal articles, general bibliographic style

Author's name. "Title of article." *Title of Periodical*. Volume and issue number (for journals only), date by month, day, year, page numbers.

The order of information and punctuation for the date differs between journals and popular magazines. For more information, see *The Chicago Manual of Style*, Chapter 15.

Printed magazine and journal articles, examples

Rosenthal, Marshal M. "Digital Cash: The Choices Are Growing." *Websmith*, May 1996, 69.

Vijayan, Jaikumar, and Mindy Blodgett. "Train Wreck at DEC." *Computerworld*, July 8, 1996, 1, 15.

Earle, Ralph, Robert Berry, and Michelle Corbin Nichols. "Indexing Online Information." *Technical Communication: Journal of the Society for Technical Communication* 43 (May 1996): 14656.

Citing electronic information

References to electronic information have the same intent and a format similar to the citations of printed material. That is, they follow the same general order of information such as author and title, but that information is followed by information such as the commercial supplier (if from an information service), the distribution medium (such as CD-ROM) or the Internet address, and the date accessed, if relevant. The important thing is to give enough information so that a user can find the source. Use lowercase for email or other logon names, or follow the protocol of the email service provider.

If the source appears both online and in print, give enough information so it can be found in either format. Rather than indicating page numbers of a magazine article that appears online, give an approximate length indication, usually in number of paragraphs.

This information is adapted from *Electronic Styles*, cited fully in the sample book citations in this topic. *Electronic Styles* itself follows Modern Language Association (MLA) style rather than *The Chicago Manual of Style*, but the kind of information to cite is accurate.

CD-ROMs and computer programs, examples

"Washington." Encarta Reference Library 2003. 2002. DVD. Microsoft Corporation, Redmond, WA.

Visual Basic 4.0. Microsoft Corporation, Redmond, WA.

Note You do not need to cite a date of access for CD-ROMs and similar media.

Internet sites, example

Buxton, Stephen, and Michael Rys (editors). "XQuery and XPath Full-Text Requirements." World Wide Web Consortium. 2003. *http://www.w3.org/TR/2003/WD-xmlquery-full-text-requirements-20030214/*

Discussion list messages and email, examples

"Top Ten Rules of Film Criticism." Online newsgroup posting. Discussions of All Forms of Cinema. Available email: listserv@american.edu/Get cinema-l log9504A. August 1995.

Higa, Sidney (someone@sample.com). "New Terminology." Email to Deborah Poe (someone2@sample.com). March 5, 1996.

See also *Cross-references*

Page layout

Topics in this section describe page layout style.

Page breaks

Do not manually break pages in print documents until all art (or art spaces) and textual changes have been added to the manuscript. Page breaks are usually inserted just before the manuscript goes to final production.

The main goal is to keep related material on one page. If this isn't possible, try to break pages in such a way that it is clear to the user that relevant material continues on the next page. Recto (right) page breaks must be handled more carefully than those on a verso (left) page of a spread. Avoid leaving a recto page so short that it looks like the end of a chapter.

- Leave at least two lines of a paragraph at the bottom or top of a page. Do not break a word over a page.

- Try to keep notes, tips, important notes, cautions, and warnings with the material to which they refer.

- Keep material that introduces a procedure or bulleted list with the list. Keep at least two steps or list entries at the bottom or top of a page. A step's explanatory paragraph should accompany the step. Try to keep all steps in a procedure on one verso-recto page spread; avoid continuing a procedure from a recto to a verso page.

- Try to keep a table from breaking across pages, especially from a recto to a verso page. If breaking is unavoidable, leave the title (if applicable) and at least two rows of the table at the top or bottom of a page. At the top of the next page, repeat the table title, followed by *(continued)* enclosed in parentheses and in lowercase letters and italic formatting. Repeat the column headings also. If an item is footnoted, the footnote goes at the end of the table. Try to keep a table's introductory sentence with the table.

- Try to keep art on the same page as the material that it illustrates. Always keep an introductory phrase with its art.

- Try to have at least five or six lines on the last page of a chapter.

- In printed indexes, if the main entry is followed by subentries, do not leave the main entry alone at the bottom of the column.

- In printed indexes, if you must break up a list of subentries, at the top of the next column include the main entry followed by *(continued)* enclosed in parentheses and in lowercase letters and italic formatting.

Line breaks

 Note This topic pertains primarily to printed content. Because users of online content can control the screen resolution, the font size, and the size of the browser window, you cannot control the appearance of screen text by explicitly inserting line breaks. You can *prevent* undesired line breaks on the screen by inserting nonbreaking spaces, but the effect on the surrounding text is impossible to predict.

Although the right text edge in printed Microsoft documents is not aligned, try to avoid very short lines that leave large amounts of white space at the end of a line. An extremely ragged right edge can distract the reader. If necessary, a copy editor and desktop publisher can break lines manually during the final stages of production.

Follow these basic rules for line breaks in Microsoft printed content:

- Do not break a word if it leaves a single letter at the end of the line.

- Do not break a word if it leaves fewer than three letters at the beginning of the next line.

Microsoft style
Be sure there are enough letters at the end of a line. Do
not leave fewer than three
letters at the begin-
ning of a line.

Not Microsoft style

Be sure there are e-
nough letters at the end
of a line. Do not leave fewer than three letters at
the beginning of the next
line.

- Do not end a page with the first part of a hyphenated word.

- Avoid leaving fewer than four characters on the last line of a paragraph, especially if a heading follows.

- Do not hyphenate *Microsoft* unless there is no alternative. If you must, the only acceptable hyphenation is *Micro-soft*.

- Do not hyphenate Microsoft product names. Avoid breaking product names at the end of a line, especially on first mention.

- Avoid breaking URLs. If you must break them, do so at the end of a section of the address immediately before the next forward slash. Do not include a hyphen.

Microsoft style

For more information, see *http://www.microsoft.com/support*
/products/developer/visualc/content/faq/

Not Microsoft style

For more information, see http://www.microsoft.com/support-
/products/developer/visualc/content/faq/

For more information, see http://www.microsoft.com/support/
products/developer/visualc/content/faq/

- Try to keep headings on one line. If a two-line heading is unavoidable, break the lines so that the first line is longer. Do not break headings by hyphenating words, and avoid breaking a heading between the parts of a hyphenated word. It does not matter whether the line breaks before or after a conjunction, but avoid breaking between two words that are part of a verb phrase.

Microsoft style

Bookmarks, cross-references,
and captions

Not Microsoft style

Bookmarks, cross-
references, and captions

- Try not to break formulas, data that should be entered without spaces, or program examples. If a break is unavoidable, break between elements.

Microsoft style

In the cell, type **=Budget!**

AH:C#+1

Not Microsoft style

In the cell, type **=Budget!$A**

$H:$C$#+1

- Try to avoid breaking function names and parameters. If hyphenating is necessary, break these names between the words that make up the function or parameter, not within a word itself.

Microsoft style

**WinBroadcast-
Msg**

Not Microsoft style

**WinBroad-
castMsg**

- Do not hyphenate a line of command syntax or code. If you must break a line, break it at a character space, and do not use a hyphen. Indent the run-over when breaking a line of syntax or code. Do not use the line-continuation character unless it is necessary for the code to compile.

Microsoft style

void CScribView::OnLButtonDown(**UINT** *nFlags, Cpoint*
    point)

Not Microsoft style

void CScribView::OnLButtonDown(**UINT** *nFlags, C-*
    point point)

For general rules about hyphenation and word division, see *Hyphens, hyphenation* (Chapter 9); *American Heritage Dictionary*; and *The Chicago Manual of Style*.

Marginal notes

In printed content, marginal notes, often labeled "Tips," usually accompany procedures to give hints, shortcuts, or background information that the user should know before proceeding. These notes should be easy to read and should help minimize long text or additional steps within the procedure. You can also use marginal notes next to tables and art.

In Help, the equivalent of these notes can be a jump to another step, a pop-up window offering additional information such as a definition, or a tip at the end of a topic.

Begin a marginal note at the first step of the procedure and end it before or at the last step. If possible, place it next to the step to which it refers.

You can include a heading to show the subject of the marginal note, as shown in the first example.

Microsoft style

About file names

Some restrictions apply to file names.

See Saving and Naming Files.

Tip If the **Formatting** toolbar does not appear, click **Toolbars** on the **View** menu, and then click **Formatting**.

The following are some basic guidelines for marginal notes:

- Do not clutter a page with too many marginal notes. Even three notes per page should be a rare occurrence.

- Try to limit marginal notes to three or four lines. They expand when localized.

- Break lines so that they are about the same length.

- Follow the design for a specific project to determine whether or not to apply character formatting in marginal notes.

See also *Marginal cross-references, Notes and tips.*

Grammar

Grammatical rules leave little room for opinion. For example, a verb must agree with its subject in person and number. However, there are grammatical concepts that are a matter of style, such as passive voice, mood, and which verb tense your documentation favors. This section focuses mainly on grammatical issues that are a matter of style and not a matter of right or wrong.

Verbs and verb forms

A sentence can do without almost anything, but no expression is a complete sentence without a verb.

In technical writing, present tense is easier to read than past or future tense. Simple verbs are easier to read and understand than complex verbs, such as verbs in the progressive or perfect tense. One-word verbs, such as *remove*, are easier for non-native English speakers than verb phrases, such as *take away*.

Don't vary voice and mood for the sake of variety. Active voice, which is generally clearer than passive voice, should predominate. Indicative mood should predominate, except in procedures, where imperative mood should predominate.

Put the action of the sentence in the verb, not in the nouns. Do not bury the action in an infinitive phrase. Do not use weak, vague verbs such as *be*, *have*, *make*, and *do*. Such verbs are sometimes necessary, but use a more descriptive verb whenever you can.

Microsoft style

By using Windows 7, you can easily organize your digital photos and create slide shows.

You can create a new folder.

If you cannot view the Security log, your user account does not have sufficient user rights.

Back up your files as part of your regular routine.

Not Microsoft style

Windows 7 enables you to easily organize your digital photos and create slide shows.

You can make a new folder.

If you are not able to view the Security log, your user account does not have sufficient user rights.

Do a backup of your files as part of your regular routine.

Do not use verbs that mean different things in different contexts. The different meanings can be a problem for non-native English speakers. Use more specific verbs instead.

Microsoft style

To solve this problem ....

When you speak to an audience, PowerPoint can help make your presentation more effective.

The issue you must resolve is the calling routine's request for additional user rights.

Not Microsoft style

To address this problem ....

When you address an audience, PowerPoint can help make your presentation more effective.

The issue you must address is the calling routine's request for additional user rights.

For information about verbs in procedures and commands, see *Procedures* (Chapter 6).

Transitive and intransitive verbs

Unlike an intransitive verb, a transitive verb must have a direct object to indicate the receiver of the action. Do not use a transitive verb without a direct object. Either supply a direct object or use an intransitive verb instead. If you are not sure whether a verb is transitive or intransitive, check the *American Heritage Dictionary*.

The following transitive verbs are often used erroneously without objects: *complete, configure, display, install, print, authenticate*, and *process*.

Microsoft style

The screen displays information.

A dialog box appears.

The printer cannot print your document.

To complete Setup, restart your computer.

Like user accounts, computer accounts provide a way to authenticate requests for access to the network and to domain resources.

Not Microsoft style

A dialog box displays.

Your document will not print.

After you restart your computer, Setup completes.

Like user accounts, computer accounts provide a way for the network to authenticate.

For related information, see *Mood, Voice*.

Agreement

It is easy to remember and apply the rule that a verb must agree with its subject in person and number. It is sometimes more difficult to apply the rule that a pronoun must agree with its antecedent, the person or thing the pronoun refers to.

Pronoun-antecedent agreement is particularly difficult with singular personal pronouns. Writers and editors do not want to give offense by using a singular pronoun of a particular gender as a general reference, so they use the gender-neutral but plural *they* to refer to a singular antecedent.

International considerations

Although using the plural *they* for a singular antecedent is gaining acceptance, it remains a problem for localizers and for non-native English speakers. Whenever possible, you should write around this problem.

Microsoft style

A user with the appropriate rights can set other users' passwords.

Authentication verifies the identity of the user.

Right-click the name of the person you want to call, click **Make a Phone Call**, and then choose from the list of published numbers.

Not Microsoft style

If the user has the appropriate rights, he can set other users' passwords.

Authentication verifies that a user is who she claims to be.

Right-click the name of the person you want to call, click **Make a Phone Call**, and then choose from the numbers they have published.

If you cannot write around the problem, do not alternate between masculine and feminine pronouns to refer to the same individual, and do not use *he/she* or *s/he*. Using the slash mark in this way is confusing for non-native English speakers, and even many native English speakers consider it confusing and annoying.

It is all right to use *he or she* occasionally, but doing so excessively may distract the user. If you need to make third-person references to more than one person in the same topic, use *he* for some individuals and *she* for others. In all cases, leave no doubt about the antecedent for each pronoun.

Voice

Voice refers to the relationship between the grammatical subject of a sentence and the verb. In active voice, the person or thing performing the action of the verb is the grammatical subject. In passive voice, the receiver of the action is the grammatical subject.

In general, active voice should predominate. Passive voice is not a grammatical error, but it has the greatest impact when you use it sparingly.

International considerations

Passive voice can be a problem for localization. Some languages use passive voice rarely, if at all, so the translation can end up sounding stilted or unnatural.

It is all right to use passive voice in the following situations:

- To avoid a wordy or awkward construction.

- When the subject is unknown or the emphasis is on the receiver of the action.

- If casting the user as the subject might sound blaming or condescending, especially in error messages and troubleshooting content.

Passive voice is more common and acceptable in programmer documentation, but active voice should still predominate.

Microsoft style (active voice)

You can divide your documents into as many sections as you want.

Data hiding provides a number of benefits.

Windows 7 includes many multimedia features.

Microsoft style (acceptable use of passive voice)

The website cannot be found. Verify that the page address is spelled correctly in the Address bar.

When the user clicks **OK**, the transaction is committed. (In content for software developers.)

Not Microsoft style (unnecessary passive voice)

Your document can be divided into as many sections as you want.

A number of benefits are provided by data hiding.

Many multimedia features are included in Windows 7.

Use active voice for column headings in tables that list user actions.

Microsoft style

To do this	Press this

For more information, see *Tables* (Chapter 7), *Verbs and verb forms*.

Mood

Mood is a way of classifying verbs according to whether the writer intends the verb to express fact, command, or hypothesis. The word *mood* as a grammatical term is an alteration of the word *mode* and is unrelated to *mood* as an emotional state.

Indicative mood expresses statements of fact and questions, *imperative mood* expresses requests or commands, and *subjunctive mood* expresses hypothetical information.

Indicative mood

Indicative mood expresses information such as facts, questions, assertions, or explanations. Declarative sentences and interrogative sentences use indicative verbs.

In technical writing, indicative mood should predominate, except in procedures. The following are examples of sentences in the indicative mood:

- Style sheets are powerful tools for formatting complex documents.

- What are the common characteristics of all interactors, including both text windows and scroll bars? They all have a size and relative position.

Imperative mood

Imperative mood expresses requests or commands and is used in procedures and other direct instructions. The subject *you* is implied. Imperative mood is always in the present tense. The following are examples of sentences in the imperative mood:

- Type a file name, and then click **OK.**

- Insert the CD in the CD ROM drive.

International considerations

Do not use imperative mood in marketing tag lines that will be localized unless you have no other choice. In many languages, the imperative mood may sound more dictatorial than intended in English.

Subjunctive mood

Subjunctive mood expresses wishes, hypotheses, and conditions contrary to fact. The most common use of subjunctive mood today is in subordinate clauses following a main clause that carry a sense of insisting or recommending. The following is an example of a sentence in the subjunctive mood:

We recommend that you be careful about opening email attachments.

8

Like passive voice, subjunctive mood is not a grammatical error, but it has the greatest impact when you use it sparingly and carefully.

Microsoft style (indicative mood)

You should complete this procedure before taking any other action.

Not Microsoft style (unnecessary subjunctive mood)

It is important that you complete this procedure before taking any other action.

Do not shift between moods.

Microsoft style (consistent mood)

Select the text, and then click **Bold**.

Type a file name, and then click **OK**.

Not Microsoft style (switches mood in mid-sentence)

Select the text, and then you can click **Bold**.

The first step is to type a file name, and then click **OK**.

Nouns

Plural nouns

In general, form the plural of a noun by adding *s*. If the noun already ends in *s*, form the plural by adding *es*. This rule applies to proper nouns as well as common nouns.

Microsoft style

the Johnsons

the Joneses

Form the plural of an abbreviation by adding an *s* with no apostrophe.

Microsoft style

ISVs

DBMSs

If an abbreviation already represents a plural, do not add an *s*. For example, the abbreviation for Microsoft Foundation Classes is *MFC*, not *MFCs*.

Form the plural of a single letter by adding an apostrophe and an *s*. The letter itself (but not the apostrophe or the ending *s*) is italic.

Form the plural of a number by adding an *s* with no apostrophe.

486s

the 1950s

International considerations

Do not add *(s)* to a word to indicate that it can be construed as either singular or plural unless you have no other choice. Such words may be difficult to translate because not all languages form plurals by adding a suffix to the root word. If a placeholder modifier can result at different times in a singular or a plural noun, use the plural form. A word to which *(s)* is added may also lead to mistranslation in machine-translated content.

Wait for *x* minutes.

Wait for *x* minute(s).

There is no fixed rule for forming the plural of words derived from Latin and Greek that retain their Latin or Greek endings. The singular forms typically end in *-a*, *-us*, *-um*, *-on*, *-ix*, or *-ex*. The plural forms often take the Latin or Greek plural endings, but they can also be formed like other English words. To verify the spelling of such plurals, see specific entries in the *Microsoft Manual of Style*, or see the *American Heritage Dictionary*.

Possessive nouns

Form the possessive of singular nouns and abbreviations by adding an apostrophe and an *s*. This rule applies even if the noun or abbreviation ends in *s*.

Form the possessive of plural nouns that end in *s* by adding only an apostrophe. Form the possessive of plural nouns that do not end in *s* by adding an apostrophe and an *s*.

the encyclopedia's search capabilities

an OEM's products

Brooks's Law

a children's encyclopedia

the articles' links

It is all right to form possessives from acronyms and abbreviations, but avoid doing so unless the abbreviation refers to a person, such as *CEO*, or generically to an organization, such as *ISV*. It is always all right to use an *of* construction instead.

Do not use the possessive form of Microsoft. Do not use the possessive form of other company names unless you have no other choice. And do not use the possessive form of a product, service, or feature name. You can use these names as adjectives, or you can use an *of* construction instead.

Microsoft style

the Windows interface

Microsoft products, services, and technologies

Word templates

templates in Word

the dictionary in the spelling checker

the **Send** command on the **File** menu

the OEMs' products

the products of OEMs

Not Microsoft style

Windows' interface

Microsoft's products, services, and technologies

Word's templates

the spelling checker's dictionary

the **File** menu's **Send** command

Do not use the possessive form of a property, class, object, or similar programming element.

Microsoft style

the **Color** property of the **Ball** object

Not Microsoft style

the **Ball** object's **Color** property

Pronouns based on possessives never take apostrophes. Correct forms are *its, ours, yours, hers, his,* and *theirs*.

Words ending in -ing

A word ending in *–ing* that looks like a verb but that is not being used as a verb can be ambiguous because such a word can be a gerund, an adjective, or a noun. If the syntax of the sentence doesn't make clear how the word is being used, non-native English speakers, localization, and machine translation may have difficulty disambiguating the word. Consider the following heading:

Meeting requirements

Will the text under this heading discuss "how to meet requirements"? Or will it discuss "requirements for a meeting"?

A gerund is an *–ing* word that functions as a noun but that expresses a verbal action or process. If *meeting* in this example heading means "the act or process of meeting a set of requirements," then *meeting* would be a gerund. An *–ing* word that functions as an adjective also expresses a verbal action or process, but in a "that is + *ing*" or "that are + *ing*" relationship with a noun. If *meeting* in this example heading means "requirements that are meeting," then *meeting* in this heading would be an adjective. An *–ing* word that functions as a noun expresses a non-verbal relationship with the noun that it modifies. If *meeting* in this heading means "the requirements for a meeting," then *meeting* would be a noun.

Based on this explanation, note that *meeting* in this example heading can be a gerund, because it can be expressed as "the act or process of meeting a set of requirements." It can also be a noun, because it can be expressed as "the requirements for the meeting." It cannot be an adjective, because it cannot be expressed as "requirements that are meeting." But because it can be either a gerund or a noun, it must be disambiguated. You could do so by using any of the following:

- Meeting the requirements

- The requirements for the meeting

- The meeting requirements

- How to meet the requirements

Here is another example heading:

Formatting templates

Note that by using the earlier explanation, you can determine that *formatting* in this heading can be a gerund ("the act or process of formatting templates"). It can also be a noun ("templates that are used for formatting"). It cannot be an adjective ("templates that are formatting").

Whenever it isn't clear from the syntax of a sentence whether a verb-like *–ing* word is functioning as a gerund, a noun, or an adjective, try to make its function explicit. For this example heading, you could do so by using any of the following:

- Formatting the templates

- The formatting templates

- How to format the templates

8

International considerations

Using gerunds to describe general concepts, such as *clustering* and *networking*, can be a problem for localization. Not all grammars allow gerunds to be used in this way, so a single word may be translated as a phrase. For example, in Dutch, *imaging* is translated as *image processing*, and *licensing* is translated as *the granting of licenses*. Further, not all gerunds are translatable in all languages, so some loss of meaning is inevitable. If you must use gerunds to describe concepts, work with your localization program manager or localization expert to keep the impact of such words to a minimum. Also, consider creating a definition of the term and adding it to your managed terminology.

For more information, see *Titles and headings* (Chapter 7); *Chapter 3, "Content for a worldwide audience"*; *Procedures* (Chapter 6); *Verbs and verb forms*.

Prepositions

Do not make the word or phrase that you want to emphasize the object of a preposition. The object of the preposition is generally considered a weak position in a sentence. Readers pay more attention to the main sequence of subject–verb–object.

There is no rule against ending a sentence with a preposition. The preposition should go where it makes the sentence easiest to read. Like other editorial decisions, the placement of a preposition depends on the rhetorical situation.

Microsoft style

Type the text that you want to search for.

Type the text for which you want to search. (More formal, but also correct.)

Do not join more than two prepositional phrases unless you have no other choice. Long chains of prepositional phrases are difficult to read and easy to misinterpret.

Microsoft style

In the lower-right corner of the **Save As** dialog box, click **Options**.

Not Microsoft style

In the lower part of the right side of the **Save As** dialog box, click **Options**.

For more information about specific prepositions, see the individual entries in the *Microsoft Manual of Style*.

8

Prefixes

In general, do not use a hyphen between a prefix and a stem word unless a confusing word would result or if the stem word begins with a capital letter. In general, when a prefix results in a double vowel and each vowel is pronounced, the word is not hyphenated. Note the following examples:

reenter

nonnegative

non-native

cooperate

coworker

un-American

For more information, see the individual entries in the *Usage Dictionary* for specific prefixes, the *American Heritage Dictionary*, or *The Chicago Manual of Style*.

A prefix affects only the word to which it is affixed. Do not use a prefix to affect an entire phrase.

Microsoft style
unrelated to security

Not Microsoft style
non-security related

International considerations

Do not coin words by adding prefixes to existing words. Such words can be difficult to translate, especially into languages that are not based on Latin. Such words may also lead to mistranslation in machine-translated content.

For additional information, see *Hyphens, hyphenation* (Chapter 9).

Dangling and misplaced modifiers

A dangling modifier is one that does not modify any element of the sentence in which it appears. A misplaced modifier is one that makes the sentence ambiguous because it is placed too far from the thing it modifies or too near to something else that it could modify.

The most common error of this type is a participial or infinitive phrase at the beginning of a sentence that does not refer to the subject. If the main clause is in passive voice, it is easy to overlook the lack of connection between modifier and subject.

To correct a dangling modifier, either change the subject of the sentence or change the modifying phrase into a clause so that its referent is clear.

For more information, see *Harbrace College Handbook* and *Handbook of Technical Writing*.

Microsoft style

By using object-oriented graphics, you can edit each element of the graphic because the structural integrity of the individual elements is maintained.

Even when you add more data, the spreadsheet calculates as quickly as before.

To add original graphics to your document, you need a scanner.

Not Microsoft style (dangling modifiers)

By using object-oriented graphics, the structural integrity of the individual elements of the graphic is maintained and can be edited.

Even after adding more data, the spreadsheet calculates as quickly as before.

To add original graphics to your document, a scanner is needed.

To correct a misplaced modifier, move the modifier so that it clearly, unambiguously modifies the thing you intend.

Microsoft style

There are files that cannot be removed on the disk.

Misplaced modifier (misplaced modifier)

There are files on the disk that cannot be removed.

CHAPTER 9

Punctuation

Punctuation is largely a matter of convention, and its rules are governed by punctuation sections in grammar books. For example, every English sentence must end with end punctuation, such as a period, a question mark, or an exclamation point. However, there are punctuation choices that are an aspect of style. This section focuses mainly on punctuation issues that are a matter of style and not a matter of right or wrong.

For information about specific punctuation marks, see the individual entries in this section, refer to the *Harbrace College Handbook* and *The Chicago Manual of Style*, or consult your project style sheet.

Periods

Use only one space after a period in both printed and online content.

When a colon introduces a bulleted list, use a period after each list element if each element completes the introduction to the list or if at least one element is a complete sentence. Do not end the entries with periods if they are all short phrases (three words or fewer), even if together with the introduction to the list, they form a complete sentence. For more information, see *Lists* (Chapter 7).

In general, format periods in the same font style in which the main content is formatted. This is especially important for a period after an element that receives different formatting to avoid the impression that the punctuation is part of the syntax. Examples are commands, options, keywords, placeholders, hyperlinks, pop-up text, and user input. However, if the period is part of the syntax of an element, such as a period that a user must type, use the formatting that is appropriate for the element. This practice may cause inappropriate line breaks online, so try to avoid the problem by rewriting as necessary.

Microsoft style

On the **Insert** menu, point to **Picture**, and then click **From File**.

Not Microsoft style

On the **Insert** menu, point to **Picture,** and then click **From File.**

When referring to a file name extension, precede it with a period, as in ".prd extension" or "an .exe file." For more information, see *File names and extensions* (Chapter 6).

If a file name appears at the end of a sentence, end the sentence with a period as usual. If ending the sentence with a period could cause confusion, rewrite the sentence so that the file name appears elsewhere in the sentence. See also *Key names* (Chapter 5), and *The Chicago Manual of Style*.

Microsoft style

To view the answer key for this lab exercise, open Answer_key.doc.

Open Answer_key.doc to view the answer key for this lab exercise.

Commas

Comma usage is governed by both convention and grammar. For more details about comma usage, see *Harbrace College Handbook*.

When to use commas

In a series consisting of three or more elements, separate each element with a comma.

Microsoft style

You need a hard disk, a VGA monitor, and a mouse.

Not Microsoft style

You need a hard disk, an EGA or VGA monitor and a mouse.

Use a comma following an introductory phrase.

Microsoft style

In Windows, you can run many programs.

Not Microsoft style

In Windows you can run many programs.

If you specify a full date in midsentence, use a comma on each side of the year.

Microsoft style

The February 4, 2003, issue of the *New York Times* reported that ....

Not Microsoft style

The February 4, 2003 issue of the *New York Times* reported that ....

When not to use commas

Do not join independent clauses with a comma unless you include a conjunction. Online documentation often has space constraints, and it may be difficult to fit in the coordinate conjunction after the comma. In these instances, separate into two sentences or use a semicolon.

Microsoft style

Click **Options**, and then click **Allow Fast Saves**.

Click **Options**; then click **Allow Fast Saves**. (Only if space is limited.)

Not Microsoft style

Click **Options**, then click **Allow Fast Saves**.

Do not use a comma between the verbs in a compound predicate.

Microsoft style

The Setup program evaluates your computer system and then copies the essential files to your hard disk.

The Setup program evaluates your computer system, and then it copies the essential files to your hard disk.

Not Microsoft style

The Setup program evaluates your computer system, and then copies the essential files to your hard disk.

Do not use commas in month-year formats.

Microsoft style

Microsoft introduced Windows 7 in October 2009.

Not Microsoft style

Microsoft introduced Windows 7 in October, 2009.

Apostrophes

Use apostrophes to form the possessive case of nouns and to indicate a missing letter in a contraction.

Form the possessive case of a singular noun by adding an apostrophe and an *s*, even if the singular noun ends in *s*, *x*, or *z*. For plural nouns that end in *s*, form the possessive case by adding only an apostrophe.

Microsoft style

insider's guide

the box's contents

Burns's poems

Berlioz's opera

an OEM's product

the Joneses' computer

> **Note** It is all right to form possessives from acronyms. Avoid forming possessives from company names. Do not use the possessive form of *Microsoft* or of product, service, or feature names.

Differentiate between the contraction *it's* (it is) and possessive pronoun *its*. Never use an apostrophe with possessive pronouns (*yours*, not *your's*).

Do not use an apostrophe to indicate the plural of a singular noun (*programs*, not *program's*).

Colons

Use colons sparingly. A colon between two statements usually signifies that what follows the colon illuminates or expands on what precedes the colon. When in doubt, use two sentences instead.

Style manuals do not agree whether the first word following a colon within a sentence should start with an uppercase letter. To ensure consistency in documentation, Microsoft style is to always use lowercase, except when:

- A colon introduces a direct quotation.
- The first word after the colon is a proper noun.

Microsoft style

Treat the unknown risk just like any other risk: identify the resources available to address it, and develop countermeasures to take if it happens.

Microsoft ActiveSync cannot recognize this device for one of two reasons: the device was not connected properly; the device is not a smartphone.

What does it mean when I see a message that asks: "Are you trying to visit this site?"

These technologies are supported on all of the operating systems that can run the Live Framework: Windows 7 and Windows Vista, Macintosh OS X, and Windows Mobile.

Use a colon at the end of a sentence or fragment that introduces a list. Do not use a colon following a procedure heading or to introduce art, tables, code, or sections.

Microsoft style for a list

The basic configuration for your computer must include the following:

- A hard disk with 24 megabytes of free disk space and at least one disk drive.
- A monitor supported by Windows.

Microsoft style for a code sample

For example, use the following code to open the external Visual FoxPro database on the network share \\FoxPro\Data in the directory \Ap.

```
... code sample
```

Semicolons

A semicolon between two independent clauses indicates less of a pause than a period. If the clauses are not joined by a conjunction, use a semicolon. Otherwise, use a comma before the conjunction. Semicolons are useful in joining two contrasting statements.

Use semicolons sparingly. They are difficult to see on low-resolution monitors.

Use semicolons within a sentence to separate phrases that contain other internal punctuation, especially commas. This practice is most common in making brief lists. Such sentences, if they include more than three elements, are often easier to read if you break them into separate sentences or use the elements to create an unordered list. For example, the following sentence is difficult to read:

In this tutorial, you will learn to quickly construct a user interface; easily implement both single-document interface and multiple-document interface applications; implement features that until now were considered difficult, such as printing, toolbars, scrolling, splitter windows, print preview, and context-sensitive help; and take advantage of many built-in components of the class library.

Instead, structure the sentence as follows:

In this tutorial, you will learn to do the following:

- Quickly construct a user interface.

- Easily implement both single-document interface and multiple-document interface applications.

- Implement features that until now were considered difficult, such as printing, toolbars, scrolling, splitter windows, print preview, and context-sensitive help.

- Take advantage of many built-in components of the class library.

Formatting semicolons

In general, format semicolons in the same font style in which the main content is formatted. This is especially important for a semicolon after an element that receives different formatting to avoid the impression that the punctuation is part of the syntax. Examples are commands, options, keywords, placeholders, and user input. However, if the semicolon is part of the syntax of an element, such as a semicolon that a user must type, use the formatting that is appropriate for the element. This practice may cause inappropriate line breaks online, so try to avoid the problem by rewriting as necessary.

In online content, do not include a semicolon in a hyperlink.

Quotation marks

The term *quotation marks*, used without modifiers, refers to double curly quotation marks (" "). In printed content, use quotation marks except in user input and code samples, which call for straight quotation marks (" "). If your project style sheet requires straight quotation marks with sans serif fonts, such as in headings, follow the project style sheet.

In online content, use straight quotation marks.

Refer to quotation marks as *quotation marks*, not as *quote marks* or *quotes*. Use the terms *opening quotation marks* or *closing quotation marks*, not *open quotation marks*, *close quotation marks*, *beginning quotation marks*, or *ending quotation marks*.

Placement of quotation marks

Place closing quotation marks outside commas and periods. For other closing punctuation, placement of the closing quotation mark depends on whether the punctuation is part of the material being quoted.

Quotation marks have specialized uses in many computer languages. Follow the conventions of the language in code examples.

Microsoft style

One Internet dictionary calls an electronic magazine a "hyperzine."

One Internet dictionary calls an electronic magazine a "hyperzine," but webzine is a common synonym.

What is a "smart device"?

A reader asks, "How scalable is .NET?"

```
/*Declare the string to have length of "constant+1".*/
```

Not Microsoft style

One Internet dictionary calls an electronic magazine a "hyperzine".

One Internet dictionary calls an electronic magazine a "hyperzine", but webzine is a common synonym.

Parentheses

In general, parentheses should be in the font style of the context of a sentence, not in the format of the text within the parentheses. For example, the text within parentheses might be italic, but the parentheses themselves would be regular type if the surrounding text is regular type. An exception to this is *"(continued),"* which is used for tables that continue on the next page or index subentries that continue in the next column or on the next page. In this usage, the parentheses and the word "continued" are italic.

Microsoft style

For a single-column array, use INDEX (*array,row_num*).

Hyphens, hyphenation

Your project style sheet and specific entries in the *Microsoft Manual of Style* are the primary sources for hyphenation of product and computer-related terms. However, rules of hyphenation are not always easily applied. In general, if there is no possibility of confusion, do not use hyphenation. Make a note of decisions about ambiguous terms on your project style sheet.

For information about hyphenation of common words, see the *American Heritage Dictionary* and *The Chicago Manual of Style*. For information about acceptable hyphenation in line endings, see *Line breaks* (Chapter 7). For information about hyphenating with prefixes, see *Prefixes* (Chapter 8). See also *Capitalization* (Chapter 7**)**, *Dashes, key combination* (Usage Dictionary), *Numbers* (Chapter 7)

Observe the following rules when hyphenating modifiers:

- Hyphenate two or more words that precede and modify a noun as a unit if confusion might otherwise result.

  Microsoft style

built-in drive	lower-left corner
high-level language	high-level-language compiler
read-only memory	floating-point decimal
line-by-line scrolling	memory-resident program
scrolling line by line (adverb)	

- Hyphenate two words that precede and modify a noun as a unit if one of the words is a past or present participle.

  Microsoft style

  copy-protected disk

  free-moving graphics

- Hyphenate two words that precede and modify a noun as a unit if the two modifiers are a number or single letter and a noun or participle.

  Microsoft style

  80-column text card

  eight-sided polygon

9

8-point font

16-bit bus

I-beam insertion point

- Do not use suspended compound adjectives unless space is limited. In a suspended compound adjective, part of the adjective is separated from the rest of the adjective, such as "first-" in "first- and second-generation computers." If you must use suspended compound adjectives, include a hyphen with both adjectives. Avoid forming suspended compound adjectives from one-word adjectives.

Microsoft style

Microsoft Project accepts any combination of uppercase and lowercase letters in a password.

Click the upper-right or lower-right corner.

Not Microsoft style

Microsoft Project accepts any combination of upper- and lowercase letters in a password.

Click the upper- or lower-right corner.

- Do not hyphenate a predicate adjective unless the *Microsoft Manual of Style* specifically recommends it. (A predicate adjective is an adjective that complements the subject of a sentence and follows a linking verb.)

Microsoft style

The DVD is copy protected.

The drive is built in.

Many viruses are memory-resident.

This type of Help is context-sensitive.

- Hyphenate compound numerals and fractions.

Microsoft style

his forty-first birthday

one-third of the page

three sixty-fourths

- Do not put a hyphen between an adverb ending in *ly* and the verb or adjective that it modifies.

Microsoft style

Most Internet browsers have a highly graphical interface.

Not Microsoft style

Most Internet browsers have a highly-graphical interface.

- Use an en dash (–) instead of a hyphen in a compound adjective in which at least one of the elements is an open compound (such as *Windows NT–based*) or when two or more of the elements are made up of hyphenated compounds (a rare occurrence).

  An exception to this guidance is MS-DOS. For example, *MS-DOS-based program* and *MS-DOS-compatible* are spelled with two hyphens, not a hyphen and an en dash.

Microsoft style

Windows 7–compatible products

Some programs have dialog box–type options for frequently used operations.

MS-DOS-compatible products

Not Microsoft style

Some programs have dialog box-type options for frequently used operations.

Some programs have dialog-box–type options for frequently used operations.

MS-DOS–compatible products

- Do not use a hyphen in key combinations. Use a plus sign instead, as in "Alt+O."

- In contexts that require title capitalization, capitalize any part of a hyphenated compound that would be capitalized absent the hyphen. Always capitalize the final part of a hyphenated compound if it is the last word in a context that requires title capitalization.

Microsoft style (title capitalization)

Installing Add-ins in Word

Installing an Add-In

Run-Time Error Codes

Find a Ready-to-Use Solution

Not Microsoft style (title capitalization)

Installing Add-Ins in Word

Installing an Add-in

Run-time Error Codes

Find a Ready-to-use Solution

9

Dashes

There are two types of dashes: the em dash (—) and the en dash (–).

Em dash

The em dash (—) is based on the width of an uppercase *M*. It is used primarily to set off sentence elements.

 Note Do not use word spacing on either side of an em dash. If your style sheet and your publishing process support it, insert a 1/4 en space on each side of an em dash.

Use an em dash:

- To set off a parenthetical phrase that deserves more emphasis than parentheses imply. Use one em dash on each side of the phrase.

    Microsoft style

    The information in your spreadsheet—numbers, formulas, and text—is stored in cells.

- To set off a phrase or clause at the end of a sentence for emphasis. Use one em dash.

    Microsoft style

    If you are not sure about the details, look at the illustrations in the wizard—they can help you figure out what type of connection you're using.

    Do not use an em dash in place of a bullet or other typographic symbol to set off items in a list.

    Do not use an em dash to indicate an empty cell in a table.

    Do not capitalize the first word after an em dash unless the word is a proper noun.

    The HTML code for an em dash is *—*.

En dash

The en dash (–) is based on the width of an uppercase *N*. At half the length of an em dash, it is slightly longer than a hyphen. An en dash is used primarily for connecting elements, especially numbers.

Use an en dash:

- To indicate a range of numbers such as inclusive values, dates, or pages.

    Microsoft style

    1993–1994

    pages 95–110

- To indicate a minus sign.

- To indicate negative numbers: –79.

- Instead of a hyphen in a compound adjective in which at least one of the elements is an open compound (such as "Windows 2000") or to join a hyphenated compound to another word.

Microsoft style

dialog box–type options

Windows NT–based programs

> **Note** *MS-DOS-based* is an exception to this guidance. *MS-DOS-based* is spelled with two hyphens, not a hyphen and an en dash. See *MS-DOS-based program* (Usage Dictionary).

Do not use an en dash to indicate an empty cell in a table.

Do not use spaces on either side of an en dash.

The HTML code for an en dash is *–*.

Ellipses

In general, do not use an ellipsis (...) except in syntax lines or to indicate omitted code in technical content. The HTML code for the ellipsis character is *…*. If you are using a font that does not support the ellipsis character, use three periods with no space between them.

In the user interface, an ellipsis is typically used to show truncation, as in a program name, or to indicate on menus and in dialog boxes that a dialog box will appear to obtain more information from the user. Do not use an ellipsis in this context in documentation.

Microsoft style

On the **File** menu, click **Open**.

Not Microsoft style

On the **File** menu, click **Open....**

In printed material, it is all right to use an ellipsis in multiple-part callouts, especially with a screen shot used in a procedure. Ensure that the user's path through the callouts is unambiguous.

9

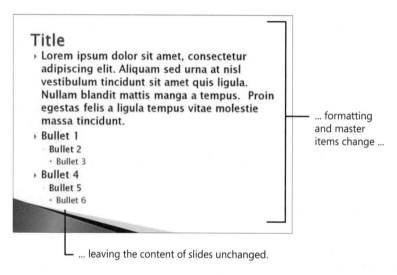

When you apply a design template ...

... formatting and master items change ...

... leaving the content of slides unchanged.

In callouts, insert one character space before and/or after the entire ellipsis, as shown in the preceding example. If the sentence or phrase ends with additional punctuation, such as a period or comma, insert a character space between the punctuation mark and the ellipsis.

In quoted material, an ellipsis indicates omitted text. If the ellipsis replaces the end of a quoted sentence, follow the ellipsis with a closing period, with no intervening space.

Microsoft style

The quick brown fox ....

If the ellipsis indicates omitted text following the end of the quoted sentence, the ellipsis immediately follows the period, again with no intervening space.

Slash mark

Do not use constructions that contain a slash mark to indicate a choice, such as *either/or* and *he/she*. However, *and/or* is all right to use if you have no other choice. Localizers and non-native English speakers may not know whether the slash mark indicates a choice, indicates that the two words are synonyms, or indicates that the two words are part of a single construction, such as client/server.

Do not use a slash mark as a substitute for *or*. If the user interface uses a slash in this way, follow the interface in describing the label, but use *or* in describing the corresponding action.

Microsoft style

Click **Automatic trapping** to add or remove a check mark.

Not Microsoft style

Click **Automatic trapping** to add/remove a check mark.

Use a slash mark in constructions that imply a combination.

Microsoft style

client/server

CR/LF, carriage return/line feed

on/off switch

read/write

Use a slash mark to separate parts of an Internet address. Use two slash marks after the protocol name, as follows: *http://mslibrary/catalog/collect.htm*. Use a backslash with server, folder, and file names, as follows: *mslibrary\catalog\collect.doc*.

To refer to a slash mark in documents, it may be useful to differentiate between a *forward slash* for URLs and a *backward slash* for servers and folders.

You can also use a slash mark between the numerator and denominator of fractions in equations that occur in text. The Word Equation Editor includes a format with a slash mark. See also *Numbers* (Chapter 7), *Names of special characters* (Chapter 7).

Microsoft style

$a/x + b/y = 1$

$x + 2/3(y) = m$

Formatting punctuation

In general, format punctuation in the same font style in which the main content is formatted. This is especially important for punctuation after an element that receives different formatting to avoid the impression that the punctuation is part of the syntax. Examples are commands, options, keywords, placeholders, hyperlinks, pop-up text, and user input. However, if the punctuation is part of the syntax of an element, such as punctuation that a user must type, use the formatting that is appropriate for the element.

Microsoft style

Type **Balance Due:** in cell A14. (User types the colon.)

On the **Insert** menu, point to **Picture**, and then click **From File**.

Not Microsoft style

On the **Insert** menu, point to **Picture,** and then click **From File.**

Format parentheses and brackets in the same font style in which the main content is formatted. Never use two different styles, such as italic for an opening parenthesis and regular type for a closing parenthesis.

9

CHAPTER 10

Indexes and keywords

Technical content is only useful to users if they can find it. One of the most important things that you can do as a content professional is to index or attribute content (or both) to ensure that it is discoverable for your users.

Indexing a printed document is different in some ways from indexing a collection of content that will be delivered online. In this section, you'll find tips and best practices for both.

Indexes

Users of printed documentation depend on indexes as their primary way of finding the information that they need. Therefore, an index must be complete, thorough, and accurate. Although the number of indexed terms per page will vary, depending on the subject and complexity of the book, a rule of thumb is that a two-column index should be about 4 to 8 percent of the total number of pages in the book.

This topic describes some indexing concepts, but it focuses more on mechanical issues such as alphabetizing, style, and cross-references. Many of the points covered pertain primarily to printed indexes. For developing search keywords and online index entries, see *Keywords and online index entries*.

Index entries

When you develop index entries, consider the tasks that the user will want to accomplish, previous versions of the Microsoft product that may have used different terms, and the terminology of similar products that the user might be familiar with. These principles are the same for both printed and online indexes.

Try to think like a user. A user who wants to delete paragraphs will probably look for the information under "paragraphs" and "deleting," possibly under "Delete command," but most likely not under "using Delete."

When you create new main entries, place the important word first. Depending on the kind of material, that word should probably be a noun (*commands, addresses, graphs*), but it can be a gerund (*copying, selecting*). Do not use nonessential words as the first in an entry and do not use vague gerunds such as "using" or "creating."

Invert entries whenever possible. For the previous example, you would include an entry for "paragraphs, deleting" and one for "deleting paragraphs." Other examples include items such as "arguments, command line" and "command-line arguments." Page numbers for inverted entries should match exactly.

Likewise, if you use synonyms to help the user find information in more than one place in the index, modifiers, subentries, and page numbers should match.

Index subentries

Consider as subentries these generic terms, especially when a topic is covered in various places in the book: defined (to refer to a term), described (to refer to an action), introduction, overview.

Avoid the use of prepositions to begin subentries. In some cases, however, prepositions can clarify relationships. Do not use articles to begin subentries.

Do not repeat a main term in the subentry.

Microsoft style

pointers
  far
  function

Not Microsoft style

pointers
  far pointers
  function pointers

Try not to use more than five page references after an entry. Subentries give more direction to the user. Do not, however, use only one subentry; there must be two or more.

Microsoft style

paragraphs, deleting 72

Microsoft style

paragraphs
  deleting 72
  formatting 79, 100

Not Microsoft style

paragraphs
  deleting 72

Not Microsoft style

  paragraphs 72, 75, 79, 100, 103, 157

If possible, use only one level of subentries, but never more than two. Localized indexes can become unreadable with two levels of subentries because entry words are often lengthy and must be broken. If your group decides to use two levels of subentries, you should inform the localization team as early as possible.

Microsoft style (one level of subentries)

paragraph formatting 75
  characters and words 63
  using styles 97
paragraphs, deleting 72

Microsoft style (two levels of subentries)

paragraphs
  deleting 72
  formatting 75
    characters and words 63
    using styles 97

If a main entry is followed by subentries, do not leave the main entry as a widow at the bottom of a column. Also, if a list of subentries is long and will run over to a second column, repeat the main entry, followed by the word *continued*, which is lowercase, in parentheses, and italic (including the parentheses), at the beginning of the second column. If the column break occurs between two second-level subentries, repeat the main entry, followed by *continued*, and the subentry, also followed by *continued*. The word *continued* is lowercase, in parentheses, and italic (including the parentheses). Avoid leaving only one subentry before or after column breaks.

Microsoft style (main entry continued)

paragraphs   paragraphs *(continued)*
  deleting 101   formatting 87–96
                                 indenting 98

Microsoft style (subentry continued)

paragraphs   paragraphs *(continued)*
  deleting 101   formatting *(continued)*
  formatting 87–96   characters and words 63
                                 using styles 97

Not Microsoft style

paragraphs   formatting 87–96
  deleting 101   indenting 98

Not Microsoft style

paragraphs   paragraphs *(continued)*
                                 deleting 101
                                 formatting 87–96
                                 indenting 98

10

Page references

Separate multiple page references with commas. Separate page ranges with en dashes. If space is limited, it is all right to use hyphens instead of en dashes to indicate page ranges. Do not abbreviate page references.

If possible, avoid long multiple-page references that list consecutive pages. A page range might better represent the topic. Likewise, avoid chapter or section length page ranges if the topic is clearly shown in the table of contents. Users prefer to be able to find more specific information.

Microsoft style

paragraphs   24, 47, 126–130
  deleting   72–76
  formatting   87

Not Microsoft style

paragraphs   24, 47, 126, 127, 128, 129, 130
  deleting   72, 73, 74, 75, 76
  formatting   87

Style and formatting

Use the index style in the same design template that you used for your document. The font should be the same as that in the book, but in a smaller point size.

In general, do not use special character formatting such as bold, monospace, or italic for entries. Use italic for cross-references (*See* and *See also* references).

Capitalization

Because many groups use the same source for both printed and online documentation, use all lowercase for all index entries except those words that require capitalization and *See* and *See also* references.

Plural vs. singular

Use the plural form of all main entries that are nouns, except where it is awkward or illogical to do so. The following table shows examples of both plural and singular uses according to Microsoft style.

Microsoft style (plural)	Microsoft style (singular)
borders	File command
files	email message
headers	ruler
paragraphs	window

Prepositions and articles

Limit the use of prepositions and articles. Use them only when they are necessary for clarity or sense. In general, do not use articles unless required for clarity.

Microsoft style

child windows
  open, list of   128
  opening   132, 137
  reading from   140
  writing to   140
structures, in programming for Windows   200

Verbs

Use a gerund rather than the infinitive or the present tense form for entries about actions, processes, or procedures.

Microsoft style

selecting
  drawing objects   22
  text   147
shapes
  drawing   37
  fitting around text   140
  fitting text into   131
substituting text   255

Not Microsoft style

select
  art   255
  text   147
shapes
  to draw   37
  to fit around text   140

Versus vs. vs.

Use the abbreviation *vs.* (including the period) in index entries.

Microsoft style

  voice, active vs. passive   98

10

Cross-references in indexes

An index can have the following types of cross-references:

See
See also
See specific (name of item)
See also specific (name of item)
See herein

Format the *See, See also*, and *See herein* phrases in italic, and capitalize *See* to avoid confusion with the actual entries. Use lowercase for the name of the entry referred to.

Place *See* cross-references on the same line as the entry, separated by two spaces. Place *See also* references on a separate line and sort them as the first subentry. (Optionally, if the main entry has no other subentries, you can place a *See also* reference on the same line. See the "pontoons" entry in the following example.)

Do not use page numbers with cross-references. Alphabetize multiple topics following one cross-reference and separate them with semicolons.

Microsoft style

airplanes   *See* planes
airports   *See specific airport*
floatplanes   101–105
planes
  See also specific plane
  rudders
    control   66–67
    types   61
  steering
    See also rudders
    guidelines   45
    taxiing *See herein* takeoff
  takeoff
    control tower   19
    steering   22, 25, 27
pontoons   98   *See also* floatplanes
seaplanes
  See also aeronautics; floatplanes; pontoons
  rudders
    controls   66–67
    types   61
steering   *See* rudders
water
  See also seaplanes
  taking off on   18

Sort order

The sequence of index entries is governed by:

1. ASCII order for special characters like spaces, periods, colons, and underscores

2. Case-insensitive alphabetical order for letters

Special characters are sorted before letters. Apostrophes, hyphens, and slashes are ignored.

Microsoft style

_name changers
name
name changers
name, changers
name taker
namechanger
NAME.CHANGERS
name:changers
name_changers
namechangers
namechanger's
name-changers
name/changers
namesake

Order of entries

Special characters appear at the beginning of the index, followed by numeric entries, sorted in ascending order. Alphabetical entries then follow. Separate the categories with headings if there are many of them; if there are only a few, no special separation is necessary. Use the heading *Symbols* for special characters if you use a heading.

Special characters

Index special characters at least twice. List each character by its symbol, followed by its name in parentheses, as the next example shows. Also list each character by name, followed by its symbol in parentheses. You might also want to index some characters under a general category, such as "operators."

Special characters that are not part of a word are sorted in ASCII sort order. The name of the character follows in parentheses. They appear at the beginning of the index, followed by numeric entries.

% (percent)

& (ampersand)

((opening parenthesis)

) (closing parenthesis)

* (asterisk)

| (pipe)

~ (tilde)

Special characters followed by letters or within a word are ignored in alphabetizing and are usually included in the alphabetical listing. Sometimes, however, you may want to include such entries in both the alphabetical list and in the list of special characters.

Microsoft style

Error

errors, correcting

^p

paragraphs

#VALUE

values

Numeric entries

Numeric entries should be placed in ascending order, with entries containing only numbers falling before those containing both numbers and letters. This requires editing to correct the computer sort. Compare these two lists of sorted numeric entries:

Computer-sorted	Edited
12-hour clock	80386
2-D chart	80486
24-hour clock	2 macro
80386	2-D chart
80486	3-D chart
1904 date system	12-hour clock
366-day year	24-hour clock
3-D area chart	366-day year
2 macro	1900 date system
1900 date system	1904 date system

Numbers follow the list of special characters and precede alphabetical entries.

Alphabetical entries

Microsoft alphabetizes word by word, not letter by letter. That is, words separated by spaces or commas are treated as two words. Alphabetizing stops at the end of a word unless the first word of two or more entries is the same. Then the first letter of the second word determines alphabetical order, and so on. Letter-by-letter alphabetization ignores spaces, treating each entry as one word. Compare the columns in the following table to see the difference. For more information, see *The Chicago Manual of Style*.

Word by word	Letter by letter
D key	Delete command
DEL key	deleting
Delete command	DEL key
deleting	D key

Keywords and online index entries

Online indexes should look similar to print indexes: they should have two levels with indented subentries. Many of the same conceptual guidelines for print indexes apply to online indexes.

The *keyword* is the term that a user associates with a specific task or set of information. The user types a keyword in the **Find** or **Index** box to locate specific information in a document. A keyword can lead to a single topic or to many related topics.

When deciding what keywords to list, consider these categories:

- Terms for a novice user of your product
- Terms for an advanced user of your product
- Common synonyms for words in the topics
- Words that describe the topic generally
- Words that describe the topic specifically
- Words commonly used in related products

Look specifically at the following elements of your document for potential keywords when you develop your index:

- Headings
- Terms and concepts important to the user
- Overviews
- Procedures and user actions
- Acronyms

10

- Definitions or new terms

- Commands, functions, methods, and properties

Order of entries

Sort HTML Help indexes in the same way as print indexes. You cannot manually sort the search keywords, so the order follows the ASCII sort order. Special characters appear first, then numbers, and then alphabetical entries. See also *print indexes*.

Style of indexed keywords

Follow most of the same general style guidelines as those used for printed indexes:

- Use gerunds (the *-ing* form) rather than infinitives (the *to* form) or the present tense of verbs for task-oriented entries, unless they are unsuitable, as they may be for languages, systems, or localized versions. Consult with your team when making this decision.

- Do not use generic gerunds that users are unlikely to look up, such as *using*, *changing*, *creating*, *getting*, *making*, and *doing*, unless you have no other choice.

- Use plural for nouns unless it is inappropriate. This applies to both single keywords *(bookmarks, not bookmark)* and keyword phrases *(copying files, not copying a file)*.

- Do not use the articles *a*, *an*, and *the*, and avoid prepositions at the beginning of a keyword.

- Keep keywords as short as practicable for clarity.

- Use synonyms liberally, especially terms that are used in competitors' products or terms that some users are likely to know. For example, list both *option* and *radio button*. Provide a cross-reference to the term that you are actually using.

- For acronyms and abbreviations, list both the spelled-out phrase followed by the acronym or abbreviation in parentheses and the acronym or abbreviation followed by the spelled-out version. For example, list *terminate-and-stay-resident (TSR)* and *TSR (terminate-and-stay-resident)*. If appropriate, provide a cross-reference at the less frequently used entry.

- Use lowercase for all keywords and index terms unless the term is a proper noun or is case-sensitive, and therefore capitalized.

Microsoft style

clearing tab stops
clip art
Close command

modems
   dialing a connection manually
   setting up
   troubleshooting

Standardize keywords across products

Some content will be shared among products. Single-sourcing, such as using the same file for both the Help topic about copying and a book chapter about copying, may extend across products instead of just occurring within a single product. Standardizing index entries across such products will simplify content reuse, and it will provide users with a consistent and predictable way of finding such information.

Topics, particularly those for technical support services and accessibility, should have standard keywords. For example, the technical support topic must include the following keywords:

assistance, customer
customer assistance
help
technical support
phone support
product support
support services
telephone support
troubleshooting

Merge keywords from multiple files

Help systems today can present a single index for multiple Help files. The keywords from the separate Help files are merged as if the main contents file specifies each Help file. If such a Help system contains an optional component that the user does not install, those keywords will not show up in the index but will be added to the index if the user installs the component later.

A merged set of keywords can be very helpful for users. However, it is essential that the keywords fit together appropriately. For example, if the main Help file uses the phrase *exiting programs*, then all Help files in the project should use this phrase rather than just *exiting*. Otherwise, when the keywords from multiple files are merged, the user will see two entries, "exiting" and "exiting programs."

Cross-references

Do not use cross-references in online indexes unless you have no other choice. They are more difficult to handle in keyword lists than in print indexes.

Because each keyword must be linked to at least one Help topic, a cross-reference keyword has to jump somewhere, perhaps to an overview, or "main," topic. It is often difficult to determine which topic that should be.

Also, cross-references *(See* and *See also)* are limited to normal keywords that jump directly to the topic that contains the K (keyword) footnote with that keyword. The cross-reference does not jump to another location in the index.

10

Instead of a cross-reference, duplicate all the subentries under both of the main keywords. For example, list all topics for "cursor" under "insertion point (cursor)" as well.

If you must include a cross-reference to other topics, you will want to force it to the top of the list of subentries. Talk to your indexer about how to do this.

10

CHAPTER 11

Acronyms and other abbreviations

Acronyms, initialisms, and other abbreviations are abundant in technical content, but they can cause confusion if they are unfamiliar to your audience or if they are used inconsistently. This section provides general guidance for using abbreviations. It also includes a collection of technical acronyms and measurement abbreviations. Acronyms that are in widespread use or that are associated with highly specialized topics have been omitted.

This topic includes the following sections:

- How to use acronyms and other abbreviations
- Table of acronyms and other abbreviations
- How to use abbreviations of measurements
- Table of abbreviations of measurements
- Process for adopting new acronyms or abbreviations

How to use acronyms and other abbreviations

First mention

In general, spell out acronyms on first mention, and include the acronym in parentheses immediately following the expanded form. On subsequent mention in the same topic or article, you can use the acronym without spelling it out. Exceptions to this guideline are indicated in the table. When you spell out the acronym, follow the capitalization given in the *Expanded form* column of the table unless noted otherwise.

Microsoft style

1-gigabyte (GB) hard disk

information stored in random access memory (RAM)

If the first mention appears in a title or heading, use your best judgment to determine how much information to include. For example, if space is limited, use the acronym without spelling it out. If the acronym and its spelled-out form are both important keywords, include them both in a title or heading to optimize their exposure to search engines. In the first sentence after the title or heading, provide the expanded form followed by the acronym in parentheses.

Articles and plurals

Choose an indefinite article (*a* or *an*) based on the acronym's pronunciation.

Microsoft style

a RAM drive

an SDK

an OEM

If an acronym represents a singular noun, add a lowercase *s* to make it plural. Do not add an apostrophe before the *s*. If an acronym already represents a plural noun, do not add an *s*.

Microsoft style

three OEMs

frequently asked questions (FAQ)

Not Microsoft style

three OEM's

Microsoft Foundation Classes (MFCs)

International considerations

In machine-translated content, be careful with acronyms that form common English words such as RAM (random access memory) and NAP (network access point). If such a word appears in text without the parentheses and without the object that it stands for, it may be translated according to its dictionary definition.

Table of acronyms and other abbreviations

In the following table, terms are listed alphabetically by acronym, not by expanded form. Many product-specific terms do not appear in this table. Exclusion of a term does not mean it is not acceptable.

When two concepts are represented by the same acronym, the concepts are numbered according to primacy of usage in the *Expanded Form* column. When a variation in wording is used to refer to a single concept, both variations are included but not numbered.

If the term you are looking for is not listed in the table, check the following resources:

- American Heritage Dictionary of the English Language (*http://education.yahoo.com/reference /dictionary/*), Fourth Edition. Boston: Houghton Mifflin Company, 2006.

- Microsoft Glossary Portal (*http://www.microsoft.com/resources/glossary/default.mspx*)

- Go Global Developer Center (*http://msdn.microsoft.com/en-us/goglobal/bb964658.aspx*) on MSDN

Acronym	Expanded form	Comments
24/7	24 hours a day, seven days a week	Spell out or replace with phrases such as *all the time* or *all day, every day*. For repeated mentions or in contexts where the abbreviation is standard, use the abbreviation after first mention.
AC	alternating current	Don't spell out.
ACL	access control list	
AD	Active Directory	Don't use either the abbreviation or the expanded form as a stand-alone term. Use *Active Directory Domain Services* (*AD DS*) instead.
ADO	ActiveX Data Objects	Not *Active Data Objects*.
ADSL	asymmetric digital subscriber line	Not *asynchronous digital subscriber line*.
AM/FM	amplitude modulation/frequency modulation	Don't spell out.
AJAX	Asynchronous JavaScript and XML	
ALM	application lifecycle management	Abbreviation for *application lifecycle management*. For repeated mention of *application lifecycle management*, spell out *ALM* on first mention. On subsequent mention, use just *ALM* or *lifecycle management*. Capitalize as *Application Lifecycle Management* when referring to Visual Studio ALM.
ANSI	American National Standards Institute	Spell out only to refer to the organization itself. Don't spell out when referring to ANSI standards or text format.
API	application programming interface	Not *application program interface*. Don't use to refer to individual programming elements. Don't use the redundant term *API set*.
APPC	Advanced Program-to-Program Communications	Note capitalization and hyphenation.
ASCII	American Standard Code for Information Interchange	Don't spell out.
ASP	1. Active Server Pages 2. application service provider	When referring to *Active Server Pages*, don't use *ASP* and *ASP.NET* interchangeably, and don't spell out in the context of ASP.NET. Otherwise, spell out if the context is not clear. When referring to *application service provider*, always spell out on first mention.
AVI	Audio Video Interleaved	Don't spell out. If the term is not familiar to your audience, use a more generic term such as *movie*.
B2B	business-to-business	Spell out unless the abbreviation is familiar to your audience.
B2C	business-to-consumer	Spell out unless the abbreviation is familiar to your audience.
BAML	Binary Application Markup Language	

11

Acronym	Expanded form	Comments
Basic	Beginners All-purpose Symbolic Instruction Code	Note capitalization. Don't spell out.
BI	business intelligence	Spell out unless the abbreviation is familiar to your audience.
bi-di	bidirectional	Always spell out.
BIFF	Binary Interchange File Format	
BIOS	basic input/output system	Don't spell out unless the abbreviation is unfamiliar to your audience.
BISYNC	Binary Synchronous Communications	Do not use *BSC*.
BSC	Binary Synchronous Communications	Don't use. Use *BISYNC* instead.
CBT	computer-based training	Don't use. Use *tutorial* instead. For additional guidance, see *CBT* (Usage Dictionary).
CD	compact disc	Don't spell out. For CD types and additional guidance, see *CD* (Usage Dictionary).
CDF	Channel Definition Format	When referring to the specification, use italic formatting and provide a version number.
CDS	Circuit Data Services	
CE	collector's edition	Always spell out. Note singular possessive. Always use title capitalization when this term is part of a product name.
CGA	color/graphics adapter	
CGI	1. Common Gateway Interface 2. computer-generated imagery	Don't spell out unless the reference is unclear.
CIS	computer information systems	
CISC	complex instruction set computer	Don't spell out unless the abbreviation is unfamiliar to your audience.
CLR	common language runtime	
CLS	common language specification	
CMC	1. Continuous Media Controller 2. Common Messaging Calls (MAPI term)	
CMS	continuous media server	Don't use. Use *MMS* instead.
CMY	cyan-magenta-yellow	Don't spell out unless the abbreviation is unfamiliar to your audience.
CMYK	cyan-magenta-yellow-black	Don't spell out unless the abbreviation is unfamiliar to your audience.
COFF	Common Object File Format	For the expanded form, use title capitalization to refer to the specification, but use lowercase to refer to the file format.

11

Acronym	Expanded form	Comments
COM **COM+**	1. Component Object Model 2. communications port 3. (all lowercase) an extension and the indicator of a commercial organization in a URL.	As *Component Object Model*, don't spell out. As the name of a communications port (also known as serial port), use all uppercase followed by a number, as in *COM1*. Be sure that the user cannot be confused about what *COM* means in your content. As an extension and the indicator of a commercial organization in a URL, use all lowercase preceded with a period, as in *.com file* and *Microsoft.com*.
CPI-C	Common Programming Interface for Communications	
CR/LF	carriage return/line feed	
CSS	cascading style sheets	Spell out unless the abbreviation is familiar to your audience.
CTI	Computer-Telephony Integration	
CTS	common type system	
CUT		Do not use as an abbreviation for *Coordinated Universal Time*. Use *UTC* instead.
DAO	Data Access Object	
DBCS	double-byte character set	
DBMS	database management system	
DCE	distributed computing environment	
DCOM	distributed COM	Don't spell out. Use this term only to refer to the DCOM wire protocol.
DDBMS	distributed database management system	
DDE	Dynamic Data Exchange	
DDI	Device Driver Interface	
DDL	data definition language	
DDNS	dynamic DNS	Don't use either the abbreviation or the expanded form. Instead, refer to a DNS server that supports the dynamic update protocol. For additional guidance, see *DNS* (*Usage Dictionary*).
DES	Data Encryption Standard	
DFS	Distributed File System	
DHCP	Dynamic Host Configuration Protocol	
DHTML	dynamic Hypertext Markup Language	Use *dynamic HTML* (*DHTML*) on first mention.
DIB	device-independent bitmap	
DIF	Data Interchange Format	

11

Acronym	Expanded form	Comments
DLC	1. Data Link Control 2. downloadable content	Spell out when referring to downloadable content.
DLL	dynamic-link library	Do not use *dynalink*. Use lowercase (.dll) when referring to the file name extension.
DMOD	dynamic access module	
DNS	Domain Name System	Not *Domain Name Server*. When referring to the DNS networking protocol, spell out on first mention. When referring to the Windows feature that implements the protocol, don't spell out. For additional guidance, see *DNS* (Usage Dictionary). Don't use this abbreviation to refer to the digital nervous system.
DoS	denial of service	Spell out unless the abbreviation is familiar to your audience. Hyphenate the spelled-out term when using it as an adjective, as in *denial-of-service attack*.
DOS	disk operating system	Don't spell out. Avoid except as *MS-DOS*. See *MS-DOS* (Usage Dictionary).
DSP	digital signal processor	
DSS	1. Digital Signature Standard 2. Decentralized Software Services	
DVD	digital versatile disc	Don't spell out. For DVD types and additional guidance, see *DVD* (Usage Dictionary).
EA	extended attributes	Always spell out.
ECC	electronic credit card	
EFI	Extensible Firmware Interface	
EGA	enhanced graphics adapter	
EISA	Extended Industry Standard Architecture	
EPS	encapsulated PostScript	
EULA	End-User License Agreement	Don't use. Use *Microsoft Software License Terms* instead. See *Microsoft software license terms* and *license terms*.
FAQ	frequently asked questions	Precede with the indefinite article *a*, not *an*. Spell out unless the abbreviation is familiar to your audience.
FAT	file allocation table	Always spell out when referring to the table. Don't spell out when referring to the file system; always use *FAT file system*.
fax	facsimile	Don't spell out. Don't capitalize as *FAX*. All right to use as an adjective, as in "fax machine" and "fax transmission;" as a noun, as in "your fax arrived;" or as a verb, as in "fax a copy of the order."
FB, fb	Facebook	Always spell out.
foo, foobar, fubar		Do not use. The word is slang derived from an obscene phrase meaning "fouled up beyond all recognition." Use another placeholder or variable name instead. For example, use *Example.exe* or *MyFile.doc*.

Acronym	Expanded form	Comments
FTP	File Transfer Protocol	Lowercase when used in an Internet address. Don't use as a verb.
FTS	1. full-text search 2. fault-tolerant system	
GAC	global assembly cache	Always spell out.
GDI	Graphics Device Interface	
GIF	Graphics Interchange Format	
GPI	graphics programming interface	
GUI	graphical user interface	Don't spell out unless the abbreviation is unfamiliar to your audience.
GUID	globally unique identifier	Don't spell out unless the abbreviation is unfamiliar to your audience.
HAL	hardware abstraction layer	
HBA	host bus adapter	
HD	high-definition	Don't spell out unless the abbreviation is unfamiliar to your audience.
HDTV	high-definition TV	Don't spell out.
HDLC	High-Level Data Link Control	
HMA	high-memory area	
HPFS	high-performance file system	
HTML	Hypertext Markup Language	Don't spell out.
HTTP	Hypertext Transfer Protocol	Don't spell out unless you are discussing protocols or URLs, or unless the abbreviation is unfamiliar to your audience. The abbreviation is lowercase when used in an Internet address. For additional guidance, see *HTTP* (Usage Dictionary).
IaaS	infrastructure as a service	Don't capitalize as *IAAS*. For additional guidance, see *infrastructure as a service (IaaS)* (Usage Dictionary).
IANA	Internet Assigned Numbers Authority	
ICP	1. independent content provider 2. International Client Pack	
ICS	Internet Connection Sharing	Always spell out.
IDE	integrated device electronics, integrated development environment	Sometimes seen as *integrated drive electronics*. Spell out on first mention, using one term consistently.
IEEE	Institute of Electrical and Electronics Engineers, Inc.	
IFS	installable file system	
IHV	independent hardware vendor	
IM	instant message, instant messaging	For additional guidance, see *instant message*.

11

Acronym	Expanded form	Comments
I/O	input/output	Don't spell out unless the abbreviation is unfamiliar to your audience.
IOCTL	I/O control	Spell out on first mention. On subsequent mention, all right to abbreviate as *I/O control* or *IOCTL*. Use only in content for a technical audience.
IP	Internet Protocol	Don't spell out.
IPC	interprocess communication	
IPX/SPX	Internetwork Packet Exchange/ Sequenced Packet Exchange	
IS	Information Services	
ISA	Industry Standard Architecture	Don't spell out unless the abbreviation is unfamiliar to your audience.
ISAM	indexed sequential access method	
ISAPI	Internet Server Application Programming Interface	If *API* has already been spelled out, use *Internet Server API (ISAPI)* on first mention.
ISV	independent software vendor	
ITV	interactive TV	
JPEG	Joint Photographic Experts Group	Refers to both the standard for storing compressed images and a graphic stored in that format. Don't spell out.
LADDR	layered-architecture device driver	
LAN	local area network	Don't spell out unless the abbreviation is unfamiliar to your audience.
LCE	limited collector's edition	Always spell out. Note singular possessive. Always use title capitalization when part of a product name.
LCID	locale identifier, locale ID	Don't abbreviate as *LCID*. Use *LCID* only as a data type.
LDAP	Lightweight Directory Access Protocol	
LDTR	local descriptor table register	
LINQ	Language-Integrated Query	
LU	logical unit	
MAC	media access control	Always spell out on first mention.
MAN	metropolitan area network	
MAPI	Messaging Application Programming Interface	If *API* has already been spelled out, use *Messaging API (MAPI)* on first mention.
MASM	Macro Assembler	
MCA	Micro Channel Architecture	
MCGA	multicolor graphics array	
MCI	Media Control Interface	

11

Acronym	Expanded form	Comments
MDA	monochrome display adapter	
MDI	multiple-document interface	
MFC	Microsoft Foundation Classes	
MIDI	Musical Instrument Digital Interface	Don't spell out unless the abbreviation is unfamiliar to your audience.
MIDL	Microsoft Interface Definition Language	
MIF	Management Information Format	
MIS	management information systems	Use *IS* instead, unless you must specifically refer to *MIS*.
MMS	Microsoft Media Server	Don't precede with a definite article. Don't use *CMS*.
MMU	memory management unit	
MOF	Managed Object Format	
MPEG	Moving Picture Experts Group	Don't spell out. For additional guidance, see *MPEG* (Usage Dictionary).
MS, MSFT	Microsoft	Always spell out, even in informal communications such as blogs or microblogs. *MSFT* is all right it use if you are referring to the stock ticker symbol.
MSMQ	Microsoft Message Queuing	Don't use. Use *Message Queuing* instead. On first mention, you can use *Message Queuing* (*also known as MSMQ*).
MSN	The Microsoft Network	
MSO	multiple service operator	
MTA	message transfer agent	
NA, N/A or	not applicable, not available	Always spell out, even in tables. For additional guidance, see *Tables* (Usage Dictionary).
NAICS	North American Industry Classification System	Pronounced "nakes." Replaces *Standard Industrial Classification* (*SIC*).
NaN	not a number	Note capitalization.
NCB	network control block	
NCSA	National Center for Supercomputing Applications	
NDIS	network driver interface specification	
NDK	network development kit	
NetBEUI	NetBIOS Enhanced User Interface	Don't spell out.
NetBIOS	network basic input/output system	Don't spell out.
NFS	network file system	
NIC	network interface card	
NLS	national language support	

11

Acronym	Expanded form	Comments
NMI	nonmaskable interrupt	
NOS	network operating system	
NTFS	NTFS file system	The redundant phrase is correct. Don't use *NT file system* or *New Technology file system*.
NTSC	National Television System Committee	
ODBC	Open Database Connectivity	
ODL	Object Description Language	
ODS	Open Data Services	
OEM	original equipment manufacturer	Don't spell out unless the abbreviation is unfamiliar to your audience.
OLAP	online analytical processing	
OLE	Object Linking and Embedding	Don't spell out.
OOFS	object-oriented file system	
OOM	out of memory	Always spell out.
OOP	object-oriented programming	
OS		Don't use as an abbreviation for *operating system*.
OSI	Open Systems Interconnection	
PaaS	platform as a service	Spell out on first mention. Don't capitalize as *PAAS*. For additional guidance, see *platform as a service* (*PaaS*) (Usage Dictionary).
PANS	pretty amazing new stuff, pretty amazing new services	Refers to telephone services. See also *POTS*.
PARC	Palo Alto Research Center	
PC	personal computer	Don't spell out. All right to use in content that is informal in tone, in UI text where space is limited, or when referring to a feature or website that includes the term *PC*. In procedures, use *computer*. For additional guidance, see *PC, PC-compatible*.
PCMCIA	Personal Computer Memory Card International Association	Use *PC Card* instead of *PCMCIA* or *PCMCIA card*, to refer to the add-in memory and communications cards for portable computers.
PDF	1. Portable Document Format 2. Package Definition File	Don't spell out when referring to the file format.
PDLC	premium downloadable content	Not *paid downloadable content*. Spell out.
PE	portable executable	When using the abbreviation, always follow with *file*, as in *PE file* or *PE file format*.
PERT	program evaluation and review technique	
PFF	Printer File Format	
PIF	program information file	

Acronym	Expanded form	Comments
PII	personally identifiable information	Always spell out.
PIN	personal identification number	Don't spell out unless the abbreviation is unfamiliar to your audience.
PnP	Plug and Play	Note capitalization. For additional guidance, see *Plug and Play*.
POTS	plain old telephone service	See also *PANS*.
PPP	Point-to-Point Protocol	
PPPoE	Point-to-Point Protocol over Ethernet	
PROM	programmable read-only memory	
PSU	power supply unit	Always spell out.
PW	password	Always spell out.
QA	quality assurance	
QBE	query by example	
QFE	quick fix engineering	Don't use. For additional guidance, see *Out-of-band release terminology* (Chapter 6).
RAID	redundant array of independent disks	
RAM	random access memory	For additional guidance about referring to memory, see *memory* (Usage Dictionary).
RAS	1. remote access server 2. Remote Access Service	*Remote Access Service* is Windows-based software. The server is a host on a LAN equipped with modems.
RDBMS	relational database management system	
RFID	radio frequency identification	
RFT	revisable form text	
RGB	red-green-blue	Don't spell out unless the abbreviation is unfamiliar to your audience.
RIFF	Resource Interchange File Format	
RIP	1. Routing Information Protocol 2. Remote Imaging Protocol 3. Raster Image Processor	Always spell out on first mention to avoid confusion.
RIPL	remote initial program load	
RISC	reduced instruction set computer	
ROM	read-only memory	For additional guidance about referring to memory, see *memory* (Usage Dictionary).
ROM BIOS	read-only memory basic input/output system	Don't spell out.
RPC	remote procedure call	
RTF	Rich Text Format	

11

Acronym	Expanded form	Comments
S+S	software-plus-services	Always spell out, but you can replace *plus* with a plus sign if space is limited. For additional guidance, see *software_plus_services* (Usage Dictionary).
SAA	Systems Application Architecture	
SaaS	software as a service	Don't capitalize as *SAAS*. For additional guidance, see *software as a service (SaaS)* (Usage Dictionary).
SAMI	Synchronized Accessible Media Interchange	
SAP	Service Advertising Protocol	
SAPI	Speech Application Programming Interface	If *API* has already been spelled out, use *Speech API (SAPI)* on first mention.
SBCS	single-byte character set	
SCSI	small computer system interface	Pronounced "scuzzy." The acronym takes the indefinite article *a*, not *an*.
SDK	software development kit	
SDLC	1. synchronous data link control 2. systems development life cycle	
SGML	Standard Generalized Markup Language	Don't spell out.
SIC	Standard Industrial Classification	Replaced by *North American Industry Classification System (NAICS)*.
SID	security identifier	
SIM	subscriber identity module	Don't spell out.
SIMM	single inline memory module	Don't spell out unless the abbreviation is unfamiliar to your audience.
SLIP	Serial Line Internet Protocol	
SMB	server message block	
SMP	symmetric multiprocessing	
SMTP	Simple Mail Transfer Protocol	
SNA	Systems Network Architecture	
SNMP	Simple Network Management Protocol	
SOA	service-oriented architecture	For additional guidance, see *service-oriented architecture* (Usage Dictionary).
SOAP	Simple Object Access Protocol	Don't spell out unless the abbreviation is unfamiliar to your audience.
SPI	service provider interface	
SQL	Structured Query Language	When referring to the language, SQL is pronounced "es-cue-el" and takes the indefinite article *an*, not *a*. When referring to Microsoft SQL Server, follow the guidance in *SQL Server* (Usage Dictionary).

Acronym	Expanded form	Comments
SSD	solid-state drive	For additional guidance about referring to drives, see *drive* (Usage Dictionary).
STB	set-top box	Always spell out.
SVC	switched virtual circuit	
SVGA	Super Video Graphics Array, Super VGA	Don't spell out. For additional guidance, see *Super VGA, SVGA* (Usage Dictionary).
SXGA	Super Extended Graphics Array, Super XGA	Don't spell out.
TAPI	Telephony Application Programming Interface	If *API* has already been spelled out, use *Telephony API (TAPI)* on first mention.
TBD	to be determined	Always spell out.
TCP/IP	Transmission Control Protocol/Internet Protocol	Don't spell out.
TIFF	Tagged Image File Format	Don't spell out.
TIP	Transaction Internet Protocol	
TP	transaction processing	Always spell out.
TSPI	Telephony Service Provider Interface	
TSR	terminate-and-stay-resident	
TTY	teletypewriter	
TV	television	All right to use without spelling out.
UDP	User Datagram Protocol	
UEFI	Unified Extensible Firmware Interface	If *EFI* has already been spelled out, introduce as *Unified EFI (UEFI)*.
UI	user interface	Don't spell out unless the abbreviation is unfamiliar to your audience.
UMB	upper memory block	
UML	Unified Modeling Language	
UNC	Universal Naming Convention	Spell out on first mention unless you are positive that your audience is familiar with the abbreviation.
UPC	universal product code	
UPnP	Universal Plug and Play	Don't spell out. This abbreviation is trademarked. For additional guidance, see *UPnP* (Usage Dictionary).
UPS	uninterruptible power supply	Spell out unless the abbreviation is familiar to your audience.
URL	Uniform Resource Locator	Don't spell out unless the abbreviation is unfamiliar to your audience. You can use *address* instead of *URL*. The acronym takes the indefinite article *a*, not *an*. For additional guidance, see *URLs, addresses* (Chapter 7).
USB	universal serial bus	Don't spell out. Don't use as a noun, only as an adjective, as in *USB storage device*.

11

Acronym	Expanded form	Comments
UTC	Coordinated Universal Time	This is the internationally recognized name for Greenwich Mean Time. Don't spell out as *Universal Time Coordinate*.
UTF-*n*	UCS Transformation Format –*n*-bit.	Don't spell out.
UUID	universally unique identifier	
UXGA	Ultra Extended Graphics Array, Ultra XGA	Don't spell out.
VAR	value-added reseller	
VB	Visual Basic	Spell out except when referring to VBA or VBScript.
VBA	Microsoft Visual Basic for Applications	
VBScript	Microsoft Visual Basic Scripting Edition	
VCPI	virtual control program interface	
VCR	video cassette recorder	Don't spell out.
VGA	Video Graphics Array, Video Graphics Adapter	Don't spell out. For additional guidance, see *VGA* (Usage Dictionary).
VIO	video input/output	
VM	1. virtual machine 2. virtual memory	Always spell out to avoid confusion. When referring to Visual Studio 2010 VM Factory, spell out as *Virtual Machine Factory* on first mention. On subsequent mention, use *VM Factory*.
VRML	Virtual Reality Modeling Language	
VSAM	virtual storage access method, virtual storage access memory	
VTP	virtual tunneling protocol, or VLAN trunking protocol	
W3C	World Wide Web Consortium	Write out as "World Wide Web Consortium" on first mention.
WAN	wide area network	
WBEM	Web-based Enterprise Management	
WEP	Wired Equivalent Privacy	Don't spell out. Don't use as a noun, only as an adjective, as in *WEP encryption key*.
Wi-Fi		Note capitalization and hyphenation. When possible, use a general phrase such as *wireless network* instead. For additional guidance, see *Wi-Fi* (Usage Dictionary).
WML	Wireless Markup Language	
WOSA	Windows Open Services Architecture	
WSDL	Web Services Description Language	
WWW	World Wide Web	Capitalize all words when using the expanded form. Otherwise, use *the web*. All lowercase (*www*) when used in an Internet address. For additional guidance, see *World Wide Web* and *Web* (Usage Dictionary).

11

Acronym	Expanded form	Comments
WYSIWYG	what you see is what you get	Don't spell out unless the abbreviation is unfamiliar to your audience.
XAML	Extensible Application Markup Language	
XGA	Extended Graphics Array	Don't spell out.
XHTML	Extensible Hypertext Markup Language	Use *Extensible HTML* (*XHTML*) on first mention.
XML	Extensible Markup Language	Don't spell out.
XMS	extended memory specification	
XSL	Extensible Stylesheet Language	
ZAW	Zero Administration for Windows	Spell out on first mention.

How to use abbreviations of measurements

Follow these guidelines when abbreviating measurements:

- As a general rule, do not abbreviate units of measure except as noted in the *Table of abbreviations of measurements*. However, if space is limited, as it might be in a table, the abbreviations in this table are all right to use without restrictions.

- Abbreviations of units of measure are identical, whether singular or plural. For example, use *in.* for both *1 in.* and *2 in.*

- When units of measure are not abbreviated, use the singular for quantities of one or less, except with zero, which takes the plural (*0 inches*).

- Insert a space between the number and the unit of measure for all abbreviations.

 Note Close up *35mm* when used in a photographic context, as in "35mm film."

- Do not insert periods after abbreviations of measurements except for *in.* (inch), which always takes a period to distinguish it from the preposition *in*.

Microsoft style

1 point	1 pt
10 points	10 pt
1 centimeter	1 cm
1 inch	1 in.
0.1 inch	0.1 in.
0 inches	0 in.

International considerations

In machine-translated content, use abbreviations of measurement with great care. Realize that abbreviations may be either mistranslated or not translated at all. For example, if you abbreviate *points* as *pt*, a Japanese version of the machine-translated content may have *pt* among all the Japanese characters, which may be confusing to the Japanese audience.

Table of abbreviations of measurements

The following table provides abbreviation guidance for common technical measurements. Terms are listed alphabetically by expanded form.

Expanded form	Abbreviation	Comments
baud	Do not abbreviate.	
bits per pixel	bpp	
bits per second	bps	Do not use *bits per second* or *bps* as a synonym for *baud*.
centimeters	cm	
days	Do not abbreviate.	
degrees	° deg	Temperature only. Angle only.
dialog unit	DLU	
dots per inch	dpi	
exabytes	EB	Spell out on first mention. On subsequent mention, all right to use the abbreviation as a measurement with numerals.
feet	ft	
gigabits	Do not abbreviate.	
gigabits per second	Gbps	Spell out as *gigabits*, not *Gb*, per second.
gigabytes	GB	Don't use G, G byte, or GByte. All right to use abbreviation as a measurement with numerals. Otherwise, spell out. See *GB*.
gigahertz	GHz	Note capitalization of *GHz*. Spell out on first mention. On subsequent mention, all right to use the abbreviation as a measurement with numerals. See *GHz*.
grams	g	
Hertz	Hz	Capitalize both the abbreviation and the word.
hours	hr	
inches	in. (or " (inch sign) if space is limited.)	Always include period with *in.* to avoid confusion with the preposition *in*.
kilobits	Do not abbreviate.	Do not use the abbreviation *Kbits*
kilobits per second	Kbps	

Expanded form	Abbreviation	Comments
kilobytes	KB	Don't use K, K byte, or KByte. All right to use abbreviation as a measurement with numerals. Otherwise, spell out. See *KB*.
kilobits per second	Kbps	Spell out on first mention. On subsequent mention, all right to use the abbreviation as a measurement with numerals. See *KBps, Kbps*.
kilobytes per second	KBps	Spell out on first mention. On subsequent mention, all right to use the abbreviation as a measurement with numerals. See *KBps, Kbps*.
kilograms	kg	
kilohertz	kHz	Note capitalization of *kHz*. Spell out on first mention. On subsequent mention, all right to use the abbreviation as a measurement with numerals. See *kHz*.
kilometers	km	
megabits	Do not abbreviate.	
megabits per second	Mbps	Spell out as *megabits*, not *Mb*, per second.
megabytes	MB	Don't use M, meg, M byte, or MByte. All right to use abbreviation as a measurement with numerals. Otherwise, spell out. See *MB*.
megabytes per second	MBps	
megahertz	MHz	Note capitalization of *MHz*. Spell out on first mention. On subsequent mention, all right to use the abbreviation as a measurement with numerals. See *MHz*.
meters	m	
microseconds	Do not abbreviate.	
miles	mi	
millimeters	mm	
milliseconds	msec (or ms)	
minutes	mins	
months	Do not abbreviate.	
nanoseconds	Do not abbreviate.	
ounces	oz	
petabytes	PB	Spell out on first mention. On subsequent mention, all right to use the abbreviation as a measurement with numerals.
picas	pi	
pixels	Do not abbreviate.	
points	pt	
points per inch	ppi	
pounds	lbs	

Expanded form	Abbreviation	Comments
seconds	sec (or s)	
terabytes	TB	Spell out on first mention. On subsequent mention, all right to use the abbreviation as a measurement with numerals.
weeks	Do not abbreviate.	
years	Do not abbreviate.	
yottabytes	YB	Spell out on first mention. On subsequent mention, all right to use the abbreviation as a measurement with numerals.
zettabytes	ZB	Spell out on first mention. On subsequent mention, all right to use the abbreviation as a measurement with numerals.

Process for adopting new acronyms or abbreviations

Before adopting a new acronym or abbreviation, follow these steps to formalize and verify it:

- Check with your content managers, writers, program managers, and product marketers or planners to determine whether the new acronym or abbreviation is necessary.

- Check the *Acronyms and other abbreviations* table to see whether the acronym is listed.

- Search the web, including Microsoft.com (*http://www.microsoft.com/en-us/default.aspx*) or MSN (*http://www.msn.com/*), for the acronym. You may find that it's in common use, either as you define it, or as the abbreviation for a different term. Also try some of the acronym search engines such as The Internet Acronym Server (*http://acronyms.silmaril.ie/cgi-bin/uncgi/acronyms*) or Acronym Finder (*http://www.acronymfinder.com/*).

11

PART 2

Usage Dictionary

Usage Dictionary

Using technical terms and common words and phrases consistently simplifies life for everyone involved in our content. It gives our customers a much more predictable experience with our content; it helps localizers and machine translation translate more accurately; and it reduces the number of decisions writers and editors are forced to make.

This usage dictionary explains standard usage at Microsoft for technical terms and common words and phrases. The terms in this section are ones that have presented the most common usage problems at Microsoft.

Numbers and symbols

35mm

Abbreviation for *35-millimeter* as a description of film or tape. In this context, *35mm* is one word, no hyphen. You do not have to spell out *35mm* on first mention.

To describe a measurement of 35 millimeters, insert a space between *35* and *mm*.

Microsoft style
You can take your pictures on 35mm film and then convert them to a digital format.

Point A is 35 mm from Point B.

8.5-by-11-inch paper

Use instead of 8.5 x 11-inch, 8 1/2 by 11-inch, or other ways of referring to the paper size.

A

A.M., P.M.

International considerations
To accommodate the worldwide audience, use the 24-hour time notation if you can. Use *00:00*, not *24:00*, to indicate midnight. If you must use *A.M.* and *P.M.*, use capital letters and periods.

Using *12:00 A.M.* or *12:00 P.M.* to refer to noon or midnight is confusing. If you are consistently using 24-hour notation, *00:00* and *12:00* are unambiguous. In any case, just specifying *noon* or *midnight* is sufficient.

Microsoft style
The meeting is at noon.

The show begins at 19:00 Pacific Time (UTC-8).

The date changes at exactly midnight.

See also *midnight, Time zones*.

-able, -ible

Adjectives ending in *-able* or *-ible* take their meaning from the passive sense of the stem verb from which they are formed. For example, *forgettable* means susceptible to, capable of, or worthy of being forgotten, not of forgetting. The same is true of words whose stem word is derived from a language other than English. For example, *portable*, which comes from the Latin *portare* (to carry), means capable of being carried.

With familiar words, this rule goes without saying. However, people sometimes coin new *-able* words, incorrectly intending them to take the active sense of the stem word. For example, *bootable disk* is defined as a disk that can start (boot) the operating system.

If you must create a new word with one of these suffixes, follow these guidelines to determine the correct spelling:

- For stem words that end in *-ce* or *-ge*, retain the final *e* to maintain the soft sound: *bridgeable, changeable*.

- For stem words that end in *-e*, drop the final *e* and add *-able*: *scalable*.

- For stem words that end in *-y*, change the *y* to *i* and add *-able*: *reliable*. An exception is that when *y* is part of a diphthong, just add *-able*: *playable, employable*.

- For verbs that end in a consonant, double the final consonant only if the participial form of the verb also takes a double consonant before the suffix: *bidding, biddable; forgetting, forgettable*. An exception is that words formed from verbs ending in *-fer* always take a single consonant: *transferable*.

The suffix *-able* is much more common than *-ible*. Do not coin words ending in *-ible*. For a detailed discussion of the use of *-ible*, see *Fowler's Modern English Usage* by R. W. Burchfield (Oxford: Oxford University Press, 2004).

International considerations

If you are not sure how to spell a word that ends in *–able* or *–ible*, look it up in *The American Heritage Dictionary*. If you cannot find it, think about writing around the word. Coinages and uncommon word formations can be problems for the worldwide audience.

abort

Do not use in content for a general audience. Instead, use *end* to refer to ending communications and network connections, *exit* for programs, *stop* for hardware operations, and *cancel* for requests and processes. If *abort* appears in a user interface that you cannot edit, it is all right to refer to abort, but use one of the preceding alternative terms to describe the user action.

It is all right to use *abort* in content for a technical audience if it is part of a function name, parameter name, or some other element of the application programming interface.

Microsoft style

To end your server connection, click **Disconnect Network Drive** on the **Tools** menu.

If you exit Setup, the program will not be installed successfully.

To stop a print job before it is finished, click **Cancel.**

The class driver calls the minidriver's StrMiniCancelPacket routine to signal that a stream request has been canceled.

Not Microsoft style

To abort your server connection, click **Disconnect Network Drive** on the **Tools** menu.

Your game has been aborted. To continue, click **Load Last Saved Game**.

above

Do not use to mean *earlier*. Do not use as an adjective preceding a noun, as in "the above section," or following a noun, as in "the code above." Use a hyperlink instead. If you cannot use a hyperlink, use *previous*, *preceding*, or *earlier*. See also *below, Cross-references, later*.

Microsoft style

See What is a copyright?

See "Connecting to the network," earlier in this chapter.

The following illustration shows the output of the preceding code.

Do not use *above* to mean *later*, as in "Windows Vista and later."

accelerator key

Obsolete term. Use *keyboard shortcut* instead. In content for software developers, it is all right to use *shortcut key* if it is necessary to distinguish from an access key. See also *access key, shortcut key*.

access

It is all right to use *access* as a verb to mean *obtain access to*. Although this usage is grating to many editors, it is well established in the context of computers.

Do not use *access* to mean *start*, *create*, or *open*. Use a more specific verb or phrase instead. See also *start, switch*.

Microsoft style

Start the program either from the **Start** menu or from Windows Explorer.

You can access your personal data from the company intranet.

You can create shortcuts to quickly switch to programs that you use often.

Services that you provide must be configured so that users can access them.

Not Microsoft style

Access the program either from the **Start** menu or from Windows Explorer.

You can create shortcuts to quickly access programs that you use often.

access key

Do not use in content for a general audience. Use *keyboard shortcut* instead. See also *keyboard shortcut, key names, key sequence, shortcut key*.

Access key is all right to use in content for software developers or in content about customizing the user interface to distinguish between an access key and a shortcut key. In such cases, use *access key* to denote a key sequence that is used to access a menu item, and provide a definition.

access privileges

Obsolete term. Use *user rights* instead. See also *user rights*.

access rights

Obsolete term. Use *user rights* instead. See also *user rights*.

accessible

Reserve *accessible* and *accessibility* to refer to things that all people, including those with disabilities, can easily use.

Do not use *accessible* as a synonym for *simple*. Instead, use terms such as *easy to learn*, *easy to use*, or *intuitive*, or refer to the specific characteristics that make something easy to use, such as *intelligent Help system*. See also *assistive*; Chapter 4, "Accessible content".

Microsoft style

A range of enhancements makes multimedia products easier to install and use and provides a great platform for home entertainment.

The availability of high-contrast color schemes enhances the program's accessibility for visually impaired users.

Not Microsoft style

A range of enhancements makes multimedia products more accessible and provides a great platform for home entertainment.

accessory

Use as a general category for programs such as Notepad, Paint, Tablet PC Input Panel, and Sticky Notes that appear in the Accessories folder of the Windows **Start** menu. It is all right to use *program* or *accessory program* to refer to such programs.

Do not refer to accessory programs as *utilities*. Do not make references such as "the Notepad accessory." Use the program name by itself. See also *tool*.

Microsoft style

Windows includes a number of accessories to help you perform routine tasks.

Notepad is a basic text editor.

Not Microsoft style

The Notepad accessory is a basic text editor.

accounts receivable

Use instead of *account receivables*.

achievement

Refers to an accomplishment that is formally recognized by a game or other program, and that is sometimes represented by a virtual badge, star, medal, or other reward for the person who earned it. Use title capitalization for achievement names. If it follows the name, use lowercase for the word *achievement*.

For Microsoft games, *achievement* should be used only if it is awarded in a player's Xbox LIVE gamer profile. Any other accomplishments that are tracked by a game should not be referred to as achievements. See also *badge*.

Microsoft style

You just earned the Superstar achievement!

Take a bow—you've earned your Superstar.

Not Microsoft style

You just earned the superstar achievement!

acknowledgment

Do not spell with an *e* between the *g* and the *m*. For a section acknowledging the contributions of other people, use the plural *Acknowledgments* even if there is only one.

action bar

Do not use. Use *menu bar* instead.

action button

Do not use. Use *button* or *command button* instead.

actionable

Do not use unless you have no other choice.

Microsoft style

Ensure that the team has access to information that they can act on.

The problem should be clearly defined and easily solvable.

Aggregate customer data to make it easier to act on.

Aggregate customer data to make it more conducive to action.

Not Microsoft style

Ensure that the team has access to actionable information.

The problem should be clearly defined and actionable.

Aggregate customer data to make it more actionable.

activate

Use only to indicate the action of verifying that a software product is a legal copy and is installed in compliance with the Microsoft Software License Terms.

Microsoft style

If you have not yet activated Windows 7, you can initiate activation at any time by clicking the **Windows Activation** icon in the notification area.

Do not use *activate* as a synonym for *open*, *start*, or *switch to*.

active player, active user

Refers to a person who is currently being tracked or recognized by a motion sensor or camera.

Microsoft style

When the game ends, the active player's score will be displayed.

Not Microsoft style

When the game ends, the score of the player in the camera's view will be displayed.

active vs. current

Use *active* or *open*, not *current*, to refer to open and operating windows, programs, documents, files, devices, or portions of the screen (such as an "open window" or "active cell"). However, use *current* to refer to a drive, directory, folder, or other element that does not change in the context of the discussion.

> **Note** If *active* causes confusion with ActiveX, try to write around it. For example, be as specific as possible in naming an active element.

Microsoft style

Change the formula in the active cell.

To switch between open documents, on the **Window** menu click the document you want to switch to.

Windows Explorer indicates the current folder.

ad hoc

Do not use *ad hoc* unless you have no other choice. It means "established only for the specific purpose or case at hand." See also *Latin and other non-English words*.

adapter

Use instead of *adaptor*.

In general, do not use *adapter* to describe hardware that supports connecting a computer to a peripheral device such as a monitor, speakers, or a camera. Use *card* instead to describe hardware that connects a computer to a device, even if the hardware is built into the motherboard. However, do use *network adapter* to describe hardware that supports connecting a computer to a network. See also *board, card, network adapter, video card*.

Microsoft style

network adapter

Not Microsoft style

display adapter

graphics adapter

sound adapter

video adapter

add

In general, do not use *add* to refer to installing software. Use *install* instead. See also *install, remove*.

add-in, add-on

Use *add-in* to refer to software that adds functionality to a larger program, such as the Analysis ToolPak in Microsoft Excel. *Add-in* can also refer to a driver or a user-written program that adds functionality to a larger program, such as a wizard, a builder, or a menu add-in.

Use *add-on* to refer to a hardware device such as an expansion board or external peripheral equipment, such as a CD-ROM player, that is attached to the computer.

In content for a general audience, use these terms primarily as modifiers. For example, say "add-in program" or "add-on modem."

adjacent selection

Do not use if you can use *multiple selection* instead. All right to use if you must emphasize that the selected items are adjacent to each other. Do not use *contiguous selection*. See also *multiple selection, nonadjacent selection*.

administer

Use instead of *administrate*.

administrator

Use *administrator* or *system administrator* unless you must specify a particular kind of administrator, such as a network administrator or a database administrator.

Do not capitalize *administrator* except in the phrase *Administrator program*. Capitalize *Administrators* only to refer to the Administrators group that is a part of Windows security.

Administrator program

Note capitalization.

affect vs. effect

As nouns and verbs, *affect* and *effect* are often confused. Part of the problem is that the verb *affect* can be defined as "to have an *effect* on."

Microsoft style

Deleting a link on the desktop does not affect the actual program.

Not Microsoft style

Deleting a link on the desktop does not effect the actual program.

The verb *effect* means "to bring about."

Microsoft style

Good software design can effect a change in users' perceptions.

Not Microsoft style

Good software design can affect a change in users' perceptions.

As a noun, *effect* means "result." The noun *affect* is a term in psychology and should not be needed in content about software.

Microsoft style

The effect of the change was minimal.

Not Microsoft style

The affect of the change was minimal.

afterward

Use instead of *afterwards*.

against

Do not use to refer to running or building a program on a particular platform or operating system. Use *on* instead.

Against is all right to use in content for a technical audience in the sense of evaluating a value *against* an expression or running a query *against* a database.

Microsoft style

Show reference queries can be run against the Guide database.

If you want a program built on the newest version of DirectX to run on an older version, define DIRECTDRAW_VERSION to be the earliest version of DirectX that you want to run the program on.

Not Microsoft style

If you want a program built against the newest version of DirectX to run against an older version, define DIRECTDRAW_VERSION to be the earliest version of DirectX that you want to run the program against.

alarm

Do not use as a general reference to a sound that is intended to get the user's attention. Use *beep* or a more specific description of the sound instead.

It is all right to use *alarm* in a specific description, such as "the low-battery alarm."

album

Refers to a collection of one or more related audio or music tracks issued together as a full-length recording. Use *album* even if the content was issued on a CD.

Use *album cover* when referring to the graphical representation of the album or CD.

alert

Do not use as a reference to a system message. Use *message* instead. *Error message* is all right to use when it is necessary to differentiate types of messages.

Use *alerts* (lowercase, plural) to refer to alert messages from .NET or from Internet sites such as MSN or eBay. Capitalize *alerts* in proper names such as MSN Alerts and .NET Alerts, and construe these names as singular.

Do not use *alert* as a synonym for *reminder*.

Microsoft style

You can receive alerts by signing up for MSN Mobile services.

These alerts appear on your desktop or mobile device.

Microsoft .NET Alerts delivers the information that you care about to your desktop, mobile device, or email.

align, aligned on

Use *align* instead of *justify* to refer to text that is aligned on only one margin. *Right-aligned* and *left-aligned* are correct usage, as are *aligned on the right* and *aligned on the right margin*.

Use *justify* only to refer to text that is aligned on both the left and right margins. If you are not sure that users will interpret *justify* correctly, define it in place or use another term.

You align text and graphics *on* a margin, but you align one object *with* another. It is all right to use a phrase such as *aligned with each other*.

Microsoft style

Align the paragraph on the left.

Left-align the paragraph.

The text is aligned on both the left and the right.

Justified text is aligned on both the left and the right.

Align the text with the headings.

Not Microsoft style

Left-justify the paragraph.

allow

Use *allow* only to refer to features such as security that permit or deny some action.

In content for a general audience, use *you can* to refer to things that a program makes easy or possible for the user. In content for a technical audience, use *the user can* or *enables the user* when you have to refer to the end user in the third person. See also *can vs. may, enable, enabled*.

Microsoft style

Windows 7 allows a user without an account to log on as a guest.

With Microsoft Word 2010, you can save files in HTML format.

Not Microsoft style

Microsoft Word 2010 allows you to save files in HTML format.

alpha

Refers to the version of a software product that is ready for structured internal testing. Alpha versions are usually not released to external testers. See also *beta*.

alphabetical

Use instead of *alphabetic*.

alphanumeric

Use to refer to character sets that include only letters and numerals or to individual characters that can be only letters or numerals.

Do not use *alphanumerical*.

alt text

The common term for the descriptive text that appears as an alternative to a graphic on a webpage. The text is indicated in the HTML file by the **alt** attribute. The code used for the graphic and the alt text looks as follows:

<img src="image.gif" alt="Add the description of the image here">

If you are not sure that your users will understand what *alt text* means, define it on first mention, and if your content has a glossary, add *alt text*.

For details about writing alt text for a specific project, consult your project style sheet.

Accessibility considerations

Because screen readers for users who are sight-impaired cannot interpret graphics, they read the alt text instead. Therefore, always provide alt text whenever you use a graphic, and always make the alt text as descriptive as possible. Do not use a word such as *graphic* or *image* by itself in alt text.

among vs. between

Use *among* when referring to three or more persons or things or when the number is unspecified. Use *between* when referring to two persons or things or when referring to relationships between two items at a time, regardless of the total number of items.

Microsoft style

Move between the two programs at the top of the list.

Switch between Windows-based programs.

You can share folders and printers among members of your workgroup.

ampersand (&)

Do not use & in text or headings to mean *and* unless you are specifically referring to the symbol on the user interface.

It is all right to use and refer to the ampersand in appropriate contexts. For example, it is all right to tell the user that in HTML, the ampersand precedes the code name or number of a special character, and in C and other programming languages, the ampersand is an operator.

Microsoft style

To show less-than (<) and greater-than (>) signs on a webpage, use the following HTML code:

- < >

or

- < >

In C and other programming languages, the & is used as an operator.

and so on

Do not use *and so on* except in situations where screen space is limited or as noted later in this topic. This phrase gives no information about the class of items that it is meant to represent, and therefore can create ambiguity. See also *etc.*

Microsoft style

Body text is most readable in Times New Roman, Palatino, and other serif fonts.

Not Microsoft style

Body text is most readable in Times New Roman, Palatino, and so on.

Do not use *and so on* to end a phrase that begins with *for example* or *such as*. These opening phrases indicate that what follows is not an exhaustive list, so adding *and so on* is superfluous.

Microsoft style

Body text is most readable in serif fonts such as Times New Roman and Palatino.

Not Microsoft style

Body text is most readable in serif fonts such as Times New Roman, Palatino, and so on.

It is all right to use *and so on* to indicate a logical progression where at least two items have been named.

Microsoft style

...a, b, c, and so on.

and/or

All right to use, but only if you cannot use either *and* or *or* by itself, or if you cannot rewrite the sentence to avoid this construction.

Microsoft style

You can save the document under its current name or under a new name.

Will the new version contain information about how to write object-oriented code and/or use the class libraries?

antialiasing

Do not hyphenate. A technique for making jagged edges look smooth on the screen.

A

antimalware

Use as an adjective, not as a noun. Do not hyphenate. Refers to a general category of software designed to detect and respond to malicious software such as viruses, worms, and trojans. Some antimalware implementations may also detect and respond to potentially unwanted software such as spyware and adware. See also *antispyware, antivirus, antispyware.*

Microsoft style

antimalware program

antispyware

Use as an adjective, not as a noun. Do not hyphenate. Refers to a computer program that is designed to detect spyware and sometimes remove it. See also *antimalware, antivirus, security, spyware.*

Microsoft style

antispyware tools

antivirus

Use as an adjective, not as a noun. Do not hyphenate. Refers to a computer program that is designed to detect and respond to malware. Responses may include blocking user access to infected files, cleaning infected files or systems, or informing the user that an infected program was detected.

This term is often used interchangeably with *antimalware* to describe any program that removes malware. However, always use *antivirus* when you want to differentiate between antispyware and other antimalware programs. See also *antimalware, antispyware, security.*

Microsoft style

Microsoft Security Essentials has both antivirus and antispyware capabilities.

app

App is an abbreviation for *application* in some Microsoft products and services. For example, you may use *app* to refer to cloud applications or programs downloaded to phones. Consult your project style sheet for guidance on using this term in your content.

International considerations

Using the abbreviation *app* does not save space when content is localized. In many languages, the full term is translated because an abbreviation is not available. See also *applet, application.*

appears, displays

Displays requires a direct object; *appears* does not. If necessary in context, you can use the passive *is displayed.*

Microsoft style

If you try to exit the program without saving the file, a message appears.

Windows displays a message if you do not log on correctly.

A message is displayed if you do not log on correctly.

Not Microsoft style

If you try to exit the program without saving the file, a message displays.

appendix, appendices

For consistency in Microsoft documentation, use *appendices* as the plural form of *appendix* instead of *appendixes*.

applet

In current usage, *applet* refers to an HTML-based program that a browser downloads temporarily to a user's hard disk. *Applet* is most often associated with Java.

In general, when referring to a small program, use the name of the program or the most appropriate term, such as *program, add-in, app,* or *applet*.

Do not refer to the individual programs that make up Control Panel as *applets*. Refer to them by their names. If you must use a generic term, refer to these programs as *items*. See also *accessory, add-in, add-on, app, Control Panel, tool, utility*.

Microsoft style

Click **Control Panel**, click **User Accounts**, and then click **Credential Manager**.

application

For a general audience, use *program* instead of *application*. *Application* is all right to use in content for a technical audience, especially to refer to a grouping of software that includes both executable files and other components. See also *app, applet, program vs. application*.

Do not use *application program*.

application developer

Do not use if you can use *software developer, web developer, developer,* or *programmer* instead.

Do not use *applications developer*.

application file

Do not use in content for a general audience. Use the specific name of the file if you can. Otherwise, use *program file* instead.

application icon

In general, do not use to refer to a program's icon. Use the specific product name, such as "the **Word** icon" instead. If you must use a general term, use *program icon*.

Application icon is all right to use in content for software developers when discussing programming elements such as the **ApplicationIcon** property.

application window

In general, do not use to refer to a specific product's window. Use the specific product name, such as "the Word window," instead.

Application window is all right to use in content for software developers when discussing programming elements such as the **WindowSize** event, which occurs when the application window is resized or moved.

arabic numerals

Use lowercase *a* for the word *arabic* when referring to numbers.

argument vs. parameter

An *argument* typically is a value or expression that contains data or code that is used with an operator or passed to a function. For example, in the following expression **x** and **y** are arguments:

```
x = y;
```

A *parameter* is a value given to a variable and treated as a constant until the operation is completed. Parameters are often used to customize a program for a particular purpose. For example, a date could be a parameter that is passed to a scheduling function.

However, these terms are often used interchangeably. In content for a technical audience, use the same term consistently to refer to the same kind of element.

In general, use *argument* in content for a general audience. The difference between an argument and a parameter is unimportant for such users because it appears so infrequently. Differentiate between the two only if necessary. See also *Command syntax, Document conventions* (Chapter 6).

arrow

In content for novice computer users, you may want to use *arrow* to identify the arrow next to a list box label. Do not use *up arrow* or *down arrow*, which refer to the **arrow keys** on the keyboard.

Microsoft style

Click the **Font** arrow to display the list.

arrow keys

The arrow keys are the keys that are labeled only with an arrow. If you need to make special mention of the similar keys on the numeric keypad, refer to the *arrow keys on the numeric keypad.*

Refer to a specific arrow key as the Left Arrow, Right Arrow, Up Arrow, or Down Arrow key. It is all right to use *arrow key* as a general term for any single arrow key.

Do not use *direction keys, directional keys,* or *movement keys.*

Use specific names to refer to other navigational keys such as Page Up, Page Down, Home, and End. See also *Key names,* (Chapter 5)

Microsoft style

To move the cursor one character, press the appropriate arrow key.

arrow pointer

Do not use. Use *pointer* instead. See also *pointer.*

article

Use *article* to refer to a topic in an encyclopedia or a similar reference program, and to the contents of magazines, journals, newspapers, and newscasts, whether online or in print. For example, you can refer to an opinion column on MSNBC or a product-related white paper as an article. You can, of course, use a more specific name for such articles.

Do not use *article* to refer to Help topics or sections or chapters of printed or online books.

International considerations

Do not use as a synonym for *because* or *while* in subordinate clauses. Both uses are grammatically correct, but they make reading more difficult for the worldwide audience.

Microsoft style

You can use the Forms Designer as a complete development environment.

Use the active voice whenever possible, because it is easier to translate.

Fill out your registration card while you wait for Setup to finish.

Not Microsoft style

Use the active voice whenever possible, as it is easier to translate.

Fill out your registration card as you wait for Setup to finish.

as well as

International considerations

Because *as well as* can be used both as a synonym for *and* and as a prepositional phrase, it can be difficult for the worldwide audience and ambiguous for machine translation. For example, does the sentence "She can play the piano as well as guitar" mean that she can play both the piano and the guitar? Or does it mean that she can play one as proficiently as she can play the other?

Microsoft style

With Word you can format whole documents, insert headers and footers, and develop an index, in addition to writing a simple letter.

With Word you can write a simple letter. In addition, you can format whole documents, insert headers and footers, and develop an index.

Not Microsoft style

With Word you can format whole documents, insert headers and footers, and develop an index, as well as write a simple letter.

assembly language

Use instead of *assembler* or *machine language*. *Assembly language* is a low-level language that uses an assembler rather than a compiler to translate the source code into machine code.

Hyphenate *assembly language* as an adjective.

assistive

Use *assistive* to refer to devices and organizations that help people with disabilities. For example, use it to refer to hardware that enables a person with a disability to interact with a program. Eye trackers and motion sensors are examples of hardware that can be used for this purpose. However, refer to these and similar devices as *assistive devices* only in the context of addressing disabilities. See also Chapter 4, "Accessible content".

Microsoft style

To calibrate your Kinect Sensor or other motion sensor, follow the instructions on the screen.

You can calibrate the Kinect Sensor or other assistive device for people with motion disabilities by using the **Options** command.

Not Microsoft style

To calibrate your Kinect Sensor or other assistive device, follow the instructions on the screen.

asterisk (*)

Use *asterisk* to refer to the * symbol. Do not use *star*, except when referring to the key on a telephone keypad. An asterisk indicates multiplication in programming languages, and it also serves as a **wildcard character** representing one or more characters.

at sign (@)

In Internet email addresses, @ separates the user name from the domain name, as in someone@ example.com. In addresses, it is pronounced *at*.

attribute

Do not use as a synonym for *property*.

In the .NET Framework, an attribute is a descriptive declaration that annotates programming elements such as types, fields, methods, and properties.

In HTML and XML, an attribute is a named value within a tagged element that can change default characteristics of the tag. For example, in a table, the attributes **width** and **height** specify the size of a table or table cells. The code for an HTML attribute looks as follows:

<table width=50% height=50%>

Files can have attributes such as **hidden** and **read-only**. See also *properties*.

audiobook

One word.

audit trail

Use instead of *audit log*.

author

In general, do not use as a verb to mean *write*.

In content for a technical audience, it is all right to mention *authoring tools* or *authoring environments* and to use *author* to refer to *authoring* in language-specific or tool-specific contexts. For example, it is all right to say *authoring in XML*.

However, in content for a general audience, a phrase such as *writing in XML* or *creating content in XML* is more suitable.

auto-

In general, do not hyphenate words beginning with *auto-*, such as *autoanswer*, *autodemo*, and *autodial*, unless it is necessary to avoid confusion. When in doubt, check the *American Heritage Dictionary*, or consult your project style sheet.

International considerations

Do not coin words beginning with *auto-*. They may confuse the worldwide audience and may lead to mistranslation in machine-translated content.

B

back end

Do not use if you can correctly use a more specific term such as *server, operating system, database,* or *network* instead.

back up, backup

Two words as a verb, one word as an adjective or as a noun.

Microsoft style

Back up the files before you turn off the computer.

Save the backup copies on a disk.

backbone

Usually, a large, fast network that connects other networks.

Do not use in content for a general audience. You do not have to define *backbone* in content for a technical audience.

backlight

One word. Refers to the lighting that makes a flat panel display, such as that on a laptop computer, easier to read.

backspace

All right to use as a verb.

backtab

Do not use. If you have to explain the procedure, refer to the Shift+Tab key combination.

backward

Use instead of *backwards*.

badge

A star, medal, or other virtual recognition that indicates an achievement in a game or other program. Use title capitalization for a badge name. If it follows the name, use lowercase for the word *badge*. See also *achievement*.

base line vs. baseline

Use *baseline* (one word) to refer to an established standard, as in "baseline data." Use *base line* (two words) only to refer to the bottom alignment of uppercase letters in print (a typographic term).

baud

Refers to the rate of signals transmitted per second. Because baud is a rate, the phrase *baud rate* is redundant.

Do not use *bits per second* or *bps* as a synonym for baud. Modems are conventionally designated by bits per second or kilobits per second, not baud. A 28.8 Kbps modem runs at a different baud, depending on how events are coded for transmission.

When designating baud, use commas when the number has five (not four) or more digits.

because vs. since

International considerations

Do not use *since* to mean *because*. The use of *since* to mean *because* can be confusing to the worldwide audience, and the possible ambiguity may lead to mistranslation in machine-translated content. In general, use *because* to refer to a reason and *since* to refer to a passage of time. If it is possible to misinterpret the meaning of *since* as referring to a reason, rewrite the sentence. For example, you can rewrite the ambiguous sentence "Since I installed the fast modem, I can download messages very quickly" in one of the following ways:

- Because I installed the fast modem, I can download messages quickly.

- Ever since I installed the fast modem, I can download messages very quickly.

- Since installing the fast modem, I can download messages very quickly.

beep

Use instead of *alarm* or *tone* to refer specifically to a beeping sound.

Microsoft style

When you hear the beep, begin your recording.

below

Do not use to mean *later* in the content. Do not use as an adjective preceding a noun, as in "the below table," or following a noun, as in "the code below." Use a hyperlink instead. If you cannot use a hyperlink, use *later* or *the following*. See also *above, cross-references, later*.

Microsoft style

The following code sample can be used without modification.

The following code displays information about the database.

See the "Installation Instructions" section later in this topic.

Not Microsoft style

The below code sample can be used without modification.

The code below displays information about the database.

See the "Installation Instructions" section below.

beta

A software product that is ready for unstructured testing by customers.

Do not refer to a beta release as a *preview*. *Preview* is often used to denote a version of a released product that will run only long enough for the user to make a purchasing decision. See also *alpha*.

bi-

In general, do not hyphenate words beginning with *bi-*, such as *bidirectional*, *bimodal*, and *bimonthly*, unless it is necessary to avoid confusion. When in doubt, check the *American Heritage Dictionary*, or consult your project style sheet.

big-endian, little-endian

All right to use in content for a technical audience. *Big-endian* refers to the method of physically storing numbers so that the most significant byte is placed first. *Little-endian* is the opposite.

bio

Bio is all right to use as the abbreviation for biography in some Microsoft products and services, such as entertainment content.

International considerations

Using the abbreviation *bio* does not necessarily save space when content is localized. In many languages, the full term is translated because an abbreviation is not available.

bitmap

One word. Refers to a specific file format for online art.

Do not use generically to refer to any graphic. Use *illustration*, *figure*, *picture*, or a similar term instead.

bitmask

One word.

bitplane

One word. Refers to one of a set of bitmaps that together make up a color image.

bits per second

Spell out *bits per second* on first mention unless you are positive that your audience is familiar with the term. On subsequent mention, use the abbreviation *bps*.

Do not use as a synonym for *baud*. See also *baud*.

bitwise

One word. Refers to a programming operation that determines the settings of individual bits in a variable. Use only in content for software developers.

black box

Do not use. It's jargon. A black box is a unit of hardware or software in which the internal structure is unknown, but its function is documented.

black hole

Do not use. It's jargon. A black hole is a condition of an internetwork where packets are lost without an indication of the error.

blacklist

Do not use. Try to write around by using wording such as in the "Microsoft style" examples.

Microsoft style

Blocked Senders list

Safe Recipients list

blocked or safe programs

Not Microsoft style

Senders Blacklist

Recipients Whitelist

Blacklisted or whitelisted programs

graylist

blank

Do not use as a verb.

blog, weblog

Blog is preferred, but *weblog* is all right to use. Use *blog* as a verb meaning "to publish or write entries for a blog," and use *blogger* to refer to a person who publishes or writes entries for a blog.

blue screen, bluescreen

Do not use *blue screen* or *bluescreen*, either as a noun or as a verb, to refer to an operating system that is not responding. As a verb, use *stop* instead. And as noun, use *stop error*.

It is all right to use *blue screen* (two words) to refer to the screen display itself, as in the following example:

The operating system stops unexpectedly and an error message appears on a blue screen.

board

Do not use *board* as a general term for hardware that provides a connection between a peripheral device and a computer. Use *card* instead. See also *card*.

Microsoft style

Video card

Motherboard

Not Microsoft style

Video board

System board

bold

Use *bold* only as an adjective, not as a noun or as a verb. Do not use *bolded, boldface,* or *boldfaced*. See also *Document conventions* (Chapter 6), *Fonts* (Chapter 3)

Microsoft style

To apply bold formatting to the selected text, press Ctrl+B.

The newly added parameters are displayed in bold type.

The selected text is bold.

Not Microsoft style

To bold the selected characters, press Ctrl+B.

The newly added parameters are displayed in bold.

 Note Use *regular type* to describe type that is neither bold nor italic.

bookmark

In general Internet usage, a saved reference in the form of a URL or link that helps users return to a particular location, page, or site. Use *favorite* to refer to a bookmark in Internet Explorer. See also *favorite*.

Boolean

Note capitalization.

boot

Do not use *boot* as a verb to mean *start* or *restart* a computer, and make clear that *start* in this context refers to the computer and not to a program. Use *turn on* to refer to turning on the power to a computer.

In content for a technical audience, it is all right to use *boot* as an adjective, as in *boot sector* and *boot sequence*. However, if you can correctly do so, use *startup* instead.

If the user interface or application programming interface uses *boot* in a label or element name, it is all right to reproduce the label or element name, but use *start* or *startup* to refer to the action or event described. See also *turn on, turn off*.

Microsoft style

The Boot.ini file is a text file that stores startup options.

bootable disk

Do not use. Use *system disk* or *startup disk* instead. It is all right to use *boot disk* in content for a technical audience.

bot

Refers to a program that performs a repetitive task, such as posting messages to newsgroups and keeping Internet Relay Chat (IRC) channels open.

This term often refers to a malicious program installed on a computer that is part of a bot network (botnet). Bots are generally backdoor trojans that allow unauthorized access and control of an affected computer.

Provide a definition if your audience might be unfamiliar with the term. For more information, see the Microsoft Malware Encyclopedia. See also *security*.

bottom left, bottom right

In general, do not use to mean *lower left* and *lower right*, which are hyphenated as adjectives. All right to use when you have no other choice, such as when discussing the **BottomLeft** and the **BottomRight** property.

For accessibility considerations, see *left*.

bounding outline

Technical term for the visible element, usually a dotted rectangle, that appears when a user selects a range of items.

Do not use *marquee* as a synonym for *bounding outline*. It is all right to use *dotted rectangle* or *dotted box* if necessary to describe the bounding outline, especially in content that is primarily for a general audience, but use the term only to describe, not to replace *bounding outline*.

box

In content about a dialog box, use *box* instead of *field* to refer to any box except a check box or a list box. For a check box, use the complete term, *check box*. For a dialog box element that displays a list, such as a drop-down list box, use *list* rather than *box* for clarity. See also *entry field*; *field*; *Webpage controls, dialog boxes and property sheets* (Chapter 5).

Microsoft style

the **Read-Only** box

the **File Name** box

the **Hidden Text** check box

the **Wallpaper** list

Not Microsoft style

the **User Name** field

bps

Abbreviation for *bits per second*. Spell out *bits per second* on first mention unless you are positive that your audience is familiar with the term.

Do not use *bps* as a synonym for *baud*. See also *baud, bits per second*.

breakpoint

One word. Technical term related to testing and debugging.

Briefcase

A Windows program for synchronizing different versions of files. Do not precede with the definite article *the* or with a possessive pronoun such as *your*.

Microsoft style

When you reconnect your portable computer to your main computer, Briefcase automatically replaces the files on your main computer with the modified versions.

Not Microsoft style

When you reconnect your portable computer to your main computer, the Briefcase automatically replaces the files on your main computer with the modified versions.

When you reconnect your portable computer to your main computer, your Briefcase automatically replaces the files on your main computer with the modified versions.

broadcast

All right to use as an adjective, as a noun, or as a verb. The past tense of the verb *broadcast* is *broadcast*, not *broadcasted*.

To refer to a broadcast delivered on the web or over an intranet, use *webcast*.

browse

Use to refer to scanning Internet sites or other files, whether in search of a particular item or only in search of something that might be interesting.

If your product refers to the ellipsis button as the **Browse** button, use *browse* to describe the user action associated with the button. Consult your project style sheet for details.

It is all right to use *browse* the Internet, but use *browse through* (not *browse*) a list, a database, a document, or a similar item.

Browsing is a manual activity. To describe using a product's search feature or using an Internet search engine, use *find* or *search*. See also *browse vs. find; ellipsis button; search, search and replace; surf.*

browse vs. find

Use *browse* to mean a user manually looking for something in a folder or tree structure, or on an Internet site.

Use *find* to mean a user instructing the computer to search for something, such as a specific file, object, computer, website, server, term, or phrase.

browser

Use *browser* or *web browser*, not *web viewer*, to refer to a program that downloads and displays HTML pages.

bug

Use without definition or apology to refer to a software or hardware error.

bug fix

Do not use. To describe the general category of fixes for an issue, use *software update*. To describe a specific fix, use one of the specific named software update types: *critical update, definition update, feature pack, hotfix, security update, service pack, update,* or *update rollup*. See also *out-of-band release terminology* (Chapter 6), *critical update, definition update, feature pack, hotfix, security update, service pack, update, update rollup.*

build

Do not use in content for a general audience to mean creating such things as documents, charts, and worksheets. Use *create* instead.

It is all right to use *build* as a verb in content for a technical audience to mean to compile and link code. It is also all right in such content to use *build* as a noun.

bulleted

In most cases, use instead of *bullet*. However, *bullet* is correct when referring to the graphical symbol for a bullet (●) or to a single item, as in a *bullet point*.

burn

All right to use to refer to recording data on a CD or a DVD. See also *rip*.

button

Use as the shortened form of *command button* or *option button*. Do not use *action button*.

In general, refer to a button only by its label without using the word *button*. If you need to use the word *button* with the label for clarity, *button* is lowercase. For example, an unnamed button such as **Maximize** may be clearer if you describe it as *the **Maximize** button*. See also *command button*; *option*; *option button*; *Webpage controls, dialog boxes and property sheets* (Chapter 5).

Microsoft style

Select the file that you want to open, and then click **OK**.

To enlarge a window to fill the entire screen, click the **Maximize** button.

C

C, C++, C#

C, *C++*, and *C#* are programming languages. It is all right to use these names as adjectives. For example, you can say "a C program." But do not form hyphenated adjective phrases with them.

C# is pronounced "c-sharp." Because not all fonts include the musical sharp sign, use the **number sign (#)** to form C#.

Microsoft style

C++ based

built with exported functions that are callable by C

Not Microsoft style

C++-based

built with C-callable exported functions

cable

Do not use as a verb.

Microsoft style

The printer is connected to the computer.

Not Microsoft style

The printer is cabled to the computer.

cabling

Do not use as a synonym for *cable* or *cables*. If necessary in a discussion of network connections, it is all right to use *cabling* to refer to a combination of cables, connectors, and terminators.

cache vs. disk cache

Differentiate between *cache* and *disk cache*. A *cache* generally refers to a special memory subsystem where data values are duplicated for quick access. A *disk cache* refers to a portion of RAM that temporarily stores information read from disk.

Do not use *cache* or *file cache* to refer to the storage location of Internet files that are downloaded as you browse the web. The Internet Explorer term is *Temporary Internet Files folder*.

calendar

Use only as an adjective or as a noun. As a verb, use *schedule, list*, or another appropriate verb instead.

call back, callback

Two words as a verb, one word as an adjective and as a noun.

In content for software developers, do not use *callback* to mean *callback function*.

call out, callout

Two words as a verb, one word as an adjective or as a noun.

Microsoft style

You should call out special features in the interface.

Add callouts to the art. The callout wording should be brief.

For information about using callouts, see *Art, captions, and callouts* (Chapter 7).

caller ID

Do not spell out *ID*.

can vs. may

Use the verb *can* to describe actions or tasks that the user or program is able to do. Use *may* to express possibility, not to imply that the user has permission to do something. Use *might* to connote greater doubt than *may* or to eliminate ambiguity when *may* could be interpreted to imply permission.

Microsoft style

You can use the **/b** option to force a black-and-white screen display.

You might receive incorrect results when you run a query in SQL.

The form might not be displayed.

You may use the **/b** option to force a black-and-white screen display.

You may receive incorrect results when you run a query in SQL.

The form may not be displayed.

Do not use *could* when you mean *can*. Like *might*, *could* conveys a tone of doubt that is best avoided in technical writing. It is all right to use *could* as the past tense of *can* when users cannot mistake its meaning. See also *should vs. must*.

Cancel button

In procedures, you do not have to use the words *the* and *button* with the button name. You can just say "Click **Cancel**."

cancel the selection

Use instead of *deselect* or *unmark*. Use *clear* to refer to check boxes.

canceled, canceling

Spell *canceled* and *canceling* with one *l*, but spell *cancellation* with two *l*'s.

card

Use as a general term to describe hardware that supports connecting a computer to a peripheral device such as a monitor, speakers, or a camera. A card can be a printed circuit board, a PC Card or CardBus device, or circuitry that is part of the motherboard itself. Do not use *board* or *adapter* with this exception: use *network adapter* to describe hardware that supports connecting a computer to a network.

Use *card* also when referring to a device that has *card* in the name, such as *smart card*, and in nontechnical ways, such as *credit card* or *business card*. See also *board, video card*.

Microsoft style

smart card

sound card

video card

Not Microsoft style

network card

Card refers to hardware. It is not the same thing as a *driver*, which is software that controls the behavior of hardware.

carriage return/line feed

Follow conventional practice and use a slash mark, not a hyphen, when referring to this ASCII character combination. Abbreviate as CR/LF for subsequent references.

carry out vs. run

Use *carry out* to describe the action that results when a user or macro issues a command. Use *run* to describe the action that results when a user or macro starts a program or macro.

Do not use *execute* for these operations in content for a general audience. *Execute* is all right to use in content for a technical audience. See also *run vs. execute*; *start, Start (the menu)*.

Microsoft style

You can use Doskey.exe to create macros that carry out one or more commands.

You can write a batch file that runs Microsoft Word.

Not Microsoft style

You can use Doskey.exe to create macros that run one or more commands.

You can use Doskey.exe to create macros that execute one or more commands.

You can write a batch file that executes Microsoft Word.

cascading menu

Do not use except in content for software developers that discusses creating menus, and only if you cannot use *submenu* in the context, or if *cascading menu* appears in the user interface or the application programming interface. See also *Ribbons, menus, toolbars*; *submenu*.

cascading style sheets

Spell out unless the abbreviation is familiar to your audience. See also *style sheet*.

catalog

Use instead of *catalogue*.

category axis

In spreadsheet programs, refers to the (usually) horizontal axis in charts and graphs that shows the categories being measured or compared. For clarity, refer to it as the *category (x) axis* on first mention. On subsequent mention, you can use *x-axis*. You can also use *horizontal (x) axis* in content for novice computer users. See also *value axis*.

caution

Advises users that failure to take or avoid a specified action could result in loss of data.

Precede a caution with the warning symbol.

Warning symbol

CBT

In general, do not use *CBT* and its spelled-out form, *computer-based training*. Use *tutorial* instead. Use *online tutorial* only to distinguish from a printed tutorial.

CBT and *computer-based training* are all right in content for software developers that discusses such things as the **CBTProc** function.

CD

Do not spell out. If you refer to a CD as a *disc*, use the correct spelling.

It is all right to use *CD* by itself as long as either the reference is general or there is no possibility of confusion as to what type of CD is under discussion: audio CD, CD-ROM, CD-R, or CD-RW. When it is necessary to be specific, be specific.

Refer to the drive for a CD as the *CD drive*, not the *CD player*. If you are referring to a specific type of drive, such as a CD-RW drive, use the appropriate name.

Do not use *CD disc*, *CD-ROM disc*, or similarly redundant constructions.

CD case

Use instead of *jewel case*.

CD key

A combination of letters and numbers that identify an individual product license. The CD key is usually found on the back of the product CD case.

Use only when necessary to refer to a key that is specific to a CD. In general, use *product key* instead.

cellular

Refers to the connectivity method in which data is exchanged over the air and not by Wi-Fi or syncing with a computer. It is also all right to use *cellular data network* or *cellular data connection*, depending on the context.

Don't use *cellular phone* or *cell phone* unless you need to call out the cellular technology. Use *mobile phone* or *phone* instead. See also *mobile phone, phone*.

center around

Do not use. Use *center on* instead.

chapter

Use only in reference to content that is written as a book or written both as a book and for online presentation. For content written only as online documentation, use *section, topic, site*, or another appropriate term. See also *article*.

character set

Do not use as a synonym for *code page*. A character set appears on a code page.

chart

Do not use as a verb when referring to entering data for a graphic. Use *plot* instead.

Use the noun *chart* instead of *graph* to refer to graphic representations of data. For example, use *bar chart*, *pie chart*, and *scatter chart*.

chat

Use as an adjective, a noun, or a verb in the context of Internet or intranet chat. Use *voice chat* and *video chat* if necessary to avoid ambiguity.

check

Use *check* or *checked* as an adjective in such phrases as "a check mark" or "a checked command."

Do not use *check* or *uncheck* as a verb meaning to add a check mark to or remove a check mark from a check box. Use *select* and *clear* instead.

Do not use *check* as a noun to mean *check mark*. See also *checked command*.

check box

Two words. Use the identifier *check box*, not just *box*, to refer to a check box. *Box* alone is ambiguous, especially for non-native English speakers.

Use *select* and *clear* with check boxes, not *turn on* and *turn off, mark* and *unmark, check* and *uncheck*, or *select* and *deselect*. See also *Webpage controls, dialog boxes, and property sheets* (Chapter 5).

check in

Do not use as a noun.

Microsoft style

The code management system requires you to check in the changes.

This change requires that you check in your code.

Not Microsoft style

This check in is required.

check mark

Two words.

checked command

A command name on a menu that follows a check mark or a bullet that appears or disappears each time that the user clicks the command or a related command. Checked commands can be either mutually exclusive or independent of each other. For example, document views in Microsoft Word are mutually exclusive. Settings on the **View** menu in Microsoft Excel are independent of each other. In the latter case, it is all right to call them *marked commands*.

Use *turn on* or *turn off* in procedures to refer to activating or deactivating the command, but use *click* as the means of turning it on or off.

Microsoft style

To turn on Outline view

- On the **View** menu, click **Outline**.
- If the **Outline** command is checked, the document is in Outline view.

child folder

Do not use. Use *subfolder* or *subdirectory* instead.

choose

Use *choose* when the user must make a decision, as opposed to selecting (not *picking*) an item from a list to carry out a decision already made.

Microsoft style

If you do not have an Internet account, click **Choose from a list of Internet service providers (ISPs)** and then click **Next**.

If you choose to encrypt only the folder, no files or subfolders contained in the folder are encrypted.

Do not use *choose* as an alternative to *click* or *double-click*. *Choose* does not convey any additional information to those who do not use a mouse, and such users normally understand the equivalent action that they must take when a procedure step says to click. See also *click, select*.

Microsoft style

On the **File** menu, click **Open**.

Not Microsoft style

On the **File** menu, choose **Open**.

clear

Use *clear* as a verb to describe the act of removing a check mark from a check box or removing a tab stop. Do not use *turn off, unmark, uncheck,* or *deselect*. See also *select, Webpage controls, dialog boxes, and property sheets* (Chapter 5).

The antonym of *clear* is *select*.

Microsoft style

Clear the **Mirror margins** check box.

click

In general, use *click* instead of *select* to refer to the user action of issuing a command or setting an option. For exceptions, see **select**.

If a user can set an option so that the user can either use a single click or a double click to perform some action, use the default mode when documenting a feature, and explain the various options.

Do not use *click on* or *click at*. However, you can say "*click in* the window." With this exception, *click* should always be a transitive verb. See also *point to; select; tap: Webpage controls, dialog boxes, and property sheets* (Chapter 5).

> **Note** It is all right to omit "Click **OK**" at the end of a procedure if it is clear that the user must click **OK** to complete the procedure.

Microsoft style

To add or remove a program, click **Start**, click **Control Panel**, and then double-click **Programs and Features**.

clickstream

One word. Do not use in content for a general audience.

clickthrough

One word. Do not use in content for a general audience.

client

In content for a general audience, use *computer* instead of *client*.

In content for a technical audience, use *client* as an adjective to refer only to a computer, object, or program that obtains data or services from a server. You can use *client*, not *client computer*, if it is clear that the context is hardware or software. See also *computer, device, machine, PC*.

Microsoft style

client workstation

client computer

Do not use *client* to refer to a person. Use *customer* instead.

client side

Do not use for a general audience, especially as an adjective. Use *client* instead.

Client side is all right to use when it refers specifically to the client part ("side") of a program or protocol that acts on both a server and a client computer. In general, such usage should be necessary only in content for a technical audience.

If you must use *client-side* as an adjective, hyphenate it. See also *client*.

client/server

Use the slash mark in all instances.

clip art

Two words.

Clipboard

Capitalize when referring to the component in both Windows and Macintosh content. Do not precede with *Windows*. Material is moved or copied *to* the Clipboard, not *onto* it.

close

Use *close* for windows, documents, and dialog boxes. For programs, use *exit*. For network connections, use *end*.

Use *close* to refer to the action a program takes when it has encountered a problem and cannot continue. Do not confuse with *stop responding*, which indicates that the program cannot close itself.

Close button

The box with an × in the upper-right corner of a window that, when clicked, closes the window.

Spell out and capitalize the word *Close* and use the word *button*. *Close* as part of *the* **Close** *button* is always bold. When possible, use an inline graphic of the **Close** button.

Microsoft style

and then click the **Close** button

and then click the **Close** button.

cloud

For technical audiences, the term *cloud computing* typically refers to a specialized, virtual environment that houses applications, data, and/or computing resources in a single location and provides access to those resources over the Internet. For a general audience, cloud computing refers simply to applications and services that are accessed over the Internet, rather than installed on a user's local computer. Define the term or give it context on the first reference, using the definition appropriate for your given audience.

Use *cloud* as an adjective. *Cloud* may be used sparingly as a noun in content for a technical audience or in informal contexts. Do not use *cloud* interchangeably with *Internet* or *web*. When referring specifically to the services provided by Microsoft, refer to *Microsoft cloud services* or *the Microsoft cloud platform* as appropriate.

For more information about referring to cloud computing, see *Cloud computing style (*Chapter 6)

co-

In general, do not hyphenate words beginning with *co-*, such as *coauthor* and *coordinate*, unless it is necessary to avoid confusion. When in doubt, check the *American Heritage Dictionary*, or consult your project style sheet.

code page

Do not use as a synonym for *character set*. A character set appears on a code page.

code point

Two words.

codec

Do not spell out as *compressor/decompressor* or *coder/decoder*. Use only in content for a technical audience or when *codec* appears in the user interface.

collaborate, collaboration, collaborator

It is all right to use *collaborate* and *collaboration* to refer to two or more people who are working on a shared document.

However, do not use *collaborator* to describe a worker in such an environment unless you have no other choice. *Collaborator* is a sensitive term in some countries. Therefore, use a synonym such as *colleague* or *coworker* instead.

color map

Two words. Refers to the color lookup table in a video card.

column format

Use instead of *columnar* or *columnlike*.

COM

As the name of a communications port (also known as serial port), use all uppercase followed by a number, as in *COM1*. As an extension and the indicator of a commercial organization in a URL, use all lowercase preceded with a period, as in *.com file* and *Microsoft.com*.

COM is also an abbreviation for *Component Object Model*. Be sure that the user cannot be confused about what *COM* means in your content.

combo box

Two words. Use in content for a technical audience to describe a box in which the user can select an item from a list or type a value directly in the box. Do not use *combo box* in content for a general audience. Refer to it as a *box* instead, using the label provided in the user interface. See also *Webpage controls, dialog boxes, and property sheets* (Chapter 5).

Use *enter* to indicate that a user can either type an item in the box or click an item in the list.

Microsoft style

In the **Size** box, enter the font size, in points, that you want.

command

In general, use *command* instead of *menu item*, *choice*, or *option* to describe a command on a menu.

In content for software developers about creating elements of the user interface, sometimes *menu item* may be the best term to use. See also *menus*.

command button

To refer to the usually rectangular button that appears in the user interface that carries out a command, use the button label without the words *command* or *button*, especially in procedures. Follow the user interface for capitalization and spelling. If it is important to identify a command button as a button, it is all right to refer to the label and the word *button*, but do not use the word *command*. See also *Webpage controls, dialog boxes, and property sheets* (Chapter 5)

Microsoft style

For information about the dialog box, click the **Help** button.

Not Microsoft style

For information about the dialog box, click the **Help** command button.

The term *command button* is all right to use in programs in which command buttons can be user-defined and created, such as Microsoft Visual Basic .NET and Microsoft Excel 2010.

Microsoft style

In Excel 2010, you can add a command button to automate the printing of a worksheet.

Do not refer to a command button as an *action button* or *push button*. It is all right to say something like "a command button, also known as a push button" if a segment of your users will be more familiar with that term.

command line

Hyphenate as an adjective. See also *command prompt, console.*

Users type commands *at a command prompt*, not *on a command line.*

Microsoft style

command-line parameter

command-line tool

command prompt

Use instead of *C prompt, command-line prompt,* or *system prompt.*

Command prompt refers only to a prompt itself. For example, C:> is a command prompt. Refer to the window in which a command prompt appears as the *Command Prompt window.* Note capitalization.

Do not refer to the Command Prompt window as a *console window* except in content for a technical audience.

Users type commands *at a command prompt*, not *on a command line.* See also *command line, console.*

Microsoft style

At the command prompt, type **certutil -setreg ca**.

Not Microsoft style

On the command line, type **certutil -setreg ca**.

communications port

Use to refer to a computer port that supports asynchronous communication one byte at a time. Spell out on first mention. It is all right to abbreviate as *COM port* on subsequent mention if you are referring specifically to the ports on a computer numbered COM1, COM2, and so on. Ensure that the context does not allow the user to confuse the *COM* in *COM port* with the abbreviation for *Component Object Model.*

It is all right to refer to a communications port as a *serial port.* If you are referring specifically to the COM ports, it is useful, especially for a general audience, to be explicit about the reference.

Microsoft style

Connect the infrared device to a serial port on your computer, and note the serial port number (typically COM1 or COM2).

compact disc

Do not spell out. Use *CD* instead. If you must spell out *compact disc*, it is *disc*, not *disk*. See also *CD*.

C

CompactFlash

Do not abbreviate. A trademark for a data storage specification.

The most common usage of *CompactFlash* is as a modifier for a specific CompactFlash device.

Microsoft style

CompactFlash memory is commonly used in digital cameras.

compare to vs. compare with

Use *compare to* to point out similarities between dissimilar items. Use *compare with* to comment on the similarities or differences between similar items. The use of *compare to*, which is often metaphorical, is generally unnecessary in technical content.

Microsoft style

People have compared a computer to a human brain.

Compared with a Pentium 4 processor, a 386 processor is extremely slow.

compile

All right to use as an adjective, as in "compile time," or as a verb. Do not use as a noun.

Microsoft style

After you save the file, compile your program.

Not Microsoft style

After you save the file, do a compile.

comprise

Do not use unless you have no other choice. *Comprise* has a history of misuse and is misunderstood even by many native English speakers. It means "to include" or "to (metaphorically) embrace." The whole *comprises* or is *composed of* its parts; the parts *compose* or are *comprised in* the whole. *Comprised of* is always incorrect.

The forms of *compose* are generally better understood than those of *comprise*, but synonyms, such as *include* and *contain*, are clearer to most users.

computer

In general, use the most generic term that describes a device. Use *computer* instead of *client*, *server*, *machine*, or *box* for most audiences.

Do not use *PC* except in content that is informal in tone, in UI text where space is constrained, or when referring to a feature or website that includes the term *PC*.

It is all right to use *machine* in content for a technical audience and in content about virtualization to describe both physical machines and virtual machines.

Use *client* or *server* as a synonym for *computer* only if it is clear to the user whether the client or server discussed is hardware or software. Otherwise, use *client computer* or *server computer*. See also *client, device, machine, PC*.

Computer icon

An icon that represents a user's private, local system. To refer to the icon in printed documents, use just *Computer* if the icon is shown. Otherwise, use *the* **Computer** *icon*.

Computer

Microsoft style
Double-click the **Computer** icon.

connect

Do not use *connect* as a synonym for *sign in* or *log on*. Do not use *connect* as a synonym for *map*, as in mapping a drive letter to a shared network folder, even though *disconnect* is the correct term for removing a mapped network drive. See also *log on, log off, logon, logoff; sign in, sign out, sign on, sign up*.

console

Do not use *console window* and *console application* except in content for a technical audience. Use *Command Prompt window* and *command-line program* instead.

Do not use *console* to describe a configuration of Microsoft Management Console (MMC) snap-ins. It is all right to refer to *console trees* and *console panes*.

Do not use *console* as a synonym for *snap-in*. See also *command line, command prompt, snap-in*.

context menu

Do not use *context menu* or *right-click menu* to refer to the menu that appears when a user clicks the right mouse button in certain areas (or "contexts"), such as in a toolbar region. If you must refer to this menu by name, use *shortcut menu* instead.

Microsoft style
Use Alt+Spacebar to display the shortcut menu for the active window.

In procedures, use *shortcut menu* only if doing so would help the customer locate the item in the user interface.

Microsoft style
Right-click the selected text, and then click **Copy.** (Preferred)

Right-click the selected text, and then click **Copy** on the shortcut menu.

It is all right to use *context menu* in content for software developers, but make clear that it refers to the shortcut menu. See also *pop-up*.

Microsoft style
The **Control.ContextMenu** property gets or sets the shortcut menu associated with the control.

context-sensitive

Always hyphenate.

Microsoft style

The Add Total command is context-sensitive.

The new context-sensitive command bar is fully customizable.

contiguous selection

Do not use. This term may be unfamiliar to many users. Use *multiple selection* instead. If it is important to emphasize that all the selected items are adjacent to each other, use *adjacent selection*. See also *multiple selection*.

control

In content for a general audience, do not use *control* to refer to a user interface object such as a text box, a check box, or a list box. It is all right to use *control* to refer to adding a user-defined control in a program such as Microsoft Office 2010.

In almost all other context, it is all right to use *control*.

Microsoft style

In the **Font** list, click the font that you want to use.

On the **Developer** tab in Word 2010, in the **Controls** group, click the **Rich Text** control or the **Text** control.

What can I control with Parental Controls in Windows 7?

Not Microsoft style

In the **Font** list box control, click the font that you want to use.

control-menu box

Use to describe the button at the far left on the title bar in Windows-based programs. This box displays the program icon in the main window and the generic window icon in secondary windows other than message boxes and dialog boxes. Do not refer to this icon and the menu that it opens by name. If such a reference is necessary, refer to the *<Program Name> icon* or the *<title bar> shortcut menu*.

Control-menu box

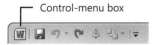

copy

Do not use to mean *photocopy*.

corrupted

Use to describe a file or data that has been damaged. Do not use *corrupt* to describe this condition.

Microsoft style

The file may be corrupted.

Not Microsoft style

The file may be corrupt.

country/region

Use instead of *country* in list headings and forms and in other contexts where specific reference may include named disputed territories.

You do not have to replace *country* with *country/region* in general discussion.

Microsoft style

This product is not available in all countries.

In the **Country/Region** box, enter your country/region.

crash

Do not use in content for a general audience unless you have no other choice.

Use *fail* for disks or *stop responding* for programs or the operating system. In content for a technical audience, *crash* may be the best word in certain circumstances, but avoid whenever possible. See also *blue screen, bluescreen*.

criteria

Plural of *criterion*. It is all right to use *criteria* in database documentation to refer to one or more instructions about records.

critical process monitor

Do not abbreviate.

critical section object

Do not hyphenate.

critical update

Use to describe a broadly released fix for a specific problem addressing a critical bug that is not security-related. Use *update* to describe a fix for a noncritical bug that is not security-related. See also *out-of-band release terminology* (Chapter 6), *update*.

current drive

Use instead of *current disk drive*.

current folder

Use to refer to the folder that the user is currently looking at, such as the Temp folder, or the folder that the user is saving something to, such as the folder that appears in the **Save in** box in the **Save As** dialog box. Do not use *active* or *open* in this context. See also *active vs. current*.

current window

Do not use. Use *active window* or *open window* instead. See also *active vs. current*.

cursor

Use to describe the point at which text or graphics will be inserted. Do not use as a synonym for *pointer*. See also *insertion point, pointer*.

cut

Do not use *cut* as a verb, even when referring to the **Cut** command. Use *delete* instead.

Do not use *cut* as an imperative in procedures involving either the **Cut** or **Delete** command. Use *delete* instead.

Do not use *cut* as a noun to refer to the action of the **Delete** command. Use *deletion* instead.

Do not use *cut-and-replace* or *cut-and-paste* as a noun or as a verb. See also *cut-and-paste*.

Microsoft style

Use the **Cut** command to delete the selected text.

Select the text you want to delete, and then click **Cut**.

Not Microsoft style

Cut the selected text.

Cut-and-paste the selected text.

Do a cut-and-paste on the second paragraph.

Do not use the verb *cut* to describe temporarily moving text to the Clipboard. Use *copy* or *move* instead.

Microsoft style

Use the **Cut** command to move the selected text to the Clipboard.

Not Microsoft style

Cut the selected text to the Clipboard.

cut-and-paste

Use only as an adjective.

Do not use as a noun phrase, with or without hyphens.

Do not use *cut and paste* as a verb phrase. The correct verb for the action of the **Cut** command is *delete*. Deleting is one act and pasting another, so *cut and paste* or *delete and paste* can be confusing.

Microsoft style

Perform a cut-and-paste operation.

In Notepad, you can delete text from one place and paste it somewhere else.

Not Microsoft style

Do a cut-and-paste.

In Notepad, you can cut and paste text.

In Notepad, you can delete and paste text.

D

data

Use as either singular or plural in meaning but always with a singular verb. That is, always use "the data is" (or another appropriate verb) whether you mean a collection of facts (plural) or information (singular). If you want to emphasize that something is plural, rewrite to use a term such as *facts* or *numbers*.

Do not use *datum* or *data are*. They are etymologically correct, but some users may not recognize *datum*, or they may see both *datum* and *data are* as pretentious.

Microsoft style

The data shows that 95% of the users prefer a graphical interface.

The data gathered so far is incomplete.

These facts contradict the earlier data.

data binding

Two words.

data center vs. datacenter

Two words except in product names such as Microsoft® Windows Server™ 2008, Datacenter Edition.

data modem

Two words. A modem that can both send and receive serial data. A data/fax modem can also send and receive faxes.

data record

Use *record* instead. *Data* in this phrase is superfluous.

database

One word both as an adjective and as a noun.

datagram

One word. Refers to one packet, or unit, of information sent through a packet-switching network.

datum

Do not use. See *data*.

deaf or hard of hearing

Use this phrase in its entirety ("deaf or hard of hearing") in accessibility information or to refer to people who are deaf. Hyphenate *hard-of-hearing* only if it precedes the noun it modifies. If space is limited, use *deaf* by itself. See also Chapter 4, "Accessible Content"

Microsoft style

The ShowSounds feature is primarily intended for deaf or hard-of-hearing customers.

People who are deaf or hard of hearing can configure Windows to use visual cues in place of sounds.

Do not use *hearing-impaired*.

debug

Debug is a valid technical term in content for software developers. Do not use *debug* in any context as a synonym for *troubleshoot*. Use *troubleshoot* or a more accurate word or phrase instead.

deceptive software

Do not use. See *unwanted software*. See also *security*.

decrement

Use as a verb only in content for a technical audience to refer specifically to decreasing an integer count by one. Do not use as a synonym for *decrease*.

In content for a technical audience, it is also all right to use *decrement* as an adjective ("the decrement operator") and as a noun ("If the result of the decrement is 0, then **Decrement** returns 0."

default

Do not use *default* as a verb unless you have no other choice. It is jargon. *Default* is all right to use as a noun or as an adjective.

Microsoft style

If you do not select a template, Word uses Normal.dot by default.

This value specifies the number of sheets to add. The default is one sheet.

Not Microsoft style

If you do not select a template, Word defaults to Normal.dot.

This value specifies the number of sheets to add. If you omit a value, the program defaults to one sheet.

definition update

Use to describe a broadly released and frequent software update that contains additions to a product's definition database. See also *out-of-band release terminology* (Chapter 6).

defragment

As a verb, use to refer to the action of the Disk Defragmenter program or similar programs. Do not use *defrag*.

Microsoft style

To defragment your files and speed up performance, use Disk Defragmenter frequently.

deinstall

Do not use unless *deinstall* appears in the user interface or the application programming interface. If *deinstall* does appear in the product interface, refer to the user action as *removing*. See also *uninstall*.

delete

As a verb, use *delete* to refer to actions that the **Delete** command takes, such as moving files to the **Recycle Bin** and moving items in Microsoft Outlook to the Deleted Items folder. You can use *delete* to describe these actions even if the user arrives at them by some other way, such as by dragging a file to the **Recycle Bin**.

Use *delete* to refer to actions that result from pressing the Delete or Backspace key on the computer, such as deleting selected text.

Do not use *delete* as a synonym for *remove*. Do not use *cut* or *erase* as a synonym for *delete*. See also *cut, erase, remove*.

Microsoft style

Delete the second paragraph.

Delete MyFile.txt from the Windows folder.

Remove the **Size** column from the Inbox.

demilitarized zone

Do not use as a technical term except on first mention, in which case use *perimeter network (also known as DMZ, demilitarized zone, and screened subnet)*. On subsequent mention, use *perimeter network*. See also *perimeter network*.

deprecated

Refers to a program or feature that is obsolete and in the process of being phased out, usually in favor of a specific replacement. Deprecated features can linger on for many years to support compatibility across product versions.

It is all right to use *deprecated* in content for a technical audience. In content for a general audience, use *obsolete*, *obsolescent*, or another appropriate word.

depress

Do not use. Use *press* for the action of pushing down a key instead. Also do not use *depressed* as a description for an indented toolbar button unless you have no other choice. See also *Key names* (Chapter 5).

deselect

Do not use. In general, use *cancel the selection*. For check boxes, use *clear*.

Designer

Name for a window with a design surface (whether it has one or more views). See also *editor*.

Microsoft style

HTML Designer has two views: Design and HTML.

Web Forms Designer has two views: Design and HTML.

XML Designer has two views: Schema and Source.

desire

Do not use. Use *want* instead.

desktop

Refers to the work area on the screen that is provided by the operating system. It has the appearance of a physical desktop.

Refer to the desktop as *client area* only in content for a technical audience and only if necessary.

Desktop is also a valid term for a computer. However, use *desktop* in this sense only if you need to differentiate the computer from a laptop or server computer. See also *laptop, workspace*.

destination

General term for an end point in some user or program actions, such as the location reached when a user clicks a hyperlink, the folder to which a file is copied or moved, or the document in which a linked or embedded object is stored. Do not use *target* as a synonym.

Destination is all right to use in content for any audience. However, use a more precise term such as *website* or *folder* if you can, and use *destination* as a modifier only if necessary for clarity.

destination disk, destination drive, destination file

Use instead of *target disk, target drive*, or *target file*. However, do not use any of these terms if you can use more specific language, such as "drag the folder to the icon for drive D."

device

Refers to any machine or component that can be attached, physically or wirelessly, to a network or computer. Examples of devices include cameras, disk drives, printers, mice, joysticks, MP3 players, and phones.

In general, use the most generic term that describes a particular device, such as *phone* or *mouse*. Use *device* when you need to refer generically to a variety or group of devices.

device driver

Use *device driver* only in the context of a driver development kit (DDK) or in a general discussion about installing peripheral devices. If you are referring to a driver for a specific device, refer to the driver for that device, such as *mouse driver* or *printer driver*.

In content for a general audience, define *driver* on first mention, and if your content has a glossary, add *driver* to the glossary.

dezoom

Do not use. Use *zoom out* instead.

dialog

Do not use as an abbreviation for *dialog box*. Do not spell as *dialogue* in the context of a dialog box. *Dialog* is all right to use in other contexts, especially in content for a technical audience.

dialog box

Always call this type of box a *dialog box*, not just *dialog*. Do not call it a *pop-up window*.

In content for all audiences except software developers, do not shorten *dialog box* to *dialog* even as a modifier.

Do not hyphenate *dialog box* if you use it as a modifier.

In content for software developers, it is all right, but not required, to use *dialog* by itself as a modifier. See also *Webpage controls, dialog boxes, and property sheets* (Chapter 5).

Microsoft style (all audiences)

dialog box option

dialog box title

Microsoft style (software developer content)

dialog class

dialog editor

dialog object

dial-up

Use only as an adjective, not as a noun or as a verb. Always hyphenate.

As an adjective, it defines a line, a modem, or a networking connection. It refers to a service. Do not use as a noun ("a dial up"). It is ambiguous.

Use *dial* as the verb to refer to placing a call or using a dial-up device.

different

Do not use *different* to mean *many* or *various*.

In comparisons, use *different from* in most cases. Use *different than* only when *than* is followed by a clause. Do not use *different to*.

Microsoft style

The result of the first calculation is different from the result of the second.

If the result is different from the result that you expected, verify that you entered your data correctly.

Not Microsoft style

The result of the first calculation is different than the result of the second.

Pay particular attention to parallelism in comparative statements that use *different*. It is very easy to make a comparison that you did not intend.

Microsoft style

The result of the first calculation is different from that of the second.

Not Microsoft style

The result of the first calculation is different from the second.

Constructions that use *different than* are often difficult to read, even if they are grammatically correct. They work best when the clauses on both sides of the comparison are balanced and parallel. If you cannot achieve such balance and parallelism, consider rewriting the sentence.

Microsoft style

The regional setting does not match the language of the localized version of the operating system.

The regional setting is different than the language of the localized version of the operating system.

dimmed

Use *unavailable* to refer to commands and options that are in an unusable state, but use *dimmed* instead of *grayed* to describe the appearance of an unavailable command or option. Use *shaded* to describe the appearance of check boxes that represent a mixture of settings. Also, use *appears dimmed*, not *is dimmed*. See also *gray, grayed; shaded.*

Microsoft style

If the option appears dimmed, it is unavailable.

Not Microsoft style

If the option is grayed, it is unavailable.

direction keys

Do not use. Use *arrow keys* instead. See also *Key names* (Chapter 5).

directory

In general, limit use of the word *directory* to references to the structure of the file system. Use *folder* to refer to the visual representation or object in the interface. You can include *directory* as a synonym for *folder* in indexes and search topics. See also *folder.*

directory icon

Do not use. This term is no longer applicable. Use *folder icon*, if necessary.

disable

All right to use in content for software developers in the sense of making a command or function unavailable.

Do not use in other content. Use *make unavailable* or something similar. See also *dimmed.*

disabled

Do not refer to people with disabilities as *disabled*. See *Chapter 4, "Accessible content".*

disc

Use only to refer to a CD or DVD. See also *CD, DVD, disk.*

discreet vs. discrete

Be sure to use these words correctly. *Discreet* means "showing good judgment" or "modest." *Discrete* means "separate" or "distinct" and is more likely to appear in technical content.

disjoint selection

Do not use except in content for a technical audience, and only if the term appears in the user interface or application programming interface. If you must use a term for selected items that do not touch each other, use *multiple selection*, or refer to the specific nonadjacent items instead. See also *multiple selection, nonadjacent selection.*

disk

In general, use *disk* to refer to both hard disks and floppy disks.

Unless necessary, use just *disk*, not *hard disk, floppy disk*, or *3.5-inch disk*. Do not use fractions or symbols when specifying a disk. Use decimals instead, and spell out *inch*.

Microsoft style
3.5-inch disk

Do not use *diskette, fixed disk, hard drive*, or *internal drive*. Do not use *hard disk system* or *floppy disk system*. Refer to the computer specifications instead.

In general, do not use *disk* in possessive constructions such as *disk's contents* or *disk's name*. Use *disk contents* or *disk name* instead.

When naming specific disks, use the disk names as they appear on the labels.

Microsoft style
The utilities disk
Disk 1

> **Note** Do not use *disk* to refer to a compact disc or DVD.

disk resource

Use to refer to a disk or part of a disk shared on a server.

disk space

Use instead of *storage* or *memory* to refer to available capacity on a disk. See also *storage, storage device*.

diskette

Do not use. Use *disk* instead. See also *disk*.

display

Use as a noun to refer generically to the visual output device and its technology, such as a flat-panel display. Use *screen* to refer to the graphic portion of a monitor.

Do not use *display* as an intransitive verb. See also *appears, displays*.

Microsoft style
The program displays the document.

You can filter the data that is displayed in a control.

Not Microsoft style
The document displays.

display adapter, display driver

Do not use. Use *video card* and *video driver* instead.

DNS

Spell out as *Domain Name System*, not *Domain Name Server*. Use to refer to the DNS networking protocol or to the Windows feature that implements the protocol. When discussing the DNS networking protocol, spell out *Domain Name System* on first mention. When discussing the Windows DNS feature, do not spell out *DNS*.

The Windows feature is *DNS*, not *DNS Server* or *Microsoft DNS Server*. If you must emphasize that you are referring to the Windows feature and not to the networking protocol, mention Windows, as in "DNS in Windows Server 2003" or "Windows Server 2008 DNS."

Do not use *dynamic DNS* or *DDNS*.

A DNS server (lowercase *s*) is a computer that is running DNS server software.

A DNS client (lowercase *c*) is a client of a DNS server.

DNS Server (capital *s*) is the Windows service that appears in the Computer Management console. In general, refer to the service only in a discussion about stopping and starting it.

DNS Client (capital *c*) is the Windows service that appears in the Computer Management console. In general, refer to the service only in a discussion about stopping and starting it.

document

You can use *document* generically to refer to any kind of item within a folder that can be edited, but it's clearer to restrict its use to Word, WordPad, and text documents. Use the specific term for "documents" in other programs. For example, say "an Excel *worksheet*," "a PowerPoint *presentation*," and "an Access *database*."

Use *file* for more general uses, such as *file management* or *file structure*.

Microsoft style

These demos will help you learn how to manage files and folders, print your documents, and use a network.

domain

Because *domain* has different meanings in database design, Windows, and Internet addresses, define the use or ensure that the context is clear. Always consult your project style sheet.

In database design, a domain is the set of valid values for a particular attribute.

In Windows, a domain is a collection of computers sharing a common database and security policy.

On the Internet, the *top-level domain* (TLD) is the last part of the address, following the dot. It identifies the type of entity owning the address, such as .com for commercial entities, or the country where the web address is located, such as .ca for Canada. The *domain* includes the top-level domain and the part of the address before the dot. For example, microsoft.com is the domain of the address www.microsoft.com.

done

Do not use *when you are done*. It's colloquial. Use *when you have finished* instead.

DOS

Don't spell out. Avoid except as *MS-DOS*.

dot-com

Do not use as a verb or noun. Always hyphenate as an adjective to reference web-based business issues. Do not capitalize the letter following the hyphen in contexts that require title capitalization.

Microsoft style

dot-com company

dot-com world

dot-com executive

dot-com stocks

dot-com sector

dot-com business

Do not use *dotcom*, *dot com*, *dot.com*, *.com*, or any other variation.

dotted rectangle

Use this term only if you are graphically describing the element that a user drags to select a region on the screen. Otherwise, use *bounding outline* (not *marquee*) instead. See also *bounding outline*.

double buffering

Two words as a noun. Hyphenate as an adjective. Do not use as a verb. Use a phrase such as *uses double buffering* instead.

Refers to the use of two temporary storage areas.

double word

Two words. Refers to a unit of data consisting of two contiguous words (bytes). DWORD is used in code.

double-click, double-clicking

Always hyphenate. Use instead of *select* and *choose* when referring to a mouse action. Do not use *double-click on*. See also *click*.

downgrade

Use this word only if absolutely necessary to express the concepts of downgrade rights, downgrading licenses, downgrading products, downgrading files, and others. Use only with an audience that would understand your use of the word in these contexts.

downlevel

Do not use. If possible, use a more precise definition of what you mean to say. Otherwise, use *earlier versions* or a similar phrase. If you are referring to versions of third-party software as well, rewrite to make this clear.

download

As a transitive verb, use *download* to describe the process of intentionally transferring data, a file, or a program to the local computer, system, or device. Do not use *download* as an intransitive verb. If necessary for the context, use the passive *is downloaded*. Do not use *downloaded* to describe the process of opening, viewing, or switching to a webpage, even though some graphics or HTML files may be transferred to the user's hard disk as a result.

As a noun, *download* is all right to use to refer to data, a file, or a program that is available for downloading or that has been downloaded.

Because *download* can be used as a noun or as a verb, be careful that the context and sentence structure make your meaning unambiguous.

Microsoft style

Design your webpage so that a user can review part of the page while your computer downloads the rest.

Not Microsoft style

Design your webpage so that a user can review part of the page while the rest downloads.

drag

Traditionally, *drag* has been used to refer to an action performed with a mouse to select or move text or other content. Although the use of *drag* remains the same in this context, the term is also now used to describe contact gestures. See also *Mouse terminology* (Chapter 5).

Microsoft style

Drag the item to where you want it.

Not Microsoft style

Move your finger on the screen to drag the item to where you want it.

Do not use *click and drag* or *drag and drop*. With a traditional mouse, the click action includes releasing the mouse button, and to drag an item, the user must hold the button down. *Press and drag* is all right to use for novice computer users.

drag-and-drop

Use only as an adjective, not as a noun or as a verb. The action of dragging includes dropping the element in place.

It is all right to use *drag-and-drop* as an adjective to describe moving objects between windows and programs or to describe behavior a programmer wants to put in a program. In these cases, use a phrase such as "drag-and-drop editing" or "drag-and-drop feature."

Microsoft style

Moving files is an easy drag-and-drop operation.

You can drag the folder to drive D.

You can move the folder to drive D using a drag-and-drop operation.

Not Microsoft style

You can drag and drop the folder in drive D.

You can use drag-and-drop to move the folder to drive D.

Drag the information from Microsoft Excel and drop it in a Word document.

drive

Distinguish among types of disks and disk drives only when necessary to avoid confusion. Make it clear whether you are talking about a disk or its associated drive.

Use these conventions when referring to drives:

- Use *drive* as the general term to refer to any type of device—internal or external, physical or virtual—that reads or writes to storage media, such as a hard drive, CD drive, DVD drive, floppy disk drive, USB flash drive, or any other removable storage device.

- Use *hard drive* to refer to a storage device—internal or external, movable or solid state—for a PC on which files and programs are typically stored. Use this term when you don't need to distinguish from other hard drive types.

- Use *hard disk drive* only when you need to mention the physical location or physical state of the hard drive, or when you need to distinguish from other hard drive types, such as solid-state drives. Use *hard disk* to refer to the disk itself.

- Use *current drive*, not *current disk drive* or *active drive*.

- Use *drive C*, not *drive C:*, *drive C>*, or *C: drive*.

- Use *network drive* to refer to a logical network drive name, such as *network drive X*.

- Use *solid-state drive* (SSD) to refer to a storage device that uses integrated circuits, or microchips, instead of a hard disk. Use only to distinguish from other hard drive types

Because Macintosh drives do not have names, it is all right in introductory content about Macintosh computers to describe a drive to be consistent with Macintosh documentation.

Microsoft style

If you have two disk drives, use the one on the right.

Do not tell users to "close the drive" unless you are writing a section introducing computers.

drive name

Use instead of *drive specification, designator,* or *designation*.

drop-down

Use only if necessary to describe how an item such as a menu works or what it looks like.

Drop-down as an adjective is all right to use in content for software developers if necessary to describe the type of item. For example, *drop-down* can be used to describe a *drop-down arrow*, a *drop-down combo box*, or a *drop-down list box*.

Do not use *drop down* as a noun to mean a *menu* or a *list*. Do not use *drop down* as a verb to describe clicking a menu or downloading a file from the Internet. See also *Webpage controls, dialog boxes, property sheets* (Chapter 5).

DVD

Do not spell out *DVD*. If you refer to a DVD as a *disc*, use the correct spelling.

It is all right to use *DVD* by itself as long as either the reference is general or there is no possibility of confusion as to what type of DVD is under discussion: video DVD, audio DVD, DVD-ROM, DVD-R, DVD-RAM, or DVD-RW. Otherwise, be specific.

Refer to the drive for a DVD as the *DVD drive*, not the *DVD player*. If you are referring to a specific type of drive, such as a DVD-RW drive, use the appropriate name.

Do not use *DVD disc*, *DVD-ROM disc*, or similar constructions.

dynamic-link library

Spell out on first mention unless you are positive that your audience knows the term. On subsequent mention, use the abbreviation *DLL*. Use lowercase (.dll) when referring to the file name extension.

Do not use *dynalink*.

dynamic service capacity

Do not use. Use *elastic service capacity* instead. See also *Cloud computing style* (Chapter 6), *elastic service capacity*.

E

e.g.

Abbreviation for *exempli gratia*, meaning *for example*. Do not use. Use *for example* instead.

earlier

Use *earlier*, *preceding*, or *previous* instead of *above* to mean earlier in a piece of content, but only if you cannot use a hyperlink, which is preferred.

Use *or earlier* or *previous* instead of *or lower* to refer to all versions of a product that precede a particular release if the statement is accurate for all preceding releases. For example, do not use "Windows 7 and earlier" unless the statement is accurate for Windows 1.0. See also *cross-references*, *later*, *version identifiers*.

Microsoft style (when the statement applies to all previous versions)
You can open files created in previous versions of Microsoft Visio.

e-book

Use *e-book* to refer to electronic books.

Use *E-book* at the beginning of a sentence or a heading. In contexts that require title capitalization, use *E-Book*.

e-commerce

Use *E-commerce* at the beginning of a sentence or a heading. In contexts that require title capitalization, use *E-Commerce*.

edit

Because the term can be confused with the **Edit** menu, do not use to refer to making changes in a document unless you have no other choice. Use *change* or *modify* instead.

Editor

Naming convention for a window that is a code or text editor only. See also *Designer*.

Microsoft style

CSS Editor

Code Editor

edutainment

Do not use. It's marketing jargon to refer to educational software, usually multimedia or web-based, that purports to entertain while it educates.

e-form

Spell out as *electronic form* on first mention if necessary for your users. Use *E-form* at the beginning of a sentence or a heading. In contexts that require title capitalization, use *E-Form*.

either/or

Do not use. Fill out the construction, as in "you can either close the document or exit the program."

elastic service capacity

The flexible allocation of computing resources over the Internet as demand changes. Define on first mention for audiences that may not be familiar with the concept.

e-learning

Any educational experience delivered electronically to the learner by means of an intranet, CD-ROM, interactive television, satellite broadcast, the Internet, or other technologies.

Use *E-learning* at the beginning of a sentence or a heading. In contexts that require title capitalization, use *E-Learning*.

ellipsis button

The *ellipsis button* has been called by a variety of names including the **Browse** button, the **Build** button, and the **Properties** button, depending on the result of clicking the button. On first mention, provide a graphic of the button, if only (...). On subsequent mention, use the graphic of the ellipsis button rather than the words. When possible, use a picture of the button rather than words. Do not capitalize *ellipsis* when used as a button name.

email

Do not use as a verb. Use *send* instead.

Use *email* to refer generically to an electronic mail program or to refer collectively to email messages. After you have established the context of electronic mail, it is all right to use *mail* instead of *email*.

Microsoft style

Check your email for messages.

Scroll through your email to find the message you want to read.

You have new mail.

Use *email message* or *message* to refer to an individual piece of email. Do not use *email* as a synonym for *message*. If you use *message* by itself, ensure that the context makes clear that you are not referring to instant messaging.

Microsoft style

Send us an email message with your comments.

You have two new messages.

Not Microsoft style

Send us an email with your comments.

Email us with your comments.

You have two new emails.

Use *Email* at the beginning of a sentence and heading.

embed

Use instead of *imbed*, which is a variant spelling.

enable, enabled

Do not use to refer to things that a program makes easy or possible for the user if you can use *you can* instead. *Enable* can lead to weak sentences in which the most important fact is buried in an infinitive phrase. See also *allow, can vs. may.*

Microsoft style

With Microsoft Word 2010, you can save files in HTML format.

Not Microsoft style

Microsoft Word 2010 enables you to save files in HTML format.

In content for a general audience, do not use *enable* with reference to commands or other program features. Use *make available*, *turn on*, or something similar, or rewrite the sentence.

Microsoft style

To turn on change tracking, click the **Tools** menu, and then click **Track Changes**.

To track changes, click the **Tools** menu, and then click **Track Changes**.

Not Microsoft style

To enable change tracking, click the **Tools** menu, and then click **Track Changes**.

In content for a technical audience, it is all right to speak of a feature or function as *enabled*. It is also all right to use *enables the user* when it is necessary to refer to the end user in the third person.

end

Use to refer to stopping communications and network connections. Use *exit* for programs.

Microsoft style

To end your server connection, on the **Tools** menu, click **Disconnect Network Drive**.

end user, end-user

In general, do not use. Use *user, customer,* or *you* instead.

It is all right to use *end user* in content for software developers to distinguish the developer from the user of the developer's program. It is all right to use *end user* in documentation for information technology professionals to distinguish the system administrator from the users of computers that the administrator is responsible for.

Use *end user* as a noun, and use *end-user* as an adjective.

End-User License Agreement

Do not use. Use *Microsoft Software License Terms*. See also *Microsoft Software License Terms, license terms.*

endline

One word.

endpoint

One word. In graphics programs, an endpoint is the beginning or end of a line segment. In content for software developers, an endpoint is a hardware port or a named pipe that a server program monitors for remote procedure calls from clients.

ensure

In common English usage, *ensure, insure,* and *assure* are interchangeable in many situations. To provide consistency and to improve readability worldwide, Microsoft style makes these distinctions:

- Use *ensure* to mean *to make sure* or *to guarantee.*

- Use *insure* to mean *to provide insurance.*

- Use *assure* to mean *to state positively* or *to make confident.*

enter

Do not use as a synonym for *type* except to indicate that a user can interact with the UI by multiple methods, such as either typing text or clicking a selection from a list.

Microsoft style

In the **Password** box, type your password.

In the **Font Size** box, enter the font size you want to use.

Not Microsoft style

In the **Password** box, enter your password.

enterprise

All right to use in client/server content to mean a *large company* or *corporation.* Use as an adjective if possible, as in *enterprise computing* or *enterprise networking* rather than as a noun to mean *corporation.* Do not use in content for a general audience unless you have no other choice.

entry

Do not use as a synonym for *topic* in reference documentation.

entry field

In general, do not use to refer to a text-entry field. Refer to the box by its label. If you must use a descriptor, use *box* instead of *entry field* or *field*.

It is all right to use *entry field* in a database context. See also *text box*.

environment variable

Use instead of *environment setting* or *environment string*.

erase

Do not use as a synonym for *delete*. It is all right to use *erase* for specialized purposes when the program requires it, as in Paint.

et al.

Abbreviation for *et alii*, meaning "and others." Do not use except in a text reference citation of three or more authors. Use *and others* instead.

etc.

Abbreviation for *et cetera*, meaning "and the rest." Do not use *etc.* except in situations where space is too limited for an alternative, such as on a button label. See also *and so on*.

EULA

Do not use. Use *Microsoft Software License Terms*. See also *Microsoft Software License Terms*, *license terms*.

euro

When referring to the currency, use lowercase. The plural of *euro* is *euros*. A euro is divided into 100 *cents*.

The euro symbol is €. The HTML code for the euro symbol is *€*. To type the euro symbol, press Alt+0128 on the numeric keypad.

When expressing an amount in euros and cents in U.S. content, use a decimal point as the delimiter. Different localities may use a decimal point or a comma, as appropriate.

In U.S. content, place the euro symbol in front of the amount. Different localities may place the euro symbol differently, as appropriate.

Microsoft style

€3.50

Use *supports the euro currency standard* rather than *euro-compatible* or *euro-ready*, both of which are best avoided.

Use the following phrases to refer to countries that have adopted the euro as their currency:

- European Union (EU) members trading in euros

E

- European Union (EU) members that have adopted the euro

- euro nations

- members of the Economic and Monetary Union (EMU)

Use references to the EMU cautiously. Many users may be unfamiliar with the organization.

> **Note** On subsequent mention, it is all right to use EU and EMU as abbreviations. It is all right to refer to EU members as EU member states and to EMU members as EMU member states.

It is all right to use *non-euro nations* to refer to EU member states that have not adopted the euro as their currency.

The terms *euroland* and *eurozone* are all right on websites where an informal tone is appropriate. Do not use in product documentation and other formal contexts, especially if the content will be localized.

e-words

In general, do not form new words with *e-* (for *electronic*). Some words that may be appropriate in certain circumstances are *e-commerce* and *e-form*.

Use lowercase for the *e* in body text, and capitalize the *e* at the beginning of a sentence or a heading. The letter following the hyphen is capitalized only in contexts that require title capitalization.

Microsoft style (beginning of sentence)
E-commerce is a very lucrative business model.

Microsoft style (title capitalization)
How to Succeed at E-Commerce

International considerations
E-words that are not in major dictionaries may cause confusion for the worldwide audience and may lead to mistranslation in machine-translated content.

executable file

A file with an .exe or .com extension.

Use *executable file* only in content for a technical audience. In content for a general audience, use *program file* instead.

Use *executable* and *.exe* as adjectives only, never as nouns. Use the indefinite article *an*, not *a*, with .exe, as in "an .exe file."

Microsoft style
an executable program

the .exe file

Not Microsoft style
an executable

the .exe

execute

Do not use *execute* in content for a general audience except to follow the user interface. Use *run* instead. If the user interface includes *execute*, the user or program action is still *run*. Always use *run* in the context of macros and queries.

Microsoft style

To run the program, click **Execute**.

You can temporarily stop Disk Defragmenter so that you can run other programs at full speed.

Not Microsoft style

You can temporarily stop Disk Defragmenter so that you can execute other programs at full speed.

Execute is all right to use in content for a technical audience, especially in the passive voice, because it has become ingrained. However, *run* is preferable when it does not cause any loss of meaning.

Microsoft style

Commands are run in the order in which they are listed in the file. (Preferred)

Commands are executed in the order in which they are listed in the file.

Execution is all right to use in technical content when there is no valid alternative.

Microsoft style

A thread is the basic unit of program execution.

exit

Use to refer to closing a program. Do not use to refer to closing a document or a window. Do not use to refer to switching from one program, document, or window to another. See also *close, quit*.

> **Note** In some circumstances, the **Close** button and the **Close** command function like the **Exit** command. Refer to the user interface elements by their correct names, but if the user is exiting the program, use *exit* to describe this action.

Microsoft style

When you are finished, close all your documents and exit Word.

To switch to the last open program or document, press Alt+Tab.

You can click the **Close** button to exit Outlook.

Not Microsoft style

When you are finished, exit all your documents and exit Word.

To exit the active window, click anywhere outside it.

You can click the **Close** button to close Outlook.

expand, collapse

Use to describe the functionality that a user can use to see more or fewer subentries in a folder or outline structure. A plus sign next to a folder indicates that it can be expanded to show more folders. A minus sign indicates that it can be collapsed to hide folders. Some programs use symbols other than a plus or a minus sign. For example, Windows 7 uses a blank right-pointing arrow to indicate a collapsed folder and a darkened down-pointing arrow to indicate an expanded folder.

expose

Do not use in the context of the user interface. Use a term such as *make available* or *display* instead.

Expose is acceptable in the context of object-oriented programming technologies such as the Component Object Model (COM), in which it means to make an object's services available to clients.

extend

In the sense of extending a selection, use instead of *grow*.

extension, file name extension

Use instead of *file extension*. For example, say "the .bak extension" or "the .bak file name extension." See also *File names and extensions* (Chapter 6).

e-zine, webzine

Do not use except to connote an underground-type of electronic magazine. It is all right to use *webzine* to refer to mainstream magazines such as *Slate* or *eWEEK* that are on the web, but it is better to call them *electronic magazines* or, if the electronic context is clear, just *magazines*. Use *E-zine* at the beginning of a sentence or heading. In contexts that require title capitalization, use *E-Zine*.

F

facsimile

Do not use to refer to the kind of document sent through a fax machine. Use *fax* instead. Use *facsimile* only to refer to an exact reproduction of something else. See also *fax*.

fail

In content for a general audience, use only to refer to disks and other hardware. Use *stop responding* to refer to programs or the operating system.

It is all right to use *fail* in content for a technical audience when necessary to describe an error condition. For example, E_FAIL is a common return value in COM programs, and it is logical to say that a function that returns E_FAIL has failed to do something or other.

Do not use *crash* in content for a general audience unless you have no other choice. In content for a technical audience, *crash* may be the best word in certain circumstances, but avoid whenever possible. See also *crash*.

Microsoft style

Backing up your files safeguards them against loss if your hard disk fails.

FALSE

In general, use all uppercase to refer to a return value in content for software developers. If you are writing about a specific programming language, follow the capitalization used in that language.

family

Use instead of *line* to refer to a series of related Microsoft products or services.

Far East

Do not use. Use *Asia* instead.

far-left, far-right

Do not use. Use *leftmost* or *rightmost* instead. See also *Chapter 4, "Accessible Content."*

Accessibility considerations

Do not use directional terms (left, right, up, down) as the only clue to location unless you have no other choice. Individuals with cognitive impairments may have difficulty interpreting them, as may blind users relying on screen-reading software. A directional term is all right to use if another indication of location, such as *in the **Save As** dialog box*, *on the **Standard** toolbar*, or *in the title bar*, is also included. Directional terms are also all right to use when a sighted user with dyslexia can clearly see a change in the interface as the result of an action, such as a change in the right pane when an option in the left pane is clicked.

fast key

Do not use. Use *shortcut key* instead. See also *Key names*, (Chapter 5)

favorite

Reference in Internet Explorer to a webpage or site the user may want to return to. Favorites can be added to the menu. Corresponds to "bookmark" in other browsers. Use lowercase when referring to a "favorite website" and uppercase when referring to the **Favorites** menu. See also *bookmark*.

Microsoft style

You can add a favorite website to the **Favorites** menu.

You can display your list of favorites at any time by clicking the **Favorites** menu.

fax

Abbreviation for *facsimile*. All right to use as an adjective ("fax machine," "fax transmission"), as a noun ("your fax arrived"), or as a verb ("fax a copy of the order"). Do not use *FAX*.

feature pack

Use to refer to new product functionality that is first distributed outside the context of a product release, and that is usually included in the next full product release. Do not confuse with *service pack* or *update*. See also *out-of-band release terminology* (Chapter 6), *service pack, update.*

field

Do not use to refer to a text-entry box. Refer to the box by its label. If you must use a descriptor, use *box* instead of *field*.

Field is all right to use to refer to Word field codes, in a database context, and in other technically accurate contexts.

Figure

Capitalize when identifying numbered art. In general reference to a figure, use lowercase. See also *Art, captions, and callouts* (Chapter 7).

Microsoft style

Figure 5.2 compares the response times of the two versions.

As the figure shows, computer prices continue to decline.

file

All right to use generically to refer to documents and programs, as well as to units of storage or file management. However, be more specific if possible in referring to a type of file. For example, say "the Word *document*," "your *worksheet*," and "the WordPad *program*."

file attributes

Use lowercase for file attributes such as *hidden*, *system*, *read-only*, and *archive*.

F

file extension

Do not use. Use *extension* or *file name extension* instead.

file name

Two words both as an adjective and as a noun when referring to the name of a file. Do not hyphenate.

Usually one word when referring to a programming term such as the **FileName** property. See also *File names and extensions* (Chapter 6).

Microsoft style

You can set the **FileName** property before opening a dialog box to set an initial file name.

Not Microsoft style

You can set the **File Name** property before opening a dialog box to set an initial filename.

file name extension, extension

Use instead of *file extension*. See also *File names and extensions* (Chapter 6).

finalize

Do not use. Use *finish* or *complete* instead.

find and replace

Microsoft applications use *find* and *replace* as standard names for search and replace features. Do not use the phrase *search and replace*.

Use *find* and *replace* as separate verbs, not as a single verb phrase. Do not use *find and replace* or *find-and-replace* as a noun. Do not use phrases such as "*search* your document." Use "*search through* your document" instead.

Microsoft style

Find the word "gem" and replace it with "diamond."

Search through your document, and replace "cat" with "dog."

Not Microsoft style

Do a find and replace.

Find and replace the word "gem" with the word "diamond."

Do not use the term *global* in reference to finding and replacing unless absolutely necessary. This term may not be clear to all users.

Microsoft style

Click **Replace All** to find all occurrences of the word "gem" and replace them with "diamond."

Replace all instances of the word "gem" with "diamond."

Use *find characters* and *replacement characters* to specify what the user types into a find or replace box.

finished

Use instead of *done* in the clause "when you have finished." "When you are done" is colloquial.

firewall

Do not hyphenate. Refers to a security solution that segregates one portion of a network from another portion, and that allows only authorized network traffic to pass through according to traffic filtering rules. Provide a definition if your audience might be unfamiliar with the term. For more information, see the Microsoft Malware Encyclopedia. See also *security*.

fixed disk

Do not use. Use *hard disk* instead.

flick

Use to refer to the contact gesture of quickly moving one or more fingers to skip through content on the screen, such as images or text. Do not use *scroll* to describe this gesture unless a user can use a traditional control on an input device, such as a wheel button or the strip on the Microsoft Arc Touch Mouse. See also *scroll*.

Microsoft style

To view more pictures, flick right and left. (Windows Phone)

To move the picture to the right, flick it. (Surface)

Flick through your contacts. (Arc Touch Mouse, Surface, Windows Phone)

Not Microsoft style

Scroll through the images with your finger until you find the one that you want to edit.

F

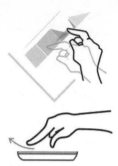

Flick gesture

flush

In content for a general audience, do not use *flush, flush to, flush left*, or *flush right* to describe text alignment. Use *even, left-aligned*, or *right-aligned*, as appropriate, instead.

In content for a technical audience, *flush* is all right to use to refer to such things as a function that "flushes the buffer."

flush to

Do not use to mean *aligned on*. See also *align, aligned on*.

folder

In content about Windows, use *folder* to refer to a container for files and for other folders. If the context is MS–DOS, use *directory*. Folders are represented on the interface by a *folder icon*. It is all right to use *directory* to mean *folder* in content for software developers if necessary to match the application programming interface.

> **Note** Not all folders represent a container for files and for other folders. For example, the Printers and Control Panel programs are also folders. Describe the nature of the folder, if necessary.

When instructing a user to click a folder, use bold formatting for the folder name. See also *directory*.

Microsoft style

You can find the file on your hard disk in C:\Windows\System\Color.

You can find the file on X:\Windows\System\Color.

You can find the file in the Color folder.

The system files are in the System subdirectory in the Windows directory.

Click the **Windows** folder.

folder icon

Use instead of *directory icon*, which is a term that is no longer applicable.

following

Use *following* to introduce art, a table, or, in some cases, a list. See also *above, below*.

Microsoft style

The following table compares the different rates.

To install the program, do the following:

If *following* is the last word before what it introduces, follow it with a colon.

font and font style

Use *font*, not *typeface*, for the name of a typeface design such as Times New Roman or Bookman. Use *font style*, not *type style*, to refer to the formatting, such as bold, italic, or small caps, and *font size*, not *type size*, for the point size, such as 12 point or 14 point.

When referring to bold formatting, use *bold*, not *bolded, boldface*, or *boldfaced*. When referring to italic formatting, use *italic*, not *italics* or *italicized*.

Microsoft style

The **Bold** option makes selected characters bold or removes the bold formatting if the characters are already bold.

Not Microsoft style

Select the **Bold** option button to bold the characters.

For information about when to use various font styles, see *Document conventions* (Chapter 6).

foobar, fubar

Do not use. The word is slang derived from an obscene phrase meaning "fouled up beyond all recognition." Use another placeholder or variable name instead. For example, use *Example.exe* or *MyFile.doc*.

footer

In content related to word-processing and publishing programs, use instead of *bottom running head* or *running foot* when discussing page layout. However, *running foot* is all right to use as a synonym in keyword lists and indexes.

foreground program

Use instead of *foreground process*.

format, formatted, formatting

Use *format* to refer to the overall layout or pattern of a document. Use *formatting* to refer to particulars of character formatting, paragraph formatting, and other types of formatting.

Fortran

Note capitalization. Do not use all uppercase *(FORTRAN)*. Do not spell out as "Formula Translation."

fourth-generation language

Spell out on first mention. On subsequent mention, it is all right to abbreviate as *4GL*.

frameset

Use this term only in content for software developers or web developers. A frames page is a webpage that is divided into independently scrollable regions called *frames*. The HTML document that describes the frame layout in a frames page is called the *frameset document*.

Use *frames page* to describe the page itself, but do not use this term in content for a general audience. In general discussions, use *frames* whenever possible.

friendly name

Do not use. Use *display name* instead to refer to a person's name as it appears in an address or email list.

from

Use *from* to indicate a specific place or time as a starting point. For example, say "Paste the text from the Clipboard" or "From the time you set the clock, the alarm is active."

If you are documenting both mouse and keyboard procedures, use *from* to indicate a menu from which a user chooses a command. For example, say "From the **File** menu, choose **Open**."

However, use *on* to indicate the starting place for clicking a command or option: "On the **File** menu, click **Open**."

from vs. than

The adjective *different* is usually followed by *from*. Use *from* when the next element of the sentence is a noun or pronoun.

Microsoft style
The result of the first calculation is different from the result of the second.

Not Microsoft style
The result of the first calculation is different than the result of the second.

front end, front-end

In content for a general audience, do not use as a synonym for the desktop interface to a database or server. Use the name of the program, or use *interface*, *program*, or another specific and accurate term instead. These terms are all right to use in content for a technical audience.

full file replacement

A technology used in hotfixes that replaces the currently installed files with new files. See *patching*.

function

A general term for a subroutine. In some languages, a function explicitly returns a value, which not all subroutines do.

Do not use *function* to mean *application programming interface (API)*. Additionally, do not use *API* to mean *function*. The API is the set of classes, interfaces, functions, structures, and other programming elements that software developers use to write programs that interact with a product, technology, or operating system.

G

G, G byte, Gbyte

Do not use as an abbreviation for *gigabyte*. Use *GB* instead. See also *GB, gigabyte.*

gallery

A gallery is a collection of pictures, charts, or other graphics that the user can select from. Use the verb *click* or *select* for the items in a gallery.

Microsoft style

Select an option from the gallery.

Click the picture that you want to select.

game pad

Two words.

Gantt chart

Note capitalization.

garbage collection

All right to use in content for a technical audience. *Garbage collection* refers to the automatic recovery of heap memory or to the automatic deletion of objects that the run-time environment determines are no longer being used. The *garbage collector* is the component of a run-time environment that performs garbage collection.

gateway

One word. Refers to software or a computer running software that enables two different networks to communicate.

GB

Abbreviation for *gigabyte*. Use the abbreviation only as a measurement with numerals. Spell out *gigabyte* on first mention. See also *gigabyte.*

Gbit

Do not use as an abbreviation for *gigabit*. Always spell out.

general protection fault

Spell out on first mention. On subsequent mention, it is all right to abbreviate as *GP fault.*

GHz

Abbreviation for *gigahertz*. Use the abbreviation only as a measurement with numerals. Do not use the abbreviation in text without a numeral. Spell out *gigahertz* on first mention. See also *gigahertz.*

gigabit

Always spell out. Do not use the abbreviation *Gbit*.

gigabyte

One gigabyte is equal to 1,073,741,824 bytes, or 1,024 megabytes.

Abbreviate as *GB*, not *G, G byte*, or *Gbyte*. On first mention, spell out and use the abbreviation in parentheses. Insert a space between the numeral and *GB*, or hyphenate if the measure is used as an adjective. See also *Measurements and units of measure* (Chapter 7).

Microsoft style
1 gigabyte (GB) of data

10-GB hard disk

> When used as a noun in measurements, add *of* to form a prepositional phrase.

Microsoft style
You will need to free 1 GB of hard disk space.

gigahertz

A *gigahertz* is a unit of frequency equal to 1 billion cycles per second.

Spell out on first mention and use the abbreviation *GHz* in parentheses. Do not use the abbreviation in text without a numeral. Insert a space between *GHz* and the numeral, or hyphenate if the measure is used as an adjective. See also *Chapter 11, "Acronyms and other abbreviations."*

Microsoft style
a frequency of 11.9300 gigahertz (GHz)

11.9300-GHz communications

given

Do not use to mean *specified, particular*, or *fixed*.

Microsoft style
Look in the specified folder.

Use the **Find** command to search for all occurrences of a specific word.

The meeting is always at a particular time.

Not Microsoft style
Look in the given folder.

Use the **Find** command to search for all occurrences of a given word.

The meeting is always at a given time.

global

In content for a technical audience, *global* refers to memory that is accessible to more than one process, to a variable whose value can be accessed and modified by any statement in a program (called a *global variable*), and to similar elements that pertain to an entire program.

Do not use *global* as a technical term in content for a general audience, especially in describing the process of replacing one text string with another throughout a document. Instead, describe the action being taken.

It is, of course, all right to use *global* to mean *worldwide*. See also *find and replace*.

Microsoft style

A cascading style sheet establishes global design formats.

Use the **Find** and **Replace** commands to find all occurrences of specific text and replace it with different text.

glyph

Do not use to refer generically to a graphic or pictorial image on a button, on an icon, or in a message box. Use *symbol* instead. All right to use in a technical discussion of fonts and characters. See also *icon, symbol*.

GP fault

Abbreviation for *general protection fault*. Spell out on first mention.

graphic, graphical, graphics

As a noun, use *graphic* to refer to a picture, display, chart, and other visual representations.

Use *graphics* to refer in general to creating pictures, displays, charts, and other visual representations using computers. An example is "graphics software."

Use *graphical* as the adjectival form of the noun *graphic*. Use *graphic* as an adjective only to mean "vivid" or "realistic" or in the phrase "graphic arts."

Noun

To import a graphic from another file, click **Picture**.

Adjective

Select the graphics file you want to open.

The image is graphic and accurate.

A tutorial offers the basics in graphic design.

The graphical user interface simulates a coliseum.

graphics adapter

Do not use. Use *video card* instead.

gray, grayed

Do not use to refer to commands or options. Use *unavailable* or *dimmed* instead. If you need to describe the appearance of check boxes with portions of a larger selection that are already selected, use *shaded*, not *grayed*. See also *dimmed, shaded, unavailable*.

Microsoft style

In the **Effects** group box, names of selected options may appear shaded.

The **Print** command on the **File** menu is unavailable.

graylist

Do not use. See *blacklist*.

grayscale

One word, both as an adjective and as a noun.

greater, better

Do not use either term to designate system requirements or versions of a program. See also *higher, later*.

Microsoft style

To run SyncToy 2.1, your computer must be running Windows 7, Windows Vista, or Windows XP.

To run Windows 7, your computer must have a 1 gigahertz (GHz) or faster 32-bit (x86) or 64-bit (x64) processor.

Not Microsoft style

To run SyncToy 2.1, your computer must be running Windows XP or greater.

To run Windows 7, your computer must have a 1 gigahertz (GHz) or better 32-bit (x86) or 64-bit (x64) processor.

gridline

One word, both as an adjective and as a noun.

Microsoft style

No gridline is displayed if the **GridLineStyle** property is set to **DataGridLineStyle**.

When the **DataList** control is displayed in a table, you can use the **GridLines** property to specify a gridline style.

Not Microsoft style

No grid line is displayed if the **GridLineStyle** property is set to **DataGridLineStyle.**

When the **DataList** control is displayed in a table, you can use the **GridLines** property to specify a grid line style.

group, newsgroup

Although these words can be synonyms, use *newsgroup* to refer specifically to an Internet discussion group focusing on a particular topic to differentiate it from other generic groups. *Newsgroup* is one word.

group box

Two words, both as an adjective and as a noun.

A group box is a rectangle drawn around a set of related controls in a dialog box. For example, in the **Print** dialog box of WordPad, page range options are grouped in the **Page Range** group box. A group box is only a visual aid; it provides no functionality.

Do not use *group box* in content for a general audience. It is generally unnecessary to include the name of the group box in a procedure unless a dialog box contains more than one option with the same name. In that case, use *under* with the group box name. For example, you can say "Under **Effects**, select **Hidden**."

It is all right to use *group box* in content for a technical audience.

groupware

Use to refer to software intended to let a group of users on a network collaborate on a project.

Do not use *groupware* as a product descriptor. For example, use "Microsoft Outlook messaging and collaboration client," not "Microsoft Outlook groupware."

grow

Do not use as a transitive verb in the sense of making something larger. Use a more specific verb such as *extend* instead.

Microsoft style

If you want to increase your business...

To extend the selection...

Not Microsoft style

If you want to grow your business...

To grow the selection...

H

hack, hacker

Use *hacker* to refer to a user who intentionally accesses a system with the intent to cause harm to the system or to use it in an unauthorized manner. Do not use *hack* to refer to improvising a solution to a programming problem. Do not use *hacker* to refer to an amateur programmer. If the intent of unauthorized access is unknown or is not malicious, use *unauthorized user*. See also *security*.

half inch

Hyphenate as an adjective. Use instead of *half an inch* or *one-half inch*. When space is limited or the measurement needs to be specific, use *0.5 in.*

International considerations

Do not use abbreviations or acronyms that form English words unless you have no other choice. Doing so may lead to mistranslation in machine-translated content. For example, if you were to abbreviate *half inch* as *0.5 in, in* likely would be mistranslated. In a machine translation from English to French, the *in* abbreviation will most likely be translated as the preposition *dans*, which of course does not mean "inch" in French.

G

handheld computer

Do not use *handheld PC*. Use *handheld computer* to refer to a portable computer that accesses, captures, and updates information in real time, such as the computers often used in line-of-business applications. Do not use *handheld* as a noun. See also *portable computer*.

handle

In programming, a handle is a pointer to a pointer or a token temporarily assigned to a device or object to identify and provide access to the device. In the latter case, insert a space between the word *handle* and the sequential number. For example, say "handle 0," "handle 1," "handle 2."

In the user interface of various programs, a handle is an element used to move or size an object. Use *move handle* or *sizing handle*. Do not use *size handle*, *grab handle*, *little box*, or similar phrases.

handshake

One word, both as an adjective and as a noun. *Handshake* refers to the connection or signal established between two pieces of hardware, such as a computer and a printer, or communications software, such as the signal to transmit data between two modems. In content for a general audience, briefly define the term on first mention.

Microsoft style

Communicating systems must use the same flow-control (or *handshake*) method. To determine whether the systems use the same handshake method...

hang

Do not use in content for a general audience. Use *stop responding* instead. In content for a technical audience, you can use *hang* by itself or to clarify the meaning of *stop responding* if necessary, but *stop responding* by itself is preferred.

Microsoft style

If the program stops responding, or "hangs," you may have to restart your computer.

Not Microsoft style

If the program hangs, you may have to restart your computer.

 Note Sometimes the computer itself stops responding, and sometimes a program does. Be sure any messages refer accurately to the problem.

hard copy

Two words. Use as a noun to mean text or images (or both) printed on paper. Do not use as an adjective unless you have no other choice. See also *soft copy*.

Microsoft style

How to scan hard copies of documents or artwork and save them as electronic files or images.

Not Microsoft style

How to scan hard-copy documents or artwork and save them as electronic files or images.

hard disk

Refer to the disk itself as the *hard disk*. Be clear whether you are talking about the disk itself or the drive, which should be referred to as the *hard disk drive*, not the *hard drive, internal drive, fixed disk drive*, or *hard disk system*. Do not hyphenate *hard disk*. See also *disk, drive*.

hard-coded

Use in content for a technical audience to describe a routine or program that uses embedded constants in place of more general user input. Do not use in content for a general audience unless you have no other choice.

hard-of-hearing

Use the phrase *"deaf or hard-of-hearing"* to refer to people who have hearing disabilities. If space is limited, use *deaf*. Do not use *hearing-impaired*. See also *Chapter 4, "Accessible Content", deaf or hard-of-hearing*

hardware

One word.

hardwired

One word. Describes a functionality that is built into a system's electronic circuitry rather than enabled through software. Do not use this technical term in content for a general audience unless you have no other choice.

he/she

Do not use. For more information about gender-neutral pronouns, see *Bias-free communication* (Chapter 1).

header

In content about word-processing and publishing, use instead of *running head* when discussing page layout. However, *running head* is all right to use if needed for clarification or as a keyword or index entry.

Do not use *header* as a synonym for *heading*.

In technical content, *header* is all right to use as a short form of the term *file header*, as in ".rtf header" or "PostScript header." Do not use *header* as a synonym for *header file*, which refers to the file at the beginning of a program that contains definitions of data types and variables used by the program's functions.

heading

Use instead of a *head* or a *header* to refer to a topic heading or chapter heading. See also *Titles and headings* (Chapter 7)

hearing-impaired

Do not use. Use the phrase *deaf or hard-of-hearing* instead. If space is limited, use *deaf*. See also *Chapter 4, "Accessible Content"*.

Help

In general, do not use *online Help*. Just use *Help* by itself. However, *online Help*, *definition Help*, *context-sensitive Help*, and *online Help files* are all right to use when necessary to describe the Help system itself or to explain how to develop a Help system.

hexadecimal

Do not abbreviate as *hex*. Use *h* or *0x* when abbreviating a number, as in "Interrupt 21h" or "addresses greater than 0xFFFE." Do not insert a space between the number and *h*, and use uppercase for alphabetical characters displayed in hexadecimal numbers.

hierarchical menu

Do not use. Use *submenu* instead. See also *submenu*.

higher

Do not use *or higher* or *or later* to refer to multiple versions of software. List each applicable version instead. It is all right to use *or earlier* to refer to all versions of a product that precede a particular release if the statement is accurate for all preceding releases. (For example, do not use "Windows 7 or earlier" unless the statement is accurate for Windows 1.0.) See also *earlier; greater, better; version identifers*.

Microsoft style
Windows 7, Windows Vista, and Windows XP

Not Microsoft style
Windows XP and later

Windows XP and higher

It is all right to use *higher* to refer to more powerful hardware.

Microsoft style
a processer speed of 2.5 Gigahertz (GHz) or higher

high-level-language compiler

Note both hyphens. Refers to a compiler for a high-level language such as C++, Visual Basic, or C#.

high-quality

Do not use *quality* by itself as an adjective. Always use *high-quality*.

Microsoft style
Use **AutoFormat** to create high-quality publications easily.

Not Microsoft style
Use **AutoFormat** to create quality publications easily.

high-resolution

Use only as an adjective. Note hyphen. Do not abbreviate as *hi-res*.

Refers to a high-quality screen display (generally 640 × 480 pixels or higher resolution) or print output (300 dots per inch or higher resolution).

highlight

In general, do not use *highlight* unless you are specifically referring to the highlighter feature in some products that users can apply to emphasize selections. Use *select* instead.

Microsoft style

Drag the pointer to select the text you want to format.

Not Microsoft style

Drag the pointer to highlight the text you want to format.

Refer to selected material as *the selection*, not *the highlight*.

Microsoft style

To extend the selection, press F6.

Not Microsoft style

To extend the highlight, press F6.

When it is necessary to be graphically descriptive, you can use *highlight* as a verb to tell the user to select such things as text in a word-processing document, a range of cells in a spreadsheet, or fields and records in a database list view. Likewise, you can use *highlight* to describe the appearance of reverse video. When using *highlight* as a verb in a procedure, include *select* in your procedure so that users won't be confused when they use other Microsoft products or services.

Microsoft style

Highlight the paragraph to select it.

Highlight to select the range of cells you want to copy.

Programmers use reverse video to highlight special items on the screen.

hint

Do not use *hint* as a heading for a type of note. Use *tip* instead. See also *Notes and tips* (Chapter 7).

hi-res

Do not use. See *high-resolution*.

hit

All right to use to refer to the number of times a file from a webpage has been retrieved. Because each file associated with a webpage counts as one hit, a single page view can result in many hits. Use *page view* or *page request* to refer to the number of times a page and all its associated files have been downloaded.

Do not use *hit* to refer to the act of pressing a key on the computer keyboard. Use *press* instead. See also *press*.

home directory

Do not use. Use *root directory* instead to refer to the starting point in a hierarchical file structure. In MS-DOS and Windows, the root directory is indicated by a backslash (\).

home page

Refers to the main page of any website, as determined by the owner or creator of the site. One website can have many home pages. For example, the Microsoft website, www.microsoft.com, has a home page, but other sites within the Microsoft site have their own home pages.

Home page also refers to the webpage that is first displayed when a user starts a web browser. Do not use *start page*.

Use lowercase to refer to the home page unless you are referring to the command.

honeypot

Do not use unless you have no other choice. It's jargon. A honeypot is a security program designed to lure and distract a network attacker with decoy data.

This term may be difficult to translate and may cause geopolitical or cultural misunderstanding.

In content that specifically addresses network decoy technology, try to write around the reference. If you cannot write around it, then define the term on first mention.

host name

Two words unless you are referring to a programming element such as the **HostName** property.

hosted service

A service, IT solution, or application that is hosted by a service provider and made available to a customer over the Internet.

hosting provider

A third-party service provider that offers scalable infrastructure services to multiple customers.

All right to use *cloud hosting provider* and *web hosting provider* if necessary to establish the context or distinguish cloud service providers from web hosts, such as Go Daddy.

Do not use *hoster*.

hot key

Obsolete term. Do not use. Use *keyboard shortcut* instead. See also *keyboard shortcut*.

hot link

Do not use. *Hot link* is jargon for a connection between programs that enables information in related databases or files to be updated when information in another database or file is changed. Do not use *hot link* to refer to a **hyperlink**.

hot spot, hotspot

Two words when used in content for a technical audience to refer to the specific pixel on the pointer that defines the exact location to which a user is pointing. Also two words when used to refer to a wireless or Wi-Fi hot spot.

One word when referring to such programming elements as the elements of the **HotSpot** class or when following the wording in the user interface.

Do not use *hot spot* or *hotspot* to refer to a hyperlink. See also *hyperlink*.

hotfix

One word. Use to describe a single cumulative package composed of one or more files used to address a defect in a product. Hotfixes address a specific customer situation and may not be distributed outside that customer organization. Do not use *QFE* (quick fix engineering) to describe a hotfix. See also *out-of-band release terminology* (Chapter 6).

hover over

Note preposition. An air gesture that refers to the action of briefly holding a finger or hand in a particular location to select an action or otherwise interact with the user interface.

Microsoft style

Hover over the item that you want until it's selected.

Microsoft style (novice computer user)

To select an object, hold your finger over it so that your finger hovers over the object until it is selected.

To start the game, hold your hand out so that it hovers over the **Start** button.

Hover over gesture

Do not use *hover*, especially in content for a general audience, to refer to the action of briefly resting the mouse pointer on an interface item to see a definition or description. Use *point to*, *pause on*, or a similar word or phrase, instead.

how-to vs. how to

Do not use *how-to* as a noun. Hyphenate as an adjective. Whether *how to* is hyphenated or not, do not capitalize *to* in contexts that require title capitalization.

Microsoft style

how-to book

how-to article

How to Format Your Hard Disk (Title capitalization)

Writing a How-to Article (Title capitalization)

Not Microsoft style

The TechNet website has how-tos for system administrators.

Writing a How-To Article (Title capitalization)

HTML

Abbreviation for "Hypertext Markup Language." Do not spell out. See also *HTML tag, element, and attribute formatting* (Chapter 6).

HTTP

Abbreviation for "Hypertext Transfer Protocol," the Internet protocol that delivers information over the World Wide Web. The protocol appears as the first element in a URL: "http://." Use lowercase for *http://* and the rest of the URL.

Don't spell out unless you are discussing protocols or URLs, or unless your audience might be unfamiliar with the abbreviation.

You do not have to include "http" in a web address if you are sure that your users will understand the context. However, if you are using another protocol such as FTP in an Internet address, you must use it. See also *Protocols* (Chapter 6).

Hub

Don't refer to a *Hub* as such unless absolutely necessary. Instead, in procedures, use the name of the Hub, such as "In Marketplace..." or "In Pictures...," to refer to the front page of a Hub for a user action. If you do refer to a Hub, capitalize Hub.

Microsoft style for Windows Phone

In Pictures, find a picture and tap to open it.

The Pictures Hub is where you go to see all the pictures on your phone and the latest pictures your friends have posted to Windows Live.

hybrid cloud

A cloud infrastructure that uses a combination of public, community, and private clouds, with each discrete entity connected to enable data and application portability between them.

A hybrid cloud addresses an organization's unique application and data storage needs and privacy concerns.

Use for a technical audience that is comfortable with cloud technology. For other audiences, it may be more useful to talk about a *hybrid model*.

Because the deployment models are not widely understood, define on first mention. See also *community cloud, private cloud, public cloud.*

hyperlink

See *link*.

I

i.e.

Abbreviation for *id est*, meaning "that is." Do not use. Use *that is* instead.

IA-32-based

Obsolete term. Use *32-bit* or *x86* instead. See also *Intel-based, Itanium-based*.

IA-64-based

Do not use *IA64* as a synonym for *64-bit*, *x64*, or *amd64*.

IA64 is an architecture that is used for Windows Server 2008 and Windows Server 2008 R2 only, and will not be available in the next version of Windows. It is all right to use *Itanium-based* instead. See also *Intel-based*, *Itanium-based*.

I-beam

Capitalize and hyphenate as shown. Do not refer to the I-beam pointer except when necessary to describe how the pointer's shape affects its function. For example, say "When you click text, the pointer looks like an I-beam."

icon

Use only to describe a graphic representation of an object that a user can select and open, such as a drive, disk, folder, document, or program.

Network   Recycle Bin

When referring to an icon, use bold for the icon name.

Microsoft style
Click the **Word** icon.

Within programs, do not use *icon* for graphical dialog box options or options that appear on ribbons, toolbars, toolboxes, or other areas of a window.

For user interface elements that are identified by a graphic instead of label text, use the most descriptive term available, such as *button*, *box*, or *check box*. To refer to the graphic itself, if there is no other identifying label, use *symbol*, as in "warning symbol."

iconize

Do not use. Use *shrink to an icon* or *minimize* instead.

if vs. when vs. whether

To avoid ambiguity, use *if* to express a condition; use *whether* to express uncertainty, and use *when* for situations requiring preparation or to denote the passage of time.

In informal writing for the web, it is all right to use *if* to express uncertainty.

Microsoft style
If you do not know whether a network key is needed, contact your network administrator.

The printer might insert stray characters if the wrong font cartridge is selected.

When Setup is complete, restart your computer.

To find out whether TrueType fonts are available....

To find out if TrueType fonts are available... (Informal style)

Not Microsoft style

If you do not know if a network key is needed, contact your network administrator.

The printer might insert stray characters when the wrong font cartridge is selected.

Do not use *whether or not* to express uncertainty.

Microsoft style

With Internet Explorer, you can save webpages and view them later, whether you are connected to the Internet or not.

Microsoft style

With Internet Explorer, you can save webpages and view them later, even if you are not connected to the Internet.

Not Microsoft style

If you are not sure whether or not a network key is needed, contact your network administrator.

illegal

Use *illegal* only in specific situations, such as notices on software that say "Do not make illegal copies of this disk" or, in local content, to reference the violation of a local law, or in reference to the violation of international law. Except for certain appropriate situations, the terms *licensed* and *unlicensed* may be better.

Do not use to mean *invalid* or *not valid*. See also *invalid, not valid*.

Microsoft style

The queue path name is not valid.

Chords cannot be composed while a segment is playing.

Not Microsoft style

The queue path name is illegal.

It is illegal to compose chords while a segment is playing.

image map

Two words unless you are referring to a programming map such as the elements of the **ImageMap** class.

imbed

Do not use. Use *embed* instead. See also *embed*.

impact

Use only as a noun. As a verb, use *affect* or another synonym instead.

Microsoft style

Sending inappropriate email can affect your career adversely.

Not Microsoft style

Sending inappropriate email can impact your career adversely.

in, into

In indicates within the limits, bounds, or area of or from the outside to a point within. *Into* generally implies moving to the inside or interior of.

Microsoft style

A word is in a paragraph, but you move the text into the document.

Data is in a cell on a worksheet.

You edit the cell contents in the formula bar.

A file name is in a list box.

A workstation is in a domain, but resources are on servers.

You open multiple windows in a document.

You insert the disk into the disk drive.

You run programs with, on, or under an operating system, not in one.

in order to

International considerations

The phrase *in order to* may be verbose in general writing, and therefore it is all right to just use *to* instead. However, in content that will be machine translated, using *in order to* avoids the ambiguity that the shorter form *to* frequently causes.

inactive, inactive state

Use instead of *not current* to refer to windows, programs, documents, files, devices, or portions of the screen that are not open and operating. See also *disable*.

inbound

Do not use in the sense of messages being delivered unless you have no other choice. Use *incoming* instead.

incent

Do not use unless you have no other choice. Use verbs such as *motivate* and *encourage*, or use a noun such as *incentive*.

Microsoft style

This pricing should encourage users to buy the new version.

Not Microsoft style

This pricing should incent users to buy the new version.

incoming, outgoing

Use to refer to email messages that are being downloaded or being sent. Do not use *inbound* and *outbound* unless you have no other choice.

increment

In content for software developers, web developers, and information technology professionals, use *increment* as a verb only to mean *increase by one or by a specified interval*. As a noun, use *increment* to refer to the specified interval.

In other content, it is all right to use *increment* in a nontechnical sense, as long as the meaning is clear.

indent, indentation

Use *indent* to refer to a single instance of indentation. For example, use *hanging indent, nested indent, negative indent*, or *positive indent*. Do not use *outdent* to mean *negative indent* or *indention* to mean *indent*.

Use *indentation* only to refer to the general concept.

indenting, outdenting

Do not use *indenting or outdenting into the margin*. Use *extending text into the margin* or *indenting to the previous tab stop* instead.

independent content provider

Use to refer to a business or organization that supplies information to an online information service such as MSN or America Online. Spell out on first mention.

index, indexes

In general, use *indexes* as the plural form of *index* instead of *indices*. Use *indices* only in the context of mathematical expressions.

infrastructure as a service (IaaS)

Flexible computing capacity such as servers, storage, and networking that is managed by a cloud services provider and made available to the customer over the Internet. In the infrastructure as a service (IaaS) model, hardware provisioning such as for compute, storage, and networking is controlled by the provider, but the customer maintains control of the operating system and applications.

All right to use *IaaS* after the full term has been spelled out on first mention. Do not capitalize as *IAAS*.

> **Note** Do not compare IaaS with common utilities such as power.

initialize

Technical term usually referring to preparing a disk or computer for use or to set a variable to an initial value. Do not use to mean start a program or turn on a computer.

initiate

Do not use to mean *start a program*. Use *start* instead.

inline

One word. Do not hyphenate. "Inline styles" are used in cascading style sheets to override a style in the style sheet itself. Inline styles are embedded in the tag itself by using the STYLE parameter.

input

Do not use as a verb. Use *type* or another appropriate verb instead. In content for a general audience, do not use as a noun unless you have no other choice.

Microsoft style

Word moves existing characters to the right as you type new text.

To verify the text that was entered... (General audience)

Not Microsoft style

Word moves existing characters to the right as you input new text.

To verify the input that was entered... (General audience)

input device

All right to use to refer generically to a mouse, pen, ball, stylus, keyboard, joystick, game controller, or other device that sends user input to a computer or console. Do not use as a synonym for *mouse* or any of the other devices mentioned in this topic when you can be specific. See also *Mouse terminology* (Chapter 5).

input/output

In content for a general audience, spell out on first mention, and then abbreviate as *I/O*. You do not have to spell out *I/O* on first mention in content for a technical audience.

input/output control

Spell out on first mention. On subsequent mention, all right to abbreviate as *I/O control* or *IOCTL*. Use only in content for a technical audience.

insecure

Do not use to mean *not secure*. Use *not secure* instead.

insertion point

Do not use. See *cursor*.

inside

Use instead of the colloquial *inside of*.

install

In general, use *install* to refer to adding hardware or software to a computer system.

Do not use *install* as a noun. Use *installation* instead. See also *add, uninstall*.

instant message, IM

IM may be used in place of *instant message* or *instant messaging* as a noun or a modifier when the audience expects an informal tone. In general, spell out *instant message* or *instant messaging* on first mention.

In general, do not use *instant message* as a verb. Use *send an instant message* instead.

Do not use *IM* as a verb. Use *send an IM* instead. However, *IM* may be used as a verb in mobile UI content or to form a parallel construction with another one-word phrase. An example is "Tap a name to call or IM a contact."

Microsoft style

To send an instant message, click **Send IM** on the toolbar.

You can customize the new instant messaging features based on your friends, family, and work contacts.

International considerations

Using abbreviations such as *IM* does not save necessarily space when content is localized. For example, in many languages, *instant message* does not have an abbreviated form, and the translation may be more than 23 characters long.

instantiate

Do not use unless you have no other choice. Use *create an instance of* (a class) instead. If you must use *instantiate*, its direct object must be the name of a class or a general reference to classes. You instantiate a class, not an object.

insure

Do not use except to refer to insurance. See also *ensure*.

Intel-based

Use to distinguish computers with processors based on the Intel IA-32 or Itanium architecture from computers based on other architectures. See also *IA-32-based, Itanium-based*.

interface

Use only as a noun, as in "user interface" and "application programming interface." Use *on* as the preposition preceding *user interface*. Use *interface* by itself only if the context is clear.

Interface as a verb is jargon. Use *interact* or *communicate* instead.

Microsoft style

It is easy to use the Internet to communicate with various interest groups.

The interface is so intuitive that even first-time users learn quickly.

The color can be adjusted on the user interface.

Not Microsoft style

It is easy to use the Internet to interface with various interest groups.

The color can be adjusted in the user interface.

In COM-based technologies and objects in the Microsoft .NET Framework, an interface is a collection of related public functions called *methods* that provide access to an object. The set of interfaces *on* (note preposition) an object composes a contract that specifies how programs and other objects can interact with the object.

Internet, intranet, extranet

The *Internet* refers to the worldwide collection of networks that use open protocols such as TCP/IP to communicate with each other. The Internet offers a number of services, including email and the World Wide Web. Always capitalize *Internet*.

An *intranet* is a communications network based on the same technology as the World Wide Web that is available only to certain people, such as the employees of a company. Do not capitalize.

An *extranet* is an extension of an intranet using Internet protocols to provide authorized outside users with limited access to the intranet. Do not capitalize.

Internet Connection Sharing

Technology that enables home and small-office computer users who have networked computers to share a single connection to the Internet. Always spell out.

Internet Explorer

Do not abbreviate *Internet Explorer*. Always use the full name.

Internet service provider

Note capitalization. Spell out on first mention.

Use to refer to an organization that provides customers with access to the Internet for such activities as web browsing, email, and newsgroup participation. Common ISPs are MSN, America Online, and EarthLink.

Interrupt

When discussing specific MS-DOS interrupts, spell out and capitalize the word *Interrupt* and use a lowercase *h*, as in "Interrupt 21h."

invalid, not valid

Both terms are all right to use, but they are sometimes vague. Replace them with a more specific term whenever possible.

International considerations

Use *not valid* instead of *invalid* whenever you can correctly do so. *Invalid* may be mistranslated in machine-translated content.

Microsoft style

There are several reasons why a product key might not be valid.

The telephone number may contain only numbers and hyphens.

Microsoft style, but vague

The telephone number is not valid.

Not Microsoft style

There are several reasons why a product key might be invalid.

inverse video

Do not use. Use *reverse video* instead. Use *highlighted* to refer to the appearance. See also *highlight*.

invoke

Do not use in content for a general audience in the sense of starting or running a program. It's jargon. All right to use in content for a technical audience to refer to a function, process, and similar elements.

IP address

Don't spell out.

issue

In content for a general audience, do not use as a verb. Use a more specific verb instead.

Microsoft style

Windows 7 displays an error message.

Click **Save As** to save a file under a new name.

Not Microsoft style

Windows 7 issues an error message.

Issue the **Save As** command to save a file under a new name.

IT as a service (ITaaS)

IT as a service describes all three layers (IaaS, PaaS, SaaS) of IT services consumed by organizations and businesses. Examples of ITaaS services include hardware selection, configuration, and optimization, in addition to software configuration and patching.

Use only in content for a technical or business-decision-maker audience. In content for a general audience, refer to the specific type of service being provided, such as applying software updates, in a cloud computing model.

All right to use *ITaaS* after the full term has been spelled out on first mention. Do not capitalize as *ITAAS*.

IT pro

Note capitalization. Abbreviation for *information technology professional*. Do not spell out.

italic

Use *italic* only as an adjective, not as a noun or as a verb. Do not use *italics* or *italicized*. See also *Document conventions* (Chapter 6), *Fonts* (Chapter 3).

Microsoft style

To make the selected characters italic, press Ctrl+I.

The newly added terms are displayed in italic type.

Not Microsoft style

Not Microsoft style

To italicize the selected characters, press Ctrl+I.

The newly added terms are displayed in italics.

> **Note** Use *regular type* to describe type that is neither bold nor italic.

Itanium-based

Use to distinguish computers with processors based on the Intel Itanium (formerly IA-64) architecture from computers with processors based on the x86 or amd64 architecture. See also *Intel-based*.

its vs. it's

Proofread your work to be sure you've used the correct word. *Its* is the possessive form; *it's* is the contraction meaning "it is."

Microsoft style

It's easy to take advantage of many new features in Office.

The easy connection to other systems is just one of its many advantages.

J

Java, JScript, JavaScript

Java is an object-oriented programming language developed by the Sun Corporation.

JScript is the Microsoft implementation of the ECMAScript scripting language specification, an open standard. Do not refer to it as *JavaScript*, which is the corresponding implementation by Time Warner.

jewel case

Do not use. Use *CD case* or *DVD case* instead.

join

All right to use as an adjective, as a noun, or as a verb. Do not use to mean *embed*. *Join*, in database terminology, refers to a relationship or association between fields in different tables and should be reserved for that meaning in documentation for database and related products.

Microsoft style

If you join numeric fields that do not have matching **FieldSize** property settings, Microsoft Access may not find all the matching records when you run the query.

When you add fields from both tables to the query design grid, the default, or inner, join tells the query to check for matching values in the join fields.

To embed one object into another, click **Paste** on the **Edit** menu.

Not Microsoft style

To join one object with another, click **Paste** on the **Edit** menu.

J

joystick

One word. Joysticks have *controls* (not options) for controlling movement on the screen.

jump

Do not use as a noun to refer to cross-references to other Help topics or to hyperlinks.

Do not use as a verb to refer to going from one link to another. Use *go to* instead.

justify, justified

Do not use as a synonym for *aligned*. Justified text is text that is both left-aligned and right-aligned. To describe alignment on one margin only, use *left-aligned* or *right-aligned*, not *left-justified* or *right-justified*.

If content that discuss text alignment has an index or glossary, include *justify* in the index or glossary with cross-references to *align*, *left align*, and *right align*, as appropriate. See also *left align, left-aligned, right align, right-aligned*.

K

K, K byte, Kbyte

Do not use as abbreviations for *kilobyte*. Use *KB* instead. Do not use *K* to refer to $1,000. It's slang. See also *KB*.

KB

Abbreviation for *kilobyte*. Use the abbreviation only as a measurement with numerals. Do not use the abbreviation in text without a numeral. Insert a space between *KB* and the numeral, or hyphenate if the measure is used as an adjective. Spell out as *kilobyte* on first mention unless you are positive that your audience is familiar with the term. See also *kilobyte*.

Microsoft style

Download size: 512 KB

500-KB hard disk space

Kbit

Do not use as an abbreviation for *kilobit*. Always spell out.

KBps, Kbps

KBps is the abbreviation for *kilobytes per second*. *Kbps* is the abbreviation for *kilobits per second*. Use the abbreviations only as a measurement with numerals. Do not use in text without a numeral. Spell out on first mention.

Kerberos protocol

Always use *Kerberos* as an adjective ("Kerberos protocol"), not as a noun ("includes Kerberos").

Always make clear on first mention what version or versions of the Kerberos protocol you are referring to. For example, the Kerberos version 5 protocol is the default authentication protocol for

Windows 7, Windows Server 2008, Windows Server 2003, Windows Vista, Windows XP Professional, and Windows 2000.

Microsoft style

Windows 7 includes support for the Kerberos version 5 protocol.

Not Microsoft style

Windows 7 includes support for Kerberos.

Windows 7 includes support for Kerberos version 5.

key combination

Do not use *key combination* in content for a general audience. Use *keyboard shortcut* instead.

Key combination is all right to use in content for a technical audience when you must distinguish between a key combination, in which two or more keys are pressed simultaneously (such as Ctrl+P), and a key sequence, in which two or more keys are pressed sequentially. In such cases, provide a definition for *key combination*. See also *keyboard shortcut, Key names* (Chapter 5), key sequence.

key sequence

Do not use *key sequence* in content for a general audience. Use *keyboard shortcut* instead.

Key sequence is all right to use in content for a technical audience when you must distinguish between a key sequence, in which two or more keys are pressed sequentially, and a key combination, in which two or more keys are pressed simultaneously (such as Ctrl+P). In such cases, provide a definition for key sequence. See also *access key, key combination, Key names* (Chapter 5), *keyboard shortcut*.

keyboard shortcut

Use to describe any combination of keystrokes that can be used to perform a task that would otherwise require a mouse or other pointing device. In content for software developers and in content about customizing the user interface, it is all right to use *access key* or *shortcut key* when you must distinguish between the two. In such cases, use *access key* to denote a key sequence used to access a menu item, and provide a definition. Use *shortcut key* to denote a key combination used to perform a command, and provide a definition. See also *access key, Key names* (Chapter 5), *key sequence, key combination, shortcut key*.

keypad

Always use *numeric keypad* on first mention. Do not use *keypad* by itself unless the context has been established and there is no possibility of confusion with the keyboard. When in doubt, continue to use *numeric keypad*.

In general, do not make a distinction between the keyboard and the numeric keypad. When the user can press two keys that look the same, be specific in directing the user to the correct key. For example, say "Press the Minus Sign on the numeric keypad, not the Hyphen key on the keyboard." Each group must resolve any problems that this approach may cause because of the way certain keyboards and keypads function.

keypress

Do not use. Use *keystroke* instead.

K

keystroke

One word. Use instead of *keypress*.

kHz

Abbreviation for *kilohertz*. Spell out on first mention and use the abbreviation *kHz* in parentheses. Use the abbreviation only as a measurement with numerals. Do not use the abbreviation in text without a numeral. Insert a space between *kHz* and the numeral, or hyphenate if the measure is used as an adjective. See also *kilohertz*.

Microsoft style

The top range of human hearing is 20 kilohertz (kHz).

8-kHz sampling rate

kilobit

Always spell out. Do not use the abbreviation *Kbit*.

kilobits per second

Spell out on first mention. On subsequent mention, use the abbreviation *Kbps*.

kilobyte

One kilobyte is equal to 1,024 bytes.

Abbreviate as *KB*, not *K, K byte*, or *Kbyte*. Use the abbreviation only as a measurement with numerals. Do not use the abbreviation in text without a numeral. Insert a space between *KB* and the numeral, or hyphenate if the measure is used as an adjective. Spell out as *kilobyte* on first mention, unless you are positive that your audience is familiar with the term. See also *Measurements and units of measure* (Chapter 7).

Microsoft style

Download size: 512 KB

Windows Vista supports up to 4-KB sector sizes.

When used as a noun in measurements, add *of* to form a prepositional phrase.

Microsoft style

A connection profile that includes the Connection Manager software uses about 800 KB of disk space

kilobytes per second

Spell out on first mention. On subsequent mention, use the abbreviation *KBps*.

kilohertz

A kilohertz is a unit of frequency equal to 1,000 cycles per second.

Spell out on first mention and use the abbreviation *kHz* in parentheses. Use the abbreviation only as a measurement with numerals. Do not use the abbreviation in text without a numeral. Insert a space between *kHz* and the numeral, or hyphenate if the measure is used as an adjective. See also *Measurements and units of measure* (Chapter 7).

Microsoft style

The top range of human hearing is 20 kilohertz (kHz).

8-kHz sampling rate

kludge, kludgy

Do not use to refer to a band-aid fix or poorly designed program or system. It is slang.

knowledge base, Knowledge Base

Use all lowercase for generic references to the "expert system" database type. Use title capitalization when referring to the Microsoft Knowledge Base. You do not have to precede *Knowledge Base* with the company name.

L

label, labeled, labeling

For consistency in Microsoft documentation, do not double the final *l*.

landscape orientation

Printing orientation so that the page is wider than it is long.

Compare *portrait orientation*.

laptop

One word. Use *laptop* to refer to a portable computer that has a flat LCD or plasma screen, an integrated keyboard, and a lid.

In general, use the most generic term that describes a device. For example, use just *computer* or *PC* unless you need to call out the mobility of the computer.

Do not use *laptop* as a modifier for computer or PC, or to refer to tablet PCs or slates. See also *computer, PC, portable computer, tablet PC*.

Microsoft style

Learn how to keep your laptop and data safe when you travel and what to do if your laptop gets stolen.

You can use the tablet pen on the tablet PC to draw in a document.

Not Microsoft style

Learn how to keep your laptop computer and data safe when you travel and what to do if your laptop gets stolen.

You can use the tablet pen on your laptop to draw in a document.

later

Use instead of *below* in cross-references. For example, say "later in this topic."

Do not use *or later* to refer to multiple versions of software. List each applicable version instead.

The phrases *or later* and *and later* may imply that the functionality or feature discussed will be included or supported in all future releases. These phrases should not be used for legal reasons.

You can use *or earlier* to refer to all versions of a product that precede a particular release if the statement is accurate for all preceding releases. For example, do not use "Windows 7 or earlier" unless the statement is accurate for Windows 1.0. See also *cross-references, earlier, Microsoft in product names* (Chapter 7).

Microsoft style
Windows Vista with SP2, Windows Vista with SP1, and Windows Vista

Not Microsoft style
Windows Vista and later

launch

Do not use to mean *start*, as in "launch a program" or "launch a form." Use *start* instead. See also *start*.

lay out, laid out, layout

Derivatives of *lay out* are commonly used in reference to formatting. Use the correct spelling and part of speech according to your meaning.

Microsoft style
You can lay out complex information in a table.

Add formatting to your table after it is laid out.

A table layout clarifies complex information.

leave

Do not use to refer to closing a program. Use *exit* instead.

left

Do not use as a directional term by itself. Use such terms as *upper left, lower left, leftmost,* and *on the left side of* instead. Include a hyphen if modifying a noun, as in "upper-left corner." Do not use *left hand*.

Accessibility considerations
Avoid using directional terms (left, right, up, down) as the only clue to location. Individuals with cognitive impairments may have difficulty interpreting them, as do blind users relying on screen-reading software. A directional term is all right to use if another indication of location, such as *in the* **Save As** *dialog box, on the* **Standard** *toolbar,* or *in the title bar,* is also included. Directional terms are also all right to use when a sighted user with dyslexia can clearly see a change in the interface as the result of an action, such as a change in the right pane when an option in the left pane is clicked.

L

left align, left-aligned

Use to refer to text that is aligned at the left margin. Hyphenate *left-aligned* in all positions in the sentence. Do not use *left-justified*. See also *justify, justified, right align, right-aligned*.

left mouse button

In general, use just *mouse button*. Use *left mouse button* only in discussions of multiple buttons or in teaching beginning skills. See also *Mouse terminology* (Chapter 5).

left-hand

Do not use. See also *left*.

left-justified

Do not use. Use *left-aligned* instead.

leftmost

One word. Use *leftmost* to refer to something at the farthest left side instead of *farthest left, far-left*, or similar terms.

For accessibility considerations, see *left*.

legacy

Do not use in content for a general audience to describe a previous version of a product or system.

Do not use in any content as an adjective, as in "a legacy system," unless you have no other choice. Use *previous, former, earlier*, or a similar term instead. Describe the earlier systems if necessary, especially when discussing compatibility issues.

legal

Use only to refer to matters of law. Do not use to mean *valid*, as in "a valid action."

less vs. fewer vs. under

Use *less* to refer to a mass amount, value, or degree. Use *fewer* to refer to a countable number of items. Do not use *under* to refer to a quantity or number.

Microsoft style

The new building has less floor space and contains fewer offices.

Fewer than 75 members were present.

Less than a quorum attended.

Not Microsoft style

Less than 75 members were present.

The new building has less offices.

Under 75 members attended.

The new building has under 10 floors.

L

let, lets

Do not use to refer to things that a program makes easy or possible for the user if you can use *you can* instead. See also *allow, can vs. may, enable, enabled*.

Microsoft style

With Microsoft Project, you can present information in many ways.

Not Microsoft style

Microsoft Project lets you present information in many ways.

leverage

Do not use as a verb to mean *take advantage of*. Use *take advantage of, capitalize on, use*, or another more appropriate word or phrase.

license terms

See *Microsoft software license terms*.

life cycle

Two words. Hyphenate as an adjective.

like

All right to use as a synonym for *such as* or *similar to* but do not use as a conjunction. Use *as* instead.

Microsoft style

In a workgroup, you can work with files residing on another computer as you would on your own computer.

Moving a dialog box is like moving a window.

Not Microsoft style

In a workgroup, you can work with files residing on another computer like you would on your own computer.

-like

In general, do not hyphenate words ending with *-like* unless the root word ends in double *l*s or the root word has three or more syllables. For example, do not hyphenate words such as *rodlike* and *maillike* But do hyphenate words such as *bell-like* and *computer-like*.

line

Do not use to refer to a series of related Microsoft products or services. Use *family* instead.

line feed

Two words. Refers to the ASCII character that moves the cursor or printer head to the next line, one space to the right of its current position. Do not confuse with the *newline character*, which is the same as the carriage return/line feed and moves the cursor to the beginning of the next line. Spell out on first mention. On subsequent mention, all right to abbreviate *LF*, as in *CR/LF*.

link

Use *link* or *hyperlink* to describe text or a graphic that users can click to go to another document or to another place within the same document. Use *hyperlink* when you refer to a UI element labeled *hyperlink*.

Do not use *hot spot*, *hot link*, or *shortcut* to refer to a link.

Use *go to* to describe the process of going to another page, and use *create* to describe writing the HTML code that forms the link.

It is all right in content for web designers to use *followed link* to refer to a destination that the user has already visited. Do not use this term in content for other audiences. See also *URLs, addresses* (Chapter 7).

Microsoft style

Click the link to go to another webpage.

On the **Insert** tab, click **Hyperlink** in the **Links** group.

linking and embedding

Do not use. Use *OLE Linking and Embedding* instead, which are two features of OLE documents. It is all right to use phrases such as "linking information" and "embedding documents." See also *object linking and embedding*.

list box

Two words. *List box* is a generic term for any type of dialog box option that contains a list of items that the user can select. In text and procedures, refer to a list box by its label and the word *list*, not *list box*. For the Macintosh, use "pop-up list" to refer to unnamed list boxes. See also *Webpage controls, dialog boxes, and property sheets* (Chapter 5).

Microsoft style

In the **Background** list, select **Coffee Bean**.

In the pop-up list, select **Microsoft Excel**. (Mac only)

Not Microsoft style

In the **Background** list box, select **Coffee Bean**.

L

load

Do not use *load* in content for a general audience. Use only to refer to dynamically calling graphics, documents, or installed programs or data such as drivers, DLLs, scripts, registry entries, and profiles into RAM or a program's virtual memory. Use *unload* or *remove* to refer to removing these items from memory.

For games, *load* is the term most commonly used to refer to continuing gameplay at the last place that a game was saved. *Load Game* and *Load Saved Game* are the industry-accepted button labels on the user interfaces of games.

Do not use *load* as a synonym for *run*, *set up*, or *download*. See also *download*.

Microsoft style

Load the device driver into the upper memory area.

Loading your personal settings...   (System status message)

When a user logs on, the system loads the user's profile.

Run the program in character mode.

Set up Word on a Network File Server   (Heading)

If a webpage is taking too long to download, click the **Stop** button.

To cancel your progress in the game, return to the main screen and load your last saved game.

Not Microsoft style

When a user logs on, the system accesses the user's profile.

Load the program in character mode.

Load Word on a Network File Server

If a webpage is taking too long to load, click the **Stop** button.

localhost

The name that is used to represent the same computer on which a TCP/IP message originates. An IP packet sent to localhost has the IP address 127.0.0.1 and does not actually go out to the Internet.

lock

In general, do not use to mean *protect*, as in "protect a document from changes." Do not confuse with *write-protect*, which is what users do to disks to protect them from being overwritten. Some programs, such as Microsoft Excel and Microsoft Word, use *locked* to indicate portions of a document that cannot be changed.

lock up

Do not use to describe a hardware failure or a program or the operating system that has stopped responding. Use *fail* instead for hardware, or *stop responding* for programs or the operating system. See also *fail*.

L

log on, log off, logon, logoff

Use *log on* or *log on to* to refer to creating a user session on a computer or a network. Use *log off* or *log off from* to refer to ending a user session on a computer or a network. Use *sign in* and *sign out* to refer to creating and ending a user session on the Internet.

Do not use *log in, login, log onto, log off of, log out, logout, sign off,* or *sign on* unless these terms appear in the user interface.

The verb form is two words, *log on* or *log off.* As a noun or adjective, use one word, no hyphen: *logon* or *logoff.* See also *sign in, sign out, sign on, sign up, connect.*

Microsoft style

You must enter your password while logging on.

Some networks support this logon feature.

A single logon gives you access to all the resources of the network.

Remember to log off from the network.

When you are finished using the network, remember to log off.

Not Microsoft style

Log in before you start Windows.

Remember to log off of the network.

Remember to log off the network.

When you logon to the network, you have access to your email.

look at

Do not use to mean viewing something that you can view by clicking a command on a **View** menu. Also do not use *look at* to mean *examine, analyze,* or *inspect.*

Microsoft style

To view the list of Help topics, click **Help.**

You can examine the log files to troubleshoot the problem.

Not Microsoft style

To look at the list of Help topics, click **Help.**

You can look at the log files to troubleshoot the problem.

look up

All right to use instead of *see* in cross-references to online index entries from printed documentation. However, if you are using common source files for both printed and online documentation, use *see.*

Microsoft style

For more information, look up "Dial-Up Networking" in the Help index.

lo-res

Do not use. Use *low-resolution* instead.

L

lower

Do not use to indicate product version numbers. Use *earlier*.

lower left, lower right

Hyphenate as adjectives. Use instead of *bottom left* and *bottom right*.

For accessibility considerations, see *left*.

lowercase

One word as an adjective and as a noun. Do not use *lowercased*. Do not use as a verb.

When *lowercase* and *uppercase* are used together, do not use a suspended hyphen.

Microsoft style

You can quickly change the capitalization of all uppercase and lowercase letters.

Change all the uppercase letters to lowercase.

Not Microsoft style

You can quickly change the capitalization of all upper- and lowercase letters.

Lowercase all the capital letters.

low-resolution

Note hyphen. Do not abbreviate as *lo-res*.

M

M, M byte, Mbyte

Do not use as abbreviations for *megabyte*. Use *MB* instead. See also *MB*.

Mac, Macintosh

According to the Apple publications style guide, *Mac* is the preferred term to describe Apple products, but *Macintosh* may also be used. When you use *Mac* as an adjective or as a noun, always precede it with an article or a possessive pronoun. For example, say *the Mac computer* or *your Mac*. Don't make *Mac* or *Macintosh* plural or possessive.

Network language for the Macintosh differs from that of other personal computers. Use the terms *zone, file server*, and *shared disk* to refer to what users select to get information shared on a network. Use colons with no spaces to separate zones, file servers, shared disks, folders, and file names. File names have no extension.

Microsoft style

Macintosh HD:My Documents:Sales

CORP-16:TOMCAT:EX130D Mac Temp:Workbook1

M

machine

In content for most audiences, do not use *machine* to mean a computer. Use *computer* instead. It is all right to use *machine* in content for a technical audience and in content about virtualization to describe both physical machines and virtual machines. See also *computer, PC.*

Microsoft style

Updates can enhance the security and performance of your computer.

This virtual machine image is designed to run on Windows Virtual PC on Windows 7.

You can move virtual machines from one physical server to another to balance the load among physical servers.

A signed machine certificate uniquely identifies the computer being used.

machine language

All right to use in content for a technical audience to refer to the language of compiled code.

Macro Assembler

A programming language. Spell out on first mention. On subsequent mention, all right to abbreviate as *MASM.*

main document

Use to refer to the document that contains the unchanging material in a merged document, such as a form letter. Do not use *core document* or other terms.

makefile

One word. Use only in content for a technical audience.

malicious code

Do not use. See *malware, malicious software, security.*

malicious user

Do not use. Use *hacker* instead of *malicious user* to refer to a user who intentionally accesses a system with the intent to cause harm to the system or to use it in an unauthorized manner. If the intent of unauthorized access is unknown or is not malicious, use *unauthorized user.* See also *hack, hacker; security.*

malware, malicious software

Potentially unwanted software that is installed without adequate user consent. For example, viruses, worms, and trojans are malware.

If your audience might not be familiar with the term *malware*, include the term *malicious software* on first mention. See also *security.*

Microsoft style

The security filter helps prevent malware (malicious software) from damaging your computer.

M

management information systems

Abbreviate as *MIS*. However, in general, use *IS* for *information systems* instead, unless the reference is specifically to management information systems.

manipulate

Do not use in content for a general audience if you can use *work with*, *handle*, or *use* instead.

manual

In general, avoid *manual* as a synonym for *book*, guide, or other specific terms referring to product documentation. Use the title of the book itself if possible. See also *titles of publications*.

marquee

All right to use *marquee* to refer to the scrolling text feature on webpages. Do not use to refer to the feature that draws a dotted line around a selection on the screen. Use *bounding outline* instead. See also *dotted rectangle*.

master/slave

This terminology, although it is standard in the information technology industry, may be insulting to some users. Its use is prohibited in at least one U.S. municipality today.

Do not use *master/slave* in content for a general audience. In content for a technical audience, we strongly recommend that you substitute *subordinate* for *slave*. Use *master/subordinate* only as an adjective. You can reference the use of *slave* as an adjective when it is necessary to clarify the concept by saying *also known as slave server*. You should continue to index *master server* and *slave server*.

We strongly discourage the use of *slave* as an adjective. Do not use *slave* as a noun. See also *master/subordinate, parent/child*.

Microsoft style (recommended)
Each subordinate device has a unique 7-bit or 10-bit address.

The architecture uses a standard master/subordinate design to replicate data from one server to many.

Microsoft style (but not recommended)
Each slave device has a unique 7-bit or 10-bit address.

The architecture uses a standard master/slave design to replicate data from one server to many.

Not Microsoft style
Each slave has a unique 7-bit or 10-bit address.

master/subordinate

Use as adjectives to refer to arrangements in which one device controls another as a *master/subordinate arrangement*, or to the controlling device as the *master server* and the controlled device as the *subordinate server*.

Do not use as a synonym for *parent/child*. These terms do not mean the same thing. See also *master/slave, parent/child*.

M

mathematical

Use instead of *mathematic*.

matrix, matrices

For consistency in Microsoft documentation, use *matrices* as the plural form of *matrix* instead of *matrixes*.

maximize

It is all right to use *maximize* as a verb.

Maximize button

Refers to the button with an open square that is located in the upper-right corner of a window when the window is not maximized. The **Maximize** button performs the same function as the **Maximize** command on a window's shortcut menu.

Do not use *Maximize box* or *Maximize icon*. Use the phrase "**Maximize** button" to refer to the button, not just "**Maximize**." However, it is all right to use *maximize* as a verb. *Maximize* as part of the **Maximize** *button* is always bold.

Microsoft style

Click the **Maximize** *button.*

To fill the screen, maximize the window.

Click *.*

Not Microsoft style

Click **Maximize.**

MB

Abbreviation for *megabyte*. Use the abbreviation only as a measurement with numerals. Do not use the abbreviation in text without a numeral. Insert a space between *MB* and the numeral, or hyphenate if the measure is used as an adjective. Spell out as *megabyte* on first mention unless you are positive that your audience is familiar with the term. See also *Chapter 11, "Acronyms and abbreviations."*

Microsoft style

512 megabytes (MB) of RAM or more

650-MB hard disk space

When used as a noun in measurements, add *of* to form a prepositional phrase.

Microsoft style

This operation can require 20 MB of disk space.

measured service

Service levels are contractually defined, and usage is metered—often per user or per hour. Customers pay only for what they use.

M

medium, media

Follow conservative practice and use *medium*, not *media*, as a singular subject. However, *media* is now gaining acceptance as a singular collective noun referring to the communications industry or the journalism profession. If usage is unclear, be conservative, but be consistent. Ensure that the verb agrees with the subject (that is, *the medium is* and *the media are*), unless you are clearly using *media* as a collective noun in the singular form.

In the computer software industry, *media* has the following meanings:

- Materials or substances, such as fiber optic cable or wire, through which data is transmitted.

- Materials on which data is recorded or stored, such as magnetic disks, CDs, or tapes.

- The mass-communications industry and its practitioners, such as publishing or broadcasting.

- Journalists as a group, whether they are published in print, on the web, or on broadcast media.

Media refers to *the means* of communication, and should not be used to mean *the content* of the communication. Use *media content, media file, media stream, media clip, media item, audio, video*, or *music* instead.

Microsoft style

The media include online broadcasts as well as newspapers, magazines, radio, and television.

The media covers news of the computer industry.

The medium now used for many large computer programs is the DVD-ROM.

Do not use *media* as a shortened form of *multimedia*.

Not Microsoft style

When the consumer plays the media...

The media is downloaded...

...technology that encrypts media with a key

meg

Do not use as an abbreviation for *megabyte*. Use *MB* instead. See also *MB*.

megabit

Always spell out. Do not use the abbreviation *Mb* or *Mbit*.

megabits per second

Spell out on first mention. On subsequent mention, only abbreviate as *Mbps* if used as a measurement with numerals. Spell out in other contexts.

megabyte

Abbreviate as *MB*, not *M*, *meg*, or *Mbyte*. Use the abbreviation only as a measurement with numerals. Do not use the abbreviation in text without a numeral. Insert a space between MB and the numeral, or hyphenate if the measure is used as an adjective. Spell out as *megabyte* on first mention, unless you are positive that your audience is familiar with the term. See also *Measurements and units of measure* (Chapter 7).

M

Microsoft style

516-megabyte (MB) disk

128 MB

650-MB hard disk space

> When used as a noun in measurements, add *of* to form a prepositional phrase.

Microsoft style

This operation can require 20 MB of disk space.

megahertz

A megahertz is a unit of frequency equal to 1 million cycles per second, or hertz.

Spell out on first mention and use the abbreviation *MHz* in parentheses. Use the abbreviation only as a measurement with numerals. Do not use the abbreviation in text without a numeral. Insert a space between *MHz* and the numeral, or hyphenate if the measure is used as an adjective. See also *Measurements and units of measure* (Chapter 7).

Microsoft style

The processor accesses memory at 50 megahertz (MHz).

900-MHz processor

member function

Do not use if you can correctly use *method* instead.

memory

To avoid confusing users, refer to a specific kind of memory rather than use the generic term *memory*, which usually refers to random access memory (RAM). That is, use the more precise terms *RAM, read-only memory (ROM), hard disk*, and so on, as appropriate. It is all right to use *memory* for RAM if you are sure your audience will understand or if you have established the connection. However, in lists of hardware requirements, use *RAM*.

Follow the standard guidelines for using acronyms and abbreviating measurements such as kilobytes (KB) with reference to memory. Spell out RAM and ROM on first mention unless you are positive that your audience is familiar with the term. See also *RAM, ROM*.

Microsoft style

Office web components require approximately 30 MB of disk space.

Each thread consumes about 1 MB of virtual memory.

A 64-bit version of Windows Vista can access from 1 GB of RAM to more than 128 GB of RAM.

> In the noun forms that refer to memory measurements, use *of* in a prepositional phrase, as in "512 MB of RAM."

memory models

Do not hyphenate when referring to various memory models such as *tiny memory model, large memory model*, and so on.

M

Do hyphenate when the term modifies *program* as in such phrases as *tiny-model program* and *large-memory-model program*.

memory-resident

Always hyphenate. Use *memory-resident program*, not *TSR*, in content for a general audience. *TSR*, which stands for *terminate-and-stay-resident*, is all right to use in content for a technical audience.

menu item

Do not use in content for a general audience. Use *command* instead. In content for software developers about creating elements of the user interface, *menu item* may be the best term to use.

message (email)

In the context of email, use *message* or *email message* to refer to an item sent or received. Do not refer to a single message as an *email*.

message box

Do not use to mean *message*. See also *Messages* (Chapter 5).

metadata

One word. Use in content for software developers, web developers, or information technology professionals to refer to data that describes other data.

metafile

One word.

MHz

Abbreviation for *megahertz*. Use the abbreviation only as a measurement with numerals. Do not use the abbreviation in text without a numeral. Spell out *megahertz* on first mention. See also *megahertz*.

mice

Use to refer to more than one mouse. See also *Mouse terminology* (Chapter 5).

micro-

In general, do not hyphenate words beginning with *micro-*, such as *microprocessor* and *microsecond*, unless it is necessary to avoid confusion or if *micro* is followed by a proper noun. When in doubt, refer to the *American Heritage Dictionary*, or consult your project style sheet.

microprocessor

Use instead of *processor* to refer to the chip used in personal computers.

Microsoft

Do not use *MS* as an abbreviation for *Microsoft*.

Microsoft Software License Terms

When referring to the license agreement, use *Microsoft Software License Terms*, instead of *End-User License Agreement* or *EULA*. On first mention, use the full name. On subsequent mention, it is all right to shorten to *license terms*. Do not use *licensing terms*.

M

Microsoft Windows AntiSpyware

Note capitalization. The name of the Microsoft antispyware product. The short form of the name is *Windows AntiSpyware*. See also *antispyware*.

midnight

Do not use *12 A.M.* or *12 P.M.* to specify midnight. Use *00:00*, or just *midnight*.

Midnight is considered the beginning of the new day, not the end of the old one. If you are concerned about ambiguity, refer to *23:59* or *00:01*. See also *A.M., P.M.*

minimize

All right to use as a verb.

Minimize button

Refers to the button containing a short line that is located in the upper-right corner of a window that has not been minimized. The **Minimize** button performs the same function as the **Minimize** command on a window's shortcut menu.

Do not use *Minimize box* or *Minimize icon*. Use the phrase "**Minimize** button" to refer to the button, not just "**Minimize**." However, it is all right to use *minimize* as a verb. *Minimize* as part of the **Minimize** *button* is always bold.

Microsoft style
Click the **Minimize** button.

To reduce a program to a button on the taskbar, minimize the window.

Click .

Not Microsoft style

Click **Minimize**.

minus sign (–)

Use an en dash for a minus sign except for user input when the user must type a hyphen. In that case, the correct key should be clearly noted.

The HTML code for a minus sign is *–*. See also *Dashes* (Chapter 9).

MIP mapping

Two words. Note capitalization. *MIP* is an acronym for *multum in parvo*, Latin meaning "much in little."

mission critical, mission-critical

Two words. Hyphenate as an adjective.

This term has many potential uses and meanings, including military and religious connotations. It is all right to use this term in a technical context when necessary to describe an application or business process. However, whenever possible, use *business-critical* or *critical* instead.

M

mobile device

In general, use the most common term that describes a particular device, such as *phone* or *tablet*. Use *mobile device* only when you need to refer generically to a variety or group of devices and to distinguish them from nonportable devices. See also *device, mobile phone, portable computer.*

mobile phone

In general, use the most generic term that describes a device. For example, just use *phone* unless you need to call out the mobility of the phone. Then use *mobile phone.*

If you are referring to a specific type of mobile phone, such as a cellular phone or a digital phone, it is all right to be specific. Use *smartphone* only when you need to make a distinction between smartphones and other kinds of phones.

Do not use *mobile telephone.*

Do not use *device* to refer to a phone unless you need to write about a generic category that includes such devices as phones, laptops, and tablet PCs. See also *phone, smartphone.*

monitor

Refers to the visual display hardware that includes the screen. Use *screen* to refer to the graphic portion of a monitor. Use *display* as a general term for any visual output device, such as a flat-panel display on a portable computer.

Microsoft style

Turn on the monitor.

Icons appear on the screen.

The newest laptops have active-matrix LCD displays.

monospace

One word. A monospace font is used primarily for examples of code, including program examples and, within text, variable names, function names, argument names, and so on. See also *Document conventions* (Chapter 6).

more than vs. over

Use *more than* to refer to quantifiable figures and amounts. Use *over* to refer to a spatial relationship or position or in a comparison in which *more* is already used. See also *over.*

Microsoft style

The Design Gallery contains more than 16 million colors.

After you compress your drive, your disk will have over 50 percent more free space.

If you want the Help topic to appear over the document you are working on, click the **On Top** button.

mouse over

Do not use as a verb phrase. To describe the action of moving the mouse over a button, use a phrase such as *point to* or, for novice users, *move the pointer over the button.*

movable

Not *moveable.*

movement keys

Do not use. Use *arrow keys* instead. See also *Key names* (Chapter 5).

MPEG

Abbreviation for *Moving Picture Experts Group* (not *Motion Pictures Experts Group*), a working group responsible for, among other things, file formats for moving pictures, with or without audio. Files in MPEG format are used on CD-ROMs, video CDs, and DVDs. Don't spell out. The extension for MPEG files is .mpg.

MS-DOS

Do not use *DOS* to refer to the MS-DOS operating system.

Do not use *MS-DOS* as an adjective before anything that is not a component or aspect of the MS-DOS operating system. Use *MS-DOS-based* instead. See also *DOS*.

Microsoft style

MS-DOS-based program

MS-DOS-based computer

MS-DOS command

Not Microsoft style

DOS program

MS-DOS program

MS-DOS computer

MS-DOS prompt

Do not use to mean *command prompt*

MS-DOS-based program

Use instead of *non-Windows program* when discussing software that runs on the MS-DOS operating system.

In content for a technical audience, it is all right to refer to programs that run only in the Command Prompt window as *console applications. Character-based application* is all right to use for generic references to programs that do not run in Windows or other graphical environments, if the audience is familiar with the term.

Note that *MS-DOS-based program* is spelled with two hyphens, not a hyphen and an en dash.

multi-

In general, do not hyphenate words beginning with *multi* unless it is necessary to avoid confusion or if *multi* is followed by a proper noun. When in doubt, check the *American Heritage Dictionary*, or consult your project style sheet. If the word does not appear there or in the following list, use *multiple* before the word instead. Do not invent new words by combining them with *multi*.

Microsoft style

multicast

multichannel

M

multicolumn

multilevel

multiline

multilingual

multimedia

multiprocessor

multipurpose

multitasking

multiuser

International considerations

Creating new words makes content more difficult for the worldwide audience and may lead to mistranslation in machine-translated content.

multiple selection

Use to refer to a selection that includes multiple items. Do not use *disjoint selection*, *nonadjacent selection*, or *noncontiguous selection*, except in content for a technical audience, and only if the term appears in the user interface or application programming interface. If you must use a term for selected items that do not touch each other, use *multiple selection*, or refer to the specific nonadjacent items instead. See also *adjacent selection*, *nonadjacent selection*.

multiplication sign (×)

In general, use the multiplication sign (×), not the letter *x*, to indicate the mathematical operation. Use an asterisk (*) if required to match the user interface.

Use × to mean *by* in referring to screen resolution or to physical dimensions.

The HTML code for the multiplication sign is *×* or *×*. See also *Chapter 11, "Acronyms and abbreviations."*

multitasking

Do not use any form of this word as a verb. It's jargon.

Microsoft style

Windows 7 supports multitasking.

Not Microsoft style

You can multitask with Windows 7.

multithreaded

Use instead of *multithread*.

M

N

n

Conventionally, a lowercase *n* in italic type refers to a generic use of a number. You can use *n* when the value of a number is arbitrary or immaterial. For example, you can say "move the insertion point *n* spaces to the right." Reserve a lowercase *x* in italic type for representing an unknown in mathematical equations (a variable) and other such placeholders. See also *x*.

International considerations

Because *n* does not refer to the generic use of a number in all languages, using *n* for this purpose may lead to mistranslation in machine-translated content.

namespace

One word.

nanosecond

Always spell out. Means one-billionth of a second.

native language

Do not use to refer to a computer system's machine language. This term could be a misleading anthropomorphism. Use *machine language* or *host language* instead.

natural user interface, NUI

Do not use *natural user interface* or *NUI* in content for a general audience unless you have no other choice. Spell out on first mention.

navigate

Do not use to refer to the act of going from place to place on the World Wide Web or on an intranet. Use *browse* instead.

To refer to the act of going directly to a webpage or website, whether by typing a URL in the Address bar of a browser or by clicking a hyperlink, use *go to*. Do not use *see* in this context.

Microsoft style

To start browsing the web, click any link on your home page when you start Internet Explorer.

To go to a webpage, type the address of the page in the Address bar, and then click **Go**.

It is all right to refer to controls or buttons on the user interface as *navigation* buttons and to Help topics or webpages that orient the user as *navigation* topics or *navigation* pages.

need

Often confused with *want*. Be sure to use the term that is appropriate to the situation. *Need* connotes a requirement or obligation; *want* indicates that the user has a choice of actions.

Microsoft style

If you want to use a laser printer, you need a laser printer driver.

Net

Note capitalization. Slang expression for *Internet*. All right to use in informal writing. Do not use in product documentation.

.NET

Note capitalization. Always begin with a dot (.). Do not spell out as *dot NET*. It is all right to begin a sentence with *.NET* if it is necessary to avoid awkwardness or ambiguity, but be aware that the consecutive periods may briefly confuse some users.

netbook

Do not use *netbook* unless you're referring to a specific make and model of a computer that includes *netbook* in its name. Use *computer* or *laptop* instead. See also *computer, device, laptop (n.), portable computer.*

network

Do not shorten to *net*. Do not use *network* as a verb to describe the action of connecting a computer to a network.

A computer is *on*, not *in*, a network, and computers on a network are linked or connected, not *networked*.

Use *network* as a verb and the noun *networking* only to refer to making personal and business connections.

network adapter

Use instead of *network card* to describe hardware that supports connecting a computer to a network. See also *adapter, board, card.*

network administrator

Use only to specifically refer to the administrator of networks. In general, use *administrator* or *system administrator* unless you must specify a particular kind. See also *system administrator, sysop.*

network connection

Use instead of *local area network connection.*

network drive

Use instead of *remote drive.*

new line, newline

Use *new line* as a noun phrase. Use *newline* as an adjective to refer to the ASCII end-of-line code (CR/ LF), which moves the cursor to the beginning of a new line. Use *newline character* instead of *end-of-line mark* to refer to the ASCII end-of-line code.

Microsoft style

Press Shift+Enter to start a new line.

Use the newline character to move to the beginning of the next line.

non-

Do not hyphenate words beginning with *non-*, such as *nonnumeric* and *nonzero*, unless a hyphen is necessary to avoid confusion, as in *non-native*, or *non-* is followed by a proper noun, as in *non-English*. When in doubt, check the *American Heritage Dictionary*, or consult your project style sheet.

Do not use *non-* to negate an entire phrase. See also *Hyphens, hyphenation* (Chapter 9).

Microsoft style

security-related

unrelated to security

Not Microsoft style

non-security related

nonadjacent selection

Do not use in content for a general audience to refer to a type of multiple selection in which items such as cells in a table or worksheet do not touch. Use in content for a technical audience only if the term appears in the user interface or application programming interface. In general, if you must use a term for selected items that do not touch each other, use *multiple selection*, or refer to the specific nonadjacent items instead. See also *adjacent selection, multiple selection, noncontiguous selection*.

Microsoft style

To select multiple adjacent cells, drag across the cells that you want to select.

To select nonadjacent cells, select a single cell, and then hold down the Ctrl key while you click other cells that you want to select.

noncontiguous selection

Do not use in content for a general audience to refer to a type of multiple selection in which items such as cells in a table or worksheet do not touch. Use in content for a technical audience only if the term appears in the user interface or application programming interface. In general, if you must use a term for selected items that do not touch each other, use *multiple selection*, or refer to the specific noncontiguous items instead. See also *adjacent selection, multiple selection, noncontiguous selection*.

Microsoft style

To select multiple adjacent cells, drag across the cells that you want to select.

nonprintable, nonprinting

Use *nonprintable* to refer to an area of a page that cannot be printed on. Use *nonprinting* to refer to characters and other data that cannot or will not be printed. Do not use *unprintable*, which means "not fit to be printed," in this context.

Microsoft style

Some text extends into the nonprintable area of the page.

When you click **Show/Hide**, Word displays all nonprinting characters, including paragraph marks and space marks.

non-Windows application, non-Windows-based

Do not use. Use the names of specific operating systems instead, such as an *MS-DOS-based program, a UNIX-based program*, and so on. Also do not use *non-Windows*. Use a "not" construction, instead. For example, say "a program that is not based on Windows."

normal, normally

Implies "in a normal manner," which may not be possible for everyone. Do not use *normal* to mean *customary, usual, typical*, or a similar term. Do not use *normally* to mean *often, usually, ordinarily, typically, generally* or a similar term.

notebook

Do not use *notebook* unless you're referring to a specific make and model of a computer that includes *notebook* in its name. Use *computer* or *laptop* instead. See also *computer, device, laptop, portable computer.*

notification area

The area on the right side of the taskbar formerly called the *system tray* or *status area*. The clock and system notifications appear here.

Do not use the following terms as synonyms for *notification area:*

- system tray

- systray

- status area

It is all right to refer to the location of the notification area, but such references should not be incorporated into the name, which is always *notification area*. Do not use the word *area* by itself to refer to the notification area. Avoid noun stacks and descriptions that might leave the impression that there is more than one notification area.

Microsoft style

The clock appears in the notification area, at the far right of the taskbar.

The notification area is located at the far right of the taskbar.

Not Microsoft style

The clock appears in the notification area of the taskbar.

The clock appears in the notification area on the taskbar.

The clock appears in the taskbar notification area.

The clock appears in the notification area at the far right of the taskbar.

The clock appears in the area at the far right of the taskbar.

NT

Do not use. Use *Windows NT* instead.

NUL, null, NULL, Null

Be sure to preserve the distinction between a *null* (ASCII *NUL) character* and a *zero character*. A null character displays nothing, even though it takes up space. It is represented by ASCII code 0. A zero character, on the other hand, refers to the digit 0 and is represented by ASCII code 48.

Use lowercase *null* to refer to a null value. Better yet, use *null value* to avoid confusion with the constant.

Use **NULL** or **Null** (depending on the language) only to refer to the constant.

null-terminated, null-terminating

Use *null-terminated* as an adjective, as in "null-terminated string." Do not use *null-terminating*, as in "null-terminating character." Use *terminating null character* instead.

number sign (#)

Use *number sign* instead of *pound sign* to refer to the # symbol. However, it is all right to use *pound key (#)*, including the symbol in parentheses, to refer specifically to telephones or telephone numbers.

Always spell out *number*. Do not use the # symbol, except as a key name. For example, use *number 7*, not *#7*. When space is limited, as in tables, it is all right to abbreviate *number* as *No.*

International considerations

Because the abbreviation No. is not used to abbreviate number in other languages, using No. for this purpose may lead to mistranslation in machine-translated content.

numeric

Use instead of *numerical*.

For the keypad, use *numeric keypad*, instead of *numerical keypad* or *numeric keyboard*. See also *keypad*.

O

object

Do not use *object* as a synonym for *item* or *thing* unless you have no other choice. Try to be as specific as possible when you refer to an object because the term means different things in different contexts.

For example, in object-oriented programming, an object is an instance of a class. It contains both methods and data and is treated as one entity. Similarly, in COM-based technologies, an object is a combination of code and data that implements one or more interfaces. However, in assembly language, *object* refers to the object module, which contains data that has been translated into machine code.

Object Linking and Embedding

Note capitalization. Spell out on first mention. On subsequent mention, abbreviate as *OLE*.

obsolete

Do not use as a verb. Use a phrase such as *make obsolete* instead.

of

Do not use *of* after another preposition in such phrases as "off of" or "outside of." It is colloquial and can be confusing for the worldwide audience.

Microsoft style

The taskbar is outside the main window area.

Save your work and then log off the network.

Not Microsoft style

The taskbar is outside of the main window area.

Save your work and then log off of the network.

offline

One word in all instances. Use in the sense of not being connected to or part of a system or network. Do not use in the slang sense of "outside the present context."

off-premises, on-premises

Terms used to distinguish local computing (in which computing resources are located on a customer's own facilities) from remote computing (in which computing resources are provided partially or totally through cloud computing).

Hyphenate in all positions. Note that *premises* is plural. Do not use *on-premise, off-premise*. Do not use *on-premises cloud* or *off-premises cloud*.

okay, OK

Use *OK* only to match the user interface. Otherwise, use *okay*. When referring to the **OK** button in procedures, do not use *the* and *button*.

Microsoft style

In the **Save As** dialog box, click **OK**.

It is okay to write passwords down, but keep them secure.

Not Microsoft style

In the **Save As** dialog box, click the **OK** button.

It is OK to write passwords down, but keep them secure.

 Note It is all right to omit "Click **OK**" at the end of a procedure if it is clear that the user must click **OK** to complete the procedure.

on

Use *on* with these elements:

- Menus ("the **Open** command is on the **File** menu")

- Taskbar, toolbar, ruler, and desktop ("click **Start** on the taskbar")

- Disks, in the sense of a program being on a disk ("the printer drivers on Disk 2")

- User interface ("on the user interface")

- The screen itself (something appears "on the screen")

- Network ("the printer is on the network")

- Hardware platforms ("on the Macintosh")

- The web ("on the web")

0

Do not use *on* with user input actions. See also *in, into; on-screen; onto; on to; procedures.*

Microsoft style
Click the right mouse button.

Click the **WordPad** icon.

Click **OK**.

Press Enter.

Not Microsoft style
Click on the right mouse button.

Click on the **WordPad** icon.

Click on **OK**.

Press on the Enter key.

In COM programming, an interface is implemented on an object.

on the fly

All right to use in content for a technical audience to refer to something that is created when it is needed instead of beforehand.

on/off switch

All right to use. Use instead of *on/off button* except when referring to a remote control device.

once

To avoid ambiguity, especially for the worldwide audience, do not use as a synonym for *after.*

Microsoft style
After you save the document, you can exit the program.

Not Microsoft style
Once you save the document, you can exit the program.

online

One word, both as an adjective and as a noun.

online Help

In general, use *Help* by itself except when necessary to describe the Help system.

Microsoft style

You have easy access to hundreds of subjects in Help.

Not Microsoft style

You have easy access to hundreds of subjects in online Help.

on-screen

Hyphenate as both an adjective and as an adverb in all instances. However, instead of using it as an adverb, try to write around by using a phrase such as *on the screen*.

Microsoft style

Follow the on-screen instructions.

Follow the instructions that appear on the screen.

on-screen keyboard

A keyboard representation on the screen that the user touches to input characters. Do not use *virtual keyboard*, *soft keyboard*, *visual keyboard*, or *keyboard display*.

> **Note** There is an add-in for some versions of Microsoft Office called the Microsoft Visual Keyboard. This program displays the keyboard for another language on your screen so that you can either click the keys on the screen or see how the keys in the second language correspond to the ones on your keyboard. This keyboard is also referred to as an on-screen keyboard.

onto, on to

Two words (*on to*) when referring to the action of connecting to a network, as in "log on to the network."

One word (*onto*) to indicate moving something to a position on top of something else, as in "drag the icon onto the desktop."

opcode

All right to use *opcode* when referring to a programming term such as the *opcode* parameter. However, do not use *opcode* as a shortened form of *operation code*. Use *operation code* instead.

open

Users open windows, files, documents, and folders. Describe the item as *open*, not *opened*, as in "an open file" and "the open document."

Do not use *open* to describe clicking a command, a menu, an icon, an option, or other similar element. See also *procedures, Ribbons, menus, and toolbars* (Chapter 5).

Microsoft style

To open the document in Outline view, click **View**, and then click **Outline**.

You double-click the **Works** icon to open Works.

You can view your document in the open window.

Not Microsoft style

Open the View menu, and then open the Outline command.

Open the Works icon.

You can view your document in the opened window.

operating environment, operating system

By conventional definitions, an *operating environment* (or just *environment*) includes both hardware and operating system software, while an *operating system* is only the software. (A *graphical environment* refers to the graphical user interface of an operating system.) However, in practice *environment* often refers only to the operating system, as in "Visual FoxPro runs in the UNIX environment."

You can use several prepositions with *operating system*. Programs can run *on*, *under*, or *with* an operating system, whichever seems more appropriate. However, do not use *run against* an operating system. See also *platform*.

Microsoft style

Word 2010 runs with the Windows operating system.

Microsoft Exchange Server runs on the Windows Server operating system.

Not Microsoft style

A number of programs run against Windows 7.

option, option button

In general, refer to items in a dialog box only by their labels. If you must provide a descriptor, use *option*. Use the exact label text, including its capitalization, but do not capitalize the word *option* itself.

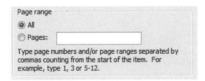

You should generally refer only to the option that the button controls. If you must refer to the button to avoid ambiguity, use *option button*. See also *control, radio button, switch*.

Microsoft style

In the **Sort Text** dialog box, click **No Header Row**.

Not Microsoft style

In the **Sort Text** dialog box, click the **No Header Row** option button.

In content for a technical audience, it is all right to use *option* instead of *switch* to refer to a command argument or compiler option, such as **/b** or **/Za**, if your project style sheet permits it.

outdent

Do not use. Use *negative indent* instead. See also *indent, indentation*.

output

Do not use as a verb. Use as a term specific to the kind of output referred to, such as *write to*, *display on*, or *print to* instead.

Microsoft style

The output provided the information needed.

A printer is a standard output device.

You can print a document to a file instead of to a specific printer.

Not Microsoft style

You can output a document to a file instead of to a specific printer.

outside

Use instead of the colloquial *outside of*.

over

To avoid ambiguity, use *over* to refer to a position or location above something. For quantities, use *more than*. Do not use to refer to version numbers. List each applicable version instead. See also *later*.

Microsoft style

A transparent viewing layer with a red border appears over the diagram.

The installed base is more than 2 million.

You need Windows 7, Windows Vista, or Windows XP.

Not Microsoft style

The installed base is over 2 million.

You need Windows 7 or over.

overtype

Use to refer to Overtype mode (note capitalization). In Overtype mode the user *types over* existing content at the cursor.

Do not use as a synonym for *overwrite*. See also *overwrite*.

overwrite

Use only to refer to replacing new data with existing data. Use *replace* to refer to replacing an existing file with a new one with the same name.

Do not use *overwrite* as a synonym for *type over*. See also *overtype*.

P

page

Refers to one of a collection of web documents that make up a website. Use *page* to refer to the page the user is on, that is, the particular document, or to a specific page such as the home page or start page.

Also, use *page* instead of *screen* to refer to an individual screen within a wizard.

palette

A collection of colors or patterns that users can apply to objects, such as the color display in Control Panel.

Users click an option in a palette. Capitalize the palette name, and use bold formatting.

Microsoft style

In the **Color** palette, click the color that you want.

pan

Use to refer to moving the screen in multiple directions at a controlled rate, as you would *pan* a camera to see different views in the environment. For contact gestures, use to refer to moving a finger, hand, or pen on the device surface to move through screens or menus at a controlled rate, rather than quickly skipping through content using the flick gesture.

Do not use *drag* or *scroll* as a synonym for *pan*.

Microsoft style

Pan up, down, right, or left by using the D-pad.

Use your finger to pan across the map.

Pan contact gesture

pane

Use to refer only to the separate areas of a split or single window. For example, in Windows Explorer, the names of all the folders can appear in one pane and the contents of a selected folder in another pane.

If a pane is not labeled in the user interface, use lowercase for pane names, as in "the *annotation pane*." If a pane is labeled in the user interface, follow the capitalization as it appears in the interface, as in "the Score pane."

panorama

All right to use *panorama* or *panoramic view* to describe the Microsoft Surround Video technology used in Expedia and other programs. However, if the view is full circle, use *360-degree* or *360° view* instead. It is all right to use the degree symbol, but the symbol may be difficult to see online.

> **Note** Surround Video, despite its name, is technically not a video presentation.

parameter

Technical term referring to a value given to a variable until an operation is completed. Do not use *parameter* to mean *characteristic, element, limit,* or *boundary.* See also *argument.*

parent/child

All right to use in content for a technical audience to refer to the relationships among processes in a multitasking environment or in content about databases to describe the relationships among nodes in a tree structure.

Do not use as a synonym for a master/slave relationship. These terms do not mean the same thing. See also *master/slave.*

parenthesis, parentheses

Use the term *opening parenthesis* or *closing parenthesis* for an individual parenthesis, not *open parenthesis, close parenthesis, beginning parenthesis, ending parenthesis, left parenthesis,* or *right parenthesis.* It is all right to use *parenthesis* by itself if it either does not matter or is unambiguously clear which parenthesis is under discussion. See also *parentheses.*

patch

Do not use as a noun or a verb. This is legacy terminology that has been replaced by specific update types such as *security update* or *software update.* See also *out-of-band release terminology* (Chapter 6), *security update, software update.*

Microsoft style

Help secure your system by applying the appropriate security updates.

You can update your system automatically with Windows Update.

Not Microsoft style

To automatically apply patches to your system, subscribe to Windows Update.

You may need to manually patch your applications server.

patch management

Industry-standard phrase that is all right to use in content for a technical audience.

patching

A method of updating a file that replaces only the parts being changed instead of the entire file.

Use only in content for a technical audience and only if this specific method for applying an update is relevant. See also *full file replacement, patch.*

path

Use *path* instead of *pathname*, both in general reference and in syntax. A path describes the route the operating system follows from the root directory of a drive through the hierarchical structure to locate a folder or file.

The path usually specifies only a drive and any folders below the root directory. When a path also specifies a file, it is called a *full path.*

In command syntax, *path* represents only the folder portion of the full path, as follows:

copy [*drive:*][*path*]*filename*

To indicate a path, first type the drive name, followed by a colon and a backslash. Then type the name of each folder in the order that you would open it, separated by a backslash, as follows:

C:\Documents and Settings\user1

Use *address* or *URL* instead of *path*, to refer to a location on the Internet.

In general, use *path of* instead of *path to*, to refer to the location of a file. See also *directory, folder, Macintosh.*

Microsoft style

The full path of my current tax form is C:\Documents and Settings\user1\My Documents\Taxes\This year's taxes.

In Macintosh documentation, use colons with no spaces to separate zones, file servers, shared disks, folders, and file names. File names have no extensions.

Microsoft style (Macintosh)

Macintosh HD:My Documentation:Sales

CORP-16:TOMCAT:EX130D Mac Temp:Workbook1

For information about capitalization of paths, see *Capitalization* (Chapter 7) and *Document conventions* (Chapter 6).

PC

PC is the abbreviation for *personal computer.* Use *PC* in the following contexts:

- In content that is informal in tone

- In UI text where space is constrained

- When referring to a feature or website that includes the term *PC*

When you use *PC*, do not spell it out on first mention.

In procedures, use *computer.*

To help avoid ambiguity, do not mix *PC* and *computer* in the same paragraph unless you have no other choice.

Microsoft style

You told us what you wanted in a PC. Here's how Windows 7 can help.

You can run multiple Windows environments by using the Windows Virtual PC feature.

To change the configuration settings on your computer, modify the configuration file.

Insert the disc into the DVD drive on your computer, and then enter the Product Key when prompted.

Not Microsoft style

Insert the disc into the DVD drive on your PC, and then enter the Product Key when prompted.

You told us what you wanted in a PC. Here's what you can do with your computer.

Do not use *PC computer*. Do not use *Windows*, with or without a version number, as a modifier for *PC* or *computer*. Instead, refer to a PC or computer that is *running Windows*.

Microsoft style

For both Mac computers and PCs....

For both Mac computers and computers running Windows 7....

To use this feature, you need a PC that's running Windows 7.

Not Microsoft style

Windows PC

Windows 7 PC

For both Mac and PC computers....

To use this feature, you must have a Windows computer.

To use this feature, you must have a Windows 7-based PC.

To make *PC* plural, add a lowercase *s* without an apostrophe.

The term *PC-compatible* is obsolete. Do not use it.

PC Card vs. PCMCIA

Use *PC Card* instead of *PCMCIA* or *PCMCIA card* to refer to the add-in memory and communications cards for portable computers.

p-code

Abbreviation for *pseudocode*. Capitalize as *P-code* when it is the first word in a sentence. Capitalize as *P-Code* in contexts that require title capitalization. Spell out on first mention. Use only in content for a technical audience.

pen

An input device that consists of a pen-shaped stylus that interacts with a computer. Use *input device* when referring generically to pens, trackballs, styluses, and so on.

Use *tap* (and *double-tap*) instead of *click* when documenting procedures specific to pen pointing devices. *Tap* means to press the screen and then to lift the pen tip.

per

Per is all right to use to mean *for each* in statistical or technical contexts. However, in other contexts, use *a* or the phrase *for each* instead of *per*.

Microsoft style

Users who log on only once a day are rare.

You can have only one drive letter per network resource.

Not Microsoft style

Users who log on only once per day are rare.

Do not use *per* to mean *by* or *in accordance with*.

Microsoft style

Find all the topics that contain a specific word by following the instructions on your screen.

Identify your computer by using the procedure in the next section.

Not Microsoft style

Find all the topics that contain a specific word, per the instructions on your screen.

Identify your computer per the procedure in the next section.

percent, percentage

One word. In general, spell out. Do not use the percent sign (%), except in tables, to save space in the user interface, and as a technical symbol. When spelling out *percent*, insert a space between the number and the word. Always use a numeral with *percent*, no matter how small.

When you are using *percent* in column headings to name the rate percent term in the percentage formula (base * rate percent = percentage), you can use *percent* without a numeral, as follows.

List price	Discount percent	Discount percentage	Sale price
$200	5%	$10.00	$190.00

When not specifying a quantity, such as in the phrase "a large percentage of system resources," or when applying the percentage formula (base * rate percent = percentage), use *percentage*.

Microsoft style

At least 50 percent of your system resources should be available.

Only 1 percent of the test group was unable to complete the task.

10.00 USD is the percentage discount calculated by applying a 10 percent discount to a list price of 100.00 USD.

$100.00 * 10% = $10.00

10% is the percent discount

$10.00 is the percentage discount

perimeter network

A collection of devices and subnets placed between an intranet and the Internet to help protect the intranet from unauthorized Internet users. On first mention, use *perimeter network* (also known as *DMZ, demilitarized zone,* and *screened subnet).* If your content has an index or glossary, include *DMZ, demilitarized zone,* and *screened subnet* with a cross-reference to *perimeter network.* See also *demilitarized zone (DMZ), screened subnet.*

peripheral

Do not use as a noun unless you have no other choice. Use *peripheral device* or a more specific term instead.

permissions

Use *permissions* only to refer to operations associated with a specific shared resource, such as a file, directory, or printer, that are authorized by the system administrator for individual user accounts or administrative groups. Permissions are *granted* or *assigned*, not *allowed*.

If you refer to a named permission, use title capitalization and regular type. Do not use *privileges* or *permission records* as a synonym for *permissions.* See also *rights, user rights.*

Microsoft style

Setting the Traverse Folder permission on a folder does not automatically set the Execute File permission on all files within that folder.

Grant Read, Read and Execute, and List Folder Content permissions to the Users group.

Whenever possible, assign permissions to groups instead of users.

phone

In general, use the most generic term that describes a device. For example, just use *phone* unless you need to call out the mobility of the phone. Then use *mobile phone.* Use *smartphone* only when you need to make a distinction between smartphones and other kinds of phones.

Do not use *device* to refer to a phone unless you need to write about a generic category that includes such devices as phones, laptops, and tablet PCs. See also *mobile phone, smartphone.*

photo

Photo is all right to use as an abbreviation for *photograph* in many Microsoft products and services. Consult your project style sheet for guidance about using this term.

International considerations

Using the abbreviation *photo* does not necessarily save space when content is localized. In many languages, the full term is translated because an abbreviation is not available.

pin

Use to refer to adding an icon to the Windows taskbar or **Start** menu or to adding a Tile to Windows Phone **Start**.

Microsoft style
Pin the **Maps** icon to **Start**.

Not Microsoft style
Add the **Maps** icon to **Start**.

pinch

Use to refer to the contact gesture or air gesture of decreasing the size of an object on the user interface by moving together two or more fingers or both hands. See also *stretch*.

Microsoft style
To decrease the size of the photograph, pinch it.

Microsoft style (novice computer user)
To decrease the size of the photograph, move your fingers together while touching the photograph.

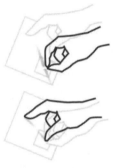

Pinch contact gesture

ping, PING

Do not use *ping* to refer generally to searching for a program. This usage is slang. *Ping* is all right to use when it refers specifically to using the PING protocol. The PING protocol is used to determine the presence of a host on the Internet. PING stands for Packet Internet Groper, but do not spell out. Describe if necessary.

pipe

Do not use as a verb in content for a general audience. Use a more specific term such as *send, move, copy, direct, redirect,* or *write* instead. Use as a verb in content for a technical audience to refer to routing data from the standard output of one process to the standard input of another.

The symbol for a pipe in programming content is a vertical bar (|).

pixel

Short for *picture element*. One pixel is a measurement representing the smallest amount of information displayed graphically on the screen as a single dot. In content for a general audience, define pixel on first mention.

placeholder

Do not use as a verb. For formatting of placeholders, see *Document conventions* (Chapter 6).

plaintext vs. plain text

Use *plaintext* only to refer to nonencrypted or decrypted text in content about encryption. Use *plain text* to refer to ASCII files.

platform

Refers to hardware architecture and is sometimes used interchangeably with *operating environment* or *environment*. But because it can be ambiguous, do not use *platform*, particularly in content for a general audience, unless you have no other choice.

Platform is all right to use in content for a technical audience if necessary to distinguish differing behaviors of a function or other API elements in various operating systems, but whenever possible use *operating system* for clarity.

Cross-platform is all right to use in content for a technical audience to refer to a program or device that can run on more than one operating system.

Use *on* to refer to a hardware platform. For example, you would say "on the Macintosh," but "in Windows 7." See also *operating environment, operating system*.

platform as a service (PaaS)

An operating environment that is made available to an organization over the Internet. Typically, a vendor manages the operating environment itself (which may include storage and servers), and the customer manages the end-user applications that are delivered in the operating environment. PaaS offerings provide a platform for the development, testing, deployment, and ongoing maintenance of applications without the cost of buying and maintaining the underlying infrastructure and operating environments.

All right to use *PaaS* after the full term has been spelled out on first mention. Do not capitalize as *PAAS*.

playlist

One word. Refers to an assembled collection of songs, movies, or other media. A user *adds* these media types to a playlist and *deletes* them from a playlist.

Plug and Play

Use only as a noun or adjective to refer to a set of specifications developed by Intel for automatic configuration of a computer to work with various peripheral devices. Note capitalization. Do not hyphenate.

All right to use all lowercase (*plug and play*) to refer to the ability of a computer system to automatically configure a device that is added to it.

Do not use as a synonym for *Universal Plug and Play* (UPnP). See also *UPnP*.

Microsoft style

Plug and Play functionality

Plug and Play printer

Plug and Play records the information in an event log.

plug-in

A component that permits a specific browser to recognize and support the file format of an object embedded in an HTML document. Do not use as a synonym for *add-in* or *add-on*. See *add-in*.

point to

Use *point to* for submenu commands that do not have to be clicked.

Microsoft style

Click **Start**, point to **All Programs**, and then click **Windows Update**.

Also use *point to* to refer to positioning the mouse pointer at the appropriate location on the screen. For example, say "Point to the window border."

pointer

Refers to the arrow or other shape that moves when the user moves the mouse, a finger or hand, or other pointing device. In general use the term pointer without descriptive labels. For more information about pointer shapes, see the Windows User Experience Guidelines.

In a programming context, a pointer is a variable that contains a memory location. In the rare case where both types of pointers are discussed, use *mouse pointer* and *pointer variable* as necessary to avoid ambiguity.

Do not use *cursor* as a synonym for *pointer*. See also *Mouse terminology* (Chapter 5).

pointing device

A mouse, tablet pen, trackball, joystick, or other hardware device that is used to move a pointer on the screen. Use *pointing device* only if users have more than one option to move a pointer on a screen. Otherwise, use the name of the specific device instead.

pop-up

Do not use as a noun. Also do not use as a verb to mean *open* or *appear*.

It is all right to use *pop-up menu* in a programming context to describe the menu that appears when the user right-clicks an item. If you must use a term to describe this type of menu in content for a general audience, use *shortcut menu*.

Pop-up window is all right to use in references to windows that pop up in context-sensitive Help. Do not use *pop-up window* as a synonym for *dialog box*. See also *context menu, shortcut menu*.

Microsoft style

Answer the questions in the wizard as they appear.

Some commands carry out an action immediately; others open a dialog box so that you can select options.

A pop-up window gives additional information about an option.

If you want to print the information in a pop-up window, right-click the window, and then click **Print Topic**.

Not Microsoft style
Answer the questions in the wizard as they pop up.

Some commands carry out an action immediately; others open a pop-up window so that you can select options.

Use "pop-up list" in Macintosh documentation to refer to unnamed list boxes.

Microsoft style
In the pop-up list, click **Microsoft Excel**.

port

As in "printer port" or "communications port." Use the verb forms *port to* and *port for* only in content for a technical audience in reference to portability. Do not use in content for a general audience unless you have no other choice.

portable computer

In general, use the most generic term that describes a device. For example, use *computer* or *PC* unless you need to call out the mobility of the computer. Use *portable computer* when you need to use a generic term that includes only laptops, notebooks, tablet PCs, and other kinds of portable computers.

Use *laptop* to refer to a portable computer with a flat LCD or plasma screen, an integrated keyboard, and a lid.

Use *device* as a generic term to include portable computers, tablet PCs, smartphones, and other mobile devices.

Do not use *portable* as a noun. See also *computer, device, laptop (n.), PC, tablet PC, phone.*

portrait orientation

Printing orientation so that the page is longer than it is wide.

 Portrait

Compare *landscape orientation.*

post office vs. postoffice

One word, lowercase, when referring to the component of an email system. Otherwise, it's two words.

pound key, pound sign (#)

Do not use either term to refer to the keyboard key name. Use *number sign* instead. However, it is all right to use *pound key (#)* when referring specifically to telephones or the telephone keypad.

power cord

Use instead of *power cable*.

power down, power up, power off, power on

Do not use. Use *turn off* and *turn on* instead. Do not use *shut down* to refer to turning off a computer. See also *shut down, shutdown, turn on, turn off*.

power user

Do not use to mean that someone must be an expert to use certain programs or features. *Power user* as a classification of expertise is vague. To some it may mean somebody who can write a macro. To others it may mean somebody who can edit the system registry by hand. It is far safer to identify the specific knowledge or skill that you are referring to.

pre-

In general, do not hyphenate words beginning with *pre*, such as *preallocate* and *preempt*, unless it is necessary to avoid confusion, as in *pre-engineered*, or if *pre* is followed by a proper noun, as in *pre-C++*. When in doubt, check the *American Heritage Dictionary*, or consult your project style sheet.

preceding

Use *preceding*, *previous*, or *earlier* instead of *above* to mean earlier in a piece of content, but only if you cannot use a hyperlink, which is preferred. See also *cross-reference*.

Preface

Do not use *Preface* as the title of the introductory section of content. Use *Introduction* or a more descriptive title appropriate to the user, such as "Before you begin."

press

Differentiate among the terms *press*, *type*, *enter*, and *use*. Use the following guidelines:

Use *press*, not *depress*, *hit*, or *strike* when pressing a key on the keyboard.

Microsoft style
Press Enter.

Press Alt+S to save your document.

Not Microsoft style
Hit Enter to begin a new paragraph.

Strike Alt+S to save your document.

Use *pressed in* and *not pressed in*, not *depressed* and *not depressed*, to refer to the position of three-dimensional toggle keys and buttons.

Use *use* when *press* might be confusing, such as when referring to the arrow keys or function keys. For example, with the statement "Press the arrow keys to move around the document," *press* might make users think that they need to press all the keys simultaneously.

Microsoft style
To move the cursor, use the arrow keys.

Not Microsoft style

To move the cursor, press the arrow keys.

Use *use* when multiple platform or peripheral choices initiate the same action or actions within a program. An example is "Use the controls on your keyboard or controller to run through the obstacle course." However, to teach beginning skills, be specific. For example, write "To run through the obstacle course, press the Spacebar on the keyboard or pull the right trigger on the Xbox controller." Consider using a table to present instructions that have more alternatives than the two that are presented in this example.

Use *type*, not *enter*, to direct a user to type information that the user cannot select from a list.

Microsoft style

Type your password.

Type the path to the server or select it from the list.

Not Microsoft style

Type in your password.

Use *press and hold* only if the program requires the user to do so because a delay is built into the peripheral/interface interaction. Do not use *press and hold* when referring to a mouse button unless you are teaching beginning skills.

Microsoft style

To open the shortcut menu, press and hold the tablet pen on the **Internet Explorer** icon.

Not Microsoft style

To adjust the volume, press and hold the **Volume** button.

Do not use *press*, *hit*, or *strike* as a synonym for *click*.

Microsoft style

On the Quick Access toolbar, click **New**.

Not Microsoft style

On the Quick Access toolbar, press the **New** button.

On the Quick Access toolbar, hit the **New** button.

On the Quick Access toolbar, strike the **New** button.

Press (Microsoft Press)

After first using *Microsoft Press*, it is all right to use *Press* to refer to Microsoft Press. Do not use *MS Press*.

print, printout

As a verb, use *print* instead of *print out*. All right to use *printout* as the result of a print job, if necessary, but try to be more specific.

print queue

Use instead of *printer queue*.

private cloud, hosted private cloud

A cloud infrastructure that is dedicated to an organization (not shared with other organizations). A private cloud can be managed by the organization or hosted by a third-party service provider, in which case it is referred to as a *hosted private cloud*. A private cloud can be located on-premises or off-premises.

Because the deployment models are not widely understood, define on first mention. See also *community cloud, hybrid cloud, public cloud*.

privileges

Do not use as a synonym for *permissions* or *rights*. See *permissions* and *rights*.

product ID

The number returned by the software after a user types the CD key or product key. Used for tracking and support.

For CD-ROM products, the product ID (PID) includes the 10-digit CD key. The user must type that number to install the product. See also *CD key, product key*.

product key

A 25-digit number on the user's CD case that identifies the product license. In general, use *product key* rather than *CD key*. See also *CD key*.

program file

All right to use, especially if necessary to avoid *executable file* in content for a general audience, but use the specific name of the file whenever you can.

program vs. application

Whenever possible, refer to a product by its descriptor, such as *database management system*, *spreadsheet*, or *publishing toolkit*, instead of by the term *program* or *application*. For example, refer to Microsoft Visual FoxPro as a *relational database development system*.

If that is not possible, follow these general guidelines:

- Use *program*, not *application*, in content for a general audience unless *application* appears in the user interface.

- It is all right to use *application* in content for a technical audience, especially to refer to a grouping of software that includes both executable files and other software components, such as a database.

- Do not use *program application*.

When in doubt, consult your project style sheet. See also *app, applet, application*.

progress indicator

A control that displays the percentage of a particular process that has been completed, such as printing or setting up a program. Do not refer to it as a "slider." A slider is a control that enables users to set a value on a continuous range of possible values, such as screen brightness, mouse-click speed, or volume.

prohibition sign

Use to describe the circle with a line through it that is commonly superimposed over another symbol to indicate an activity that is not permitted.

prompt

Do not use *prompt* as a synonym for *message*. A prompt is a signal, which may or may not be a message, that a program or the operating system is waiting for the user to take some action. In general, restrict the use of *prompt* as a noun to the command prompt.

Use *prompt* as a verb to describe the act of requesting information or an action from the user. See also *command prompt*.

Microsoft style

If you receive a message that the association information is incomplete...

When you run Setup, you are prompted to insert disks one by one.

Not Microsoft style

If you receive a prompt that the association information is incomplete...

prop

Do not use as a slang form of *propagate* in such phrases as "propping files to a server" or "propping information to a database."

properties

Properties are attributes or characteristics of an object used to define its state, appearance, or value. For example, the **Special Effect** property in Microsoft Access determines the appearance of a control on a form, such as sunken, raised, or flat.

Outside a programming context, *property* can be a vague term. Do not use it except for a specific reference to something named as a property. Use *value* or *setting* instead to refer to a specific characteristic a user can set (such as the specific color of a font) or *attribute* for the general characteristic (such as "color is an attribute of fonts"). See also *attributes*.

property sheet, property page

Property sheet refers either to a secondary window that displays the properties of an object after carrying out the **Properties** command or to a collection of tabs or *property pages* that make up a dialog box.

In general, do not use the terms *property sheet* or *property page* in content for a general audience. Use *dialog box* or *tab* instead. If your product uses *property sheets*, consult your project style sheet for specific usage of the term. See also *Webpage controls, dialog boxes, and property sheets* (Chapter 5).

protected mode

Use instead of *protect mode*.

public cloud

A cloud infrastructure typically owned and managed by an organization that provisions cloud services to the general public or to a large group.

Because the deployment models are not widely understood, define on first mention. See also *community cloud, hybrid cloud, private cloud*.

pull quote

Two words. Refers to a brief excerpt visually set off from the main text, usually in large type, to draw the user's attention to the content.

pull-down

Do not use *pull-down* as an adjective to describe a menu or a list except in content for software developers. Do not use *pull down* as a noun to mean a menu or a list. Do not use *pull down* as a verb to describe clicking a menu or downloading a file from the Internet. See also *drop-down*.

purge

In general, do not use because of negative associations in ordinary English usage. Use *delete, clear*, or *remove* instead. It is all right to use *purge* if it is a programming term such as the **Purge** method.

push button, push-button

Two words. Hyphenated as an adjective.

Do not use as a synonym for *button* or *command button*. In content for software developers, *push button* can be included parenthetically and in glossaries, if necessary. In content for software developers, it is also all right to use when describing programming elements such as the **PushButton** class. See also *command button; Webpage controls, dialog boxes, and property sheets* (Chapter 5).

push-to-talk

Do not capitalize in body text. In contexts that require title capitalization, capitalize as *Push-to-Talk*.

P

Q

quality

Do not use *quality* by itself as an adjective. Always use *high-quality*. See also *high-quality*.

Microsoft style
Microsoft Word is a high-quality word processor.

Not Microsoft style
Microsoft Word is a quality product.

quarter inch

In general, use *a quarter inch*, instead of *quarter of an inch* or *one-quarter inch*.

quick key

Do not use. Use *keyboard shortcut* instead. See also *keyboard shortcut.*

quit

Do not use *quit* to refer to any of the following:

- A user closing a program. Use *exit* instead.

- A user closing a document or a window. Use *close* instead.

- The action a program takes to close itself when it has encountered a problem and cannot continue. Use *close* instead. (Do not confuse with *stop responding*, which indicates that the program cannot close itself.)

- Ending a user session on a computer or on a network. Use *log off* instead.

- Ending a network connection. Use *end* instead.

R

radio button

International considerations

Radio button is a problem term for the worldwide audience. Do not use *radio button* except in content for software developers in which the application programming interface includes the term. In that case, use wording such as *<name> option button (also known as a radio button)*. If your content has an index, include *radio button* in the index with a cross-reference to *option button.*

In other content, refer to a *radio button* by its label. If you must provide a descriptor, use *option.* Use the exact label text, including its capitalization, but do not capitalize the word *option* itself. You should generally refer only to the option that the radio button controls. If you must refer to the button to avoid ambiguity, use *option button.* See also *option; option button; Webpage controls, dialog boxes, and property sheets* (Chapter 5).

ragged right

All right to use to refer to the uneven right edge in documents. Opposite of *right-aligned.*

RAM

Abbreviation for *random access memory.* For guidance about referring to memory, see *memory.*

range selection

Do not use unless you have no other choice. In content for a general audience, use a phrase such as *a range of cells* or a *range of dates* to refer to a selection of adjoining cells, dates, and so on.

Use the same type of phrasing in content for a technical audience, but if you are describing the feature, use *adjacent selection.*

The selection of more than one nonadjacent item is called a *multiple selection.* See also *adjacent selection, multiple selection, nonadjacent selection.*

re-

In general, do not hyphenate words beginning with *re-* unless it is necessary to avoid confusion or *re-* is followed by a proper noun. When in doubt, check the *American Heritage Dictionary*, or consult your project style sheet.

Microsoft style

reenter

recover (to get back or regain)

re-cover (to cover again)

recreate (to take part in a recreational activity)

re-create (to create anew)

read/write

Use instead of *read-write*, as in "read/write permission."

read/write permission

Use instead of *read/write access*. Files and devices have read/write properties, but users have the permission to access those files and devices.

read-only

Always hyphenate.

Microsoft style

read-only memory

This file is read-only.

real-time, real time

Two words. Hyphenate as an adjective.

Microsoft style

Real-time operations happen at the same rate as human perceptions of time.

In chat rooms, users communicate in real time.

reboot

Do not use. Use *restart* instead, and make clear that *restart* in this context refers to the computer and not to a program.

Microsoft style

After Setup is complete, restart your computer.

Not Microsoft style

After Setup is complete, reboot your computer.

Restart after Setup is complete.

If the user interface or application programming interface uses *reboot* in a label or element name, it is all right to reproduce the label or element name, but use *restart* to refer to the action or event described.

Microsoft style

The **Reboot** method shuts down the computer and then restarts it.

recommend

It is all right, but not required, to make recommendations directly by using a phrase such as *we recommend*. Alternate phrasings are also all right to use. Do not use *recommend* when something is required.

Do not use *Microsoft recommends*. It injects an inappropriately corporate tone that some users might interpret as arrogant. Do not use *it is recommended*. It sounds both corporate and evasive. See also *should vs. must*.

Microsoft style

We recommend at least 256 MB of RAM to run this program.

This program performs best with at least 256 MB of RAM.

You must have at least 128 MB of RAM to run this program, but for best performance you should have at least 256 MB.

Not Microsoft style

Microsoft recommends at least 256 MB of RAM to run this program.

It is recommended that you have at least 256 MB of RAM to run this program.

Recycle Bin

Precede with the definite article *the*, as in "the **Recycle Bin**." In Windows, the **Recycle Bin** is a temporary storage place for deleted files until they are permanently deleted.

Recycle Bin

refresh

Use *refresh* to refer to updating a webpage. Do not use to describe the action of an image being restored on the screen or data being updated. Use *redraw* or *update* instead. To refer to the **Refresh** command, use wording such as "To update the screen, click **Refresh**."

registry, registry settings

The *registry* is a database that stores configuration data about the user, the installed programs and applications, and the specific hardware. The registry has a hierarchical structure, with the first level in the path called a subtree. The next level is called a *key*, and all levels below keys are *subkeys*.

Use lowercase for the word *registry* except when it is part of a named system component, such as the Registry Editor. The first-level subtrees are system-defined and are in all uppercase letters, with words separated by underscores. Registry subtrees are usually bold.

Microsoft style

HKEY_CLASSES_ROOTHKEY_LOCAL_MACHINE

Keys are developer-defined and are usually all uppercase or mixed caps, with no underscores. Subkeys are usually mixed case.

Microsoft style

SOFTWAREApplicationIdentifierApplication Identifier *Name*

stockfile

the **new program** subkey

An entire subkey path is referred to as a *subkey*, not a *path*. The following is a typical subkey:

Microsoft style

\HKEY_LOCAL_MACHINE\SOFTWARE\Microsoft\Jet\3.5\Engines\Xbase subkey

For a subkey, the items in the **Name** column are *entries*. The items in the **Data** column are *values*.

reinitialize

Do not use to mean *restart*. See *initialize*.

release notes

Provides information about test and beta versions of a product. See *Readme files and release notes* (Chapter 6).

REM statement

Short for "remark statement," which is the term for a comment in Visual Basic and some other programs. Do not use generically to refer to a comment. Use *comment* instead.

remote

All right to use to as an adjective to describe a person or computer at another site. In programming, a remote computer is usually a computer connected, directly or indirectly, to the computer that a program is running on.

Do not use *remote drive* to describe a disk drive on a remote computer. Use *network drive* instead.

Do not use *remote* as a noun except to refer to a remote control device, such as that used to operate a TV set.

Do not use *remote* as a verb.

remove

Do not use *remove* to mean *delete*. *Remove* is correct in technical contexts such as the following:

- To refer to taking an item off a list in a dialog box that has **Add** and **Remove** buttons.

- To refer to taking a toolbar button off a toolbar, or hiding displayed data without deleting the data, such as columns in Windows Explorer.

- As a synonym for *unload*.

- As a synonym for *uninstall* in a context that talks about *adding* instead of *installing* software or hardware.

See also *delete, load, uninstall.*

replace

Use *replace* only as an adjective or as a verb, not as a noun. See also *find and replace.*

Microsoft style
You can replace all instances of an incorrect term at one time.

The **Replace** method replaces text found in a regular expression search.

Not Microsoft style
You can do a replace of all instances of an incorrect term at one time.

Replace replaces text found in a regular expression search.

In general, use *replace* instead of *overwrite* to mean replacing a file.

Microsoft style
Replace the selected text with the new text.

Replace the file with the changed file.

restore

Use as a verb instead of *undelete* to refer to restoring an item that was deleted.

Use as a verb to describe the action of restoring an item or condition to its previous state, such as a window that was previously maximized or minimized.

Do not use as an adjective or as a noun in content for a general audience except to follow the user interface. See also *restore (SQL Server), undelete*

Microsoft style
Restore the file.

Restore the window to its minimized state.

For more information about System Restore, see "What is System Restore?"

Not Microsoft style
Perform a system restore.

Keep the restore disk in a safe place.

Restore button

Refers to the button containing the image of two windows that is located in the upper-right corner of a window near the **Close** button.

Do not use *Restore box* or *Restore icon*. *Restore* as part of the **Restore** *button* is always bold. The **Restore** button can replace either the **Minimize** or, more often, the **Maximize** button. Clicking it restores a document to its previous size.

restore (SQL Server)

Use to refer to restoring a series of one or more database backups.

Do not use as a noun unless you have no other choice. It is all right to use *restore* as an adjective if necessary. For example, it is all right to say "restore operation" or "RESTORE statement." However, it is preferable to use *restore* only as a verb. See also *restore*.

Microsoft style
Under the full recovery model, first restore one or more data backups, and then restore the subsequent log backups to roll the database forward in time.

Restore the database.

You can restart an interrupted restore operation. (If necessary)

Use the RESTORE statement to specify the restore operation. (If necessary)

Not Microsoft style
Perform a database restore.

right

Do not use as a directional term by itself. Use a term such as *upper right, lower right, rightmost,* or *the right side of* instead. Include a hyphen when modifying a noun, as in "upper-right corner." Do not use *right hand.*

Accessibility considerations
Avoid using directional terms (left, right, up, down) as the only clue to location. Individuals with cognitive impairments may have difficulty interpreting them, as do blind users relying on screen-reading software. A directional term is all right to use if another indication of location, such as *in the* **Save As** *dialog box, on the* **Standard** *toolbar,* or *in the title bar,* is also included. Directional terms are also all right to use when a sighted user with dyslexia can clearly see a change in the interface as the result of an action, such as a change in the right pane when an option in the left pane is clicked.

right align, right-aligned

Use to refer to text that is aligned at the right margin. Hyphenate *right-aligned* in all positions in the sentence. Do not use *right-justified.* See also *justify, justified, left align, left-aligned.*

right mouse button

In most content, use this term instead of *secondary mouse button, mouse button 2,* or other terms. Even though a user can program a mouse to switch buttons, usability studies show that most users understand this commonly used term. See also *Mouse terminology* (Chapter 5).

right-click

Use to describe clicking the secondary (usually the right) mouse button. In content for novice computer users, define the term if necessary.

Microsoft style

Using the right mouse button (right-click)...

Right-click to select the file.

right-hand

Do not use. See *right*.

rightmost

One word.

Use *rightmost* to refer to something at the farthest right side instead of *farthest right*, far-right, or similar terms.

For accessibility considerations, see *right*.

rights

Use *rights* only in a nonspecific way to refer to system actions that are authorized by the system administrator. For specific references, use *user rights*.

Do not confuse *rights*, which apply to system operations, with *permissions*, which apply to specific system resources such as files or printers.

Do not use *privileges* as a synonym for *rights*. See also *permissions, user rights*.

Microsoft style

Domain administrators should use a primary user account, which has basic user rights in the domain.

rip

Avoid in the sense of transferring music or video from a CD or DVD to a hard disk. If you must use *rip*, define on first mention, and provide a glossary entry.

ROM

Abbreviation for *read-only memory*. For guidance about referring to memory, see *memory*.

root directory

Use this term, not *home directory*, to refer to the directory or folder (indicated in MS-DOS with a backslash: \) from which all other directories or folders branch. Do not shorten to *root* when you mean the directory.

Microsoft style

Change to the root directory and type the following command: **edit autoexec.bat**

RTFM

Abbreviation for "read the manual," sometimes interpreted as using an expletive term. Do not use.

running foot, running head

Do not use. Use *footer* and *header* instead. *Running foot* and *running head* are all right to use if needed for clarification or as keywords or glossary entries.

run time, runtime, run-time

Run time is the time during which an application is running.

Microsoft style

You can enter and modify data at run time. During design time, you create objects and modify their design.

A *runtime* is an environment that is required to run programs that are not compiled to machine language. Do not use *runtime* as a synonym for reader programs such as Microsoft Office file viewers.

The adjective *run-time* describes a thing that is occurring or relevant at run time.

Microsoft style

Microsoft Access file viewer

The common language runtime is a key element of the .NET Framework.

run-time error

run-time state

Not Microsoft style

Microsoft Access runtime

In contexts that require title capitalization, capitalize as *Run Time*, *Runtime*, and *Run-Time*.

run vs. execute

Do not use *execute* in content for a general audience except to follow the user interface. Use *run* instead. If the user interface includes *execute*, the user or program action is still *run*. Always use *run* in the context of macros and queries.

Microsoft style

While Windows defragments your disk, you can use your computer to carry out other tasks.

You can temporarily stop Disk Defragmenter so that you can run other programs at full speed.

Execute is all right to use in content for a technical audience, especially in the passive voice, because it has become ingrained. However, *run* is preferable when it does not cause any loss of meaning.

Microsoft style

Commands are run in the order in which they are listed in the file. (Preferred.)

Commands are executed in the order in which they are listed in the file.

runs vs. runs on

A computer runs an operating system such as Windows Server 2008, but a program runs on the operating system.

R

Microsoft style

Many companies are configuring their computers to run Windows Server 2008.

They may have to install upgraded programs to run on Windows Server 2008.

S

(s), (es)

Do not add *(s)* or *(es)* to a singular noun to indicate that it can be singular or plural. In general, use plural, but be guided by meaning. If it's important to indicate both, use *one or more*.

Microsoft style

To add rows or columns to a table,...

To add one or more rows or columns to a table,...

Not Microsoft style

To add a row(s) or column(s) to a table,...

sample vs. preview

A *sample* is a graphic representation of something that might show up on screen, not an exact representation of what is in the file that the user is working on.

A *preview* is a graphic representation of exactly what the user will see on screen.

Microsoft style

This displays a sample of what the control will look like with the scheme applied. To preview what the control will look like with the scheme applied, click **Preview**.

save

Do not use as a noun.

Microsoft style

Before you turn off your computer, save your files.

Not Microsoft style

Before you turn off your computer, do a save of your files.

Use these prepositions with save: "save *on* a disk," "save *to* a file," and "save *for* a rainy day."

scale up

In general, use *scale up*, instead of *upsize*, even though *upsize* has become common in client/server products.

scan line

Two words. Refers to either the row of pixels read by a scanning device or one of the horizontal lines on a display screen.

screen

Use instead of *screenful* or *full screen*. However, it is all right to say that a program is running in *full-screen mode*.

Use *screen* to refer to the graphic portion of a visual output device. Use *display* as a general term for visual output devices such as a flat-panel display. See also *display, monitor*.

screen resolution

For screen resolutions, use *number × number* instead of *number by number*. For example, use *640 × 480*, instead of *640 by 480*. Use the multiplication sign (×) instead of the letter *x*. See also *multiplication sign (x)*.

screened subnet

Do not use, except on first mention of *perimeter network*, in which case *screened subnet* should be placed in parentheses as follows: *perimeter network (also known as DMZ, demilitarized zone, and screened subnet)*. On subsequent mention, use *perimeter network*. If your content has an index or glossary, include *DMZ, demilitarized zone*, and *screened subnet* with cross-references to *perimeter network*. See also *perimeter network*.

ScreenTip

Generic term for any tip that appears on the screen, such as a tooltip. Used especially in content for Microsoft Office.

script, scripting language

Whenever possible, refer to a script generically. That is, just use *script* when you are referring to the code. See also *Java, Jscript, JavaScript, scriptlet*.

scriptlet

Use only to refer to the web component called a scriptlet. Use *script* in all other cases, or use a more specific term if necessary.

scroll

Scroll does not take a direct object. Use directional signals or prepositions with *scroll*.

If the concept of scrolling is already clear, use a verb phrase such as *move through*.

The user scrolls within the document by rotating the wheel of the mouse. It is all right to use *scroll up* and *scroll down* to describe this behavior. See also *flick, swipe*.

Microsoft style
You can scroll through the document to get to the end.

Drag the scroll box to move through the information.

Scroll down until you see the new folder.

Not Microsoft style
You can scroll the document to get to the end.

Drag the scroll box to scroll the information.

Do not use *scroll* to describe interacting with a device unless a user can use a traditional control on that device, such as the wheel button on the Microsoft Arc Touch Mouse.

scroll arrow, scroll bar, scroll box

A *scroll bar* is a control that enables users to bring into view information that extends beyond the borders of a window. A *scroll bar* contains *scroll arrows* and a *scroll box*.

Do not use *arrow* to refer to a *scroll arrow*. It can be confused with an up or down arrow.

Do not use *slider* or *slider box* as a synonym for *scroll box*. See *slider*.

Do not use *gray* or *shaded area* to refer to the *scroll bar*.

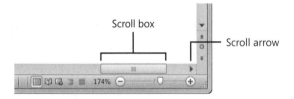

Scroll box

Scroll arrow

search, search and replace

Do not use for the find and replace features. Use *find* and *replace* instead.

Use *search, find*, and *replace* as verbs, not as nouns. Do not use *search your document*. Use *search through your document* instead.

Microsoft style

Find the word "gem" and replace it with "jewel."

Search through your document for comments in red.

Not Microsoft style

Do a search and replace.

Search your document for comments in red.

secondary menu

Describes the menu that appears when the user selects a command that has a small arrow on its right side. Do not use in content for a general audience. If the way that the menu works needs to be emphasized as a feature of the product, use *submenu*.

In content for software developers, use only in content that discusses creating menus, and only if you cannot use *submenu* in the context.

security patch

Do not use. Use *security update* instead. See also *out-of-band release terminology* (Chapter 6), *security update*.

security update

Use to describe a broadly released fix for a product-specific, security-related vulnerability. Security vulnerabilities are rated based on their severity, which is indicated in the Microsoft security bulletin as *critical, important, moderate*, or *low*.

Do not use *patch* or *security patch* to describe a security update. See also *out-of-band release terminology* (Chapter 6).

select

Use *select* to refer to marking text, cells, and similar items that will be subject to a user action, such as copying text. Items so marked are referred to as *the selection* or the *selected* text, cells, items, and so on.

Use *select* to refer to adding a check mark to a check box or to selecting an item in a list box or a combo box list.

Do not use *select* as a general term for selecting other options in a dialog box. Use *click* instead.

Do not use *highlight* as a synonym for *select*. Selecting is a standard procedure, and *highlight* can often be confused with product features such as text highlighters that provide only visual emphasis.

Do not use *pick* as a synonym for *select*. See also *choose, click, controls, highlight*.

selection cursor

In general, do not use this term, which refers to the marker that appears where the user is working in a window or dialog box or indicates what is selected. Use *cursor* or *pointer* instead. See also *cursor, pointer*.

service-oriented architecture

Note the hyphen. A software architecture that uses policies, practices, and frameworks to enable application functionality to be provided and consumed as sets of services.

All right to use the acronym *SOA* after the full term has been spelled out on first mention.

service pack

Use to refer to a cumulative set of all product updates, including fixes for problems found since the release of a product. A service pack might also contain design changes or features that are requested by customers. Do not use *service release*; it is an obsolete term.

Do not confuse *service pack* with *update rollup*, which contains multiple bug fixes but is not as comprehensive as a service pack.

When using *service pack* in a general sense, always spell it out and do not capitalize the term.

When referring to the service packs for specific products, capitalize the term. On first mention, spell it out unless space is limited. Thereafter, use the abbreviation *SP* to identify a particular service pack.

Consult your project style sheet for the correct way of referring to the service packs for particular products.

When discussing functionality that is included in multiple service packs, do not use *or later, or greater*, or similar phrases that could refer to unreleased service packs or products. List each released service pack separately.

When discussing functionality that was included in earlier service packs, use a phrase such as *with SP2 or earlier service packs* to avoid implying that the functionality applies to all earlier versions of the product. See also *earlier, later, out-of-band release terminology, update rollup*.

S

Requirements: Windows 7 SP1

This program requires Windows 7 Service Pack 1.

If you are using Windows Vista with SP2 or earlier service packs, you can...

If you are using Windows Vista with SP2 or SP1, you can...

This service pack includes...

Not Microsoft style

This SP addresses all known security vulnerabilities.

We recommend that you install service pack 2.

We recommend that you install Service Pack 2.0.

If you are using Windows Vista with SP2 or earlier, you can...

If you are using Windows Vista with SP1 or later, you can...

You can install more than one Service Pack.

set up, setup, Setup

Two words as a verb, one word as an adjective and as a noun. Capitalize *Setup* when it refers to the Setup program. Do not hyphenate. See also *install*.

Verb

Have everything unpacked before you set up your computer.

Adjective

The setup time should be about 15 minutes.

Noun

Your office setup should be ergonomically designed.

Run Setup before you open other programs.

Insert the Setup CD in the CD drive.

set vs. specify

It is worth avoiding words such as *set* and *specify* that make general reference to user actions. A better approach is to be specific about the action that the user should take.

Microsoft style

Select a color for an appointment or a meeting.

Right-click an appointment or meeting, point to **Label** on the shortcut menu, and then click a color in the list.

Not Microsoft style

Specify the color of an appointment or a meeting.

Right-click an appointment or a meeting, point to **Label** on the shortcut menu, and then specify a color in the list.

Do not use *set* to indicate the user action of entering or selecting a value in a dialog box. Because *set* has so many potential meanings, it is a difficult word for non-native English speakers. If you must make a general reference to such a user action, it's all right to use *specify* instead.

Software developers are accustomed to, and expect to see, references to getting and setting properties, so it is all right to use *set* in content for software developers to indicate the action of entering or selecting the value of a property, whether through code or through the user interface.

setting

Use *setting* or *value* in content for a general audience to refer to a specific value that the user can set, such as the specific color of a font. See also *properties*.

Microsoft style

You can choose blue as the setting for your font.

Differentiate from *attribute*, which is the general characteristic that can be set.

Not Microsoft style

Color is one attribute of fonts.

Do not use *property* in content for a general audience to mean a setting or a value unless you are discussing something that is specifically identified as a property.

set-top box

Note hyphen. Do not use the abbreviation *STB*. Standard industry term for the computer that sits on top of a TV set to create two-way communication.

shaded

Use *shaded*, not *grayed* or *dimmed*, to describe the appearance of a check box that may occur when there is a mixture of settings for a selection in a group of options. The shaded appearance indicates that some previously checked options may make parts of the selection different from the rest. See also *dimmed, gray, grayed*.

General

- ☐ Provide feedback with sound
- ☑ Provide feedback with animation
- ☐ Confirm file format conversion on open
- ☑ Update automatic links at open
- ☐ Allow opening a document in Draft view
- ☑ Enable background repagination
- ☐ Show add-in user interface errors
- ☑ Show customer submitted Office.com content

Shaded options

shell

All right to use as a noun in content for a technical audience. Do not use in content for a general audience.

Do not use a verb, such as *shell* or *shell out*, unless you have no other choice. Use more precise terminology instead, such as "create a new shell" or "return to the operating system."

S

ship

Do not use *ship* to refer to releasing software or services to the public. It's jargon. Use *release* instead.

Microsoft style

Windows 7 was released in October 2009.

Not Microsoft style

Windows 7 shipped in October 2009.

The ship date slipped by three weeks.

shortcut

One word as an adjective or as a noun. Use lowercase unless *shortcut* is uppercase in the user interface.

Do not use as a synonym for *hyperlink*.

shortcut key

Do not use in content for a general audience. Use *keyboard shortcut* instead.

All right to use in content for software developers and in content about customizing the user interface when you must distinguish between an access key and a shortcut key. In such cases, use *shortcut key* to denote a key combination used to perform a command, and provide a definition. Use *access key* to denote a key sequence used to access a menu item, and provide a definition. See also *access key, key combinations, keyboard shortcut, Key names* (Chapter 5).

shortcut menu

The shortcut menu appears when the user right-clicks an item. It lists commands that pertain only to the item that the user clicked.

It is all right to use *shortcut menu* if you must refer to this menu by name.

Microsoft style

Use Alt+Spacebar to display the shortcut menu for the active window.

In procedures, use *shortcut menu* only if doing so would help the user locate the item in the user interface.

Microsoft style

Right-click the selected text, and then click **Copy**. (Preferred.)

Right-click the selected text, and then click **Copy** on the shortcut menu.

should vs. must

Use *should* only to describe a user action that is recommended, but optional. Use *must* only to describe a user action that is required.

Microsoft style

You should periodically back up your data.

Your computer must have at least 128 MB of RAM to run this program, but for best performance your computer should have at least 256 MB.

In Windows, you cannot have multiple versions of a file with the same name. To save different copies of a document, you must save each copy with a different file name.

Do not use *should* to indicate probability. Wherever possible, express certainty. When that is not possible, use *may* or rephrase. See also *can vs. may*.

Microsoft style

When you click **Submit**, the data is sent to Microsoft, and you will get a confirmation email message within 24 hours.

Not Microsoft style

When you click **Submit**, the data is sent to Microsoft, and you should get a confirmation email message within 24 hours.

It is all right, and often better, to use alternate ways of specifying recommendations or requirements. For example, for required actions, you can use the imperative mood; for optional actions, you can use a phrase such as *we recommend*.

Do not use *Microsoft recommends*. It injects an inappropriately corporate tone that some users may interpret as arrogant. Do not use *it is recommended*. It sounds both corporate and evasive.

Microsoft style

We recommend at least 256 MB of RAM to run this program.

Whatever phrasing you use, be sensitive to the tone that your words convey.

Microsoft style

Free technical support is available when you register with Microsoft.

shut down, shutdown, Shut Down

Two words as a verb, one word as an adjective and as a noun. The **Shut down** command on the **Start** menu of Windows is two words.

Shut down refers to the orderly closing of the operating system. Do not use *shut down* to refer to turning off the power to a computer. Do not use *shut down* as a synonym for *close* or *exit*. See also *close; exit; turn on, turn off*.

S

Microsoft style

Shut down your computer before you turn it off.

This action shuts down Windows so that you can safely turn off the computer power.

Many computers turn the power off automatically.

The accidental shutdown may have corrupted some files.

To turn off your computer, click **Start**, and then click **Shut down**.

sign in, sign out, sign on, sign up

Use *sign in* and *sign out* to refer to creating and ending a user session for an Internet account. You *sign in to* (not *sign into*) a MyMSN account, an Internet service provider account, or an XML web service. Use *log on* and *log off* to describe creating and ending a user session for a computer or intranet user account.

Use *connect*, *make a connection*, and similar phrases to refer to the act of physically attaching a computer to a network, whether intranet or Internet.

Use *sign on* only as part of the term *single sign on* (SSO). The user action is still *signing in*, even though the technology is called *single sign on*. Use *sign off* only informally to refer to getting approval. Otherwise, do not use *sign on* and *sign off* unless these terms appear in the user interface.

Use *sign out* to refer to closing a user session on the Internet.

Use *sign up* to refer to enrolling in a service.

Hyphenate these terms only when they are used as adjectives. See also *connect*; *log on, log off, logon, logoff.*

Microsoft style

Type your sign-in name here.

Sign in here.

You can sign up for Internet Explorer by filling in the following information.

You can connect your server to the Internet.

simply

Do not use to mean that something is easy to do. It is generally unnecessary and can sound condescending if the user does not find the task as simple as you do. If you must have the meaning that *simply* conveys, use *just* instead.

Microsoft style

To publish your files to the web, click **Publish to the Web** on the **File** menu. When you see a clip that you like on the site, just click the clip and drag it into your document.

Not Microsoft style

To publish your files to the web, simply click **Publish to the Web** on the **File** menu. When you see a clip that you like on the site, simply click the clip and drag it into your document.

site

Collection of webpages developed as part of a whole, such as the Microsoft website, the MSDN Library website, and so on. Use *website* instead of *site* if necessary for clarity.

Information is *on* a website, but the address of a site is *at* http://www. See also *page*.

site map

Two words.

size

It is all right to use *size* as a verb, as in "size the window." It is also all right to use *resize* to mean *change the size of.*

slate

Do not use *slate* as a modifier for *computer* or *PC*.

In general, use the most generic term that describes a device. For example, use *computer* or *PC* unless you need to differentiate from other kinds of devices.

Slate typically refers to a tablet PC without an integrated physical keyboard. See also *portable computer.*

slider

Control that enables users to set a value on a continuous range of possible values, such as screen brightness, mouse-click speed, or volume. In content for software developers, sometimes referred to as a *trackbar control.*

Do not refer to the scroll box or a progress indicator as a slider. See also *progress indicator*; *Webpage controls, dialog boxes, and property sheets* (Chapter 5).

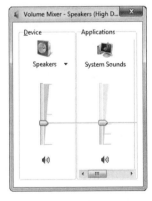

Microsoft style
Move the slider to the left to decrease pointer speed.

small caps

Do not use small caps for key names or for A.M. and P.M. They are awkward to designate in code such as HTML.

It is all right to use the term *small caps*. If necessary for clarity, refer to them as *small capitals* on first mention, followed by a phrase such as *often referred to as "small caps."*

smart card, Smart Card

Use lowercase for generic references to smart cards or smart card technology. Capitalize as part of proper names, but not in general references to smart card implementations.

smartphone

One word. In general, use the most generic term that describes a device. For example, use just *phone* unless you need to call out the mobility of the phone. In that case, use *mobile phone*. Use *smartphone* only when you need to make a distinction between smartphones and other kinds of phones.

Do not use *device* to refer to a phone unless you need to write about a generic category that includes such things as phones, laptops, and tablet PCs.

snap-in

A program that runs in the context of Microsoft Management Console. In contexts that require title capitalization, capitalize as *Snap-in*.

soft copy

Do not use. It's jargon formed by analogy with *hard copy*. Use a more specific term such as *electronic document* or *file* instead.

software as a service (SaaS)

Software that is consumed over the Internet rather than installed on-premises. Typically, a vendor manages the cloud infrastructure, including hardware, storage, operating system, and applications. Organizations pay for the use of the service.

All right to use *SaaS* after the full term has been spelled out on first mention. Do not capitalize as *SAAS*.

software-plus-services

Software-plus-services is a computing model that includes both locally installed, full-package software and Internet-delivered or hosted applications. In general, use *Microsoft Cloud Services*, not *software-plus-services*, to refer specifically to the cloud platform and services provided by Microsoft.

When the term *software-plus-services* is used, spell it out and lowercase it in body text and captions. Hyphenate *software-plus-services* both as a noun and as a modifier. The term *software-plus-services* takes a singular verb and pronoun. See also *Cloud computing style* (Chapter 6).

Microsoft style

The software-plus-services approach combines client software and services delivered over the Internet.

In contexts that require title capitalization, do not capitalize *plus*.

Microsoft style

Software-plus-Services

Do not use the plus sign unless space is limited, such as on the screens of mobile devices. Note that there is a space before and after the plus sign.

Microsoft style (if space is limited)
software + services

When you refer generically to software and services, as opposed to the Microsoft vision or the offerings manifested by that vision, use *and* instead of *plus* and do not use hyphens.

Microsoft style
You have more flexibility when you combine software and services.

Do not use *S + S*. This construction is geopolitically sensitive.

software update

Use to describe any update, update rollup, service pack, feature pack, critical update, security update, or hotfix used to improve or fix a software product released by Microsoft. See also *out-of-band release terminology* (Chapter 6).

sound card

Use instead of *sound adapter.*

spam

Spam is a problem for everyone, but not everyone interprets it in the same way. Nevertheless, it is in wide use and is all right to use in certain circumstances.

Use *spam* only to refer to unsolicited commercial email. Do not use *spam* to refer generally to commercial email, such as bulk email sent to a customer list. Do not use *spam* to refer to an inappropriate posting to a large distribution list or newsgroup.

Do not use *spam* as a verb.

specification

Do not use the informal *spec* in any content unless you have no other choice.

speed key

Do not use. Use *keyboard shortcut* instead. See also *shortcut key.*

spelling checker

Refer to the tool as the *spelling checker* instead of as the *spell checker* or the *Spell Checker.* Do not use *spell check* as a noun or as a verb.

Microsoft style
Use the spelling checker to check the spelling in the document.

Not Microsoft style
Spell check the document.

Run the spell checker.

spider

Refers to an automated program that searches the Internet for new web documents and places information about them in a database that can be accessed by a search engine. If you are not sure that your users will understand what *spider* means, define it on first mention, and if your content has a glossary, add *spider*.

spin box

Use only in content for a technical audience to describe a control that users can use to move ("spin") through a fixed set of values, such as dates.

In content for a general audience, refer to a spin box by its label. For example, say "the **Start time** box." See also *Webpage controls, dialog boxes, and property sheets* (Chapter 5).

split bar

All right to use in content for all audiences. Refers to the horizontal or vertical double line that separates a window into two panes. In some programs, such as Windows Explorer, the window is already split, but the user can change the size of the panes. In other programs, such as Excel, the user can split the window by using the split box.

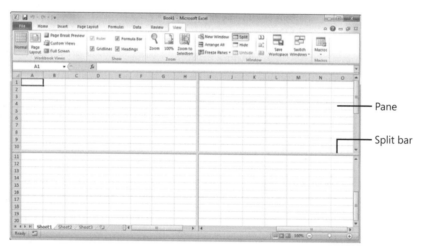

Pane

Split bar

split box

Refers to the control at the upper right-side of the vertical scroll bar (for horizontal splitting) or the rightmost side of the horizontal scroll bar (for vertical splitting). Users point to the split box to drag the split bar. The term is all right to use in content for all audiences.

S

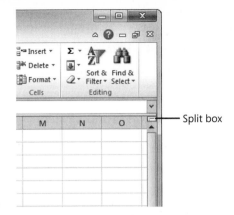

Split box

spoofing

Refers to various practices that conceal the identity of a user account, an email account, or a computer's Internet Protocol (IP) address that is taking some action. For example, email spoofing involves forging the header of an email message so that the message appears to come from someone other than the true sender.

Spoofing is a valid technical term, and it is all right to use if you are sure that your users will understand the meaning. If you are not sure that your users will understand what *spoofing* means, define it on first mention, and if your content has a glossary, add *spoofing*.

Where appropriate to avoid ambiguity, use a modifier to be as specific as possible about the kind of spoofing that you are referring to, such as email spoofing or IP spoofing.

spreadsheet

A spreadsheet is a computer accounting program, such as Microsoft Excel. The document produced by a spreadsheet program is a worksheet, also commonly called a spreadsheet.

spyware

Refers to software that can display advertisements such as pop-up ads, collect information about you from your computer, or change settings on your computer, usually without appropriately obtaining your consent.

When you are using this term to describe specific software, ensure that the software has been identified as spyware. For a list of spyware detected by Microsoft security products, search for "spyware" in the Microsoft Malware Encyclopedia. See also *antispyware, security*.

Microsoft style

Your computer may have spyware and other unwanted software installed.

SQL

When you are referring to Structured Query Language as *SQL*, *SQL* is pronounced "es-cue-el" and takes the indefinite article *an*. An example is "an SQL database."

When you are referring to the product or the server that is running the product, *SQL* is pronounced "sequel."

SQL Server

Use *Microsoft SQL Server* on first mention and occasionally thereafter. Also on first mention, include the descriptor *data management software* unless you are referring to a specific feature.

When you are referring to a computer that is running Microsoft SQL Server, use *a computer running SQL Server* or *a computer that is running SQL Server.* (Note the capital *S* in *Server.*)

Never refer to a computer that is running Microsoft SQL Server as any of the following:

- *the SQL Server*
- *a SQL Server*
- *SQL Servers*
- *SQL server*

When you are referring to the product or the server that is running the product, SQL is pronounced "sequel."

When you are referring to Structured Query Language as *SQL, SQL* is pronounced "es-cue-el" and takes the indefinite article *an*. An example is "an SQL database."

stand-alone

Use only as an adjective.

Microsoft style

You can use Microsoft Word either as a stand-alone word processor or as a shared processer on a network.

Not Microsoft style

Some early word processors were stand-alones.

start, Start (the menu)

Use *start* to mean "to start a program" instead of *boot, initiate, initialize, issue, launch, turn on,* or similar words and phrases.

Capitalize references to the **Start** menu and the **Start** button on the taskbar in Windows.

Don't refer to the **Start** button as the *Windows* **Start** *button*.

Use **Start**, rather than *Start screen* or *Home screen* to describe the initial screen on Windows Phone. See also *boot; initiate; initialize; issue; launch; turn on, turn off.*

Microsoft style

You'll find the **Start** button on the taskbar.

Start Windows, click the **Start** button, and then, on the **Start** menu, right-click **Control Panel**.

On **Start**, tap **Messaging**. (Windows Phone)

Not Microsoft style

Boot Windows, and then click the **Start** button to launch your programs.

On the taskbar, click the Windows **Start** button, and then click **Run**.

start page

Do not use to refer to the webpage that appears when the user starts the browser. Use *home page* instead. See also *home page*.

startup, start up

Do not use *start up* as a verb. Use *start* instead.

Do not use *on startup* and similar noun phrases in content for a general audience. It is all right to use *on startup* in content for a technical audience.

It is all right to use *startup* as an adjective in phrases such as *startup disk* and *startup screen*. See also *bootable disk, start, Start (the menu)*.

Microsoft style

To start the program, click the icon.

When the program starts, a startup screen appears.

If there is a catastrophic failure, use the emergency startup disk to start Windows.

Not Microsoft style

To start up the program, click the icon.

On startup, a splash screen appears.

If there is a catastrophic failure, use the emergency boot disk to start Windows.

status bar

Use instead of *status line* or *message area*. Refers to the area at the bottom of a document window that lists the status of a document and gives other information, such as the meaning of a command. Messages appear *on*, not *in*, the status bar.

Microsoft style

The page number is displayed on the status bar.

Writing status messages

Follow these guidelines for writing effective status bar messages:

- Use parallel constructions and begin the message with a verb.

  For example, the message describing the **View** menu should read something like "Contains commands for customizing this window" and the message describing the **Internet folder** icon should read something like "Changes your Internet settings."

- Use the indicative mood (with *this item* understood), not the imperative mood (with *you* understood).

  For example, use "Changes your Internet settings," not "Change your Internet settings."

- Ensure that the text is constructive. Don't repeat the obvious.

For example, even though the **File** menu is quite basic, a message such as "Contains commands for working with the selected items" gives some useful information with the inclusion of the phrase "selected items."

- Use complete sentences, including articles, and end with a period.

stop

Do not use to mean *exit a program*.

storage, storage device

Do not use *storage* to refer to available space on a disk. Use *disk space* instead. *Storage device* is all right to use as a generic term to refer to things such as disk and tape drives.

stream, streaming

All right to use as a noun or as a verb to refer to audio and video or graphics coming to a browser or media player over the Internet. *Stream* is also an I/O management term in C programming.

Do not use in other metaphorical senses.

stretch

Use to refer to the contact gesture or air gesture of enlarging an object on the user interface by separating two or more fingers or both hands. See also *pinch*.

Microsoft style

To enlarge the photograph, stretch it.

Microsoft style (novice computer user)

To enlarge the photograph, separate your fingers while touching the photograph.

strike

Do not use to refer to keyboard input. Use *press* or *type* instead. See also *press*.

strikethrough

Use instead of *strikeout* or *lineout*. Refers to the line crossing out words in revisions.

struct

Do not use in text to refer to a data structure identified by the **struct** language keyword. Use *structure* instead.

style sheet

Two words. Can refer to a file of instructions for formatting a document in word processing or desktop publishing, or to a list of words and phrases and how they are used or spelled in a particular document.

In Internet use, refers to a cascading style sheet (a .css file) attached to an HTML document that controls the formatting of tags on webpages. The browser follows rules (a "cascading order") to determine precedence and resolve conflicts.

In an XML context, *XSL* is the abbreviation for Extensible Stylesheet Language. Even so, refer to an .xsl file as a *style sheet*. See also *cascading style sheets*.

sub-

In general, do not hyphenate words beginning with *sub-*, such as *subheading* and *subsection*, unless it is necessary to avoid confusion or if *sub* is followed by a proper noun, as in *sub-Saharan*. When in doubt, check the *American Heritage Dictionary*, or consult your project style sheet.

subaddress

Do not use to refer to parts of an address that go to a specific place in a file, such as a bookmark. Use the specific term instead.

subclass

Do not use as a verb. Use a standard verb, such as *create a subclass*, instead.

submenu

Describes the menu that appears when the user clicks a command that has a small arrow on its right side. In content for a general audience, do not use the term *submenu* unless the way that the menu works needs to be emphasized as a feature of the product.

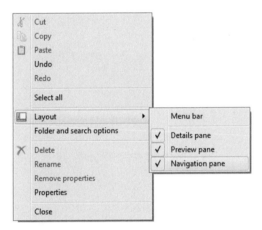

In content for a general audience, also do not use the terms *cascading menu, hierarchical menu,* or *secondary menu* to mean a submenu. *Submenu, cascading menu, hierarchical menu,* or *secondary menu* are all right to use in content for a technical audience if you must detail specific kinds of menus.

Microsoft style

On the **Edit** menu, point to **Clear**, and then click the item that you want to clear.

Not Microsoft style

On the **Edit** menu, point to **Clear**, and then on the submenu click the item that you want to clear.

Super VGA, SVGA

Use *Super VGA (SVGA)* on first mention. On subsequent mention, it is all right to use *SVGA*. Do not spell out *SVGA* and related graphics specifications such as *VGA, XGA, UXGA, SXGA,* and *QXGA*.

surf

In the context of browsing the web, generally implies a more random browsing than the less informal *browse*. All right to use in informal contexts if accurate.

swipe

Use only as a verb to refer to the contact gesture or air gesture of moving from object to object on the user interface with a hand or arm. See also *flick, pan, scroll.*

Microsoft style

In *Kinectimals*, swipe left or right through your decorating options.

Not Microsoft style

Swipe left and right through your decorating options.

For novice computer users, it is all right to describe this gesture as "a swiping motion."

Microsoft style

Move your arm right and left to swipe through the items.

switch

As a verb, use instead of *activate* or *toggle.*

Microsoft style

To embed the new object, switch to the source document.

You can easily switch between open windows.

Not Microsoft style

To embed the new object, activate the source document.

You can easily toggle between open windows.

All right to use as a noun in content for a technical audience to refer to command-line and compiler options, such as **/Za**. Because some groups use *option* instead, consult your project style sheet.

symbol

Use the word *symbol* to refer to a graphic or special character that represents something else, but differentiate a symbol from an icon. (An icon represents an object the user can select and open. A symbol can appear on an icon.) See also *Measurements and units of measure* (Chapter 7), *Names of special characters* (Chapter 7).

Follow these guidelines for discussing symbols:

Write out the name of the symbol in text and, if the symbol itself is important, enclose the symbol in parentheses. Use a symbol by itself only in tables and lists where space is limited or in mathematical expressions.

Microsoft style

You can type a backslash (\) to return to the previous directory.

Only 75 percent of the students attended.

Not Microsoft style

You can type a \ to return to the previous directory.

Only 75% of the students attended.

For screen elements such as buttons, you can use a graphic of the button by itself after it has been named once or if clicking it brings up a definition.

Microsoft style

Click the **Minimize** button ( ).

Click .

Spell out *plus sign, minus sign, hyphen, period,* and *comma* when referring to them as key names.

Microsoft style

Press Comma.

Type a comma.

Press the Plus Sign (+).

Not Microsoft style

Press ,.

Press +.

Write out plurals of symbols, showing the use in parentheses. Do not add *s* or *'s* to a symbol.

Microsoft style

Type two backslashes (\\) to show a network connection.

Not Microsoft style

Type two \'s to show a network connection.

Type \\s to show a network connection.

Do not insert a space between a number and the symbol it modifies.

Microsoft style (to conserve space)

75%

<100

Not Microsoft style

75 %

< 100

sync

It is all right to use *sync* as an abbreviation for the verb *synchronize* in some Microsoft products and services. Consult your project style sheet for guidance about using this term.

When you use it as a verb, spell it as *sync, syncing,* and *synced,* not *synch, synching,* and *synched.*

Do not use *sync* as a noun; always use *synchronization* instead.

International considerations

Using the abbreviation *sync* does not necessarily save space when content is localized. In many languages, the full term is translated because an abbreviation is not available.

sysop

Even though *sysop* is jargon for "system operator," it is all right to use to refer to the person who oversees or runs a bulletin board system or online communications system in content about such products. Define on first mention. Do not use in other documentation.

system

Use generically to refer to computer hardware configurations instead of to the computer itself. The system includes the computer and peripheral devices. It is not synonymous with, but can include, the *system software*.

system administrator

Use only to refer to the person responsible for administering the use of a multiuser computer system. Generally, use *administrator* unless you must specify a particular kind. Use *network administrator* only to specifically refer to the administrator of networks.

system prompt

Do not use to mean *command prompt*. Also do not use to mean *system message*.

system software

In general, use *system software* (singular) instead of *systems software* (plural).

system tray

Do not use. Use *notification area* instead. See also *notification area*.

T

tab

Do not use as a verb. As a noun, use only to refer to tabs on a ribbon, a webpage, in a dialog box, and so on.

For other uses, clarify the meaning with a descriptor. For example, say "the Tab key," "a tab stop," or "a tab mark on the ruler." See also *Webpage controls, dialog boxes, and property sheets* (Chapter 5).

Microsoft style
Use the Tab key to move through a dialog box.

Set a tab stop on the ruler.

Click the **View** tab.

Not Microsoft style
You can tab through a dialog box.

Set a tab on the ruler.

table of contents

Do not use *Table of Contents* as the heading for the list of contents at the beginning of a document or file. Use just *Contents* instead. However, it is correct to refer generically to the *table of contents*.

tablet, tablet PC

Lowercase. In general, use the most generic term that describes a device. For example, use *computer* or *PC* unless you need to differentiate from other kinds of devices.

A tablet is a portable computer that has a screen with which someone can interact by using a tablet pen or contact gesture. A tablet may or may not have an integrated keyboard.

It is all right to use *tablet PC* when referring in general to tablets running Windows. Do not spell out as *tablet portable computer*.

If it aids comprehension, use *convertible tablet* to describe a portable computer that has an integrated keyboard and a display that can be positioned for use as a laptop or as a tablet. See also *portable computer*.

Taiwan

Refer to Taiwan only as *Taiwan*, never as *Republic of China* or *ROC*. If you must abbreviate *Taiwan*, the ISO abbreviation is *TWN*.

tap

Use *tap* and *double-tap* instead of *click* and *double-click* when writing content specific to touching a screen or using a pen pointing device. *Tap* means to press the screen with a finger or pen tip and then to lift it, usually quickly.

Use *tap and hold* if required by the program to achieve a specific interaction. Do not use *press and hold* or *touch and hold*.

Microsoft style

Tap the **Internet Explorer** icon.

Tap **Internet Explorer**.

Tap and hold the album that you want to remove, and then tap **Delete**.

Tap gesture

target disk, target drive, target file

Do not use. These terms can be ambiguous and difficult to translate. If you must use the idea of "target," use *destination disk*, *destination drive*, or *destination file* instead. But it is better is to be specific about the disk, drive, or file under discussion. See also *destination disk, destination drive, destination file*.

taskbar

One word.

TB

Do not use as an abbreviation for *terabyte*. See also *terabyte*.

telnet, Telnet

Use lowercase to refer to a client program that implements the Telnet terminal-emulation protocol.

It is all right to use *telnet* to refer to using the protocol. Use lowercase for this usage.

Capitalize *Telnet* to refer to the protocol itself. In UNIX usage, the protocol is usually all uppercase (TELNET).

terabyte

One terabyte is equal to 1,099,511,627,776 bytes, or 1,024 gigabytes.

Do not abbreviate. Insert a space between the numeral and *terabyte*, or hyphenate if the measure is used as an adjective. See also *Measurements and units of measure* (Chapter 7).

Microsoft style

36 terabytes

36-terabyte database

When used as a noun in measurements, add *of* to form a prepositional phrase.

Microsoft style

This database contains 36 terabytes of information.

terminal

Use *terminal* only in the context of terminal emulators. Do not use as a synonym for *client*, *workstation*, or *computer*.

terminate

Do not use as a synonym for *close* or *exit*. It is all right to use *terminate* in content for a technical audience in phrases such as "null-terminated string" or "terminate a process." See also *close, exit*.

text box

In general, refer to a box in which the user types text only by its label. If you must use a descriptor, use *box*. Do not use *field* or *entry field*, except in content about database programs.

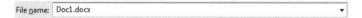

In content for software developers, it is all right to use *text box* in content about designing and developing the user interface. See also *Webpage controls, dialog boxes, and property sheets* (Chapter 5).

that vs. which

That and *which* are often confused. Be sure to use the appropriate word.

That introduces a restrictive clause, which is a clause that is essential for the sentence to make sense. A restrictive clause often defines the noun or phrase preceding it and is not separated from it by a comma.

Microsoft style

You will need to supply information about applications that you want to run with Windows.

Not Microsoft style

You will need to supply information about applications which you want to run with Windows.

Which introduces a nonrestrictive clause, which is a clause that could be omitted without affecting the meaning of the sentence. It is preceded by a comma. Nonrestrictive clauses often contain auxiliary or parenthetical information.

Microsoft style

Your package contains the subsidiary information card, which you can use to obtain device drivers or local technical support.

International considerations

In general, do include the word *that* in restrictive clauses, even though the sentence may be clear without it. Including *that* prevents ambiguity and makes the sentence easier for non-native English speakers and machine translation to interpret.

Microsoft style

Open the document that you just created.

Not Microsoft style

Open the document you just created.

Do not use *that* or *which* to refer to a person. Use *who* instead. See *who vs. that*.

then

Then is not a coordinate conjunction. Therefore *then* cannot correctly join two independent clauses. Use *and then* or *then* with a semicolon to connect two independent clauses. You can also begin a new sentence with *Then* or, in a procedure, make the *then* clause a separate step without using *then*.

Microsoft style

On the **File** menu, click **Save As**, and then type the name of the file.

On the **File** menu, click **Save As**; then type the name of the file.

On the **File** menu, click **Save As**. Then type the name of the file in the **Save as** box.

Microsoft style

1. On the **File** menu, click **Save As**.
2. Type the name of the file in the **Save As** box.

Not Microsoft style

On the **File** menu, click **Save As**, then type the name of the file.

Avoid using *then* at the beginning of the clause that follows an *if* clause (an "if...then" construction).

Microsoft style

If you turn off the computer before shutting down all programs, you may lose data.

Not Microsoft style

If you turn off the computer before shutting down all programs, then you may lose data.

thread

All right to use to describe a series of articles or messages on the same topic in a newsgroup or email discussion. In content for a technical audience, *thread* is all right to use in the context of threaded programming models.

three-dimensional, 3-D

Spell out on first mention. On subsequent mention, *three-dimensional* is preferred, but *3-D* is all right to use. Use *3-D* when space is limited and to follow the user interface.

Hyphenate both the spelled out and abbreviated versions. Use *3D* (no hyphen) only as specified by product names.

Tile, Live Tile

Use *Tile* to refer to the objects on the screen that the user can move around, such as the Phone Tile and the Calendar Tile on Windows Phone. Tiles are shortcuts to apps, Hubs, or other links. Always capitalize *Tile*.

Use *Live Tile* to refer to a Tile that updates automatically and shows content updates on **Start**.

Tiles on Windows Phone

time bomb, timebomb

Do not use. Use *expiration date* instead.

time stamp

Two words.

time-out, time out

Always hyphenate as an adjective or as a noun. Do not hyphenate as a verbal phrase.

Microsoft style

A time-out occurs if the connection can't be made.

If the connection isn't made, a time-out event occurs.

The connection timed out.

title bar

The horizontal bar at the top of a window that shows the name of the document or program. All right to use in content for all audiences.

titled vs. entitled

For consistency, do not use *entitled* to mean *the given title* of something, such as a book. Instead, use *entitled* to mean "is owed." For such things as a book, use *titled*.

Do not use the phrase "the book titled" or a similar phrase if the phrase is not necessary. If you do use *titled*, the word is not followed by a comma.

Microsoft style

Look in the book titled *User's Guide*, which accompanies your software.

Look in the *User's Guide* that accompanies your software.

toggle

Use as an adjective, as in *toggle key*. A toggle key turns a particular mode on or off.

Do not use as a verb. Use *switch, click,* or *turn on* and *turn off* to describe the action instead. For example, use the specific name of a toggle key or command to refer to what the user should do to switch between modes.

Microsoft style

Use the Caps Lock key to switch from typing in capital letters to typing in lowercase letters.

To turn the Ruler on or off, click **Ruler** on the **Edit** menu.

Not Microsoft style

Toggle the Caps Lock key on or off to switch from capital letters to lowercase letters.

To turn the Ruler on or off, toggle **Ruler** on the **Edit** menu.

tone

Do not use *tone* to refer to a beeping sound. Use *beep* instead. All right to use in other contexts dealing with sound, such as a dial tone or a tone coming from a speaker.

tool

Use *tool* instead of utility to describe a feature that aids in accomplishing a task or set of tasks.

toolbox

Generically, a toolbox is a collection of drawing or interface tools such as paintbrushes, lines, circles, scissors, and spray cans. In programming applications such as Visual Basic, the toolbox also includes controls that users can add to programs, such as command buttons and option buttons. Tools in a toolbox differ from the commands on a toolbar in that the shapes or controls often can be dragged to a document and manipulated in some way.

Treat elements in a toolbox like any other options in dialog boxes. That is, use bold formatting for toolbox labels, and in procedures, tell users to click a particular option. Do not capitalize *toolbox* except to match the interface or if it's a specifically named product feature. See also *Webpage controls, dialog boxes, and property sheets* (Chapter 5).

Microsoft style

Insert a **Combo Box** control in the dialog box.

toolkit

One word.

tooltip

One word. See also *ScreenTip*.

top left, top right

Hyphenate as adjectives. Do not use to mean *upper left* and *upper right*.

For accessibility considerations, see *left*.

topic

Use Help *topic* instead of Help *entry* or Help *article*.

toward

Use instead of *towards*.

trailing

Use instead of *following* in such phrases as *trailing periods, trailing slashes, trailing spaces* and others that may occur at the end of strings, parameters, or other values. *Trailing* in this context is the opposite of *leading*.

trojan horse, trojan

Refers to a program that appears to be useful or harmless but that contains hidden code designed to exploit or damage the system on which it is run. Also called *trojan code*.

In content for a technical audience, the term can be shortened to *trojan*. See also *hack, hacker; security*.

Microsoft style

A trojan horse is a type of malicious software.

TRUE

In general, use all uppercase to refer to a return value in content for software developers. If you are writing about a specific programming language, follow the capitalization used in that language.

turn

Use to refer to the contact gesture or air gesture of rotating an object on the user interface with either the fingers or hand, as if turning a knob.

Microsoft style

Touch the **Volume** knob on the screen with your thumb and at least one finger, and then turn it clockwise or counterclockwise.

Hover over the knob, and then turn it clockwise or counterclockwise.

turn on, turn off

Use instead of *power on, power off; start, stop;* or *switch on, switch off* to mean turning the computer on and off.

Use instead of *enable, disable* to refer to commands or other program features.

Do not use to refer to selecting or clearing check boxes in procedures. Use *select* and *clear* or *click to select* and *click to clear* instead. It is all right to use *turn on, turn off* to refer to the status options on webpages, such as those for multimedia, as in, "You can turn off graphics."

turnkey

One word.

tutorial

Use instead of *CBT.*

two-dimensional, 2-D

Spell out on first mention. On subsequent mention, *two-dimensional* is preferred, but *2-D* is all right to use. Use *2-D* when space is limited and to follow the user interface.

Hyphenate both the spelled out and abbreviated versions. Use 2D (no hyphen) only as specified by product names.

type vs. enter

Use *type* instead of *type in* or *enter* for information that a user must type, such as a password. For information that a user can either type or select from a list, use either *type* or *enter.* You can also use a combination of words such as *type or select.* See also *press.*

Microsoft style

Type your password.

Enter the file name.

Type the path to the server or select it from the list.

Not Microsoft style

Type in your password.

Enter your password.

U

U.K.

All right to use as an abbreviation for *United Kingdom* as an adjective or as a noun, but only when space is limited. Otherwise, do not use unless you have no other choice.

U.S.

All right to use as an abbreviation for *United States* but only as an adjective and only when space is limited. Otherwise, do not use unless you have no other choice. Do not use *US*, *USA*, or *U.S.A.*

If you use the abbreviation, you do not have to spell out *U.S.* on first mention. Always use periods and no space.

Spell out *United States* as a noun except when third-party, legally required content specifies otherwise.

un-

In general, do not hyphenate words beginning with *un-*, such as *undo* and *unread*, unless it is necessary to avoid confusion, as in *un-ionized*, or unless *un-* is followed by a proper noun, as in *un-American*. When in doubt, check the *American Heritage Dictionary*, or consult your project style sheet.

unavailable

Use *unavailable* instead of *grayed* or *disabled* to refer to unusable commands and options on the user interface. Use *dimmed* only if you have to describe their appearance. See also *dimmed, disable*.

Microsoft style

You cannot use unavailable commands until your file meets certain conditions, such as having selected text. These commands appear dimmed on the menu.

UNC

Abbreviation for *Universal Naming Convention*, the system for indicating names of servers and computers, such as *\\Servername\Sharename*. Spell out on first mention unless you are positive that your audience is familiar with the abbreviation. Use only in content for a technical audience.

uncheck, unmark, unselect

Do not use for check boxes or selections. Use *clear the check box* or *cancel the selection* instead.

undelete

Do not use except to follow the user interface or the application programming interface. Use *restore* instead.

Even if the product interface uses *undelete*, the action is still to *restore*. See also *restore*.

Microsoft style

To restore the deleted text, click **Undelete** on the **Edit** menu.

underline, underscore

Use *underline* to refer to text formatting with underlined characters or to formatting. Use *underscore* to refer to the underscore character (_).

undo

Do not use the command name **Undo** as a noun to refer to undoing an action, especially in the plural. Write around instead, as in "to undo multiple actions" or "select the actions that you want to undo." It is all right to say that a command *undoes* an action.

U

uninstall

In general, use *uninstall* to refer to removing hardware or software from a computer system. However, if the context talks about *adding* (rather than *installing*) software or hardware, the preferred term is *remove*.

Do not use *uninstall* as a noun. See also *remove*.

unprintable

Do not use. Use *nonprinting* instead.

unregister

All right to use in content for software developers.

unwanted software

Use as a general term for spyware, adware, and similar software.

Do not use *deceptive software*. See also *security*.

update

Use *update* as a noun to describe a broadly released fix for a specific problem addressing a noncritical bug that is not security-related. Use *critical update* to describe a fix for a critical bug that is not security-related.

Use *update* as a verb to describe the action of installing a software update or service pack. Also use *update* as a verb instead of *refresh* to describe the action of an image being restored on the screen or data in a table being updated. See also *critical update, out-of-band release terminology* (Chapter 6), *refresh*.

update rollup

A tested, cumulative set of hotfixes, security updates, critical updates, and updates packaged together for easy deployment. A rollup generally targets a specific area, such as security, or a component of a product, such as Internet Information Services (IIS). See also *out-of-band release terminology* (Chapter 6).

upgrade

Use to refer to a software package that replaces an installed version of a product with a newer version of the same product. The upgrade process typically leaves existing customer data and preferences intact while replacing the existing software with the newer version.

Do not use *upgrade* as a synonym for *update, service pack,* or any other release that occurs between product versions.

Microsoft style

To upgrade your operating system to Windows 7, place the CD in the drive.

To install the upgrade version, you must already have a previous version of the program on your computer.

The upgrade was successful.

UPnP

Do not spell out as *Universal Plug and Play*. Do not use as a synonym for *Plug and Play* or *PnP*.

Use the trademark bug on first mention. Include the following in trademark lists: "UPnP™ is a certification mark of the UPnP™ Implementers Corporation."

Use as an adjective followed by "certified," if appropriate, and a specific term, such as "device," "architecture," or "standards." For example, say, "This UPnP certified device features..." Do not use *UPnP* to refer to an uncertified device.

Do not use as a noun by itself. For example, do not say "UPnP is an architecture for pervasive peer-to-peer network connectivity." Rephrase the sentence as "The UPnP architecture enables pervasive peer-to-peer network connectivity" instead.

Do not use in the name of any product, and do not use in the trademark of any device.

For any other guidelines required by the UPnP™ Implementers Corporation, see the UPnP Implementers Corporation website. (You must register to be able to use this website.)

upper left, upper right

Hyphenate as adjectives. Use instead of *top left* and *top right*.

For accessibility considerations, see *left*.

uppercase

One word both as an adjective and as a noun. Do not use *uppercased*. Do not use as a verb.

When lowercase and uppercase are used together, do not use a suspended hyphen.

Microsoft style
You can quickly change the capitalization of all uppercase and lowercase letters.

Change all the lowercase letters to uppercase.

Not Microsoft style
You can quickly change the capitalization of all upper- and lowercase letters.

Uppercase all the lowercase letters.

uppercase and lowercase

When *uppercase and lowercase* is used as a compound adjective, do not use a suspended hyphen. That is, use *uppercase and lowercase*, not *upper- and lowercase*. See also *uppercase, lowercase*.

upsize

In general, use *scale up* instead of *upsize*, even though the jargon *upsize* has become common in client/server products.

upward

Use instead of *upwards*.

usable

Use instead of *useable*.

use terms

Do not use in public content to mean *license terms*. All right to use in internal content. See also *Microsoft Software License Terms*.

Usenet

Sometimes seen all capped. The collection of computers and networks that share news articles. Overlaps with the Internet, but not identical to it. From "User Network."

user name

Two words unless describing a label in the user interface. If the user interface uses the one-word form *username*, use *username* to describe the interface element, but use *user name* in the rest of the text.

Microsoft style

In the **Username** box, type your user name.

Not Microsoft style

In the **Username** box, type your username.

user rights

Use *user rights* only to refer to Windows security policies that apply to individual user accounts or administrative groups. The system administrator manages user rights through the User Rights Assignment snap-in. User rights are *assigned*, not *granted* or *allowed*.

When you refer to a named user right, use sentence-style capitalization and bold formatting for the name itself.

If an operation requires that the user be logged on to an account that is a member of a specific administrative group, refer to the group instead of to the associated user rights.

Do not use *privilege* as a synonym for *user right*. See also *permissions, rights*.

Microsoft style

You must have the **Perform volume maintenance tasks** user right to perform this task.

You must be logged on as a member of the Administrators group to perform this task.

Not Microsoft style

You must have the **Perform volume maintenance tasks** privilege to perform this task.

using vs. by using

International considerations

To help the worldwide audience and to reduce the possibility of ambiguity that makes localization more difficult, use *by using* instead of using by itself, even if the preposition seems unnecessary. Notice that the sentence, "You can change files using the Template utility" can mean either of the following, very different, things:

You can change files by using the Template utility.

You can change files that use the Template utility.

See also *using vs. with, Words ending in -ing*

using vs. with

International considerations

To help the worldwide audience and to reduce the possibility of ambiguity that makes localization more difficult, do not use *with* to mean *by using*. See also *using vs. by using*.

U

Microsoft style

You can select part of the picture by using the dotted rectangle selection tool.

Not Microsoft style

You can select part of the picture with the dotted rectangle selection tool.

With is all right to use in some marketing materials and sometimes with product or service names.

Microsoft style

With Home Essentials, you can create professional documents quickly and easily.

utility

Do not use. Use *tool* instead.

utilize

Although *utilize* is a synonym for *use* that means "to find a practical use for," this shade of meaning is seldom necessary in software documentation.

Microsoft style

Some applications are unable to use expanded memory.

This content shows you how to use the Visual Studio 2010 features.

Not Microsoft style

Some applications are unable to utilize expanded memory.

This content shows you how to utilize the Visual Studio 2010 features.

V

value axis

In spreadsheet programs, refers to the (usually) vertical axis in charts and graphs that shows the values being measured or compared. For clarity, refer to it as the *value (y) axis* on first mention. On subsequent mention, it is all right to use *y-axis*. You can also use *vertical (y) axis* in content for novice computer users. See also *category axis*.

VCR

Abbreviation for *video cassette recorder*. Don't spell out.

versus, vs.

In headings, use the abbreviation *vs.*, all lowercase. In text, spell out as *versus*.

Microsoft style (in headings)

Daily vs. weekly backups

VGA

Do not spell out *VGA* and related graphics specifications such as *SVGA*, *XGA*, *UXGA*, *SXGA*, and *QXGA*.

Do not use *VGA+* to describe graphics specifications of higher resolution than VGA; there is no such thing.

It is all right to use the abbreviation for a graphics specification as a modifier for a graphics device such as a card or a monitor. See also *Chapter 11, "Acronyms and abbreviations."*

Microsoft style

QXGA video card

SVGA monitor

VGA device

vibration

Refers to physical feedback provided by a controller's motor. Do not use *rumble*.

video adapter

Obsolete term. Use *video card* instead.

video board

Do not use. Use *video card* instead.

video card

Use instead of *video adapter* or *display adapter* to describe the hardware that converts image data into electronic signals processed by a computer monitor. Do not use *graphics adapter*, *graphics card*, or *graphics board*.

video display

Do not use. Use *screen* to refer to the graphic portion of a monitor and *display* to refer generically to a visual output device. See also *display, screen*.

video driver

Use to describe the software that sends image data to a video card.

video game, video-game

Two words. Hyphenate as an adjective.

viewport

One word. Refers to a view of a document or image in computer graphics programs.

virtual

Do not use in content for a general audience unless you have no other choice.

In other content, use to describe a device or service that appears to the user as something that it actually is not or that does not physically exist. For example, a virtual disk performs like a physical disk but is actually a part of the computer's memory. Some other virtual devices or services are virtual machine, virtual memory, and virtual desktop. Use the term only to refer to a specific element.

virtual root

All right to use to refer to the root directory that the user sees when connected to an Internet server. It is actually a pointer to the actual root directory. Do not use *virtual directory* as a synonym.

virtual server

All right to use in content for a technical audience to refer to a server that appears to a browser like a physical server. Sometimes used as a synonym for website. In that case, use *website* instead if possible.

virtualize

Do not use in content for a general audience.

In content for a technical audience, do not use as a synonym for *simulate*. If you must use *virtualize*, use it only to mean creating a virtual implementation. For example, "to virtualize storage" would mean to create virtual storage, which makes many physical storage devices appear to be one device.

visit

In the context of the Internet, use *visit* only to talk about going to a website for the purpose of spending time at that site. You may also use *go to* in this context.

To talk about going to a specific webpage, use *go to*.

Microsoft style

Visit our website at www.microsoft.com.

For information about Windows and Microsoft .NET programming, visit the Microsoft Developer Network Website.

When you visit a retail website, you can often put items that you want to purchase into a shopping basket.

For information about Windows and Microsoft .NET programming, go to the Microsoft Developer Network Website.

To learn how to convert text to numbers in Microsoft Excel 2002, go to http://support.microsoft.com/default.aspx?scid=kb;en-us;Q291047&sd=tech.

Not Microsoft style

To learn how to convert text to numbers in Microsoft Excel 2003, visit http://support.microsoft.com/default.aspx?scid=kb;en-us;Q291047&sd=tech.

voice mail

Two words. Do not abbreviate as *v-mail* or *vmail*.

vulnerability

Refers to any product weakness, administrative process or act, or physical exposure that makes a computer susceptible to exploit by a threat. Because *vulnerability* covers so many types of security problems, its misuse can easily confuse users on the very sensitive topic of security. Follow the guidelines in this topic to help ensure that your users do not misunderstand the security-related information that you are giving them. See also *security*.

On first mention, use a modifier to identify what kind of vulnerability you are discussing:

- *Product vulnerability.* A set of conditions that violates an implied or explicit security policy. A product vulnerability is usually addressed by a Microsoft security bulletin or a service pack.

- *Administrative vulnerability.* Failure to observe administrative best practices, such as when a user uses a weak password or logs on to an account that has more user rights than the user requires to perform a specific task.

- *Physical vulnerability.* Failure to provide physical security for a computer, such as when an authorized user leaves an unlocked workstation running in a workspace that is available to unauthorized users.

Microsoft style

Do not expose your system to administrative vulnerabilities. For example, do not log on as an administrator unless you are doing a task that requires the user rights of an administrator.

This security update resolves a product vulnerability in Internet Explorer that could allow remote code execution if the user views a specially crafted webpage.

After the context is established, you can use *vulnerability* without a modifier on subsequent mention. However, it is a good idea to use the modifier again occasionally in your content.

For other security issues, use the most specific term that describes the issue, and define it if users might be unfamiliar with the term. If there is no specific term, use *security issue*.

Don't describe intentionally designed behavior as a vulnerability.

Microsoft style

In Active Directory Domain Services, the administrator of any domain within a forest is trusted to control any other domain within the forest.

Not Microsoft style

There is a vulnerability within Active Directory Domain Services that can allow the administrator of any domain within a forest to gain control of any other domain within the forest.

W

W3C

Abbreviation for *World Wide Web Consortium*, the organization that sets standards for the web and HTML. Write out as "World Wide Web Consortium" on first mention.

want

Use instead of *wish* or *desire*. Do not confuse with *need*. Be sure to use the term that is appropriate to the situation. *Need* connotes a requirement or obligation; *want* indicates that the user has a choice of actions.

Microsoft style

If you want to use a laser printer, you need a laser printer driver.

Not Microsoft style

If you wish to format the entire word, double-click it.

Add the controls and functionality that you desire.

we

In general, do not use, except in the phrase *we recommend*.

web

All uses of *web* as a modifier are lowercase except when following the user interface and in feature names such as *Web Slice*. Capitalize all words in the phrase *World Wide Web*, but the shortened form *the web* is lowercase.

The following are among the web-based terms that are one word:

webpage

website

webcam

webcast

webmaster

webzine

The following are among the web-based terms that are hyphenated:

web-centric

web-based

web-enabled

The following are among the web-based terms that are two words:

web address

web browser

web content

web crawler

web document

web folder

Web Apps

Office Web Apps are online companions to the Microsoft Office client applications (programs) Microsoft Word, PowerPoint, Excel, and OneNote. With Office Web Apps, customers can use the familiar Office user interface in a browser, either on the Internet or on a SharePoint site. The

W

documents are stored on a website and viewed in a browser. Office Web Apps are compatible with Office 2010 programs that are locally installed.

Office Web Apps offer most, but not all, the features of the Office 2010 client programs. Therefore, in any discussion or mention of Office Web Apps, it is important that you not mislead users. In essence, the user's "experience" of Office is extended to the web, but Office is still a suite of desktop programs. You cannot promise or imply that there is 100% fidelity between the client programs and Office Web Apps, and you cannot say or imply that the online experience will be identical to the desktop experience.

The following table contains examples of the kinds of things that you can and cannot say about Office Web Apps.

What you can say:	What you cannot say:
Office Web Apps are online companions to Microsoft Office applications, such as Word or Excel.	Office Web Apps are a feature of Office.
Office Web Apps extend your Office experience to the web.	Office Web Apps are a tool of Office.
With Microsoft Office Web Apps, you can use the familiar Office user interface.	Office Web Apps are "Office in the cloud."
By using Office Web Apps, you can access your files from almost any computer that has an Internet connection.	Office Web Apps extend the Office client.
With Office Web Apps, you can quickly and easily save your documents to the web directly from the Office applications on your computer.	Office Web Apps are lighter versions of Word, Excel, PowerPoint, or OneNote.
Office Web Apps work with the Microsoft Office programs that you already know and use.	Office Web Apps are online versions of Word, Excel, Power Point, or OneNote.
Enjoy great interoperability between Office 2010 and Office Web Apps.	Office Web Apps are versions of Word, Excel, PowerPoint, or OneNote.
Web Apps provide "high fidelity," "great fidelity," or "excellent fidelity."	Office Web Apps are integrated with the Office client to provide a better experience.
By using Office Web Apps, you can view your documents on your PC, mobile phone, and on the web with great document fidelity and consistent formatting.	Office Web Apps let you know your content will be preserved and your data retained even though you edited the files online.
View and perform basic editing functions on your online documents even from a computer that doesn't have Microsoft Office installed.	Office Web Apps eliminate the loss of data and formatting that can occur when files are transferred and accessed through different desktop or web-based applications.
Easily store files and documents online in a password-protected environment.	Office Web Apps provide "perfect" fidelity.
Easily share documents with others who use different versions of Microsoft Office.	Office Web Apps provide "full" fidelity.
Easily share documents with people who don't have Microsoft Office installed on their PCs.	Office Web Apps render content "exactly as intended."
Control who has permission to view or edit your documents.	All formatting remains intact.
Office Web Apps let multiple users make changes to one document in a central location and keep track of revisions.	Office Web Apps work with Office 2003 or Office XP without any additional download.

W

What you can say:	What you cannot say:
Create amazing documents by using the rich features that are available in Microsoft Office Word 2010, and then easily upload them to the web and share them with others by using Office Web Apps.	With Office Web Apps, you can easily transfer, share, and convert documents with perfect fidelity.
	SkyDrive access to Web Apps is for consumers only.
	Customers may use Office Web Apps only after they have purchased the Office suite.

How to refer to the Web Apps

The category title Microsoft Office Web Apps applies to the following four Web Apps:

- Microsoft Excel Web App

- Microsoft OneNote Web App

- Microsoft PowerPoint Web App

- Microsoft Word Web App

Microsoft Outlook Web App is licensed separately; therefore, it is not included under the category title Microsoft Office Web Apps.

On first mention

On first mention of the category title or an individual product name, precede the title or name with *Microsoft* and use appropriate trademarks, as follows:

- Microsoft® Office Web Apps (for the category)

- Microsoft® Excel® Web App (for an individual program name)

> **Note** Trademarks are required only in printed documentation.

On second mention

On second mention, *Microsoft* is not required:

- Office Web Apps (for the category)

- Excel Web App (for an individual program name)

On subsequent mentions

On subsequent mentions of the category title or the individual product names, you may omit *Microsoft*, but do not omit *Web App*, because this name distinguishes the Web App from the desktop application. The only exception to this rule is that *Web App* may be omitted in the user interface if space is limited.

On subsequent mentions, it is also all right to shorten *Office Web Apps* to *Web Apps*, especially if the use of "Office" is becoming repetitive. *Web Apps* is capitalized. For example, it is all right to say "Office 2010 includes a plug-in for opening Office documents directly from the Web Apps."

Version numbers

Office Web Apps do not have version numbers.

Use of an article

In general, when *Office Web Apps* is used as a noun to mean the product, do not precede it with the definite article *the*. When it is used as an adjective, you can precede it with the definite article *the*. It is all right to precede *Web Apps* with the definite article *the*. In addition, when you are referring to Office Web Apps collectively or generically, you may precede the term with the definite article *the*.

Microsoft style

If Office desktop applications are not installed on your computer, you can use Office Web Apps to create documents.

When you use Office Web Apps, all your documents are created, edited, and stored on a server.

Use your web browser and Internet connection to access Office Web Apps.

There are some differences between the features of the Office Web Apps and the Office 2010 applications.

In general, when a specific Web App is used as a noun, do not precede it with the definite article *the*. When it is used as an adjective, you can precede it with the definite article *the*.

Microsoft style

Office Web Apps are available on SkyDrive for free.

The Word Web App ribbon is familiar if you're used to working in Word 2007 or Word 2010.

The document opens for editing in the appropriate Web App.

In smaller organizations, you can deploy the Office Web Apps components on a single SharePoint 2010 Products server.

In Reading view, Word Web App displays all content and formatting.

Open the Excel Web App spreadsheet from SkyDrive.

Not Microsoft style

The Office Web Apps are interoperable with the Office client.

The Word Web App is familiar if you're used to working in Word 2007 or Word 2010.

Open the Excel Web App from SkyDrive.

webpage

Use *webpage* instead of *Web page* unless you must follow the user interface. See also *web*.

W

website

Use *website* instead of *Web site* unless you must follow the user interface. See also *web*.

weblication

Jargon for "web application." Do not use. It could be confused with "web publication."

where

Use to introduce a list, as in code or formulas, to define the meaning of elements such as variables or symbols.

Microsoft style

Use the following formula to calculate the return, where:

r = rate of interest
n = number of months
p = principal

while

Use to refer only to something occurring in time. Do not use as a synonym for *although* or *whereas*.

Microsoft style

Fill out your registration card while you wait for Setup to be completed.

Although the icon indicates that the print job is finished, you may have to wait until a previous job is finished.

Not Microsoft style

While the icon indicates that the print job is finished, you may have to wait until a previous job is finished.

whitelist

Do not use. See *blacklist*.

white paper

Two words.

white space, white-space

Two words as a noun. Hyphenated as an adjective.

who vs. that

Although there is no linguistic basis for not using *that* to refer to people, as in "the man that was walking," it is considered more polite to use *who* instead of *that* in references to people. Therefore, use *who*, not *that*, to introduce clauses referring to users.

Microsoft style

Custom Setup is for experienced users who want to alter the standard Windows configuration.

Not Microsoft style

Custom Setup is for experienced users that want to alter the standard Windows configuration.

Wi-Fi

Use instead of *WiFi*, *wifi*, or *Wifi*. Capitalize and hyphenate when referring specifically to Wi-Fi technologies. When possible, use a general phrase such as *wireless network* instead.

This term is a proper noun and a registered trademark. However, do not include the registered trademark symbol.

When possible, use a general phrase instead, such as *wireless network*, or refer to the specific wireless technology that you are describing, such as *wireless LAN*.

wildcard character

Always use the word *character* with *wildcard* when referring to a keyboard character that can be used to represent one or many characters, such as the * or ? keyboard character.

Wildcard is one word.

window

Do not use as a verb.

Microsoft Windows AntiSpyware

Note capitalization. The name of the Microsoft antispyware product. The short form of the name is *Windows AntiSpyware*. See also *antispyware*.

Windows 7

Always use the entire name. Do not precede the name with *Microsoft*.

Windows Events

Generic term encompassing events occurring in the various versions of Windows.

Microsoft style

The Windows 7 Event Log service writes Windows Events to one of several log files that reside on the user's computer.

You can also refer to the version number when referring to version-specific events. For example, you can say *Windows 7 Events* or *Windows Server 2008 Events*.

Windows Explorer

Do not use as a synonym for Internet Explorer. Windows Explorer is a feature of Windows operating systems that shows the hierarchical structure of the files and folders on a computer.

Do not precede with *the* and do not shorten to *Explorer*.

Windows Installer

Note capitalization.

Windows NT Server, Windows NT Workstation

Do not use *Windows NT* as a modifier for aspects or elements of Windows NT Server or Windows NT Workstation products unless you have no other choice. Instead, say that a product or process *runs on* one of these products, not *is on* one of them.

W

Microsoft style

The printer is attached to a computer running Windows NT Server.

The Microsoft Exchange Client software is on a computer running Windows NT Workstation.

Not Microsoft style

Windows NT Server server

Windows NT system

Windows Vista

Always use the entire name. Do not shorten to *Vista*. Do not precede the name with *Microsoft*.

Windows, Windows-based

Use *Windows* as a modifier for aspects or elements of the Windows operating system itself. Do not use *Windows* to modify the names of programs, hardware, or development methods that are based on or run on the Windows operating system. Use *Windows-based* or *running Windows* instead. To avoid a ridiculous construction, the term *Windows user* is all right to use.

Microsoft style

Windows-based application

Windows-based device

the Windows **Recycle Bin**

a computer running Windows

Not Microsoft style

Windows application

Windows computer

Winsock

All right to use to refer to the Windows Sockets API. Do not use *Sockets* unless you have no other choice.

wireframe

One word. Refers to a type of three-dimensional graphic.

want

Use instead of *wish* or *desire*. Do not confuse with *need*. Be sure to use the term that is appropriate to the situation. *Need* connotes a requirement or obligation; *want* indicates that the user has a choice of actions.

Microsoft style

If you want to use a laser printer, you need a laser printer driver.

Not Microsoft style

If you wish to format the entire word, double-click it.

Add the controls and functionality that you desire.

wizard

Always use lowercase for the generic term *wizard*. Capitalize *wizard* if it is part of a feature name that appears in the user interface. Refer to an individual screen in a wizard as a *page*.

Use bold formatting for wizard page names. Use bold formatting for wizard names only in procedures and only if the name is clicked.

Microsoft style

Click **Start**, point to **All Programs**, point to **Administrative Tools**, and then click **SharePoint Products Configuration Wizard**.

In the SharePoint Products Configuration Wizard, on the **Welcome to SharePoint Products** page, click **Next**.

On the **Identify Fact and Dimension Tables** page, the fact and dimension tables identified by the wizard are displayed.

word processing

Use the following guidelines for *word-processing* terms:

- As an adjective, use the hyphenated form *word-processed* or *word-processing*.
- As a noun, use *word processor* or *word processing*.
- As a verb, do not use *word process* or *word processing*. Use *write, format,* or another term instead.

wordwrap, wordwrapping

One word.

work area

Two words. Do not use *work area* unless the term has a specific meaning in a particular product. Use *workspace* to refer to the area within a window where the user interacts with the program.

workgroup

One word.

working memory

Do not use. Use *available memory* instead.

worksheet

A tabbed section of a workbook that you use in Excel to store and work with data. Also called a spreadsheet. A worksheet consists of cells that are organized into columns and rows. A workbook can contain one or more worksheets, also called spreadsheets.

workspace

One word. Refers to the area within the application window where the user interacts with a program. See also *desktop*.

W

workstation

One word. Use to refer to a personal computer used by an individual in a network. A workstation is the client in a client/server system.

World Wide Web

Capitalize all the words of the phrase *World Wide Web*. However, if you use *the web*, use lowercase.

Use *on* to refer to material existing on the web. You can use *to* or *on* to refer to the action of creating and publishing something *to the web* or *on the web*.

write-only

Always hyphenate. Related to *read/write*, but *write-only* and *read-only* refer to properties of files, whereas *read/write* refers to a level of permissions granted to users.

write-protect, write-protected

Always hyphenate. When used as a verb, use *write-protect*. When used as an adjective, use *write-protected*. Use *write-protect*, not *lock*, to refer to the action of protecting disks from being overwritten.

Microsoft style

to write-protect a disk

a write-protected disk

a disk that is write-protected

WWW

Abbreviation for *World Wide Web*. Capitalize all words when using the expanded form. Otherwise, use *the web*. All lowercase (www) when used in an Internet address. For additional guidance, see *World Wide Web* and *web*.

X

x

Use a lowercase *x* in italic type as a placeholder number or variable. Do not use *x* to refer to a generic unspecified number. Use *n* instead. Do not use *x* to refer to a multiplication sign. See also *multiplication sign (×), n*.

Microsoft style
version 4.*x*

R4*x*00

Not Microsoft style
Move the insertion point *x* spaces to the right.

x86

Refers to the generic concept of 32-bit processing.

When describing a computer, it refers to a computer that uses any of the family of Intel and AMD 32-bit processors.

When referring to software, it refers to 32-bit versions of software. For example, "C:\Program Files (x86)\" refers to a folder that stores 32-bit programs.

x-axis

Use lowercase, hyphen, and regular type. In general, use *category (x) axis* to refer to the (usually) horizontal axis in charts and graphs that shows the categories being compared. Include a reference to the horizontal axis if it will clarify the meaning.

Xbase

Use instead of *xBASE*.

x-coordinate

Lowercase, hyphenated, and regular type.

XON/XOF

Note capitalization and slash mark. Refers to the handshake between two computers during transmission of data. See *handshake*.

Y

y-axis

Use lowercase, hyphen, and regular type. In general, use *value (y) axis* to refer to the (usually) vertical axis in charts and graphs that shows the values being measured or compared. Include a reference to the vertical axis if it will clarify the meaning.

y-coordinate

Lowercase, hyphenated, and regular type.

Z

z-

Hyphenate all words referring to entities that begin with *z* used as a separate letter, such as *z-axis, z-coordinate, z-order,* and *z-test*. Consult your project style sheet for capitalization.

z-axis

Use lowercase, hyphen, and regular type. In 3-D charts, the z-axis shows depth. It generally represents values. Refer to the z-axis as the *value axis*, where both the x-axis and y-axis are category axes, but include *z-axis* in parentheses if it will clarify the meaning.

zero, zeros

For consistency in Microsoft documentation, use *zeros* instead of *zeroes* as the plural of *zero*.

In measurements, when the unit of measurement is not abbreviated, zero takes the plural, as in "0 megabytes."

zero character

In the ASCII character set, a zero character represents the digit 0 but is ASCII code 48. Differentiate it from the NUL character (ASCII code 0). See also *NUL, null, NULL, Null.*

ZIP Code

In general text, use the generically international term *postal code* instead of *ZIP Code.* In forms or fill-in fields, include both *ZIP Code* and *postal code* whenever you can. Do not use a slash mark (/) as a substitute for *or* unless space is limited. It is all right to combine the two terms if space is limited.

Microsoft style

ZIP Code or Postal Code: _____

ZIP or Postal Code: _____

Postal Code: _____

Microsoft style (if necessary for space reasons)

ZIP Code/Postal Code: _____

ZIP/Postal Code: _____

> **Note** Use an uppercase *C* for *Code* in accordance with the U.S. Postal Service trademark.

zoom in, zoom out

Use instead of *dezoom* or *unzoom.*

Z

Index

Tools tab, 61
tooltip, 375, 400
top left and *top right*, 400
topic, 400
top-level domain (TLD), 281
touch procedures, referring to, 104
toward, 400
Trace Research and Development Center, University of Wisconsin, 48
trackbar controls, 82
trademark information, 45, 72, 129
trademark symbol (™), 166
trailing, 400
transcripts, 48
transitive verbs, 178
translation, 33. *See also* global content guidelines
  abbreviations, 230
  acronyms, 216
  clauses, wording, 397
  consistent terminology and, 3
  directional terms, 49
  error messages, 76
  gerunds, 186
  jokes, slang, and sarcasm, 5
  Machine translation, 35–37
  plurals, 183
  short, plain words, 6
  text in graphics, 40
  voice and, 180
  web content, 32
trojan and *trojan horse*, 400
troubleshoot, 275
troubleshooting, 21
TRUE, 400
turn, 400
turn on and *turn off*, 101, 263, 399
turnkey, 401
tutorial, 261, 401
24-hour time notation, 153
two-dimensional, 401
type, 59, 67, 101, 315, 361–362, 401

U

U.K., 401
un-, 402
unauthorized user, 331
unavailable, 68, 279, 301, 402
UNC, 402
uncheck, *unmark*, and *unselect*, 402
undelete, 402
under, 325–326
underline, 402
underscore (_), 166, 402
undo, 402
unfold buttons, 82
uninstall, 370, 403
United States, 402
United States resources, references to, 43
United States standards, globalization and, 41

units of measurement, 161–162
  abbreviations of, 162, 229–230
  number of, 156
Universal Naming Convention, 402
Universal Plug and Play (UPnP), 359
unload, 328, 370
unnamed buttons, referring to, 83
unnumbered lists, 141–142
unprintable, 403
unregister, 403
unwanted software, 275, 403
Up Arrow key, 89
update, 125, 272, 368, 403
update identifiers, referring to, 124
update rollup, 125, 377, 403
upgrade, 403
UPnP (Universal Plug and Play), 359, 403
uppercase and *lowercase*, 404
upper left and *upper right*, 404
upsize, 374, 404
upward, 404
URLs, 163–164
  formatting conventions, 110
  line breaks, 174
U.S., 402
usable, 404
use, 361–362
use terms, 404
use-case scenarios in global content, 41
Usenet, 405
user, 288
user actions, referring to, 379
user expectations, consistent syntax and, 3
user input, formatting, 103, 110
user interface
  anthropomorphism, 15
  Backstage view, 72–73
  capitalization, 94–95, 102–103, 133, 134
  contractions, 11
  Control Panel, 74–75
  controls, 78–83
  dialog boxes, 71
  on different devices, 92
  elements, 59–60, 94–98
  ellipses, 199
  formatting, 94–98
  gesturing, 83–84
  Help content, linking to, 93
  interaction with, modes of, 49, 83–85
  key names, 87–92
  keyboard shortcuts, 90
  menus, 63–66
  messages, 75–78
  mouse terminology, 85–87
  for multiple platforms, 92
  property sheets, 71–72
  ribbons, 60–63
  special character names, 90
  syntax, 3, 59–60
  terminology, 59
  text, 93–94

toolbars, 66–70
  types of, 51
  UI text checklist, 94
  voice commands, 84–85
  webpage controls, 70
  Windows, 51–54
  Windows Phone, 54–58
user location, globalization and localization for, 44. *See also* global content guidelines; localization
user name, 405–406
user rights, 238, 372, 405
user session, ending, 366
users
  communicating with, 19
  focusing discussion on, 9
  inspiring, 4
  text scanning by, 21–22
users with disabilities, accessible content, 47–50
using, 405
utilities, 110, 238
utility, 406
utilize, 406

V

value axis, 406
values, formatting, 110
variables, formatting, 109, 110
VCR, 406
verbs, 177–178
  capitalization, 132
  converting to nouns, 8
  gerunds, 185
  imperative, 181
  indicative, 181
  mood, 177, 181–182
  for mouse actions, 86
  present tense, 8
  punctuation and, 191
  single-word vs. multiple-word, 7
  subject-verb agreement, 179
  subjunctive, 181–182
  tense, 177
  transitive and intransitive, 178
  voice, 177, 179–180
version identifiers, 123–125, 302, 306, 324, 325
versus, 406
vertical bar (|), 166
VGA, 406–407
vibration, 407
video, 19, 23–24
  accessibility guidelines, 48
  alternative text, 48
  screen-capture, 20
  text descriptions, 29
video adapter, 407
video board, 407
video card, 280, 301, 407

What do you think of this book?

We want to hear from you!

To participate in a brief online survey, please visit:

microsoft.com/learning/booksurvey

Tell us how well this book meets your needs—what works effectively, and what we can do better. Your feedback will help us continually improve our books and learning resources for you.

Thank you in advance for your input!